LET'S GO

www.letsgo.com

ISTANBUL, ATHENS & THE GREEK ISLANDS

researcher-writers
Michal Labik
Elyssa Spitzer

staff writers
Sophie Arlow
Taylor Nickel
Ansley Dawn Rubenstein

research manager
Anna E. Boch

editors
Jonathan Rossi

managing editor
Marykate Jasper

RESEARCHER-WRITERS

MICHAL LABIK. Michal was really looking forward to wearing a fez in Istanbul, but was saddened to hear that the Ottoman Empire wouldn't be reinstated in time. However, he made do with cavorting in the bazaars, eating more kebab than he thought possible, and being hit on in a gay hammam. Though as Michal likes to say, being hit on is always better than being hit.

ELYSSA SPITZER. The quintessential straight shooter, Elyssa didn't put up with BS. No sub-par orange juice or cigarette-burned bed was going to slip into her listings. If this ball-busting research weren't enough to make her an champ, Elyssa's always pleasant calls and hilarious stories about old, pants-less Greek dudes made her editors love her.

CONTENTS

ISTANBUL, ATHENS & THE GREEK ISLANDS

Newsflash! A giant meteor is headed straight toward Earth, and Ben Affleck is too busy playing with animal crackers and Liv Tyler to save our existence. The government gives everyone ten days before this apocalyptic armageddon will wipe the Earth out of our galaxy. Where does Let's Go think you should go for the final days of your existence? Start by killing two birds with one stone with trip to Istanbul, the Turkish city straddling two continents and almost three millennia of history. From the Hagia Sophia's beautiful dome to the expansive Topkapı Palace complex, there's enough history here to make you feel like you've been living for centuries. Still got the blues about the world ending? Seek atmospheric solidarity at Sultan Ahmed's Blue Mosque to check out the beautiful navy tiles that line its interior.

When you've had your fair share of kebabs, head to the hometown of western philosophy, literature, art, and athletics in Athens, Greece. Explore some of the oldest landmarks in history by traversing the relics around the Parthenon, the Acropolis, and the Agora. Regain some faith in humanity in one of the famous Byzantine churches, or kick back and relax in one of the cafes dotting the Exarhia and Plaka neighborhoods.

Whatever you do, make sure to end your whirlwind trip by island-hopping along Greece's Cyclades, where sun-drenched beach parties and centuries of habitation make for a perfect mix of history and hangovers. Orange and black sands coat the shoreline of Santorini, celebrated archaeological sites testify to the mythical and historical legends surrounding Delos, and notorious party spots uncork some of the wildest nightlife anywhere on Ios and Mykonos. Who knows, hopefully the government will figure this whole armageddon thing out and cover it up with a late '90s Hollywood blockbuster.

when to go

High season in Istanbul and Greece takes place in the summer months between late June and early September. Flora aficionados and history buffs alike should visit Istanbul in April and May to catch the indigenous tulips' blossom before the summer sun and masses of tourists arrive. Museums, sights, and local transportation have their longest hours during these summer months, but accommodations and air travel are at their peak prices. The Greek islands heat up during the summer months—particularly August—as party animals pack these sea spots for sun, sand, and sin. To be safe, make sure to book **reservations** if you plan to travel to these destinations during these warm months.

If the crowds and frantic pace of summer travel aren't your style, consider visiting in May, early June, or September when the crowds are lighter. While public transportation and hours of operation might be somewhat limited, sights won't be jam-packed and accommodations will be less expensive. The winter is **off-season** in Istanbul, Athens, and the islands, but **ski season** at nearby Mt. Parnassos, Karpenisi, and Kalavrita, brings tinted-goggled masses to its slippery slopes. If traveling during the winter, make sure to check hours of operation and accommodation availability.

what to do

HOARDING AND HAGGLING

If there's only one thing Let's Go enjoys on this green earth, it's finding a great deal on the road. If there's another thing Let's Go enjoys, it's *making* a great deal on the road. No, all ye aspiring capitalists looking to exploit foreign laws with sketchy transactions, we are not advocating anything illegal—especially in a country where the word misdemeanor isn't even in the national vocabulary. Instead, we are telling you to get your frugal selves over to the outdoor markets in Athens and Istanbul to find the best deals on everything from trinkets and baubles to fresh produce and livestock. Before bringing out your wallet, make sure to haggle your way to a price within your budget—because nothing makes a purchase better than a bargain.

- **GRAND BAZAAR:** With over 60 streets and 1200 stores, Istanbul's Grand Bazaar is asking you to get lost in order to find some of its fantastic deals.

- **SPICE BAZAAR:** Encounter a true Turkish sneeze by getting too close to the goods at this marketplace that sells everything from international spices and dried fruits to nuts locally referred to as "Turkish Viagra."

- **VARNAKIOS:** Like an outside supermarket with one aisle and a rougher crowd of customers, Varnakios has everything needed to stock an Athenian kitchen.

TASTES OF THE ROAD

Backpackers need energy to keep a steady pace on their routes, and Let's Go knows no better power booster than local cuisine. Turkish favorites like *pides*, *köfte*, and kebabs are served in local restaurants throughout Istanbul, and cultural traditions like sipping tea and smoking *nargile* (hookah for you westerners) make for a great nightcap on the road. In Athens, ubiquitous mini-marts sell yogurt, spanakopita, and fresh fruit next to vendors that roast souvlaki by the bushel and gelaterias that serve the iciest of treats. After nightfall, *tavernas*serve up honey-induced wine or *ouzo* to patrons looking to wind down. Even the islands have their own distinct specialty beverages and local fare.

top five places to blossom your romance

- **SULTANAHMET PARK:** Head to this park in late March and early May to see the local tulips blossom as you whisper some sweet nothings in your honey's ear.
- **ACROPOLIS:** Take a walk along the Acropolis and the Philopappos Hills through Dimitri Pikionis' landscape project, making sure your sweetie doesn't trip over a rock.
- **SANTORINI:** Help your honey forgive and forget with some apology roses from Santorini Florists, the only flower shop on the entire island.
- **TULIP HOUSE:** Break the bank and celebrate an anniversary or special occasion at the Tulip House, a mansion-turned-boutique hotel in the heart of Old Istanbul.
- **ATHENS NATIONAL GARDEN:** Let the general havoc of Athens fade into the soft paths and bird sounds within this expansive patch of peace as you win over your snickermuffin with some marigolds.

- **PAŞAZADE RESTAURANT:** Try Ottoman empire specialtieslike *mahmudiye*, a combination of chicken, potato, and fruit, at this fancy Turkish restaurant that doesn't break the bank.
- **CEZAYIR:** Try the grilled lamb tenderloin and *hallumi* cheese at this Turkish treasure to get a taste of some of the national delicacies.
- **BENETH:** Sample some of the best baklava in all of Greece at this bakery in the Plaka neighborhood.
- **BARBA YIANIS:** Sit down with the manager of this family-owned *taverna* to learn about its history and experience classic Greek cooking.
- **CLUB CAVO PARADISO:** With everything from beach drinks and *ouzo* to dozens of Red Bull-inspired beverages, this club offers just about any booze to get you in the mood to dance.

A NIGHT OUT IN ISTANBUL

As a majority of the native population abstains from drinking alcohol, Istanbul's nightlife is a breath of fresh air from the intoxicated masses in most of western Europe. Experience ultimate relaxation in cafes and restaurants that offer *nargile* and tea along the Bosphorous, or head to a local wateringhole for a few beers. Dance enthusiasts can visit theaters and bars that showcase traditional Turkish moves, and theater connoisseurs can buy tickets to shows put on by Istanbul's internationally acclaimed performing arts groups.

- **SETÜSTÜ ÇAY BAHÇESI:** With a breathtaking view of the Bosphorous breaking Istanbul into three distinct areas, this cafe serves up traditional tea and regional specialties.
- **HOCAPAŞA ART AND CULTURE CENTER:** Dervishes, or Sufi mystics, engage in whirling that has become as much Turkish art as religious practice.
- **GALATA TOWER:** Come to this 14th century tower's Turkish nights for a showcase of belly dancing and other traditional dances—as well as an open bar.
- **SÜREYYA OPERASI:** Show your lover you've got class and culture by buying tickets to shows at this home of the Istanbul State Opera and Ballet group.

BEYOND TOURISM

That last guided tour put you to sleep? Need to take a break from schlepping your baggage around cobble stone streets? Or maybe you're broke beyond belief and in need of some spare cash to prolong your trip? Whatever the case may be, use our Beyond Tourism section that shows how to study, work, or volunteer in these countries to spice up your trip and help you get closer to the local way of life.

- **COLLEGE YEAR IN ATHENS:** The oldest English study-abroad program in Greece, CYA offers Greek language classes as well as study travel programs to Crete, Peloponnesse, and other parts of Greece within its curriculum.
- **ISTANBUL UNIVERSITY:** With over 60,000 undergrads at this 557 year old institution, there's everything from a radio station to athletic teams for international students.
- **ARCHELON SEA TURTLE PROTECTION SOCIETY:** Help save turtle nesting sights at a rehab center in Athens and live free of charge during your work.
- **ANGLONANNIES:** Use this database to find au pair and nanny openings in Istanbul and Athens.

student superlatives

- **BEST PLACE TO STEAL (LOOK AT) FERRARIS:** Head to Istanbul Park Circuit in August to see the Turkish Grand Prix.

- **BEST PLACE TO RUN A MARATHON:** Sorry, Boston. The Athens Classic Marathon from the city of Marathon to Athens' Panathenaic Stadium started in 490 BC and remains the most famous distance route in the world.

- **BEST PLACE TO MAKE A NEW FEATHERED FRIEND:** Meet Petros, the official mascot of Mykonos in the capity city of this Greek island.

- **BEST PLACE TO GET SO FRESH AND SO CLEAN, CLEAN:** Head to Istanbul's Çemberlitaş Hamamı bathhouse for a tradional bath that is sure to leave you squeaky clean.

- **BEST PLACE TO FEEL LIKE A KING:** Head to Istanbul's Topkapı Palace to see the home of the powerful—and where their harem hung out.

- **BEST PLACE TO HAVE YOUR BAKLAVA AND EAT IT TOO:** Eat your own body weight in this Greek pastry at Beneth Bakery.

- **BEST PLACE TO DRINK ALONGSIDE A MOVIE STAR:** Head to Athen's Cine Paris Rooftop Cinema for an outdoor bar and theater that plays recent blockbusters.

suggested itineraries

BEST OF ISTANBUL, ATHENS, AND GREEK ISLANDS IN 14 DAYS

Take a crash course in classical history in two of its most culturally significant countries with this trip that is sure to astonish both academic noobs and learned individuals.

1. ISTANBUL (5 DAYS): Straddling two continents and almost three millennia of history, two worlds collide in this ginormous city chock-full of historical happenings.

2. ATHENS (4 DAYS): From the classics to feta cheese, this Greek capital houses some of the oldest structures known to man and will entertain even the most tired travelers.

3. ANDROS (1 DAY) : Known today as a beach getaway, this island actually aided Xerxes with supplies of ships before rejoining the Delian League.

4. MYKONOS (2 DAYS): Watch the sea and dancing bodies glisten in the sun on this hedonistic island known for its booze and bouncing bass.

5. SANTORINI (2 DAYS): Whitewashed towns, scorching black-sand beaches, and sharply stratified geological rock formations make this island's landscape nearly as dramatic as the volcano that created it.

BULGARIA

BEST OF ISTANBUL, ATHENS, AND GREEK ISLANDS IN 14 DAYS

1 Istanbul

GREECE

Aegean

TURKEY

Sea

3
Athens
Andros

2
Mykonos
4

N
LG

| 0 | 50 kilometers |
| 0 | 50 miles |

5 Santorini

RUINS, RELICS, AND REALLY OLD GREEK STUFF

1. ATHENS (2 DAYS): Head to the Acropolis and the Agora to scope out two of the most historically significant structures in Greece.

2. CAPE SOUNION PENINSULA (1 DAY): With a temple and cape dedicated to mythical badass Poseidon, this historic landmark also is home to a gorgeous beach close to Athens.

3. DELOS (2 DAYS): While only 20% of the city has been excavated, this former home of the Delian League is also home to timeless frescoes, mosaics, and architectural masterpieces.

4. EPHESUS (1 DAY): A major city for both the Greeks and the Romans, Ephesus houses the Temple of Artemis, one of the 7 Wonders of the Ancient World.

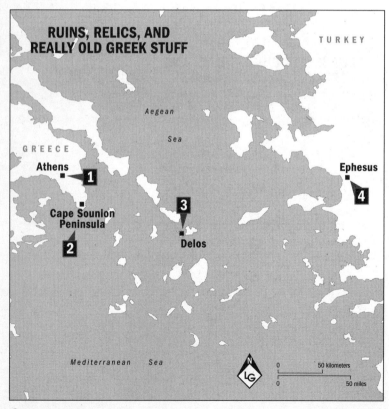

ISTANBUL'S HISTORIC NEIGHBORHOODS IN 2 WEEKS

1. SULTANAHMET (3 DAYS): With the Hagia Sophia and other popular historical sites to its name, Sultanahmet is the center of Istanbul's tourism and a great first stop in the city.

2. FATIH (2 DAYS): This conservative neighborhood centered around the Fatih Mosque houses many government officials and holds the Siirt Bazaar, a square rampant with small eateries.

3. FENER AND BALAT (2 DAYS): Historic home to Greek, Jewish, and Armenian minorities, this district today showcases the mosaic-filled Chora Church and the Eyüp Sultan Mosque around a developing neighborhood.

4. MODA, KADIKÖY, AND ÜSKÜDAR (3 DAYS): Make your way to this center of lively alternative art on the Asian side of Istanbul for an exciting bar street and historical neighborhood that's home to a number of mosques.

5. BEYOĞLU (2 DAYS): This heart of modern Istanbul is a major leisure district with authentic restaurants, sights like the Galata Tower, and a ton of recently renovated accommodations.

6. BEŞIKTAŞ AND ORTAKÖY (2 DAYS): While Beşiktaş' pedestrian center is popular with local students, nearby Ortaköy is Istanbul's hub of conspicuous consumption where the rich and powerful come for expensive shopping, eating, and partying.

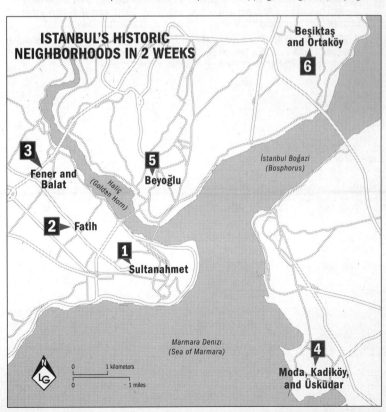

ISLAND TRIPPIN' IN 2 WEEKS

1. ANDROS (2 DAYS): With coveted beaches perfect for bronzing and three different museums in its small namesake town, burn and learn on the northernmost island in the Cyclades.

2. TINOS (2 DAYS): Head to the Panagia Evangelistria Church for this island's main attraction, but leave the town and see some nearby villages and mountains like Mount Exobourgo for a lofty experience.

3. MYKONOS (2 DAYS): Get more than sand in your pants at this debauchery-filled island's beach clubs and downright dirty discos.

4. DELOS (1 DAY): Steeped in history and home to the Delian League, this island's sightseeing will be a Mythology 101 refresher and makes it the sacred center of the Cyclades.

5. NAXOS (1 DAY): Home to the famous Portara arch, delicious produce, and world-class linens, this island's Chora neighborhood is a materialist's, just a moped ride away from small villages.

6. IOS (2 DAYS): This hangover-haven rivals Mykonos in nocturnal Dionysian rites and boasts 36 beaches along its coast for rejuvenation after a night out on the town.

7. SANTORINI (2 DAYS): Some believe this island's volcanic past to be proof of the lost continent of Atlantis. True or not, Santorini's 4000 years of history make its whitewashed towns and black-sand beaches a must-stop for travelers.

8. MILOS (2 DAYS): The small towns of Plaka and Trypiti hold some interesting catacombs and Orthodox churches, but the coast's dramatic views and beautiful shorelines highlight some of the best beaches in the Cyclades.

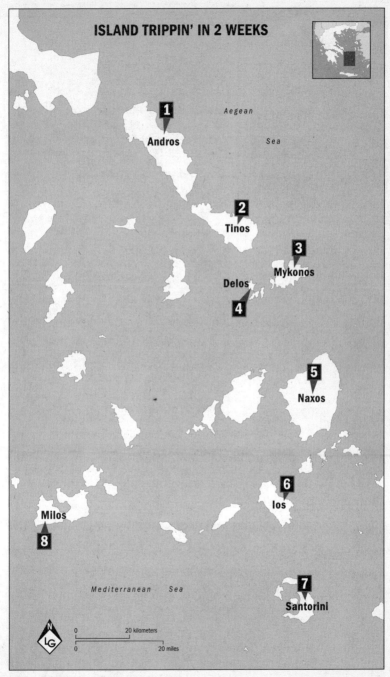

ISLAND TRIPPIN' IN 2 WEEKS

Aegean

Sea

1 Andros

2 Tinos

3 Mykonos

Delos

4

5 Naxos

6 Ios

Milos

8

Mediterranean   Sea

7 Santorini

N
LG

0   20 kilometers

0   20 miles

how to use this book

CHAPTERS

In the next few pages, the travel coverage chapters—the meat of any *Let's Go* book—begin with Istanbul, head to Athens, take detours to places like the Cape Sounion Peninsula and Troy in the Excursions chapter, and finish up in the Greek Islands.

But that's not all, folks. We also have a few extra chapters for you to peruse:

CHAPTER	DESCRIPTION
Discover Istanbul, Athens & the Greek Isles	Discover tells you what to do, when to do it, and where to go for it. The absolute coolest things about any destination get highlighted in this chapter at the front of all *Let's Go* books.
Essentials	Essentials contains the practical info you need before, during, and after your trip–visas, regional transportation, health and safety, phrasebooks, and more.
Beyond Tourism	As students ourselves, we at *Let's Go* encourage studying abroad, or going beyond tourism more generally, every chance we get. This chapter lists ideas for how to study, volunteer, or work abroad with other young travelers in Istanbul, Athens & the Greek Isles to get more out of your trip.

LISTINGS

Listings—a.k.a. reviews of individual establishments—constitute a majority of *Let's Go* coverage. Our Researcher-Writers list establishments in order from **best to worst value**—not necessarily quality. (Obviously a five-star hotel is nicer than a hostel, but it would probably be ranked lower because it's not as good a value.) Listings pack in a lot of information, but it's easy to digest if you know how they're constructed:

ESTABLISHMENT NAME 💳 [cash] ♿ [no ♿] 📶 🍸 ❄ ☀ ▼ type of establishment ❶
Address ☎phone number 🖥website
Editorial review goes here.
⇆ Directions to the establishment. ***i*** *Other practical information about the establishment, like age restrictions at a club or whether breakfast is included at a hostel.* *$ Prices for goods or services.* *⏰ Hours or schedules.*

ICONS

First things first: places and things that we absolutely love, sappily cherish, generally obsess over, and wholeheartedly endorse are denoted by the all-empowering 👍**Let's Go thumbs-up.** In addition, the icons scattered throughout a listing (as you saw in the sample above) can tell you a lot about an establishment. The following icons answer a series of yes-no questions about a place:

💳	Credit cards accepted	[cash]	Cash only	♿	Wheelchair-accessible
[no ♿]	Not wheelchair-accessible	📶	Internet access available	🍸	Alcohol served
❄	Air-conditioned	☀	Outdoor seating available	▼	GLBT or GLBT-friendly

The rest are visual cues to help you navigate each listing:

☎	Phone numbers	🖥	Websites	⇆	Directions
i	Other hard info	$	Prices	⏰	Hours

OTHER USEFUL STUFF

Area codes for each destination appear opposite the name of the city and are denoted by the ☎ icon. Finally, in order to pack the book with as much information as possible, we have used a few **standard abbreviations.** The Turkish *caddesi* is abbreviated as "Cad," and *sokak* is abbreviated as "Sok."

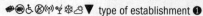

PRICE DIVERSITY

A final set of icons corresponds to what we call our "price diversity" scale, which approximates how much money you can expect to spend at a given establishment. For **accommodations,** we base our range on the cheapest price for which a single traveler can stay for one night. For **food,** we estimate the average amount one traveler will spend in one sitting. The table below tells you what you'll typically find in Athens, Istanbul, and the Greek Isles at the corresponding price range, but keep in mind that no system can allow for the quirks of individual establishments.

ACCOMMODATIONS	GREECE RANGE	TURKEY RANGE	WHAT YOU'RE LIKELY TO FIND
❶	under €22	under €35	Campgrounds and dorm rooms in hostels. Expect bunk beds and a communal bath. You may have to provide or rent towels and sheets.
❷	€22-33	€36-50	Upper-end hostels or lower-end hotels. You may have a private bathroom, or there may be a sink in your room and a communal shower in the hall.
❸	€34-45	€51-70	A small room with a private bath. Should have decent amenities, such as phone and TV. Breakfast may be included.
❹	€46-60	€71-100	Should have bigger rooms than a ❸, with more amenities or in a more convenient location. Breakfast probably included.
❺	over €60	over €100	Large hotels or upscale chains. If it's a ❺ and it doesn't have the perks you want (and more), you've paid too much.

FOOD	GREECE RANGE	TURKEY RANGE	WHAT YOU'RE LIKELY TO FIND
❶	under €6	under 10TL	Probably street food or a fast-food joint, but also inexpensive bakeries (yum). Usually takeout, but you may have the option of sitting down.
❷	€6-12	11-16TL	Sandwiches, pizza, appetizers at a bar, or low-priced entrees. Most ethnic eateries are a ❷. Either takeout or a sit-down meal, but only slightly more fashionable decor.
❸	€13-19	17-25TL	Mid-priced entrees, seafood, and exotic pasta dishes. More upscale ethnic eateries. Since you'll have the luxury of a waiter, tip will set you back a little extra.
❹	€20-25	26-40TL	A somewhat fancy restaurant. Entrees tend to be heartier or more elaborate, but you're really paying for decor and ambience. Few restaurants in this range have a dress code, but some may look down on T-shirts and sandals.
❺	over €25	40TL+	Your meal might cost more than your room, but there's a reason—it's something fabulous, famous, or both. Slacks and dress shirts may be expected. Offers foreign-sounding food and a decent wine list.

ISTANBUL

Istanbul is a city like no other. With stray cats running around sloping cobblestone streets, lean minarets of centuries-old mosques piercing the sky, and ferries hurtling across the stunning waters of the Bosphorus, this city of two continents seems never to run out of steam or surprises. There is something for everyone—foodies will love sampling Turkish *meze* and desserts, history buffs will wander in awe through the city's palaces and places of worship, shopaholics will bargain-hunt in the immense bazaars and markets, party animals will dance their nights away in the clubs on **İstiklal Avenue** and in **Ortaköy**, hipsters will chatter their way through **Beyoğlu's** burgeoning art scene, the homesick will hobnob with expats in **Cihangir**, idlers will rest inside the city's hamams, and all travelers will experience the city's spectacle firsthand. Naturally, it's not all exhilarating. Istanbul is also a minefield of tourist traps and shameless rip-offs, and you can't avoid making a few mistakes before you learn how to navigate it. But once you get a hang of the confusing street plan, buy an Akbil to commute like a local, and learn a few Turkish words (Kebab! Rakı!), you'll be in for much more than what all those peddlers of "Turkish culture" offer you. Take a ferry to the Asian side, at sunset. Learn about the city's history. Find your own best way to avoid a rakı hangover (a late-night çorba is a safe bet). Take a walk among the decrepit houses of **Tarlabaşı** or **Fener**. Pretend you're rich or beautiful at **Reina** or another prestigious club in Ortaköy. Spend a day down at the **Princes' Islands,** riding horse carriages or hiking up to a monastery. Stay up all night and watch a sunrise over the misty Bosphorus. Whatever you want to do, Istanbul is waiting.

greatest hits

- **BIKE PRINCES' ISLANDS.** Tour Heybeliada Island on two wheels, while enjoying its beaches, beer, and the beautiful vista of Istanbul (p. 34).

- **GET STEAMED.** Head to Sofular Hamamı and experience a real Turkish bath (p. 67).

- **EAT FRESH-OFF-THE-BOAT FISH.** Go to Sıdıka for grilled octopus. If that's too tentacle-y for your taste, get something else off their handwritten, chalkboard menu (p. 56).

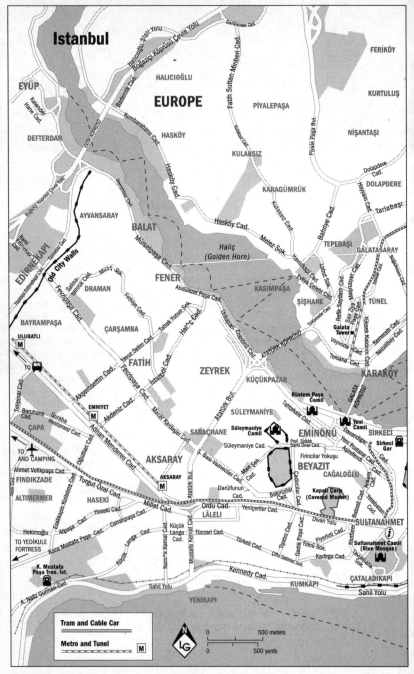

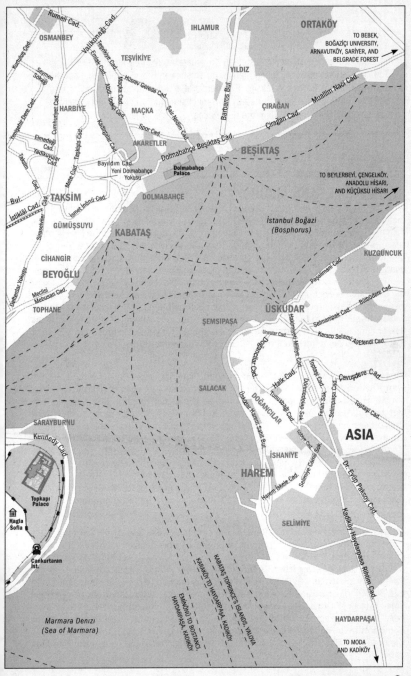

orientation

SULTANAHMET AND AROUND

With the **Hagia Sophia** and other popular historical sights to its name, Sultanahmet is the center of Istanbul's tourism and the first stop for anyone who wants to explore the city. Sultanahmet proper is the area teeming with tourists around the **Blue Mosque**, where many of the budget accommodations and historical sights can be found. To the north there are the **Sirkeci** and **Eminönü** neighborhoods, home to the **Spice Bazaar**, bustling streets, and some decent eating options. The **Galata Bridge** above Eminönü connects the historic peninsula with **Karaköy** on the European side. The eastern tip of the peninsula is occupied by **Topkapı Palace** and the **Gülhane Park,** one of the few areas around that have greenery. To the west from Sultanahmet are **Çemberlitaş** and **Beyazıt Square,** home to nice tea places and cheap restaurants. Above Beyazıt is the **Grand Bazaar,** a maze-like area perfect for some shopping with your haggling. Below Beyazıt is the **Kumkapı** neighborhood, renowned for its fish restaurants.

FATIH ☎0212

There are two Fatihs talked about in Istanbul. The municipality of Fatih covers the entire historical peninsula and includes Sultanahmet, Beyazıt, and all the nearby neighborhoods. Fatih proper, on the other hand, is a small neighborhood around **Fatih Mosque** where government officials dwell and fun goes to die. It's more conservative than other neighborhoods, which can be a refreshing change from **İstiklal Cad.** One of the liveliest roads here is **Fevzi Paşa Cad.,** which runs northwest from **Fatih İtfaiye Park.** If you follow the **Valens Aqueduct** from its southern end, to the right you'll find the **Siirt Bazaar,** a square with plenty of small restaurants. A marginally classier cluster of restaurants can be found on **Atpazarı,** a square just a few blocks east of the mosque, but no establishment in Fatih serves alcohol. To the north of the Fatih Mosque is the **Çarşamba** neighborhood, next to which Fatih looks like a hippie commune.

FENER AND BALAT

Fener and Balat used to be a home to the Greek, Jewish, and Armenian minorities of Istanbul, but today they're populated mostly by poor Muslim migrants. It's a very dilapidated area, but doesn't feel unsafe. The fastest way to get here is by bus, but the prettiest is by ferry from Eminönü. The street plan is rather confusing, so use landmarks to navigate the area. **Vodina Cad.** runs parallel to the shore between Fener and Balat and has a number of local stores as well as the impressive, red-brick **Phanar Greek Orthodox College** (Özel Fener Rum Lisesi) some 300m inland from the Fener ferry jetty. The **Edirnekapı** neighborhood is a 15min. walk inland, close to the city walls, home to the mosaic-filled **Chora Church.** **Eyüp** is a neighborhood a few kilometers to the north of Balat, where you can find the **Eyüp Sultan Mosque** as well as the **Pierre Loti Cafe.**

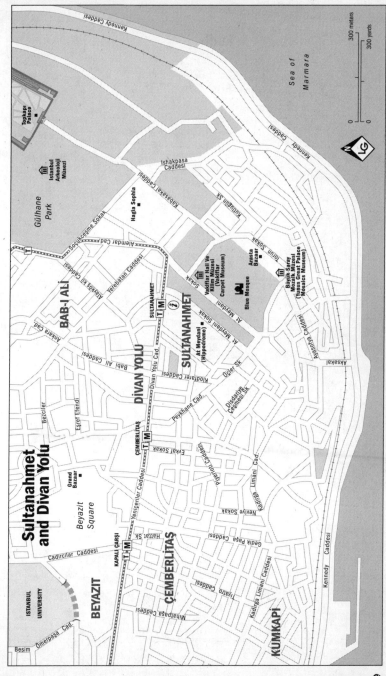

Sultanahmet and Divan Yolu

BEYAZIT

BAB-I ALİ

DİVAN YOLU

SULTANAHMET

ÇEMBERLİTAŞ

KUMKAPI

ISTANBUL UNIVERSITY

Besim

Ömerpaşa Cad.

Çadircılar Caddesi

Beyazit Square

Grand Bazaar

KAPALI ÇARŞI

Minarpaşa Caddesi

Bezciler

Eşref Efendi

Ankara Cad.

Babı Ali Caddesi

Yeniçeriler Caddesi

Hattat SK.

CEMBERLİTAŞ

Divan Yolu Cad.

Peykhane Cad.

Kıodlararı Caddesi

Evkat Sokak

Gedik Pasa Caddesi

Tiyatro Caddesi

Kadirga Limanı Caddesi

Piyerloti Caddesi

Neviye Sokak

Disdariye Cennesi Sk.

Üçler SK.

Kennedy Caddesi

SULTANAHMET

At Meydanı (Hippodrome)

At Meydanı Sokak

Sokak

Vakıflar Halı Ve Kilim Müzesi (Vakıflar Carpet Museum)

Blue Mosque

Arasta Bazaar

Büyük Saray Mozaik Müzesi (Yunus Great Palace Mosaics Museum)

Torun Sokak

Aksakal Caddesi

Aksakal

Akbıyık Caddesi

Kaleagasi SK.

Kulluğün SK.

Hagia Sophia

Yerebatan Caddesi

Alemdar Cad.

Alayköşkü Caddesi

Soğukçeşme Sokak

Kabasakal Caddesi

Ishakpaşa Caddesi

Gülhane Park

Istanbul Arkeoloji Müzesi

Topkapı Palace

Kennedy Caddesi

Kennedy Caddesi

Sea of Marmara

300 meters

300 yards

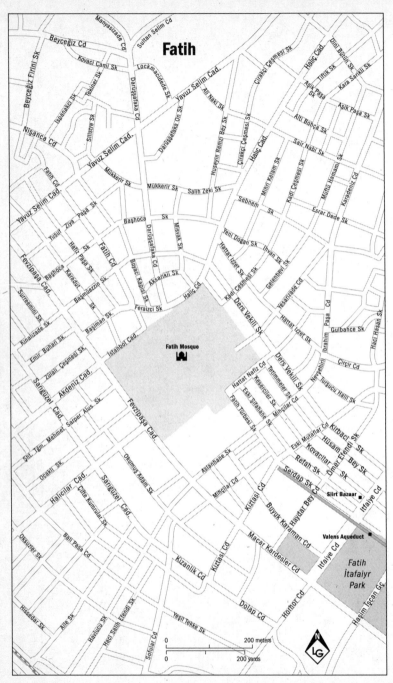

Fatih

Fatih Mosque

Siirt Bazaar

Valens Aqueduct

Fatih İtafaiyr Park

istanbul

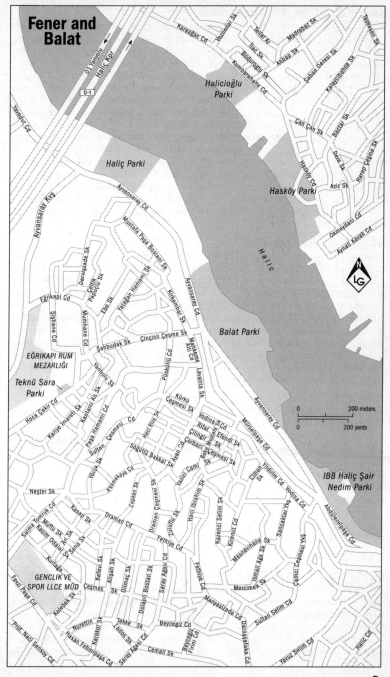

Fener and
Balat

Karaağaç Cd
Yenadar Sk
Tellar Ar
Madrabaz Sk
Başçeşme Sk
İlaç Sk
Ahbap Sk
Boğuroğlu Sk
Şaban Deresi Sk
Kumbarahane Cd
Kataycıbahçe Sk

O1 Yanyolu
Haliç Kpr

Halicioğlu Parki

O-1

Çan Çan Sk
Badiar Sk
Dere Sk
Harap Çeşme Sk

Yavedut Cd

Haliç Parki

Hasköy Cd
Aziz Sk

Ayvansaray Kvş

Ayvansaray Cd

Hasköy Parki

Okmeydanı Cd
Aynalı Kavak Cd

Mustafa Paşa Bostanı Sk

Ayvansaray Cd

H a l i ç

N
LG

Dervişzade Sk
Çeltik Paşalıç Sk

Yatağan Hamam Sk

Eba Sk

Kirkmbal Sk

Eğrikapı Cd

Ayvansaray Cd

Balat Parki

Mumhane Cd
Şişhane Cd

Sahbudak Sk
Çinçinli Çeşme Sk

Mahkeme Altı Cd

EĞRİKAPI RUM MEZARLIĞI

Pisküllü Cd

Lavanta Sk

Teknü Sara Parki

Yahyolu Sk

0   200 meters
0   200 yards

Hoca Çakır Cd
Kariye İmareti Sk
Kantarcı Ali Sk

Kürkü Çeşmesi Sk

Paşa Hamamı Cd

Cd

Vodina Cd

Ayvansaray Cd

Mürselpaşa Cd

Sultan Çeşmesi Sk

Haci Rıza Sk

Rifat Efendi Sk

Çilingir Sk

Yörük Sk

Soğutlu Bakkal Sk

Ayan Cd

Çorbacı Çeşmesi Sk

IBB Haliç Şair Nedim Parki

Kesmekaya Cd

Yazıcı Camii

Çimen Sk

Yıldırım Cd

Vodina Cd

Neşter Sk

Cepken Sk

Draman Çeşmesi Sk

Zülüflü Sk

Hacı İbrahim Sk

Kazancı Selim Sk

Kiremit Cd

Sancaktar Kvş

Abdülezelpaşa Cd

Salma Tomruk Cd
Murtu Sk
Kasap Sk
Draman Cd
Fethiye Cd

Mesnevihane Sk

Kasım Odaları Sk
Arı Sk
Sena Sk

Kurtağa

Saray Ağası Sk

Fethiye Cd

İsmail Ağa Sk

Çamcı Çeşmesi Ykş

GENÇLİK VE SPOR İLÇE MÜD

Ketevi Sk

Alişah Sk

Dilmaç Sk

Saray Ağası Sk

Dolaplı Bostan Sk

Manyasizade Cd

Sultan Selim Cd

Mercimek Sk

Fevzi Paşa Cd

Kelebek Sk

Çeşmesi Sk

Nurettin Sk

Tekke Sk

Beycegiz Cd

Darüşşafaka Cd

Prof. Naci Şensoy Cd

Hasan Fehmipaşa Cd

Karakol Sk

Loços Sk

Saray Ağası Cd

Cemali Sk

Beycegiz Firini Cd

Yavuz Selim Cd

Haliç Cd

KADIKÖY, MODA, AND ÜSKÜDAR

The Asian side of Istanbul tends to be more confusing for travelers, because it isn't laid out like most European cities. However, make your way through this confusing part of town to discover the center of a lively alternative art scene, with an abundance of cafes and restaurants free from the hordes of tourists in other parts of the city. There are a few streets in historical **Kadıköy** whose location you should keep in mind. The **Söğütlüçeşme Cad.** runs from the ferry terminal inland and intersects with Kadıköy's important pedestrian street **Bahariye Cad.** This intersection is home to the well-known statue of a bull. Parallel to Bahariye Cad. is **Kadife Sok.**, the "bar street," where most of the local nightlife is located. Intersecting with Söğütlüçeşme near the ferry terminal is the **Güneşlibahçe Sok.**, where **Kadıköy Market** and many restaurants with live music can be found. **Moda** is a well-to-do residential area to the south of Kadıköy with some romantic beaches that people often use to watch the sunset. Within walking distance, Moda is also accessible by a nostalgic shoebox-of-a-**tram** that follows a circular route around Kadıköy into suburbia. **Üsküdar** is a rather sleepy historical neighborhood some kilometers north of Kadıköy that is home to a number of mosques. The easiest way to travel between Kadıköy and Üsküdar is to take public bus #12 or #12A.

BEŞİKTAŞ AND ORTAKÖY

Beşiktaş, a village a few local kilometers up from Kabataş, has a small pedestrian center popular with students. The **eagle statue** (there are two—we mean the bigger one), which is near the triangular **fish market,** is a good orientation point. There are a few expensive places here, but it's **Ortaköy** that is notorious as Istanbul's leading site of conspicuous consumption—the rich and powerful flock here to shop, eat, and party. Ortaköy's small center is near the water, around the **Ortaköy Mosque.** The city's famous clubs are mostly concentrated on **Muallim Naci,** a road running up from Ortaköy to **Kuruçeşme.** One main road (at various points called Dolmabahçe, Çırağan, and Muallim Naci) runs along the shore, connecting Kabataş with these neighborhoods. You can take one of the many buses, though the road is often clogged with traffic, so we suggest walking when possible.

BEYOĞLU

Beyoğlu is the real heart of modern Istanbul, pulsing with tons of galleries, eateries, bars, and clubs. Many of these establishments are located off **İstiklal Cad.**, a throbbing promenade connecting **Taksim Square** in the north with **Tünel Square** in the south. A bit below Tünel is the **Galata Tower,** the most recognizable landmark of the entire European portion of the city. Don't confuse this with **Galatasaray Lisesi,** which is about halfway into İstiklal, near where **Yeni Çarşı** intersects the avenue. Just above Galatasaray is the **Nevizade Sokak,** where much of Beyoğlu's nightlife takes place. **Cihangir,** a bohemian neighborhood popular with expats, is between the **Alman Hastanesi** (German Hospital) and **Firuzağa Mosque.** The Sultanahmet tram doesn't run to İstiklal, so to get there, you can either go to Karaköy and take a funicular to Tünel, or go to Kabataş and then take the funicular to Taksim.

accommodations

Most of Istanbul's budget accommodations are concentrated in **Sultanahmet,** but **Beyoğlu** is becoming more and more popular with travelers looking for cheap rooms. The main advantage to staying in Sultanahmet is being close to the major historical sights, while residing in Beyoğlu gives you easier access to the city's culture and nightlife. In Sultanahmet, boutique hotels and small guesthouses often provide the

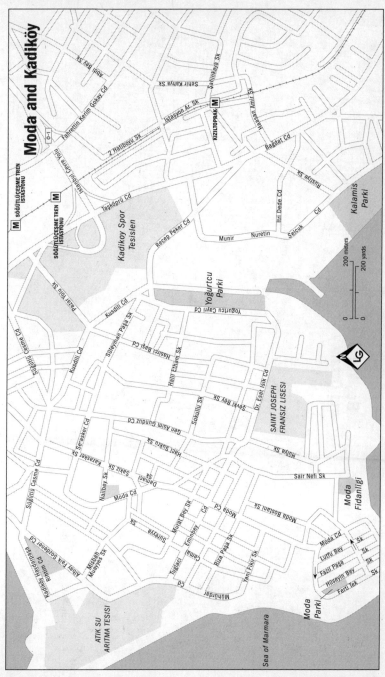

Moda and Kadiköy

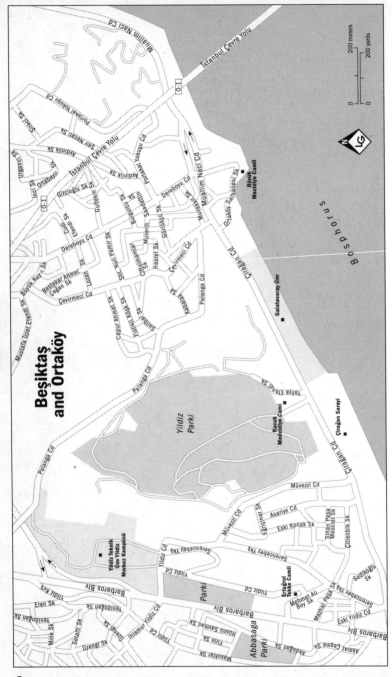

Beşiktaş and Ortaköy

best value, but they usually fill up quickly. There are only a few suitable accommodations on the Asian side and in the more conservative districts like **Fatih** or **Fener**, while Beşiktaş is home to mostly upscale hotels. Avoid staying in hotels in the **Aksaray** area, the city's seedy red light district.

The prices of Istanbul's hostels can change faster than you can say "Çekoslovakyalılaştıramadıklarımızdanmışsınız" (which, by the way, means "are you one of those whom we couldn't have possibly turned into a Czechoslovak?"). All the prices quoted here were collected during the **high season** (Mar-May, Aug-Sept, Christmas-New Years), but they may be much lower at other times. Not all hostels change their prices at the same time, and some maintain the same prices year-round. Often the deal you get depends on what kind of room is available at the moment, so the best way to find a **bargain** is to ask at multiple hostels in person, or to look for current prices on the internet.

SULTANAHMET AND AROUND

✓ METROPOLIS HOSTEL — 🚭 📶 ❄ HOSTEL ❷

Akbıyık Cad. Terbıyık Sok. 24 ☎212 518 1822 💻www.metropolishostel.com

Though skeptical of everything in Sultanahmet that's under than 400 years old, *Let's Go* still found an accommodation option that it can wholeheartedly recommend—Metropolis Hostel seems to really know what international travelers need. The rooms are clean and welcoming, the beds are comfortable (a rarity in the hostel scene here), and the terrace view beats much of the competition. Spend your evening with *nargile* on the rooftop bar, or join in on a pub crawl organized by the hostel.

*‡ [M]Sultanahmet. Near İshak Paşa Mosque. **i** Breakfast included. $ Co-ed dorms €14-17; all-female €17. Singles €37; doubles €54, with bath €66; triples €72; quads €72. ⏰ Reception 24hr.*

CORDIAL HOUSE — ♿ 📶 HOSTEL ❶

Peykhane Sok. 29 ☎212 518 0576 💻www.cordialhouse.com

One of the best budget options on the historical peninsula, this big hostel near *Çemberlitaş* is cheap, close to a tram stop, and very conveniently located for walking to both the Grand Bazaar and Sultanahmet. Since it has so many rooms, you might get a lower price even at a time when other hostels are still charging their high-season prices. It's not quite the social hotspot that hostels with terrace bars aspire to be, but if that aspect of hostel culture isn't too important to you, this is the place to stay.

*‡ [M]Çemberlitaş. 50m south from the tram stop. **i** Breakfast €4. $ Dorms €12; singles €24; doubles €30, with bath €60; triples with bath €70; quads with bath €80. ⏰ Reception 24hr.*

TULIP GUESTHOUSE — 🚭 📶 ❄ GUESTHOUSE ❶

Akbıyık Cad. Terbıyık Sok. 15/2 ☎212 517 6509 💻www.tulipguesthouse.com

With a tiny kitchen in which to cook, cheerful and clean rooms, and an owner with a university education, this guesthouse offers better value than many bigger hostels. Twice a week there are community dinners prepared by the staff and the guests in the upstairs breakfast area, and there's a shower available in the basement for people who already checked out but are staying until the end of the day. Even the name reflects the management's desire to cater to the comfort of its guests—it was changed to "Tulip" after they realized it was more memorable than the original, unpronounceable one.

*‡ [M]Sultanahmet. Near İshak Paşa Mosque. **i** Breakfast included. Bathrooms ensuite. $ Dorms €10; singles €35; doubles €45; triples €55. ⏰ Guests get their own key.*

CHEERS HOSTEL — 🚭 📶 HOSTEL ❶

Alemdar Mahallesi Zeynep, Sultan Camii Sok. 21 ☎212 526 0200 💻www.cheershostel.com

Among the more expensive accommodations, Cheers Hostel offers great value for your money. The rooms are decorated with objects that could be mistaken for Ottoman relics by people not in the know, the showers are inside glass cubicles (not as common around here as you might think), and there's a killer view of Hagia Sophia from the terrace. The dorm beds have their own storage containers (most places only have safety boxes at the reception desk), but the dorms themselves aren't usually locked.

❧ *From ⓂGülhane, continue up Divan Yolu, turn right after Zeynep Sultan Mosque, and continue for 30m.* ⓲ *Breakfast included. All doubles and triples with ensuite bath.* Ⓢ *Dorms €16-20; doubles €60; triples €80.* Ⓐ *Reception 24hr.*

NOBEL HOSTEL
⚓⊗(ᵗᵖ)❄ HOSTEL ❶

Mimar Mehmet Aga 32   ☎212 516 3177 ▣www.nobelhostel.com

Yet another good hostel that combines relatively low prices with acceptable quality. A vertigo-inducing staircase leads to the terrace upstairs that offers a great view of the Blue Mosque. Guests get a 15% discount in the restaurant downstairs, and a beer for just 4 TL upstairs. Here's a joke: Knock, knock. Who's there? Nobel. Nobel who? Nobel, so I rang. *Let's Go* doesn't know how long (if at all) the reception will find this joke funny.

❧ *From ⓂSultanahmet, head down Akbıyık Cad.* ⓲ *Breakfast included.* Ⓢ *Singles €30; doubles €40, with bath €50; triples €50, with bath €60.* Ⓐ *Reception 24hr.*

BIG APPLE HOSTEL
⚓♿(ᵗᵖ) HOSTEL ❶

Akbıyık Cad. Bayram Fırını Sok. 12   ☎212 517 7931 ▣www.hostelbigapple.com

Not very tuned into the whole let's-name-our-hostel-after-something-related-to-the-Ottomans mindset in this area, the Big Apple Hostel is a reliable place to spend a few nights. It didn't get the best end of the stick when it comes to its terrace view, but the hostel is doing what it can to make sitting up there pleasant. Not as cramped for space as most other hostels around, the Big Apple's rooms are clean and pleasant, and the reception desk offers the standard combination of bellydancing (F) and disco trips to Taksim.

❧ *ⓂSultanahmet. Go past Aya Sofya, and enter the hostel neighborhood; it's located off Akbıyık Cad.* ⓲ *Breakfast included.* Ⓢ *Dorms €12-15; singles with bath €40; doubles with bath €50; triples with bath €75; quads with bath €80.* Ⓐ *Reception 24hr.*

ORIENT HOSTEL
⚓⊗(ᵗᵖ)⚲ HOSTEL ❶

Akbıyık Cad. 13   ☎212 517 9493 ▣www.orienthostel.com

Allegedly the first hostel in Turkey and one of the biggest ones in Istanbul, Orient Hostel is a safe bet for young travelers and offers a decent view of the sea from the terrace, a daily happy hour, and many common spaces in which to meet fellow backpackers. The rooms are small and reasonably clean, even if the stairs and the underground spaces can feel a bit musty. With a capacity of 152 guests, you're probably not going to get turned down when you show up fresh off the plane at 3am.

❧ *From ⓂSultanahmet, walk past the Hagia Sophia; it's located in the middle of the hostel district.* ⓲ *HI member. Breakfast included. Happy hour beer 5TL.* Ⓢ *Dorms €10-15; singles €30; doubles €40, with bath €55.* Ⓐ *Reception 24hr.*

BOUTIQUE BEST TOWN HOTEL
⚓♿(ᵗᵖ)❄ BOUTIQUE HOTEL ❷

Nöbethane Cad. 34   ☎212 528 1515 ▣www.besttownhotel.com

This is one of the best options among the cluster of hotels near the Sirkeci Train Station. Just a 10min. walk away from Hagia Sophia, it's also conveniently located for walks around Eminönü and Karaköy. The rooms feel comfortable, and the hostel is one of the few cheaper places around with a working elevator. Unless you are bringing a children's choir with you (there are only 10 rooms), staying here is a good alternative to Sultanahmet.

❧ *ⓂSirkeci. Go away from the sea, down Muradiye Cad.; Nöbethane Cad. will be on the left.* ⓲ *Breakfast included. All rooms with ensuite bath.* Ⓢ *Singles €50; doubles €60.* Ⓐ *Reception 24hr.*

Cankurtaran Mah. Amiral Tafdil 18 　　　　　☎212 458 6664 ▣www.hoteloceans7.com.tr

For travelers less willing to forego their sense of dignity, there's Ocean's 7 (*Let's Go* has no idea where the other 4 went—or why Brad Pitt isn't at this hotel). For a price that's comparable with what many of the hostels charge during the high season, you can get rooms that are so aesthetically appealing they may make a

the "weast"

Unlike most countries in the world, Turkey bears the unique distinction of belonging to two continents. Straddling the line of both Europe and Asia, 97% of the country lies in Asia, while the remaining 3% lies in Europe. Though 3% may seem pretty insignificant, this latter percentage consists of Istanbul, the country's most recognizable and lively city. Simply because it's better known, Istanbul comes to define the whole country in the eyes of many outsiders. Yet, Turkey should perhaps be better described as "weast" – the crucible of West and East captured in a single noun. Over the centuries Greek warriors, Arab invaders, Crusaders, and Mongolian traders have all passed through or settled in the region, and their legacies live on today, bridging the old and new, the east and west, and ultimately embodying the "weast."

In particular, the city of Istanbul best illustrates this melting pot. It's simplest to think about the city as a historical core surrounded by modern, cosmopolitan growth. The southern shores of the Golden Horn peninsula are home to the city's historic districts – the old Sultan's palace, citadel, ancient religious sites like the Blue Mosque, and the tangy aromas of the Spice Bazaar. Beyond this core, rising residential buildings, tall offices and companies, and banks sketch a New York City skyline farther out on the western, European side of the city, while a mirroring layout of skyscrapers have also shot up on the Asian side. As a visitor, you can haggle for jewels and leather in the Grand Bazaar or peruse the designer shops at a modern-day mall. In addition to the intriguing combination of new and old seen in the physical architecture, this element of the "weast" is also embedded in the attitude of the people. There is crazy driving and a blatant lack of punctuality. Foreigners will undoubtedly be charged "tourist prices" in markets and bazaars, and might be surprised that the largest religious community is Islam.

Yet as the meeting point of west and east, Istanbul is also the place where common ground lurks beneath superficial differences. One commonality is the 500-year reign of the Ottoman Empire, which influenced the heritage of over 31 countries all over Europe, western Asia, and North Africa. In 1928, after the Empire's decline, Turkey's first president Mustafa Kemal wanted to model Turkey's relatively new nation on the West—Arabic script was discarded and replaced by the Latin alphabet, and turbans were banned. After such heavy influence from an Islamic empire, these changes set the stage for the many future identities within Turkey, yet also created controversy over how the nation should define itself.

The desire for a clear identity has continued to be a struggle for this relatively young nation, and Istanbul is the locus of this activity. In recent years, an explosion of creativity and renewed appreciation of Anatolian culture has swept the young generation. There are Turkish traditional jazz and rock fusion groups, mystic Sufi dancers, fashion designers using native cloths in distinct styles, and filmmakers earning recognition abroad. The "weast" is no longer just a blend of west and east, but rather a defining characteristic that can't be found anywhere else.

sweaty backpacker feel out of place. While the covered seating area upstairs is more formal than the *nargile* terrace lairs you find elsewhere, there's nothing haughty about the staff.

➜ [M]Sultanahmet. One street west of Akbıyık Cad. ℹ Breakfast included. All rooms with ensuite bath. $ Singles €40; doubles €65; triples €85; family rooms €95. ⏰ Reception 24hr.

HOTEL ERENREL 💳🚭📶 HOSTEL [1]

Hoca Paşa Tayahatun Sok. 11 ☎212 527 3468 💻www.hotelerenler.com

A great choice for cheapskates who don't want to stay in a dorm, this hostel has single rooms that are half the price and half the size of what one tends to expect. The wireless connection is erratic, the English at the reception desk is intermittent, and the hostel is tucked away in a small street in Sirkeci that could look eerie at night—but hey, you get to stay in your own room for the price of an upscale kebab. The place isn't dirty or unsafe, so it can be used as a base for sleeping, because your waking hours will be spent in the magnificent streets of Istanbul.

➜ [M]Gülhane. Follow the tram tracks north along the Gülhane Park walls. When the tram tracks turn left, keep to the right and continue for two blocks. $ Dorms €10; singles €13; doubles with bath €33. ⏰ Reception 24hr.

BEST ISLAND HOSTEL 💳🚭📶 HOSTEL [1]

Cankurtaran Mah. Kutlugün Sok. 5 ☎212 518 0170 💻www.bestislandhostel.com

Best Island is one of the cheaper places still within a short walk from all the famous old mosques that you came to ogle, and the degree of comfort accords to that. Avoid staying in the basement rooms, but definitely go check out the terrace, which has a full view of the Hagia Sophia and is a pleasant place for hanging out. If you ignore the occasional patch of peeling paint and the small shared bathrooms, you can save a few euros and take advantage of this hostel's good location.

➜ [M]Sultanahmet. Walk past Hagia Sophia and toward Akbıyık Cad; it will be in a street to the left. ℹ Breakfast included. $ Dorms €10-13; singles €32; doubles €37. ⏰ Reception 24hr.

istanbul

KADIKÖY, MODA, AND ÜSKÜDAR

HUSH HOSTEL 💳🚭📶 HOSTEL [1]

Miralay Nazım Sok. 20, Kadıköy ☎216 330 9188 💻www.hushhostelistanbul.com

Decrepit but charming, this hostel housed within an Ottoman mansion seems to have a monopoly on budget accommodations in this area. The cracked paint and gloomy feel aren't for everybody, but the location next to Bar Street is great, and there's an art gallery downstairs. If you want to stay on the Asian side and close to all the nightlife, say no more than "hush."

➜ From the bull statue, head south down Bahariye Cad. After passing the Süreyya Opera House, turn right, and then another right. The hostel will be on your left. $ Dorms €11-12; doubles €34-38; triples €45; quads €52. ⏰ Guests get their own key.

HOTEL GRAND AS 💳♿📶❄ HOTEL [4]

Nüzhetefendi Sok. 27, Kadıköy ☎216 346 9160 💻www.grandashotel.com

Despite the unfortunate name, this is one of the better options from among the cluster of hotels near the ferry terminal, which range from completely unmemorable to unforgettably terrible. You won't write home about this place, but at least the staff speaks some English and the rooms have ensuite bathrooms.

➜ From the ferry terminal, head up Söğütlü Çeşme Cad. Turn left at Osmanağa Mosque, and it's two blocks ahead. ℹ Breakfast included. $ Singles 75TL; doubles 110TL; triples 140TL. ⏰ Reception 24hr.

HUSH HOSTEL LOUNGE 💳🚭📶 HOSTEL [1]

Rıhtım Cad. Iskele Sok. 46, Kadıköy ☎216 450 4363 💻www.hushhostelistanbul.com

This very recent offshoot of the HUSH Hostel is a bit more expensive, a bit more modern, and a bit farther from everything interesting. The rooms are large and

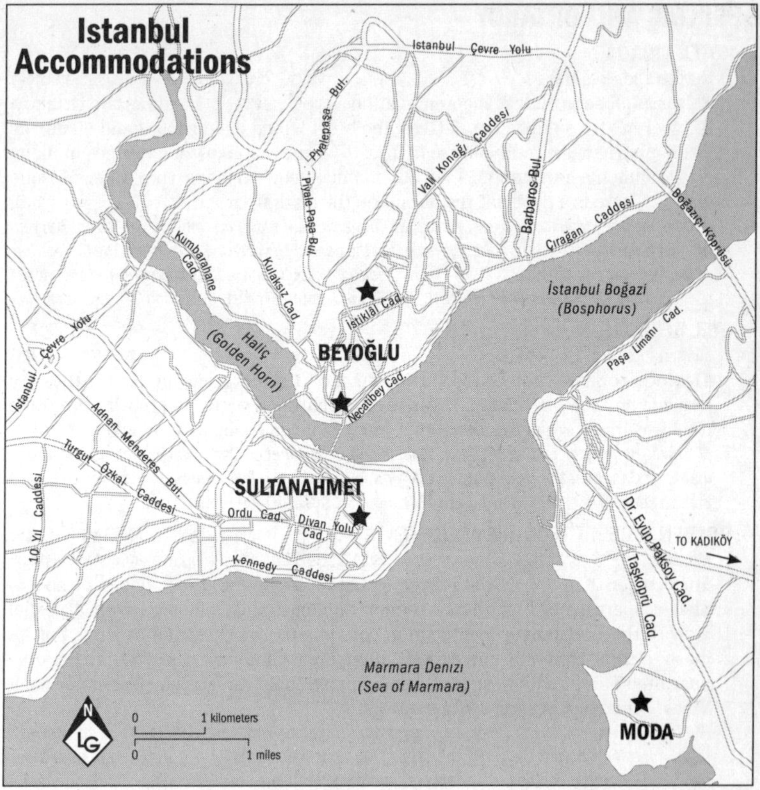
Istanbul Accommodations
Istanbul Çevre Yolu
Piyalepaşa Bul.
Piyale Paşa Bul.
Vali Konağı Caddesi
Barbaros Bul.
Boğaziçi Köprüsü
Çırağan Caddesi
Kumbarahane Cad.
Kulaksız Cad.
İstiklâl Cad.
İstanbul Boğazi (Bosphorus)
Paşa Limanı Cad.
Haliç (Golden Horn)
BEYOĞLU
Necatibey Cad.
Istanbul Çevre Yolu
Adnan Menderes Bul.
Turgut Özkal Caddesi
10. Yıl Caddesi
SULTANAHMET
Ordu Cad.
Divan Yolu Cad.
Kennedy Caddesi
Dr. Eyüp Paksoy Cad.
Taşkoprü Cad.
TO KADIKÖY
Marmara Denızı (Sea of Marmara)
MODA
0 1 kilometers
0 1 miles
N
LG

take the word "bare" to new extremes, but there are a couple of cool lounges downstairs that make up for it. The empty walls are slowly being populated by art that's left over from exhibitions at the other HUSH hostel, so the charisma of this place can only go up.

➜ *From the terminal that serves ferries from Eminönü, cross the street and head north. Instead of continuing on the bridge, turn right on Iskele Sok. and continue up the hill. It will be to your right.* ℹ *Breakfast included.* $ *Dorms €12-13; singles €33-35, with bath €44; doubles €34-38, with bath €50; triples €48-54, with bath €66; quads €60-64, with bath €72.* ⏰ *Reception 24hr.*

ZÜMRÜT OTEL 💳♿📶❄ HOTEL [5]

Rıhtım Cad. Reşitefendi Sok. 5 ☎216 450 0454 💻www.kadikoyzumruthotel.com

The prices quoted here are the hotel's normal rates, but if it's not Formula 1 time, Zümrüt might give you a discount. English at the reception desk is a plus, as is the fact that they made the effort to add themselves into the databases of a few English-language hotel-search websites despite serving mostly locals. While the hotel itself is pretty sparse, rooms do have bathrooms ensuite.

➜ *3 streets north from Söğütlü Çeşme Cad. The sign is hard to miss.* ℹ *Breakfast included.* $ *Singles 110TL; doubles 150TL.* ⏰ *Reception 24hr.*

BEŞIKTAŞ AND ORTAKÖY

HOTEL ÇIRAĞAN
💳📶 HOTEL [2]

Müvezzi Cad., Beşiktaş ☎212 260 0230 🖳www.ciraganhotel.com

This is as close to budget accommodation as you can get in Beşiktaş and Ortaköy. If it weren't for some very tall trees, the hotel would have what could qualify as a "Bosphorus view" (the phrase that justifies unreasonably high prices in many establishments in Istanbul—its Sultanahmet equivalent is the "Blue Mosque view"). There is a pleasant restaurant on the sixth floor.

➜ Take the ferry or bus to Beşiktaş. Walk down Çirağan toward Yıldız Park until you see Müvezzi on your left, just before the park walls start. The hotel is at the base of Müvezzi Cad. on the left. The Çirağan bus stop is very close to the hotel. ℹ Wi-Fi is available in the lobby and in the restaurant. The staff speak some English. [$] Singles with bath 75TL; doubles with bath 95TL. ⏰ Reception 24hr.

OTEL BEŞIKTAŞ
💳📶 HOTEL [2]

Ihlamurdere Cad. 19, Beşiktaş ☎212 261 0346

This locals-oriented hotel is right in the center of Beşiktaş, relatively close to the ferry terminal and the bus station. If you're an unmarried couple, you might have some trouble getting a room together, but if you act foreign enough you should be fine.

➜ Take the ferry or bus to Beşiktaş. Walk inland on Ortabahçe Cad., which intersects with Dolmabahçe Cad. near the Naval Museum. After a few blocks, the hotel will be to your left. ℹ Little English spoken. [$] Singles with bath 70TL; doubles 90TL. ⏰ Reception 24hr.

GOLDEN STREET EXECUTIVE APARTMENTS
⊗📶 APARTMENTS [4]

Müvezzi Cad. 33, Beşiktaş ☎212 259 2384 🖳www.apartmentinistanbul.co.uk

Much nicer than any of the hostels you'd be staying at, these dozen or so furnished apartments have living rooms, kitchens, and balconies with a partial view of the Bosphorus. The location could be more pedestrian-friendly, but it's close to three different universities in the area. Of course, these aren't the only apartments in Istanbul for rent—many individuals sublet their places. Consult 🖳www.craigslist.org for the best offers.

➜ Take the ferry or bus to Beşiktaş. Walk down Çirağan toward Yıldız Park until you see Müvezzi to your left, just before the park walls start. The apartment building is a 4min. walk up a steep hill. ℹ Washing machines, dishwashers, and cooking utilities available. [$] 2-person studios €100; 4-person apartments €120. ⏰ Guests receive a key to the building.

FOUR SEASONS HOTEL
💳📶 HOTEL [5]

Çirağan Cad. 28, Beşiktaş ☎212 381 4000 🖳www.fourseasons.com/bosphorus

Let's admit it: most people who choose to stay in Beşiktaş or Ortaköy stay in places like this. The rooms are spacious, clean, and have their own bathrooms. The staff speaks English and are generally helpful. Also, the rooms start at €400.

➜ Take the ferry or bus to Beşiktaş. Walk down Çirağan toward Yıldız Park until you see it on your right. ℹ Breakfast €32. Among the facilities are a fitness center, heated outdoor pool, two ballrooms, and a private dock. [$] Singles €400; doubles €430. 3-bedroom Atik Pasha Suite €20,000. 8% tax is not included. ⏰ Reception 24hr.

BEYOĞLU

👍 RAPUNZEL GUESTHOUSE
💳📶 HOSTEL [1]

Bereketzade Camii Sok. 3 ☎212 292 5034 🖳www.rapunzelistanbul.com

This hostel is run by three charming people fresh out of university and very willing to give you advice on where to go and what to see in the city. What's more, every week they compile a list of concerts and events that might be of interest to travelers. The mattresses are orthopedic, and the location right below the Galata Tower is great, provided that you don't mind having to climb some steep slopes in the nearby streets. Rapunzel is quite new, so let's hope its owners never lose their current youthful enthusiasm.

✈ ⓂTünel or ⓂKaraköy. Get as close to Galata Tower as you can, then head down the hill on Came-kan Sok. and take a right turn at the Berekzade Mosque; the hostel will be on right. *i* Breakfast included. ⓢ 4-bed dorms €16; singles with bath €40; doubles with bath €50. ☼ Reception 24hr.

NEVERLAND HOSTEL

Boğazkesen Cad. 96

☎212 243 3177 🖳www.hostelneverland.com

⊛⁽ᵖ⁾ HOSTEL ❶

With posters calling for the fall of neoliberalism, a giant yin and yang seat, and handpainted walls, this is one of the most charismatic hostels in the city. Its enactment of the word "alternative" is very thorough—few other places in Istanbul

accommodations · beyoğlu

the bosphorus

It is impossible to visit Istanbul without gazing over the 30km of iridescent blue known as the Bosphorous. Besides its magical shimmer, it is also one of the most fascinating strips of water in the world—past, present, and future.

Connecting the Aegean and the Black Sea, the Bosphorous has been linked to the tale off Noah's Ark and the history of the flood. Though no wreckage of the ark is anywhere in sight, archaeologists can confirm that the Black Sea was once upon a time a freshwater lake. Then, during the last ice age, sea levels all over the world rose and caused the rock walls at the northern edge of the Bosphorous to collapse. Seawater surged in, mixing and permanently altering the lake to saltwater. According to legend, the villagers living around the lake built boats to survive the deluge, and they took animals, water, and supplies on board to survive.

From its enlightened beginnings, the Bosphorous now ranks as the second-busiest waterway in the world. Ferries carry commuters from their homes in Asia to their work in Europe, while tankers whisk oil and gas to a fuel-hungry West. A trip up (or down) the Bosphorous is not complete without passing under the strait's two main bridges - the Bosphorous Bridge and the quite predictably named Second Bosphorous Bridge. (The full name for the Bosphorous II is the Fatih Sultan Mehmet Bridge, although it is recognized as both). The Bosphorous Bridge is a steel suspension bridge illuminated by an array of LED lights that change colors and patterns at night. With around 200,000 automobiles traversing the bridge daily, it's no wonder there is a slight sagging at the very middle of the bridge when it is weighed down with traffic. Hopefully, the small toll charged when passing from Europe to Asia ensures that you will at least make it to the other side, though the absence of a toll in the reverse direction perhaps does not guarantee the same safe crossing the other way. It seems that the first Bosphorous Bridge was a difficult act to follow—the same designers were commissioned for the Fatih Sultan Mehmet, but it did not achieve quite the same standard the second time around. Although a bit longer, the Bosphorous II is not nearly as picturesque, and spans only 4 lanes, instead of the first bridge's eight.

It's hard to say exactly what lies in store for the Bosphorous in the future. Unfortunately, the quality of Bosphorous water has continued to degrade due to the heavy traffic and increasing pollution of the neighboring Marmara Sea. It's unlikely this pollution will clear anytime soon, so for those city dwellers in need of a swim, the Black Sea beaches offer the cleaner option. However, the cold water and dangerous undercurrents there remain an equally ominous alternative to the filth. Needless to say, the Bosphorous is not for swimming, but it can still offer a leisurely escape from the bustling city.

care about recycling paper and plastics and usually just leave it to the poor who make a living out of it. There are many pleasant common spaces, free tea and coffee from the kitchen, and a collective management that is set on creating an ecovillage one of these days. If you're nice, maybe they'll let you join.

⚑ Ⓜ*Tophane. Walk uphill on Boğazkesen Cad. for 5min. The hostel will be on your right.* *i* *Breakfast included.* Ⓢ *Dorms €9-12; singles €20; doubles €28, with bath €34; triples €36.* Ⓠ *Reception 24hr.*

CHILL OUT CENGO HOSTEL
Halas Sok. 3

⊕⊕((ŗ)) HOSTEL ❶

☎212 251 3148 🖳www.chillouthc.com

Perhaps the most atmospheric of hostel from among the five Chill Out hostels in Beyoğlu, Cengo is also the biggest. It features some innovative interior design—the stairs to some of the attic rooms look like something you'd encounter in an obstacle course. The furniture in the common rooms is very pleasant to sit on, but you can also choose to sit on the indoor swing. If this one is full, you can try the **Chill Out Lya Hostel** (*Toprak Lüle Sok. 1* ☎*212 244 7400*) or the **Chill Out Hostel Classic** (*Balyoz Sok. 3A* ☎*212 249 4784*), which is closer to Tünel and a bit more impersonal. All five Chill Out hostels have crazily painted stairs and affordable prices.

⚑ *From* Ⓜ*Taksim, walk down İstiklal, turn right after the Ağa Camii mosque, and continue down Atif Yilmaz. Take the 2nd left, and the hostel's unmarked gate will be to your left.* Ⓢ *Dorms €15; singles €25; doubles €35.* Ⓠ *Reception 24hr.*

HOSTELON
Boğazkesen Cad. 68

⊕⊕((ŗ)) HOSTEL ❶

☎212 252 7413 🖳www.hostelon.net

Clean, quiet, and rather forgettable, this hostel is a safe bet if you're tired of socialist-leaning alternative burrows. The downstairs kitchen could use some ventilation, but who wants to cook with so many cheap eateries around anyway? The hostel's main advantage is that it's fairly close to a tram station, which

can't go back

The city of Istanbul has existed since 667 BCE, but not always as Istanbul. As a site of frequent conquest and springboard into the Middle East from Europe, this city has changed hands, religions, and names once every couple hundred years. Here is a etymological history so you can know why exactly, you can't go back to Constantinople.

- **BYZANTIUM:** This was the name of the original Greek settlement on the Bosphorous, derived from their King Byzas. This also was the adopted name of the Eastern Roman Empire, after the fall of the West in 395 CE—even though the city itself was known as Constantinople by then.

- **NEW ROME:** Okay, this one's cheating. Constantine might have named his new capital after himself, but apparently a lot of people gave it a more functional name—New Rome. You can still find this name on the inscription of the title of the Archbishop of Constantinople-New Rome.

- **CONSTANTINOPLE:** On May 11, 330, Emperor Constantine gave the city its classical name. This meaningful mouthful of a name made Constantinople the new capital of the Eastern Roman Empire. This name even lasted in Ottoman Turk times, called Kostantiniyye, and continued until the fall of the empire in 1923.

- **ISTANBUL:** This was the common name of the city since before the conquest in 1453 by the Turks. It was officially re-dubbed by Atatürk in 1923. The name change was expedited by the Turkish Postal Service by refusing to send packages marked with Constantinople as the destination.

makes it much easier for you to go to Sultanahmet. Guests at hostels around İstiklal Avenue usually have to walk a lot or transfer at least once.

From [M]Tophane, walk uphill on Boğazkesen Cad. for 4min.; the hostel will be on your right.
[$] Dorms €9-12; doubles €30. Reception 24hr.

CHAMBERS OF THE BOHEME — HOSTEL [1]

Küçük Parmakkapı Sok. 11/13 ☎212 251 0931

Chambers of the Boheme has a great location for raiding bars in İstiklal, Çukurcuma, and Cihangir. The hostel's style is more old-fashioned than alternative, but it's nevertheless interesting: many private rooms, and even some of the dorm rooms, feature antique furniture. Guests get a 10% percent discount at the cafe on the ground level. Some website gave this place a "Best Hostel in Turkey" award in 2009, and the management equates this with winning an Oscar—we suggest you remain a bit skeptical.

From [M]Taksim, walk down İstiklal and take the 2nd left turn; the hostel will be to your left.
[i] Breakfast included. [$] Dorms €15-18; 4-person family room €120. Reception 24hr.

midnight express, not fun

If there were ever a reason to not smuggle drugs out of Turkey, the story of **William Hayes** (not the football or baseball player) is at the top of **Let's Go's** list, right under the reason that its illegal.

William Hayes was in Turkey in 1970, traveling as a student. He decided that it would be an awesome idea (it wasn't) to smuggle hashish out of the country. The airport police caught him with bricks of hash strapped to his body in a pat down. He was sentenced to jail for 4 years in the less-than-cushy Turkish prison system.

After serving 4 years, he was told that the authorities had decided to make an example out of him and extended his sentence to life in prison. He was subject to beatings and isolation. Luckily, he was moved to another prison, from which he later escaped by sea. In 1975, he escaped to Greece, and within 72 hours of escaping, he arrived at JFK airport, in New York City.

In the end, he wrote a book, sold a screenplay, and made a lot of **money**. But we still never advise engaging in any illicit activity, no matter how famous you might become thereafter.

INTERNATIONAL HOUSE ISTANBUL — HOSTEL [1]

Zambak Sok. 5 ☎212 244 3773 www.ihouseistanbul.com

Among the hostels in Beyoğlu, this one is probably the closest to Taksim Square, which makes traveling to other parts of the city easier. At the same time, it's well-positioned for exploring İstiklal's bars. Apart from the location, there's not that much that distinguishes it, as the walls are bare and the rooms are standard. Like many hostels in Beyoğlu, there is an elevator.

From [M]Taksim, walk down İstiklal and take the 1st right turn; the hostel has an unmarked black door on the left side of the street. [$] 4-bed dorms €14; doubles with bath €45. Reception 24hr.

SOHO HOSTEL — HOSTEL [1]

Süslü Saksı Sok. 5 ☎212 251 5866

It's not the neatest of hostels (there isn't much space and the bathrooms can look a bit unappealing), but there's a sense of free-spiritedness to its color and common room. It's not one of the many bland, unmemorable hotels that clutter the streets in this area. Soho is one of the cheapest hostels near İstiklal Cad. and close to all the nightlife, so it can be a good base for sleeping and perhaps for connecting with similar-minded travelers.

✚ ⓂTaksim. From Taksim walk down İstiklal and take the fifth right turn (on İmam Adnan Sokak). Continue to the end and turn left, the hostel will be on your left side. Ⓢ Dorms €6-10; singles €20; doubles €34. 🕐 Reception 24hr.

WORLD HOUSE
📶⧉⁽ᵠ⁾ HOSTEL ❶

Galipdede Cad. 85 ☎212 293 5520 🖥www.worldhouseistanbul.com

This is one of the better options if you want to stay in the Galata area. Galipdede is an especially well-positioned street; take two steps north and you're at Tünel, take two steps south and you're at the Galata Tower. The common spaces don't feel very intimate when employees of the downstairs cafe run to and from the adjoining kitchen, but if all you want is to watch TV, you'll be fine.

✚ ⓂTünel. From Tünel Square walk down on Galipdede for a few blocks; the hostel will be on your left side. 𝑖 Breakfast included. Wi-Fi only in the lobby. Ⓢ Dorms €10-15; doubles with bath €50; triples with bath €60. 🕐 Reception 24hr.

GALATALIFE
📶⧉⁽ᵠ⁾ HOTEL ❷

Galipdede Cad. 75 ☎212 251 5866

The prices at this hotel are slightly higher than those at the hostels that it competes against, and we haven't yet figured out why. Maybe it's the title "hotel," or maybe it's that each room has its own name, written on a mother-of-pearl board on the door. Whatever the reason for the price jump, the location is good and the place does seem marginally more polished than your average hostel.

✚ From ⓂTünel, walk down Galipdede for a few blocks; the hotel will be on your left side. 𝑖 Breakfast included. Ⓢ Doubles with bath €60; quads with bath €120. 🕐 Reception 24hr.

sights 👁

PRINCES' ISLANDS Kızıl Adalar

Originally inhabited by monks and exiled aristocracy and later by wealthy merchants and writers, the Princes' Islands are today a popular escape spot for locals and tourists who want to take a break from Istanbul's busy streets. Of the nine islands, four have a daily ferry service to Istanbul, while the others are mostly uninhabited. Cars are not allowed on the islands, so people either walk, bike, or use *faytons* (horse-drawn carriages). These islands are not in the Caribbean—the paid beaches are often ugly with limited sand and sea overflowing with chaise lounges. If the traditional beach experience is what you're after, you'll be disappointed. However, there are fish restaurants, monasteries, forests, picnic areas, and hills overlooking the sea, so it's worth the daytrip if you're staying in Istanbul for at least a few days.

The easiest way to get to the islands is to take a **ferry** from ⓂKabataş. Ferries may stop in Kadıköy before continuing to **Kiliada, Burgazada, Heybeliada, and Büyükada.** If you hop off at one island and then take a ferry to another one, you'll have to pay the fare again. The ferry system is mildly confusing because there are three kinds of ferries with separate schedules that leave from ⓂKabataş—**IDO seabus, IDO passenger ferry,** and **Dentur Avrasya ferry.** The first two are operated by IDO, cost 2.5TL per ride, and can be paid for with Akbil, but each differ in their speed and routes. While the seabus may take you straight to Büyükada in 35 min., the passenger ferry may take up to 1½hr. by stopping at the smaller islands first. The Dentur Avrasya ferry (☎212 227 7894 Ⓢ 4TL one way, 6TL return ticket) leaves from behind the gas station and is faster than the passenger ferry. Free schedules are available at the ferry terminals—consult them so that you don't miss the last ferry home.

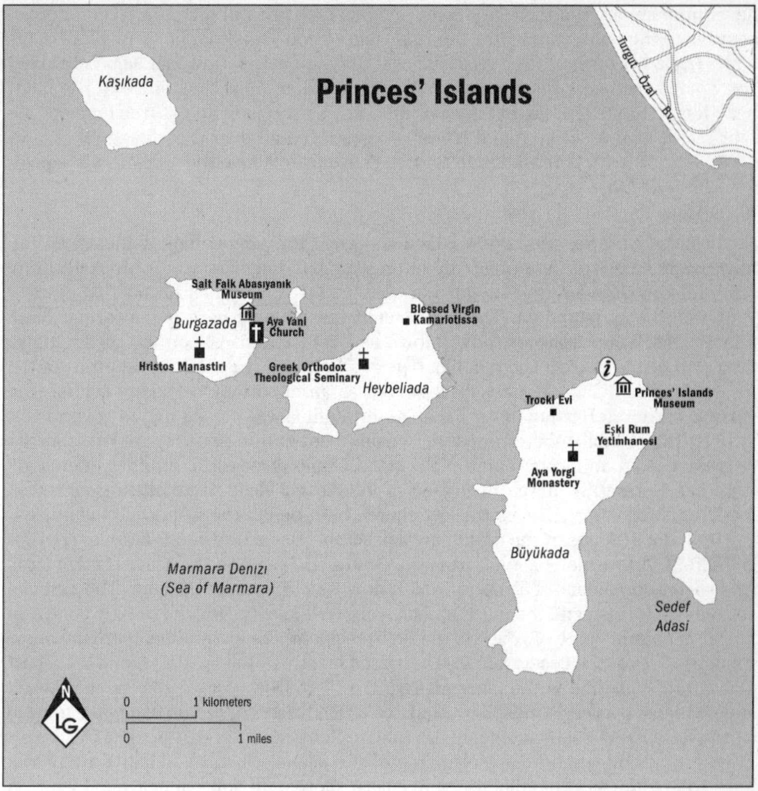
Princes' Islands
Kaşıkada
Turgut Özal Bv.
Sait Faik Abasıyanık Museum
Burgazada
Aya Yani Church
Hristos Manastiri
Blessed Virgin Kamariotissa
Greek Orthodox Theological Seminary
Heybeliada
Princes' Islands Museum
Trocki Evi
Eşki Rum Yetimhanesi
Aya Yorgi Monastery
Büyükada
Marmara Denızı (Sea of Marmara)
Sedef Adasi
0
1 kilometers
0
1 miles

Büyükada *Prinkipo*

This is the largest and the most touristy of the islands. It can get unbearably crowded on weekends and during the summer, so your best bet is to visit midweek. The main attraction is the **Aya Yorgi Monastery** *(☎216 382 3939 🕐 Open daily 9am-6pm. $ Free)*, located on top of a hill that offers a great view of the surrounding archipelago. To get here, first go to the Luna Park square (*fayton* costs 20TL, walking there should take about 30min.) and then walk up a very steep hill for about 20min. If you're into miracles, try the ascent without shoes while wishing something—word on the street is that the wish might come true after you reach the top (just don't wish for a pair of shoes). The monastery's church is rather new (it was built in 1906), but the interior is enthusiastically decorated with Christian imagery. The monastery used to function as a place for healing the mentally ill, who would spend their nights chained to the ground in front of Saint George's icon. Unfortunately, the chain rings were removed during a restoration some years ago. Nearby the church is the pleasant **Yücetepe Kir Gazinosu restaurant** *(☎216 382 1333 💻www.yucetepe.com)*, where you can refuel after the hike. Other things to do here include visiting the **Princes' Islands Museum,** which will contain much more information about the islands than you'll ever need. There are three paid **beaches** *(15-25TL)* which run their own free shuttle boats from the docks, but don't set your expectations too high. A nice, if a bit barren spot for a **picnic** is the Dilburnu peninsula *(Piknik Alani ☎216 382 4301 $ 3TL per person)*. The authorities and entrepreneurs are working on transforming the island into the new Sultanahmet, but there are many sights which are still dilapidated and not accessible to the public, including the villa where Leon Trotsky spent four years of his exile, **Trocki Evi,** *(down a steep cul-de-sac near Çankaya Cad. 59)* and **Eşki Rum Yetimhanesi** *(an abandoned orphanage on the hill opposite Aya Yorgi)*. As you exit the ferry, head left to the useful **tourist information** booth, where you can get free maps of the four major islands. Bike rental stores are scattered all over the village *(Ⓢ 2.5-5TL per hr., 7.5-15TL per 24hr.),* while the *faytons* leave from above the clock tower square *(Ⓢ Tours 40TL-50TL).*

Heybeliada *Halki*

Heybeliada is the second-largest island and great for independent exploration. Unfortunately, many of the potentially interesting buildings are either blocked off by scary-looking soldiers holding guns or simply closed, so you'll have to do most of your sightseeing from afar. The most significant building here is the former **Greek Orthodox Theological Seminary** (now known as Özel Rum Lisesi) on top of the hill to the north of the docks. The building dates to 1896 and was built in the ruins of the former Haghia Triada Monastery. It served as an important Orthodox school (the current Patriarch Bartholomew I is an alum) until it was closed by the government in 1971. The Halki Seminary's closure remains a hot-button issue for the West, and its reopening is an important point in EU membership discussion. Another interesting sight is a Byzantine church dedicated to the **Blessed Virgin Kamariotissa** (marked as Aya Yorgi Monastery). It was the last church built before the Conquest, but since it is within the grounds of the off-limits **Naval School** (Deniz Lisesi), all one can see of it is the roof. A few blocks uphill from the center you can find the **house of İsmet İnönü** (the second president of Turkey), which now functions as a museum. The exhibits are only in Turkish and the museum isn't very well-known, which strongly contrasts the all-pervading fame of Atatürk, the first president. For swimming, there are some small beaches at the **Çam Limani Koyu**, attended mostly by the locals. One of the nicest places on the island is the **Akvaryum** *(☎535 294 4622 Ⓢ 5TL),* a tiny pebbly beach amidst crags. It's very atmospheric and not well advertised, so you can come to have a little Robinson Crusoe moment here (unlike Robinson, you can sip on a 5TL beer). The beach is on the northwestern side of the island, close to Alman Koyu. From here, follow the road parallel to the northern shore until you reach a small wooden sign pointing you to the beach. A **biking** tour of the island *(Ⓢ 3-5TL per hr., 10-15TL per day, cheapest options near the fayton park)* can be very pleasant, provided that you're prepared to push the bike along on the steeper slopes. There are a number of *fayton* stands in the center *(Ⓢ Tours 25-35TL),* and to the north of the ferry docks is a small **tourist information** booth.

Burgazada *Antigoni*

Rather unmarked by tourism, this is by far the most authentic of the three islands (the fourth major island is Kinaliada, generally agreed to be a boring landmass). There is no tourist office, so get your map in advance at one of the two bigger islands. There are two well-known fish restaurants, so head to **Barba Yani** *(☎215 381 2404* 🖳*www. burgazadabarbayani.com)* right at the docks, or **Kalpazankaya Restaurant** *(☎216 381 1504* 🖳*www.kalpazankaya.com)* on the opposite side of the island. Kalpazankaya is especially charismatic, with a great view of the sea and a small pebbly beach right below it (the drinks are cheaper at the beach than in the restaurant upstairs). A *fayton* will take you here for 20TL, or you can walk following the shore, which could take around 45 minutes. Burgazada's main landmark is the **Hristos Manastiri** (Christ Monastery) which is on top of the central hill. Many trees on the island were destroyed in a forest fire in 2003, giving the walk up to the monastery one of the best views that the Prince's Islands offer. Unobstructed by trees, you can see three other islands (including the uninhabited **Kaşıkada,** the "Spoon Island") and Istanbul in the distance. In the town near the docks you can find the **Aya Yani Church** dating back to 1896 and the **Sait Faik**

Abasıyanık museum, the former residence of this Turkish short story writer. There's a **bike rental** store to the south of the docks *($ 5TL per hr., 15TL per day)*, while *faytons* wait to the north *($ Tours 30-40TL)*.

SULTANAHMET AND AROUND

👍 HAGIA SOPHIA — MUSEUM

Aya Sofya ☎212 522 0989

In our cynical age of the internet, few things can truly impress. However, Hagia Sophia is an exception. Built as a Christian basilica in the 6th century, later converted into a mosque by the Ottomans, and finally turned into a museum 500 years later, this place has an overpowering aura that everyone who visits Istanbul should experience. Hagia Sophia had two predecessors that were destroyed—nothing remains from the first basilica, and the only remains from the second are the marble blocks depicting **12 lambs** (symbolizing the 12 apostles) near the entrance. Hagia Sophia is most famous for its **dome**—it seems to be suspended in the air, with no pillars cluttering the space in the middle. Notice the mosaics of the Archangel Gabriel and the Virgin Mary holding Jesus that can be seen in the semi-dome of the apse. The enormous **calligraphied medallions** were added during the building's stint as a mosque in the 19th century, and bear the names of Allah, Prophet Muhammad, the first four caliphs, and two of Muhammad's grandsons. When your neck starts hurting from staring up, walk up the stone ramp to the upper gallery. Here you can find the 13th-century **Deesis mosaic** depicting Jesus, Mary, and Joseph, and the **Loge of the Empress,** with a green stone marking the place where the empress used to watch the proceedings downstairs from her throne. Near the entrance is the sweating pillar, which can supposedly make your wish come true—just put in your thumb and rotate your hand 360 degrees.

➜ From Ⓜ Sultanahmet, walk south. $ 20TL, under 12 free. Guides from €40 per group.
⏰ Open T-Su 9am-7pm. Last entry with 6pm.

blue mosque vs hagia sophia

Don't feel like going to two mosques that are right across the street from each other? Read this quick guide to determine which, once and for all, is the best mosque.

Number of Minarets: The Blue Mosque has an unprecedented 6, while the Hagia Sophia only have 4. Winner: Blue Mosque

Age: Hagia Sophia was originally built as a church in 330CE dedicated by constantine the Great, which is a whole 1200 years before the Blue Mosque. Hagia Sophia was converted to a moqsue in 1453. Winner: Hagia Sophia

Being a Mosque: The Hagia Sophia was converted into a museum in 1935 by Atatürk, while the Blue Mosque is still in use as a place of worship today. Winner: Blue Mosque

Entrance Fee: Who knew money could incentivize religion? Well, because it's a museum, you do have to pay entrance fee to Hagia Sophia, while the Blue Mosque is free to enter for anyone covering their legs. Winner: Blue Mosque.

Size: Hello? We already told you it had 6 minarets. Are you even paying attention? Winner: Blue Mosque

Well, as it turns out, the free, larger, fully functioning mosque won. We do reccomend visiting Hagia Sophia, since all those entrance fees have been used to painstakingly peel back plaster revealing mosaics of 1000+ peices and marble that hasn't seen Christian eyes since the 1400s.

TOPKAPI PALACE

PALACE

Topkapı Sarayı ☎212 512 0480 ▦www.topkapısarayi.gov.tr/eng/indexalt.html

To do justice to this sprawling palace complex, you need to spend at least a few hours exploring what it has to offer. If that seems like too much, consider that some people had to spend their entire lives within its walls. The palace used to serve as the official residence for the sultans between the Conquest and 19th century, and today there are **four courtyards.** The First Courtyard contains the grounds outside of the Palace, including the **Archaeological Museums** and **Hagia Eirene.** The Second Courtyard is known as the place where the **Divan meetings** took place and where legal decrees were discussed. The Third Courtyard is the real heart of the Palace—there's the **Privy Chamber** where the sultan used to receive foreign dignitaries, and the **Holy Relics Apartment** exhibiting some of Islam's most valued items—a sword, a cloak, a tooth, and other belongings of Prophet Muhammad. The Fourth Courtyard is a **small garden** with pavilions and kiosks. There's also the fascinating **Harem** where all the important women in the sultan's life used to dwell.

⚑ Ⓜ*Sultanahmet or* Ⓜ*Gülhane. Enter the grounds down the hill from Hagia Sophia.* ***i*** *Audio tours 10TL. Guided group tours around €80.* Ⓢ *20TL, with harem tour 35TL.* ☒ *Open M 9am-6pm, W-Su 9am-6pm.*

BASILICA CISTERN

CISTERN

Yerebatan Sarayı, Yerebatan Cad. 13 ☎212 522 1259 ▦www.yerebatan.com

Much more atmospheric than its cousin Binbirdirek Cistern, this underground structure was built more than 1400 years ago under Emperor Justinian, the same guy who was responsible for Hagia Sophia. Even though it was once used to store water, today you can take a walk through its innards and listen to dripping water, feed the fish swarming underneath, or take invariably blurred photos of the beautifully lit columns. In the back of the cistern, there are two medusa heads forming the bases of two columns. These craniums were supposedly brought here from pagan Roman temples, but nobody seems to know why they are positioned upside-down and sideways, respectively.

⚑ Ⓜ*Sultanahmet. The entrance is across the street from Hagia Sophia, near the Million Stone.* ***i*** *Audio tours 5TL.* Ⓢ *10TL.* ☒ *Open 9am-7:30 pm.*

SULTANAHMET MOSQUE (BLUE MOSQUE)

MOSQUE

Sultanahmet Camii ☎212 518 1319

While people say Hagia Sophia is less remarkable on the outside than on the inside, the Blue Mosque is often said to have the opposite effect on visitors. Even if this tidbit were true, it wouldn't mean that much—the mosque's exterior is quite difficult to match. Some say that when the Blue Mosque was constructed in the early 17th century, its six impressive minarets caused an uproar, as the Haram Mosque in Mecca was the only place of worship with the same number. In what was quite a smart move, the sultan allegedly sent his architect to Mecca to build a seventh minaret for their mosque. Decorated with the blue Iznik porcelain tiles responsible for the mosque's name, the dome is supported by four "elephant feet," enormous pillars 5m in diameter. Since the Blue Mosque is still in use, visitors have to enter through a separate entrance, keep to a designated area, and stay out during prayer times.

⚑ Ⓜ*Sultanahmet.* ***i*** *No shoes or shorts allowed. Women must wear head cover.* Ⓢ *Free.* ☒ *Open in summer M-Th 8:30am-12:30pm, 2-4:30pm, and 5:30-6:15pm; F 8:30am-noon and 2:30-6:15pm; Sa-Su 8:30am-12:30pm, 2-4:30pm, and 5:30-6:15pm.*

ISTANBUL ARCHEOLOGY MUSEUMS

MUSEUM

İstanbul Arkeoloji Müzeleri ☎212 520 7740

Aside from the occasional schoolboy giggling at a nude statue, the atmosphere in this complex, which houses some of world's oldest artifacts within its three museums, is quite serene. The **Museum of Islamic Art** (i.e. the Tiled Kiosk) houses tiles and ceramics. The **Archaeological Museum** is home to a collection of statues, sarcophagi, and the mummy of the Sidonian king Tabnit—who currently doesn't look too happy about the world's state of affairs. Finally, the **Museum of the Ancient Orient** holds the oldest preserved written international agreement, the Kadesh Peace Agreement, a treaty between the Hittites and Egyptians from 1258 BCE.

✠ ⓂSultanahmet or ⓂGülhane; it's in the First Courtyard of Topkapı Palace. Ⓢ 10TL. ⌚ Open Tu-Su 9am-7pm.

SULTANAHMET SQUARE (HIPPODROME)
Sultanahmet Meydanı

^{((ᵠ))} SQUARE

Very little remains from the Hippodrome (chariot racing stadium) that used to stand here, and what does remain was originally brought here from other places for adornment. The Greek **Serpent Column** (5th century BCE) was made from the melted shields of Persian soldiers in honor of Greek victory in the Battle of Plataea. The **Obelisk** (1490 BCE) was built by the Egyptian pharaoh Thutmose III. In fact, the only monument still around today that was actually constructed here is the **Walled Obelisk** that looks pretty decrepit (blame the Fourth Crusade—they took all the gilded plates off it). Speaking of old phallic monuments, don't miss the **Million Stone** right by Hagia Sophia—all distances in the Byzantine Empire used to be measured from this starting point; contrary to popular belief, the US hasn't always been the center of the universe. If you tire of historical monuments, Sultanahment Square is also a great place to people-watch.

✠ ⓂSultanahmet; it's the square north from the Blue Mosque.

LITTLE HAGIA SOPHIA
Küçük Aya Sofya

MOSQUE
☎212 458 0776

Older than its bigger sister, this charming mosque is a bit like Baby Taj Mahal in Agra, India—not quite the real deal, but worth a visit once you're done with all the big names. One of the first historical buildings built during Justinian's reign, Little Hagia Sophia has many architectural features similar to its counterpart, which it preceded by only a few years. After the Conquest, it took decades before it was converted into a mosque by the chief *eunuch* Hüseyin Ağa. After a long period of decay, it was finally restored a few years ago. It's located in a quiet neighborhood, so come here to have a tea in the garden nearby, or stop by on your way toward Kumkapi.

✠ ⓂSultanahmet. From the Blue Mosque, walk down Küçük Aya Sofya Cad. for 5min. Ⓢ Free.

SÜLEYMANIYE MOSQUE
Süleymaniye Camii

MOSQUE
☎212 514 0139

This mosque has been under renovation for a few years now and is currently still closed to the public. However, if the tourist brochures are telling the truth, a visit here is nothing short of life-altering. Designed by the architect Mimar Sinan (a big deal in Istanbul's architecture world), it is one of the seven structures that adorn the seven hills of Istanbul. The mosque used to be heated with oil lamps—a process which usually would have left layers of soot on the walls; however, Sinan solved this conundrum by designing airflow which collected the soot in a small room. What's more, the soot was later used to produce ink for books in the Süleymaniye Library. Despite such inventiveness, this wasn't Sinan's favorite mosque, but he did choose to be buried here. If you're in town and the mosque is still closed, come see the tombs of Sultan Süleyman and others outside.

✠ ⓂBeyazit or ⓂEminönü. From ⓂBeyazit, walk north to the gate of Istanbul University, turn right and follow its walls all the way up. From ⓂEminönü, exit the Spice Bazaar on Sabuncuhanı Sok., turn left on Vasit Çinar Cad., and continue up the hill. ⓘ Mosque closed for restoration at time of writing. Tombs open daily 9am-5pm.

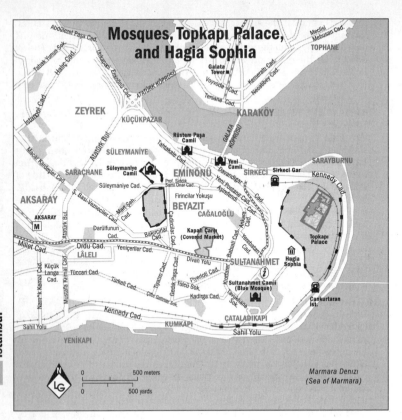

Mosques, Topkapı Palace, and Hagia Sophia

BEYAZIT SQUARE   SQUARE

Beyazit Meydani

This square is a good place to relax after finally finding your way out of the Grand Bazaar. Notice the impressive gate of **Istanbul University** (unfortunately, the university is not accessible), and try talking to some of the students who sit around. There used to be a giant triumphal arch here, but it was destroyed in a 1509 earthquake and only some fragments remain. Visit the **Beyazit Mosque** nearby, one of the oldest mosques in Istanbul that was inspired both by Hagia Sophia and the Fatih Mosque. You can also go take a look at the **Sahaflar Bazaar** (Old Book Bazaar) to see an obscure collection of foreign books. Behind the university walls, look for the **Beyazit Tower,** another off-limits structure that is used as a fire tower.

⚓ Ⓜ*Beyazıt.*

GALATA BRIDGE   BRIDGE

Galata Köprüsü

Allegedly, the walk down this bridge isn't quite what it used to be before 1992, when the current structure replaced an earlier, iron version, but it still offers a great view of mosques and other landmarks on both the historical peninsula and the European side. Today, the upper level is populated by anglers with fishing rods catching fish in the Golden Horn, and the lower level is populated by ang...um, waiters catching tourists and making sure they eat at their overpriced seafood restaurants. Choose the upper level, and if you're hungry, try one of those famous fish sandwiches *(4TL)* that are sold on both sides.

🪧 *[M]Eminönü or [M]Karaköy.*

FATIH

FATIH MOSQUE ♿ MOSQUE

Fatih Camii, Fatih ☎212 631 6723

A few years after the Ottomans conquered Constantinople, Sultan Mehmet the Conqueror decided to have the Church of the **Holy Apostles** (an important Byzantine basilica) demolished and built the **Fatih Mosque** in its place. The mosque was completed in 1470 and was the first of its kind in the city. Unfortunately, what you'll see today is a completely different mosque: the original building was destroyed by an earthquake in 1766 and had to be completely rebuilt by Sultan Mustafa III. As of 2010, Fatih Mosque is undergoing an extensive restoration project, but this should not deter you from visiting—the temporary metal walls inside make the mosque resemble a warehouse, which, combined with the fact that people still come to pray here, makes for an interesting experience. Even more memorable is **the tomb of Sultan Mehmet the Conqueror** just outside the mosque. Its interior is effusively decorated, and it contrasts with the bareness of his wife's tomb nearby. There's also a short bio of the Sultan at the entrance that states that he was poisoned by a "Jewish doctor" in the services of a Venetian king, even though the cause of the Sultan's mysterious death remains disputed.

🪧 *Take bus to Fatih. The mosque is behind the tall walls near the bus stop. If you're walking here by following the aqueduct, keep walking northwest until you see an entrance to your left.* ℹ *Mosque etiquette applies. According to staff, the reconstruction will be over by 2012.* $ *Free.* ⏰ *Open dawn to dusk, closed for prayer times.*

VALENS AQUEDUCT 🚫♿ ☀ RUINS

Bozdoğan Kemeri, Fatih

This is not a very interactive historical sight. Unless you're one of the local hoodlums who are not afraid to climb its steep walls, you'll just have to walk beside it. However, stretching almost 1km, the aqueduct is one of Istanbul's more distinct landmarks. Dating back to the 4th century, it was completed under the Roman Emperor Valens to supply the city with water. Going from one end to the other can make for a pleasant short walk: start at the Şehzade Mosque, which lies at the aqueduct's southeastern end, and continue northwest, crossing the **Atatürk Bulvari,** a major road that passes right underneath the aqueduct and gives you the best view of the structure. Continuing further up, there will be the **Siirt Bazaar** on the right and a few cafes with small tables set up against the aqueduct's walls. If you walk all the way to its end and then continue for a few more blocks, you'll reach the **Fatih Mosque.**

🪧 *Take the bus to Müze or İtfaiye or take the tram to Laleli-Universite or Aksaray.* $ *Free.*

FENER AND BALAT

CHORA CHURCH MUSEUM

Kariye Müzesi, Kariye Camii Sok. 29, Edirnekapı ☎212 631 9241

Chora Church requires some serious ceiling-gazing skills—the most beautiful Byzantine mosaics and frescoes are on the domes. The church's history goes back to the fourth century, when Constantinople was so small then that this church stood outside the city walls—hence the name *Chora,* meaning "countryside" in Old Greek. However, most of the mosaics date to the early 14th century, when the church was restored following an earthquake. A few decades after the Ottoman conquest in 1453, the building was converted into a mosque. Fortunately, the Christian images were not destroyed. Instead, they were covered over with plaster and wooden panels and stayed that way for over four centuries. In 1945 the

mosque was converted into a museum and the artwork was restored and brought back into the daylight. The mosaics and frescoes depict various events in the busy lives of Virgin Mary and Jesus, which range from the Annunciation to Jesus healing the blind and paralyzed. Sometimes it's difficult to understand what goes on in individual mosaics and frescoes, so feel free to consult our list in the table below.
🚌 Bus to Edirnekapı. As you get off the bus, turn left and walk, then take the nearest right turn. Walk for 3 blocks, but before you reach the city walls, turn right and walk 2 blocks down the slope until you see the museum. If you're getting here from Fener or Balat, the walk takes around 15min. with a map and 45min. without one. $ 15TL, Turkish students 10TL, under 12 free. ⏰ Open in summer M-Tu 9am-6pm, Th-Su 9am-6pm; in winter M-Tu 9am-4:30pm, Th-Su 9am-4:30pm.

SCENES IN MOSAICS AND FRESCOES			
1	Jesus Pantocrator	41	Deteriorated
2	The Prayer of Mary and the Angels	42	The Healing of a Paralyzed Person and the Samaritan Woman
3	Jesus and Theodore Metochites	43	The Healing of a Blind and Dumb Man
4	St. Peter	44	The Healing of Two Blindmen
5	St. Paul	45	The Healing of the Mother-In-Law of St. Peter
6	The Khalke Jesus	46	The Woman Asking for a Restoration of Her Health
7	Jesus and his Ancestors	47	The Healing of a Young Man with an Injured Arm
8	Mary and the Child Jesus	48	he Healing of the Leprous Man
9	Rejection of Joachim's Offerings	49	The Dispersion of Good Health to the People
10	Joachim in the Desert	50	St. Andronicus
11	The Annunciation Scene	51	St. Trachos
12	The Meeting of Joachim and Anne	52	The Death of the Virgin
13	The Birth of the Virgin Mary	53	Jesus
14	The First Seven Steps of Virgin Mary	54	Mary of Hodegetria
15	The Blessing of the Virgin	55	The Resurrection Scene
16	The Virgin Given Affection	56	Archangel Michael
17	The Presentation of Mary to the Temple	57	The Healing of the Daughter of Jairus
18	The Feeding of the Virgin	58	The Raising of the Widow's Son
19	The Virgin Taking the Skeins of Wool from the Temple	59	The Depiction of Six Saints
20	Zachariah In Front of the Twelve Sticks	60	The Last Judgment Scene
21	The Virgin Given to Joseph	61	An Angel Carrying the Heaven
22	Joseph Bringing the Virgin into His House	62	Abraham with Lazarus On His Lap
23	The Annunciation Scene	63	The Rich Man Burning In Hell's Fire
24	Joseph Bidding Farewell to Mary	64	The Angel and the Child
25	The Visit to Betlehem	65	The Angels and The Dead
26	The Enrollment for Taxation	66	The People Burning In Hell's Fire

BULGARIAN ST. STEPHEN CHURCH CHURCH
Sveti Stefan Kilisesi, Balat ☎212 635 4432
What makes this church interesting is that it's got none of that stone-and-concrete

nonsense. Instead, it's all made of iron parts that were manufactured in Vienna, sent down by boat on the Danube, and assembled here in 1898. Iron was in vogue back then (the church is just a few years younger than the Eiffel Tower), but it's not today—St. Stephen Church is one of the few surviving cast-iron churches in the world. Interestingly enough, it was built on the site of a previous wooden church, taking over as the new home of the Bulgarian Exarchate. The Exarchate was an autocephalous Orthodox church that seceded from the Ecumenical Patriarchate of Constantinople as a result of the increasing nationalist sentiment of ethnic Bulgarians in the Ottoman Empire during the 19th century. The Exarchate didn't last long. In 1913 it relocated to Sofia, and in 1915 it lost autonomy for three decades. However, even today St. Stephen Church remains important for the Bulgarian minority in Istanbul. Inside, the church is wonderfully decorated, and its internal structures are made completely out of iron.

 # Bus or ferry to Fener. The church is located in the park between Fener and Balat ferry jetties. If you're arriving by ferry at Fener, turn right and walk along the shore until you see the church across the road to the left. $ Free. ⏰ Open daily 8am-5pm.

EYÜP SULTAN MOSQUE — MOSQUE

Eyüp Sultan Camii, Eyüp

This mosque is one of Islam's most important pilgrimage sites because it's the burial place of Ayyoub Al-Ansari (Eyüp Sultan in Turkish), a friend of Prophet Muhammad and the standard-bearer of Islam who died during the Muslim siege of Constantinople. The mosque was the first one built by the Ottomans after the Conquest, and the giant plane tree that grows in the mosque's courtyard was supposedly planted around that time. The mosque has a separate entrance for women, who generally pray in the upper gallery, but it should be possible for female tourists to enter through the main entrance provided that they stick to the usual mosque etiquette. The main attraction of the complex, however, is the **Tomb of Eyüp Sultan,** a wonderfully decorated burial site that's even more beautiful on the inside. Within

LET THE
RABBİT TO
TELL YOUR
FORTUNE

the tomb you can find exhibited the footprint of Prophet Muhammad, a strange white object inside a glass display in the wall. The place is almost constantly full of believers showing their respect, so make sure to act accordingly. You'll see many young boys in curious white costumes—they are visiting the tomb as a part of their *sünnet*, the circumcision ritual that most Turkish boys have to undergo. Due to their religious significance, the mosque grounds became a popular burial place for government officials. When you're done with the tomb, go for a walk up the hill through the cemetery, preferably all the way to **Pierre Loti Cafe.**

🚏 Bus or ferry to Eyüp. Cross the road and head inland, following the 1 visible minaret of Eyüp Mosque. You'll have to pass through a long bazaar street and by a fountain. ℹ *Standard mosque etiquette applies.* $ *Free.* 🕐 *Mosque open in summer daily 4am-11pm. Tomb open in summer daily 9:30am-6:45pm.*

KADIKÖY, MODA, AND ÜSKÜDAR

👍 ISTANBUL TOY MUSEUM 💳♿ MUSEUM

Ömer Paşa Cad. Dr. Zeki Zeren Sok., Göztepe ☎216 359 4550 💻www.istanbultoymuseum.com

Alright, it's no Hagia Sophia, but Istanbul's Toy Museum is unlike any other museum you'll visit in this city. This multi-story villa houses a collection of mostly European and American antique toys, the oldest dating back to 1817. Each room is dedicated to different kinds of toys, with music and lighting to complement the theme (the space exploration room has a particularly fierce disco flicker). The museum has got its share of kitsch, but there are many memorable exhibits. Come see what are supposedly the first Mickey Mouse toy (Performo Toy Company, 1926) and the first Mickey Mouse toy (Disney, appears in cartoons in 1928) standing side-by-side, throwing some suspicion on how Mr. Disney was inspired to create his world-famous mouse character. Bild Lilli, the German doll that inspired the creation of Barbie dolls, is here as well, alongside a rather hideous toy made by the Mattel toy company before it took up Barbies. The most interesting part of the collection is the army of 300 toy Nazi soldiers produced in Germany just before World War II. This exhibit proves that running a "toy museum" isn't just a frivolous waste of time, but instead a different way of documenting history. After all, children's toys often reflect adults' dreams.

🚏 Take the suburban train from Haydarpaşa Train Station to Göztepe (10 min). After you leave the station, cross and walk down the street that faces the train exit. After the street turns right, take the nearest left turn and go straight. There are giant giraffe statues in front of the museum. $ *8TL, students 5TL.* 🕐 *Open daily 9:30am-6pm.*

MAIDEN TOWER 💳⊗ TOWER

Kız Kulesi, Üsküdar ☎216 342 4747 💻www.kizkulesi.com.tr

Maiden Tower is like a mountain—it looks more interesting from afar. Located on a tiny islet near the Asian side, it's been a legend-inspiring landmark for a few millennia. The oldest of the many legends by **Ovidius** claims a nun named Hero from the temple of Aphrodite used to live here. She used to receive secret visits from **Leander,** the love of her life who would swim to her at night by following the light coming from the tower. One night a storm blew the light out, and as a result Leander got lost in the Bosphorus and drowned. When Hero found out, she threw herself from the tower. It's a nice story, but since the islet is within spitting distance of the Asian side, one cannot escape the impression that Mr. Leander must have had a very poor sense of direction. Legends aside, the first structure here was built by the Greeks around 400 BCE, but what you see today is a much more modern product of numerous reconstructions. The tower has served a variety of purposes over time, acting as a military center, a lighthouse, an infirmary, and, since 2000, a restaurant. Beautifully lit at night, the tower looks best from a ferry to Kadıköy after dark. If you decide to come here in person, you'll be able to climb the stairs to the top and enjoy the view of Istanbul's two sides. There's a restaurant in the base of the tower and a tiny cafe up on top, and neither is as ridiculously overpriced as you'd expect them to be.

➡ To get here from Üsküdar's ferry terminal, walk around the huge construction site and then follow the shore south until you see the tower (15 min). Shuttle boats run every 20min. or so from a pier to the south of the tower. There are hourly shuttle boats from Kabataş as well. $ Tickets from Üsküdar 5TL, from Kabataş 7TL. ⏰ Shuttle boats run daily 9am-6:45pm.

TURK BALLOON — BALLOON

Kadıköy Meydanı Deniz Otobüsleri İskelesi, Kadıköy ☎216 347 6703 🖥www.turkbalon.net

Among the meager selection of tourist attractions on the Asian side of Istanbul, this is perhaps the best known. With the capacity of 30 people, this big yellow balloon rises 200m into the air and allows you to experience Istanbul from a rather unusual perspective. The balloon doesn't move once it reaches its maximum height, but instead stays up for 15min. before descending. In the past couple of years, there have been problems with the availability of the balloon, and it wasn't operating at the time of writing. However, according to the staff, it should be back up soon. When you're in town, look up and search for a big yellow object in the sky that's not the sun to see if it's in service.

➡ From the Kadıköy ferry terminal, head west along the shore; the balloon should be on top of a white building that resembles an anemone. $ 20TL, students 15TL. ⏰ Open 9am-8pm; schedule dependent on weather.

MIHRIMAH SULTAN MOSQUE — ♿ MOSQUE

Mihrimah Sultan Camii, Üsküdar

There's really not that much to say about the Mihrimah Sultan Mosque (also called İskele Mosque), aside from the fact that it's pretty. Designed by Mimar Sinan and completed in 1548 at the order of Mihrimah Sultana, the daughter of Sultan Süleyman the Magnificent, it's one of more than 180 mosques that can be found in the Üsküdar neighborhood. If you're in the mood for walking from one mosque to another and admiring the architecture, start your journey here and work your way inland. Be on the lookout for **Şemsi Pasha Mosque, Yeni Valide Mosque, Atik Valide Mosque,** and **Çinili Mosque** to see a sampling of the best mosques around. The streets themselves aren't that interesting, so if you're in Istanbul for only a few days, make sure you hit the more charismatic neighborhoods first.

➡ The mosque is clearly visible from Üsküdar's ferry terminal. ℹ Usual mosque etiquette applies. $ Free.

BEŞIKTAŞ AND ORTAKÖY

DOLMABAHÇE PALACE — MUSEUM

Dolmabahçe Sarayı, Beşiktaş ☎212 236 9000 🖥www.millisaraylar.gov.tr

Topkapı may be the most historically significant of imperial palaces, but Dolmabahçe is probably the most impressive one. It was commissioned by Sultan Abdülmecid I, and upon completion in 1854, it replaced Topkapı as the official residence of the sultans. The palace is a real exercise in architectural and decorative overkill (think bear pelts, crystal chandeliers, and man-sized Japanese vases) and has 285 rooms, 43 salons, and six hamams. The most impressive part is the central **Ceremonial Hall,** which features the heaviest chandelier in Europe and which is still in use for special government events. During the tour you can also see the room where Mustafa Kemal Atatürk died on November 10, 1938—many clocks in the palace are set to five minutes after nine, the exact time of Atatürk's death. The place where the palace now stands was originally a bay—by the order of the sultans it was filled in with stones and turned into imperial gardens. Before the Conquest, the Byzantines had an enormous chain strung across the mouth of the Golden Horn to prevent enemy ships from entering it. It was in this former bay that Mehmet the Conqueror's ships started their journey on land (through Pera and Kasimpaşa) to circumvent this obstacle. The palace is a very popular tourist attraction, and the lines for tickets can be very long and very slow. Your best bet will be to come on a weekday early in the morning.

✈ ⓜKabataş. *The palace is a short walk northeast from Kabataş. Just walk parallel to the shore toward the Dolmabahçe Mosque and past it. To get here from Beşiktaş, you'll have to walk for approx. 7min. toward Kabataş down Dolmabahçe Cad.* ✦ *Guided tours are mandatory. Tours in Turkish or English, 40min., start every 15min. No photos. Come on a weekday early morning for shortest lines.* ⓢ *20TL, student with ISIC card 1TL.* ⚙ *Open Tu 9am-5:30pm, W 9am-5:30pm, F-Su 9am-5:30pm. Box office closes at 4pm.*

ORTAKÖY MOSQUE   MOSQUE
Büyük Mecidiye Camii, Ortaköy

This Ortaköy landmark was designed by the Balyans, the Armenian father-son tandem that contributed to the design of Dolmabahçe Palace. The inside is pretty, but you probably won't spend more than five minutes there. The mosque is best viewed from the outside—get a *kumpir (potato stuffed with cheese and various other fillings—if there's one place in Istanbul where you should try this snack, it's here; 8TL)* from one of the nearby stalls. Sit near the water and watch Ortaköy's beautiful and well-to-do youth promenade in front of the mosque and the Bosphorus.

✈ *Take the bus to Ortaköy. The mosque is right by the sea, to the east of the ferry terminal.* ✦ *Usual mosque etiquette (no shorts, women cover hair) applies.* ⓢ *Free.* ⚙ *Open daily 4am-midnight.*

ISTANBUL NAVAL MUSEUM   MUSEUM
Deniz Müzesi, Hayrettin Iskelesi Sok., Beşiktaş   ☎212 327 4345
                                                                  🖳www.denizmuzeleri.tsk.tr

For those who retain an interest in ship models from their early childhood, this museum might make for a diverting visit. It has exhibits from different eras of Ottoman and Turkish naval history—the top floor has some old boat escutcheons and monograms, while the bottom floor holds some relatively modern naval weapons. Atatürk's death certificate and a copy of his will can be found here as well. There's a TV screen showing the modern Turkish navy doing some cool things (exploding ships, etc.), all set to the main theme from Michael Bay's film *The Rock.* On the square opposite the museum is the tomb of Barbaros Hayrettin Paşa (known as Barbarossa), an Ottoman admiral who once dominated the Mediterranean sea. Don't flaunt your camera too much when entering the museum—the exhibits aren't worth paying extra to immortalize them on film.

✈ *Take the ferry or bus to Beşiktaş. The museum is on the square in front of the ferry terminal.* ⓢ *4TL. Students 1TL. Camera 8TL. Videocamera 16TL.* ⚙ *Open daily W-Su 9am-5pm.*

YILDIZ ŞALE   MUSEUM
Yıldız Park   ☎212 259 8977 🖳www.millisaraylar.gov.tr

This stuffy guesthouse built by Sultan Abdülhamit II once hosted important state visitors, like Kaiser Wilhelm II or Charles de Gaulle. The Balyan family had its share in the construction of this building as well, but the guesthouse pales in comparison with Dolmabahçe Palace, or with any other interesting place really. However, it's got its highlights—the carpet in the **ceremonial hall** is 450 sq. m large and was rolled into such a huge roll that a hole had to be made in the walls in order to allow the carpet to be brought inside. Aside from that, there's plenty of gold, mother-of-pearl, and crystal. Yıldız Şale isn't the only interesting structure inside the Yıldız Park—there's the **Malta Köşkü,** where the rather paranoid Abdülhamit II kept his brother Murad V and their mother as prisoners. Now it functions as a restaurant. With trees, flowers, and kitschy animal statues, the park itself is worth some aimless walking.

✈ *Take bus to Beşiktaş. Buses running between Beşiktaş and Ortaköy usually stop near the entrance to Yıldız Park, so you can either walk there or take a bus. Once inside the park, follow the signs up the hill. The walk there takes about 20min.* ✦ *Guided tours are compulsory. 20min. tours in English every 15min. No photos.* ⓢ *4TL, students 1TL, on weekends 2TL.* ⚙ *Open Tu-W 9:30am-5pm, F-Su 9:30am-5pm.*

BEYOĞLU

ISTANBUL MUSEUM OF MODERN ART ♿❄ MUSEUM

Meclis-i Mebusan Cad. ☎212 334 7300 💻www.istanbulmodern.org

Almost every corner in Beyoğlu has its own tiny gallery, but if there's one place for modern art, it's here. The upper floor hosts the permanent collection chronicling the development of modern art in Turkey over the past century, and the lower level hosts temporary exhibits by local and international artists. Even the staircase that connects these two floors is supposedly a work of art, one that "attacks" the "modernist logic" of "latently oppressive" sleek surfaces. There are a lot of big words on the explanatory signs, but many of the paintings, video projections, photographs, and installations are genuinely interesting. Don't miss the auto portrait gallery on the upper level, or the "False Ceiling" installation downstairs (it's a layer of books suspended from above, forming an artificial ceiling. Profound, isn't it?). For a schedule of the museum's frequent film screenings (mostly classics and modern Turkish films), check their website. Don't miss the awesome view of Istanbul Modern through the glass walls and from the museum's cafe.

🚏 From ⓂTophane, walk in the direction of Kabataş, and after passing the Nusretiye Mosque, turn right and follow the signs. $ 8TL, students 3TL; free on Th. ⏰ Open Tu-W 10am-6pm, Th 10am-8pm, F-Su 10am-6pm.

PERA MUSEUM ♿❄ MUSEUM

Meşrutiyet Cad. 65 ☎212 334 9900 💻www.peramuzesi.org.tr

Run by the Suna and İnan Kıraç Foundation, this museum is worth visiting both for its temporary exhibits (which occupy the top three floors and have included works by Picasso, Chagal, and Kurosawa) and its permanent collection. The museum's best-known painting is the rather funny *The Tortoise Trainer* by Osman Hamdi Bey, which the Pera bought for $3.5 million in 2004. It is exhibited on the second floor, along with other Orientalist paintings depicting scenes from life in the Ottoman Empire. These paintings are mostly by Western painters infatuated with the East's mystique, and if their obsession seems hilarious today, think about how many of your friends are into yoga or Buddhism. The first floor holds collections of Kütahya tiles, ceramics, and old measuring instruments.

🚏 ⓂTünel. Walk up İstiklal until you reach a silver statue resembling a sea urchin (opposite Nuruziya Sokak). Turn left into the passage, and at the end turn left. The museum will be in front of you. $ 7TL, students 3TL. Students free on W. English audio tours 4TL. ⏰ Open Tu-Sa 10am-7pm, Su noon-6pm.

food

Contrary to popular belief, food in Istanbul isn't all kebabs. Start your day with a generous Turkish breakfast plate (usually bread, cheese, olives, egg, tomatoes, cucumbers) or, even better, with *kaymak* (cream) and honey. If you don't have time for a breakfast, just grab a *simit* (Turkish bagel with sesame) from a street vendor. For lunch, pop into a *lokanta* to choose from among the ready dishes that are waiting for workers on their lunch breaks, or go to a restaurant and order a thin *pide*, the so-called "Turkish pizza." To combat your afternoon slump, find a patisserie and have a baklava, or any one of the many types of syrup-soaked pastries on sale. For dinner try a fish restaurant—if you don't want to spend too much money, just order some *meze* (vegetable or seafood appetizers) and share them among yourselves. At night, find a fast-food joint that sells *dürüms* (kebab wraps), *tantuni* (diced meat), or, if you're feeling frisky, *kokoreç* (chopped lamb intestines). Some of the nicest places to experience the authentic Turkish cuisine are small 👍homefood restaurants, so be on a lookout for those—they are generally not very well advertised. Few things are better than a late-night *çorba* (lentil soup), while *börek* (phyllo-dough pastry) is a choice breakfast staple. And these are just the basics—over time, you'll discover many more options. Oh, and let's not forget about *çay* (black tea), without which no Turkish meal can be complete.

SULTANAHMET AND AROUND

👍 HOCAPAŞA PIDECISI — 🍴 PIDE ❶

Hocapaşa Sok. 19 ☎212 512 0990

Don't let any of the mantis-like waiters around this well-known restaurant street direct you into their own place instead of this one—Hocapaşa Pidecisi is one of the few eateries here that isn't slowly turning into a tourist trap. With a menu only in Turkish, it serves excellent cheap *pides* to the locals who know their order by heart. There is more seating upstairs, but it's probably not the best option for taller travelers. Be on the lookout for other tourists—once they start coming here, everything is lost.

➜ Ⓜ Sirkeci. Go south (up the slope), and then turn left on Hocapaşa Sok.; the restaurant will be on your left. Ⓢ Pide 6-10TL. ⏰ Open daily 9am-9pm.

TARIHI SULTANAHMET KÖFTECISI SELIM USTA — 🍴 KÖFTE ❷

Divan Yolu Cad. 12 ☎212 520 0566 💻www.sultanahmetkoftesi.com

Even with only two meat items on its 10-item menu, this place still manages to be one of Istanbul's most famous restaurants. Serving meatballs with vinegary bean salad since 1920, the restaurant attracts both tourists and the kind of Istanbul natives who would otherwise avoid Sultanahmet like a stinking toe. All three floors get wonderfully crowded, so give in to peer pressure and enjoy what locals and visitors alike agree is one of Istanbul's best offerings. While therere are a few imitators nearby, you'll know you are in the original if they only accept cash.

➜ Ⓜ Sultanahmet. Ⓢ Bean salad 5TL. Köfte 10TL. ⏰ Open daily 11am-11pm.

BEREKET SOFRASI — 🍴 TURKISH ❶

Binbirdirek Mah. Peykhane Sok. 15/17 ☎212 518 7111 💻www.bereketsofrasi.com

Foodwise, the real question in Sultanahmet isn't how to find an exhilarating restaurant, it's how to find a good, honest one. Berek Sofrası, a short walk from

no beans about it

You may have heard about infamous Turkish coffee–strong dark coffee served in a little cup (about the size of a shot glass), loaded with sugar and marked by a layer of grainy sludge at the bottom. Prevalent all over eastern Europe and the Arab world, Turkish coffee is the super-strong start to every Istanbul native's morning. The name refers to the specific method of preparation used, rather than to a specific type of bean. Freshly ground coffee beans are saturated in hot water for just the right amount of time, then poured from a copper pot with a long thin neck. If the beans are left for too long or are put in boiling water rather than hot, it can leave the coffee with an unpleasant burnt taste that will likely spoil your appetite for a future tasting of this distinctive drink. However, even if your coffee's been perfectly prepared, don't drink that sludge at the bottom–these nasty-tasting dregs are best left for *kahve fali*, Turkish coffee fortune-telling.

the center down Divan Yolu, is as authentic as they come and serves excellent *pide* and kebabs *(6-13TL)* to the locals for a local price. Tourists are welcome to eat here, but they aren't the main clientele. Have the *sütlaç (rice pudding; 3 TL)* after a heavy meal.

🧭 [M]Çemberlitas. From the tram stop, head south 2 blocks. [$] Entrees 6-13TL. ⏰ Open daily 6:30am-11pm.

ORIENT EXPRESS RESTAURANT 💳♿🍸 TURKISH [3]

İstasyon Cad. 2 Gar İçi Sirkeci ☎212 522 2280 💻www.orientexpressrestaurant.com

When it's empty, this restaurant inside the Sirkeci train station seems like it's from a time when the century of electricity was merely beginning. The station was the last stop of the famous Orient Express, and the restaurant tries to imitate that cosmopolitan feel with waiters in bowties that speak French, German, and English. Don't just come to take a picture, however—sit down under the tall, arching ceiling and eat. Roast lamb shoulder *(25 TL)* is the specialty, but appetizers such as *Imam Bayildi (10TL)* are good as well. Come when there aren't many people and let your imagination roam free. Then get on the Orient Express and solve a particularly convoluted murder case.

🧭 [M]Sirkeci. Enter the train station, and the restaurant is on your left. [$] Entrees 16-25TL. ⏰ Open daily 10:30am-10:30pm.

HAMDI RESTAURANT 💳♿❄ TURKISH [3]

Tahmis Cad. Kalçın Sok. ☎212 528 0390 💻www.hamdirestorant.com.tr

With only a parking lot and some roads separating its building from the river, this restaurant is well-known for the view of Galata that it offers to the early birds who reserve the best seats. The food is traditional southeastern Turkish cuisine (kebabs) and worth the few extra liras. But even without a reservation, you can end up with some of the best seats—just sit one floor below the terrace, where there are fewer people, a great view, and the most potent A/C. Come for a dinner during the golden hour to see the entire town illuminated during sunset.

🧭 [M]Eminönü. Exit the station in the direction of Sultanahmet, turn right, continue until you see Hamdi on your left. ℹ Reservations are encouraged, but not necessary. [$] Kebabs 16-22TL. ⏰ Open daily 11am-11pm.

BAB-I HAYAT 💳🍸 TURKISH [2]

Mısır Çarşışı Haseki 47 ☎212 520 7878 💻www.babihayat.com.tr

Originally used as a stable, a tax collector's office, and a warehouse, this restaurant was renovated by the people responsible for the restoration of Topkapı Palace. Featuring tiled walls and hand-painted ceilings, Bab-ı Hayat offers local dishes worth their price. Come after a haggling session in the Egyptian Bazaar to enjoy their entrees *(10-21TL)*.

🧭 From [M]Eminönü, head toward the New Mosque; the restaurant is at the southeastern exit of the Egyptian Bazaar. ⏰ Open daily 8am-10pm.

YENI YILDIZ 💳🍸⛱ TURKISH, PIDE [2]

Cankurtaran Meydani 18 ☎212 518 1257

Down a crooked cobblestone path from Sultanahmet, this *pide* and kebab restaurant is a decent alternative to all of the tourist-filled eateries uphill. Originally owned by the late Erol Taş, a popular Turkish actor to whom much of the wall space is now devoted, this place offers expansive, colorful outdoor seating where you can eat, play backgammon, and smoke *nargile (hookah, 15TL)*. The restaurant is split into different parts as a result of alcohol licensing regulations, but don't let that confuse you. Come during the day and take a walk through the decrepit surrounding streets before enjoying this location's standard Turkish fare.

🧭 [M]Sultanahmet. From the hostel neighborhood, go south down the steps; it's 50m down the road on the right. [$] Kebabs 10-15TL. ⏰ Open daily 8am-midnight.

PAŞAZADE RESTAURANT 🍴 TURKISH ❸

Ibn-i Kemal Cad. 13 ☎212 513 3757 💻www.pasazade.com

In certain pricey restaurants, you pay for an unbelievable view and cope with the usually mediocre food. In Paşazade, you don't get much of a view, which should be a good sign. Come to this restaurant to find tasty Ottoman dishes that you can't find on the street—no grilled kebabs here, just boiled or cooked food that is arranged in artistic-looking shapes. Try the *Mahmudiye (15TL)* with chicken, mashed potatoes, and fruit. This is one of the few places where you can get the upscale decor (candle and all) and not pay more than you'd like.

➡ ⓂGülhane. Follow the tracks toward Sirkeci, turn left as soon as you can, and then turn right. Paşazade will be on your left. $ Entrees 13-23TL. Dessert 6-7.50TL. ⏰ Open daily noon-11pm.

DOY-DOY 🍴 TURKISH ❷

Şifa Hamamı Sok. 13 ☎212 518 1280 💻www.doydoy-restaurant.com

Recommended by perhaps every travel guide that has ever passed through this area, Doy-Doy might soon be on the brink of flipping from underrated to overrated. But don't let that discourage you from coming here for a meal—Doy-Doy's popularity is apparent from how often their delivery motorbikes zip around the town. If you climb three flights of stairs, you can sit on a terrace, enjoy a view of the Blue Mosque, and have some reasonably priced kebabs or pizza. Shoo away the sparrows trying to hop toward your plate, and make use of the photo op with the mosque in the background.

➡ ⓂSultanahmet. Two blocks down from the southern corner of the Blue Mosque. i Free delivery within Sultanahmet. $ Kebabs 8-14TL. Desserts 4TL. ⏰ Open daily 8am-10:30pm.

SARNIÇ RESTAURANT 🍴🚭 TURKISH ❹

Soğukçeşme Sokağı ☎212 512 4291 💻www.sarnicrestaurant.com

If you're a rich, elderly German tourist and you just happen to be reading a budget travel guide to amuse yourself, feel free to go to Sarnıç Restaurant. If you're a student and feel like eating inside a renovated water cistern from 1500 years ago (and are willing to shell out some serious dough for said experience), you should also eat here—and maybe pick up a mainstream hobby. With lit candles and acoustics worthy of a bat cave, an atmosphere like this is hard to imitate. If the cost of entrees *(25-57 TL)* scares you but you still feel an urge to eat inside a centuries-old water cistern, there's an easy fix—have a hamburger in the cafe that's inside the Byzantine Cistern.

➡ ⓂSultanahmet. Find it in the small street behind Hagia Sophia. $ Appetizers 20-35TL; entrees 25-57TL. Desserts 16-22TL. ⏰ Open daily 7:30-10:30pm.

FATIH

ESKI KAFA 🌿📶☀ CAFE, ORGANIC ❷

Atpazarı 11/A, Fatih ☎212 533 4291 💻www.eski-kafa.com

There aren't many items on the menu here, but every one is worth a try. Order the *gulaş (12TL)*, one of the Hungarian contributions to the greatness of the Ottoman Empire. All food here is organic, so the place is bound to be popular with all the yoga-lovin' hipsters who might happen across it. You can enjoy your cup of hibiscus tea either in the crammed interior or outside as you sit at one of the blocks of concrete that serves as a table.

➡ Take bus to Fatih. Leave the Fatih Mosque grounds through the southeastern exit. Turn left and walk for 3 blocks. Turn right into Atpazarı, and Eski Kafa will be to your right. i Free Wi-Fi. $ Meals 10-12TL. Desserts 4-7TL. Tea 1.50-4TL. ⏰ Open daily 10am-11pm.

SUR OCAKBAŞI 🍴📶☀ TURKISH ❷

İtfaiye Cad. 19, Fatih ☎212 533 8088 💻www.surocakbasi.net

Apparently, Anthony Bourdain visited this place in 2009, and the food gave him an orgasm or something—so it's about time tourists started crowding this eatery. The specialty here is the *büryan kebab (11TL)* which is made from lamb back cooked in an underground pit. If one regional dish isn't enough for you, try the *bütün (7TL)*, a dessert made from ice cream and rice. The mascot of this restaurant is a nude, bewildered child standing inside a huge watermelon. Don't ask why.

➡ Take bus to Fatih. From the mosque walk, southeast until you reach the aqueduct. Walk along it, then turn left into Siirt Bazaar and go straight. The restaurant will be to your left. ℹ Free Wi-Fi. $ Kebabs 10-17.50TL; pide 11TL. ⏰ Open daily 8am-1am.

SELAM 💳❄ TURKISH [2]

Fevzi Paşa Cad. 69, Fatih ☎212 631 2595 💻www.selam.com.tr

This multi-story chameleon of a restaurant offers something different on every floor: it serves sweets in the basement, fast food on the first floor, and kebabs and all that jazz on the second. As the quality of A/C varies by floor, choose where to dine based on what you feel like having as well as your preferred temperature. If you haven't tried it yet, order the *soslu manti (9-10TL)*, a handmade pasta with tiny bits of meat inside. Its preparation is a fascinating, machine-like process. Come in at the right time, and you'll see some of it take place inside the cubicle near the entrance.

➡ If you're walking northwest on Fevzi Paşa, Selam will be on your left, close to where the Fatih Mosque's walls end. $ Kebabs 11-18TL. Pides 6.50-10TL. Pastries 4.50-6.50TL. ⏰ Open daily 11am-11pm.

SARAY MUHALLEBICISI 💳📶❄ SWEETS [1]

Fevzi Paşa Cad. 1, Fatih ☎212 521 0505 💻www.saraymuhallebicisi.com

If you want to have a substance-induced state of altered consciousness in Fatih, your best bet will be to go for a sugar high. Take the elevator to the terrace on Saray's top floor, where you can feed on *kazandibis*, *muhallebis*, profiterols, and baklavas while taking in a view of the city. Sugar hangover? It's also a good spot for breakfast *(5-7TL)*.

➡ Leave the Fatih Mosque grounds through the southeastern exit, turn right and walk to Fevzi Paşa. Saray will be right across the road. $ Desserts 5-6TL; pastries 4.50-7.50TL. Sandwiches 6TL. Coffee 4TL. ⏰ Open daily 6am-1am.

KÖMÜR LOKANTASI 💳♿ LOKANTA [1]

Fevzi Paşa Cad. 18 ☎212 521 9999 💻www.komurlokantasi.com

Kömür is one of the more pleasant *lokantas* spots, with four floors and a lot of busy waiters, but the food is nothing to write home about. If you're feeling important, go sit in the VIP lounge on the top floor, which looks quite similar to all the other floors—apart from the fact that it's VIP.

➡ If you're walking northwest on Fevzi Paşa, Kömür will be to your right, on the first corner after the mosque's walls end. $ Kebabs 7-12TL. Pilaf 3-5TL. Desserts 3-5.50TL. ⏰ Open daily 4am-11pm.

BEYOĞLU

👍 MANGAL KEYFI 💳 DÜRÜM [1]

Öğüt Sok. 8 ☎212 245 1534

This charismatic, unpretentious place is attended mostly by young locals, and it's got better *dürüms* than you'll get at any touristy restaurant in Taksim. Try the excellent chicken *dürüm (4TL)*, and have a cup of frothy *ayran* with it. It's surprising that this place is so cheap without being a dump. The dark red walls, the plethora of posters, and the nonstop rock music make eating here very agreeable.

➡ From [M]Taksim, walk down İstiklal. Take a right onto Ağa Camii, then take the 2nd right onto Öğüt Sok; the restaurant will be to your left. $ Dürüms 4-4.50TL. Kebabs 8-12TL. Ayran 1.50TL. ⏰ Open daily 8am-midnight.

VAN KAHVALTI EVI 💳⛅ BREAKFAST [2]

Defterdar Yok. 52/A ☎212 293 6437

Cihangir is the best area in Beyoğlu for a lazy breakfast, probably because most of its inhabitants are a lazy lot (artists, expats, and the like), and Van Kahvaltı Evi offers the best deal, making excellent scrambled eggs with cheese and sausage *(8TL)* and mixed breakfast plates with varieties of cheese. Tea is served in big cups, but *Let's Go* recommends one of the organic fruit juices *(4TL)*. It's a simple place, but on weekend mornings it's hard to find an empty table.

➡ From [M]Taksim, walk down Sıraselviler Cad.; this breakfast place is 1 block after the Firuzağa Mosque. $ Eggs 5-8TL. Breakfast plates 8-15TL. Coffee 3-4TL. ⏰ Open daily 7am-7pm.

ZENCEFIL 💳📶 VEGETARIAN [2]

Kurabiye Sok. 8-10 ☎212 243 8234 💻www.zencefil.org

If you're vegetarian and have been navigating the kebab minefield that is Istanbul, you should definitely come to this Taksim eatery for a meal. Its "vegetable-oriented" menu changes according to season and tastes a cut above the standard at many restaurants that focus on meat. Zencefil cans its own vegetables, makes its own butter and bread, and even had its own homemade lemonade before this drink became a popular fare in the city's restaurants. Eating here isn't dirt-cheap, but it is worth your money.

➡ [M]Taksim. Walk down İstiklal, take the 1st right and then the 1st left turn; walk straight until you see the restaurant on your right. ℹ Free Wi-Fi. $ Full entrees 11.50-13.50TL; small entrees 7.50-10.50TL. Lemonade 8TL. ⏰ Open M-Sa 8:30am-11:30pm.

SOFYALI 9 💳🍸⛅ SEAFOOD, TURKISH [2]

Sofyalı Sok. 9 ☎212 245 0362 💻www.sofyali.com.tr

This is one of the best-known establishments in the Tünel area, and it's worth coming here for the *meze*. This Arabic specialty is on the expensive side, but you can always find some cheaper items in the daily-special section of the menu. Despite its poshness and reputation, the restaurant still has something of a *meyhane* feel, so don't hesitate to just come for *rakı* and some cheese.

➡ [M]Tünel. Walk up İstiklal from Tünel, take the first left turn, walk to the end of the street and turn left. The restaurant will be to your left. $ Meze 2.50-10TL. Salads 8-11TL. Entrees 13-25TL. Desserts 5-7.50TL. ⏰ Open daily noon-11pm.

KIVAHAN 💳📶 TRADITIONAL [2]

Galata Kulesi Meydanı 9 ☎212 292 9898 💻www.galatakivahan.com

Right in Galata Tower's backyard, this restaurant is almost a tourist trap, but the food is original enough to make it worth a visit. The recipes were collected from all over Turkey, and since the names on the menu aren't too familiar (where are the kebabs, Kivahan?), you'll probably just have to walk up to the counter and point at things you'd like to have. The portions are quite small, so if you're starving, get a street *dürüm* first.

➡ [M]Tünel or [M]Karaköy. The restaurant is in the square right next to Galata Tower. $ Salads and meze 5-6TL. Vegetarian dishes 8-10TL. Entrees 10-20TL. Desserts 5TL. 10% service charge not included in price. ⏰ Open daily 9am-midnight.

CEZAYIR 💳📶🍸⛅ TURKISH [4]

Hayriye Cad. 12 ☎212 245 9980 💻www.cezayir-istanbul.com

Cezayir is housed by an old Italian building that used to function as a school, and today the eatery is among Galatasaray's best known restaurants. The cuisine is Turkish, with a degree of innovation—the hallumi cheese with tomato pesto *(10TL)* and the grilled lamb tenderloin *(30.50TL)* are among the more popular dishes. If this place is too expensive for you, try the Cezayir Sokak nearby, a narrow, steep street with plenty of atmospheric, lesser-known restaurants.

➡ [M]Taksim or [M]Tünel. From Galatasaray Lisesi, go down Yeni Çarşı and take the 1st left turn;

the restaurant will be to your right. $ *Appetizers 10-18TL. Starters 17-36.50TL. Beer 8-13TL.* ⏰ *Open daily 9am-2am.*

EMINE ANA SOFRASI 💳 TANTUNI ❶

Billurcu Sok. 5/A ☎212 292 8430

Kebab might be the default fast food in Istanbul, but leaving without trying *tantuni* (diced meat) would be a mistake—a grave one, at that. This visually unappealing eatery serves excellent and cheap *tantuni dürüms*, which taste far better than most of their kebab cousins. The only problem is that one *tantuni dürüm* is never enough, so you'll have to get two or three to be satisfied.

➔ *Ⓜ Taksim. Billurcu Sok. is a small street off Kücükparmakkapı Sokak.* $ *Tantuni dürüm 4.5TL. Tantuni sandwich 5TL.* ⏰ *Open daily 11am-6am.*

KAFE ARA 💳📶⛅ CAFE ❷

Tosbağa Sok. 2 ☎212 245 4105

The cosmopolitan Kafe Ara is owned by Ara Güler, a respected Turkish photographer whose giant black-and-white photographs of Istanbul adorn the walls. If you come from 1-5pm, you might get to see the old man himself, now in his eighties, chilling in his shrine. The interior design is interesting, and ambient jazz music sets the mood. If you're hungry, try the Balkan *köfte (18TL)*, or just come for a coffee.

➔ *Ⓜ Taksim or Ⓜ Tünel. From Galatasaray Lisesi, go down Yeni Çarşı and take the 1st right.* $ *Breakfast buffet 15TL. Sunday brunch 22.50TL. Entrees 16-20TL. Desserts 7-10TL.* ⏰ *Open M-F 7:30am-midnight, Sa 10:30am-1am, Su 10am-midnight. Su brunch 10am-2pm.*

GALATA HOUSE 💳🍸 GEORGIAN ❸

Galata Kulesi Sok. (61) 15 ☎212 245 1861 💻www.thegalatahouse.com

A former British jail, this building in Galata was restored by its architect owners and later converted into a restaurant. Apart from offering the (potential) thrill of eating in a former exercise yard, Galata House is also unique in Istanbul for serving Georgian and Russian cuisine. There aren't many tables, supposedly because the owners are against the industrialization of food consumption. A history lesson on Galata ("the Empire within an Empire") comes along with the menu.

➔ *Ⓜ Tünel or Ⓜ Karaköy. From Galata Tower, head down the hill on Galata Kulesi Sokak; the restaurant will be on your left.* $ *Entrees 17-23TL. Desserts 8-10TL.* ⏰ *Open daily noon-midnight. Kitchen open noon-11pm.*

FENER AND BALAT

👍 **FINDIK KABUĞUNDA KÖFTE** 💳📶 KÖFTE ❶

Mürsel Paşa Cad. 89, Balat ☎212 635 3310 💻www.findikkofte.com

It's surprising to find such a tourist-friendly restaurant with such reasonable prices in Balat. With a clean interior, free Wi-Fi, and a terrace offering a view of the Bulgarian St. Stephen Church and the Golden Horn, this spot makes for a great lunch. Try one of the three varieties of meatballs, the artichoke, or the saffron-tinged lentil soup.

➔ *Bus or ferry to Fener. From the ferry jetty, go inland, cross the road, turn right, and walk until you see the Bulgarian St. Stephen Church on the right. The restaurant is opposite the church.* $ *Köfte 6-7.50TL. Sides and salads 3TL. Desserts 3TL.* ⏰ *Open daily 9am-10pm.*

PIERRE LOTI CAFE 🌐⛅ CAFE ❶

Gümüşsuyu Balmumcu Sok. 5, Eyüp ☎212 581 2696

Positioned on top of a hill overlooking the Golden Horn, this used to be the favorite hangout place of Julien Viaud, the 19th-century French writer working under the penname Pierre Loti, whose detail-oriented style allegedly influenced the even more detail-oriented Marcel Proust. Viaud's first novel was based on his romantic adventures with a harem girl called Aziyade here in Istanbul. Come to this cafe to have some tea and enjoy the magnificent view—perhaps it will inspire you to write a blog post or something.

➜ *Bus or ferry to Eyüp. To get here from the Eyüp Sultan Mosque, you can either take a cable car (Piyerloti teleferik) or walk. It's a 15min. hike up the hill through the cemetery. The path begins with a flight of stairs to the side of the mosque.* [$] *Tea 1.90TL. Coffee and soda 3.80TL.* ⏰ *Open daily 7am-midnight.*

MEKTEB-I CAFE ⊛ CAFE [1]

Vodina Cad. Akçin Sok. 3/A, Fener ☎535 953 1293

Quite close to the Fener ferry jetty, this small cafe seems like the intuitive place to have a tea or coffee before setting out to explore the neighborhood. It's pleasantly decorated, and the upper level with soft cushions and low ceilings is especially appealing. After you're done here, go find the castle-like Greek College.

➜ *Bus or ferry to Fener. From the ferry jetty, go inland, cross the road, turn right, and walk. Then take the first available left turn; the cafe will be on the corner to your left.* [$] *Tea 2TL. Coffee 4TL. Toast 3TL.* ⏰ *Open daily 8am-8pm.*

HALIÇ SOSYAL TESISI 🍴☀ TURKISH [2]

Abdülezel Paşa Cad., Kadir Has Üniversitesi Karşısı, Fener ☎212 444 1034 💻www.ibb.gov.tr

A government-run restaurant, this place exists as a result of the many attempts of the local authorities to turn Fener and Balat into a hip, gentrified place like Cihangir. The restaurant is clean, spacious, and reasonably priced. The fish or the chicken casserole *(10TL)* is worth the money, but the government is going to need to do a lot more to make this a tourist spot.

➜ *Bus or ferry to Fener. Head southeast along the shore (toward Sultanahmet) for some 300m. The restaurant is right by the water.* [$] *Fish 10-18.5TL. Köfte 7.5-8.5TL. Desserts 4-5TL.* ⏰ *Open daily 8:30am-11pm.*

KADIKÖY, MODA, AND ÜSKÜDAR

ÇIYA KEBAP 🍴☀ TURKISH [2]

Güneşlibahçe Sok. 48/B, Kadıköy ☎216 336 3013 💻www.ciya.com.tr

Arguably the best-known restaurant on the Asian side, Çiya has three branches right next to each other—two focus on kebabs, while the third one, Çiya Sofrası, has more vegetarian dishes. The daily offerings changed based on what's available, so if you're interested, check out the menu in advance on their website; otherwise, just stop by and pick something. Çiya's chef Musa Dağdeviren is celebrating one success after another with his obscure ingredients, and it's surprising that this doesn't translate into unbearably high prices. Sit outside and let the wind bring you the sound of live music coming from one of the less distinguished restaurants down the street.

➜ *Take the ferry to Kadıköy. It's a few blocks down from Kadıköy market. To get there from the ferry terminal, go on Söğütlüçeşme, turn right, and make a quick left. Walk up 2 blocks, then take a right and go straight until you see it.* [$] *Kebabs 12-20TL. Salads 5-6TL. Desserts 5-6TL.* ⏰ *Open daily 10am-11pm.*

ALI USTA 🍴 ICE CREAM [1]

Moda Cad. 264/A, Moda ☎216 414 1880

This small ice cream joint doesn't look like much, but the lines of locals that you can sometimes see here are a bit more telling. In fact, it's one of the best-known ice cream places in Istanbul. Get a scoop or two with some caramel sauce, chocolate chips, and chopped nuts on top, and set out for Moda's beaches.

➜ *The ferry to Kadıköy. Get off the nostalgic tram near Moda Cad. and walk down the street. Ali Usta is on the right side, close to where Moda forks.* [$] *One scoop 2TL, 2 scoops 4TL, 3 scoops 6TL.* ⏰ *Open daily 8am-2am.*

MEŞHUR MENEMENCI ⊛☀ MENEMEN [1]

Pavlonya Sok. 22, Kadıköy ☎216 336 6308

Preparing almost exclusively *menemen*—a popular scrambled egg dish—this tiny eatery is a great place to kick off your day. It's not exactly tourist central, but *Let's Go* likes its authenticity. The dishes are custom-made, so you can choose whether you want cheese, sausage, or chili inside your menemen (you want it all, by the way). Don't forget to use bread to wipe the pan clean—leaving any of it would be an act of barbarism.

➜ Take the ferry to Kadıköy. Walk up Söğütlüçeşme, turn right immediately after Osmanağa Mosque, and walk straight. It will be on your right. Ⓢ Menemen 4-5TL. ⏰ Open daily 7am-8pm.

PIDE SUN 💳☀ PIDE [1]

Moda Cad. Şükran Apartmanı 97, Kadıköy ☎216 347 3155 💻www.pidesun.com

Pide Sun is an unassuming place that hits all the important points for an easy meal—it's cozy, cheap, and tasty. The *pides* here are so thin that even the most devoted pizza aficionados will be forced to suck up their pride and eat the *pides* the Turkish way, i.e. with utensils. It's easy to pass by the restaurant without noticing it, but the food is worth the extra time you'll spend searching for it.

➜ Take the ferry to Kadıköy. Pide Sun is in the Kadıköy portion of Moda Cad., very close to a Migros supermarket. If you're walking from Kadıköy market, it will be to your left. Ⓢ Pides 7-10.50TL. ⏰ Open daily 11:30am-11pm.

İSKENDER İSKENDEROĞLU 💳 KEBAB [3]

Rıhtım Cad. PTT yanı, Kadıköy ☎216 336 0777 💻www.iskenderkebabi.com.tr

Who could have guessed that the famous İskender kebab was named not after a Turkish village but after a person? Well, it was. A century or so ago, Mr. Mehmet Oğlu İskender invented the dish in Bursa and later passed the recipe to his descendants. This restaurant is run by third- and fourth-generation İskenders who seem to be taking their legacy pretty seriously. The place itself is not very charismatic and the *İskender* kebabs are a bit overpriced, but it's a must-see for anyone who feels strongly about İskender kebabs or the İskender family pedigree. Next on the list: Mr. Döner and his grandchildren.

➜ Take the ferry to Kadıköy. From the ferry terminal, head southwest on Faik Sözen; it will be on your left next to Benzin Cafe. Ⓢ İskender kebabs 18TL. Desserts 5-6TL. ⏰ Open daily 11:30am-10pm.

AGAPIA 💳☀ INTERNATIONAL [2]

Miralay Nazim Sok. 10, Kadıköy ☎216 418 3636

With a wonderfully atmospheric garden and creatively arranged dishes, this is one of the nicest dinner restaurants around. If you're not in the mood for international dishes like chicken fajitas *(9.50TL)* or grilled veal, come for a cocktail *(12TL)* complete with a funny-looking straw and umbrella. And if you order a dessert, much of the plate will be sprinkled with a layer of cocoa powder—which is a creative way of distracting you from how small the desserts look on their huge plates.

➜ Take the ferry to Kadıköy. It's on the same street as HUSH Hostel. If you're walking down Bahariye from the bull statue, turn right just before the Süreyya Opera House and go straight. Ⓢ Entrees 9.50-14TL. Salads 7.50-11.50TL. Desserts 4.50-6TL. ⏰ Open daily 8am-2am.

KANAAT LOKANTASI ◉ LOKANTA [2]

Selmanipak Cad. 25, Üsküdar ☎216 553 3791

For some reason, this is one of the best-known restaurants in Üsküdar. The place looks like a very normal Ottoman *lokanta* and serves basic food to locals, but don't let that trick you into underestimating the bill at the end. The most impressive part of the restaurant is the desserts counter, so save some space for a *kazandibi* after your meal.

➜ Take the ferry to Üsküdar. It's quite close to the ferry terminal. Cross the street and head toward Seyh Mosque. Ⓢ Meat entrees 7.50-13.50TL; vegetarian entrees 7.50-9TL. Pilaf 4.50TL. Desserts 5-7TL. ⏰ Open daily 6am-11pm.

MOLA YEMEKEVI

⊜⌂ TRADITIONAL ❶

Damacı Sok. 8/3, Kadıköy   ☎216 348 6310

Small places like this are a good bet for travelers who want to see what food really tastes like in a Turkish home. Mola Yemekevi has a distinctly domestic feel due to its tiny kitchen, several child-made drawings pinned up on its walls, and an old Hi-Fi system playing CDs. Order something in the back and while they prepare it, go sit outside under the enthusiastically sprouting roof of climbing plants.

✈ *Take the ferry to Kadıköy. From Rexx Cinema go one block down Sakiz Gülü and turn left. The restaurant will be to your left, tucked into a small corner.* Ⓢ *Entrees 4.50-8TL. Soup 3TL. Salads 5-7TL.* ⓣ *Open daily 9am-9pm.*

MODA TERAS

✐✦♔⌂ INTERNATIONAL❹

Mektep Sok. 1, Moda   ☎216 338 7040 ▤www.modateras.com.tr

The wedding albums at the entrance and the restaurant's motto (encouraging you to say your *romantik evet*, or proposals, here) may make this a bad choice for less-than stable couples. Otherwise, Moda Teras is a pleasant place: the interior is trendy and the terrace overlooks the sea. There's a decent selection of international dishes, with one lonely kebab repping among all the Thai chickens and veal medallions. The prices are on the higher side, but if you don't want to dine here, you can always come for a cold drink sometime midday.

✈ *Take ferry to Kadıköy. Go south on Moda Cad., go left when the road forks, then take another left and walk for three min.* Ⓢ *Entrees 19-35TL. Desserts 8.50-13TL. Drinks 3.50-7.50TL.* ⓣ *Open M-F 10am-midnight; Sa breakfast buffet 10am-1pm, Su brunch 10:30am-2:30pm.*

BAYLAN PASTANESI

✐❀⌂ SWEETS❷

Muvakkıthane Cad. 9, Kadıköy   ☎216 346 6350 ▤www.baylanpastanesi.com

Another culinary landmark, Baylan is the last remaining branch of a pastry shop started by Greek immigrant Philip Lenas. The patisserie's most decadent creation is the decadent *Kup Griye (11TL)*, which contains vanilla ice cream, caramel sauce, chopped almonds, ground pistachios, Chantilly cream, and a ladyfinger biscuit. As good as this concoction is, there's no reason to limit yourself to just one dish—there are kilograms of other sweets and pastries to be tried. The interior isn't that appealing, but there's an artificial-looking garden in the back that's more pleasant.

✈ *Take ferry to Kadıköy. It's in a small street that intersects Kadıköy Market around where the restaurants start. From the intersection go two blocks down the slope, Baylan will be on your right.* Ⓢ *Kup Griye 11TL. Tea 3.25TL. Coffee 5-6TL.* ⓣ *Open daily 7am-9pm.*

BEŞIKTAŞ AND ORTAKÖY

▨ SIDIKA

✐♔ SEAFOOD ❸

Şair Nedim Cad. 38, Beşiktaş   ☎212 259 7232 ▤www.sidika.com.tr

Many seafood restaurants in Istanbul put candles on their tables, hire some *fasil* musicians, and then think they are entitled to charge a lot for mediocre food. Sıdıka, on the other hand, serves delicious fish dishes in a low-key, stylish environment. Let the energetic owner Sıdıka recommend a dish to you, or choose at random from the menu written on a blackboard. The *meze* are wonderful, but the house specialties are the grilled octopus *(8-12TL)* and the grilled fish in grape leaves *(16-20TL)*.

✈ *Take the ferry or bus to Beşiktaş. From the big eagle statue, walk down Şehit Asim, cross Orta-bahçe Cad., and continue until you get to Şair Nedim. Turn right at Şair Nedim and continue up the road until you see the restaurant on your right side.* ⓘ *Free Wi-Fi.* Ⓢ *Meze 3-10TL. Fish 14-20TL. Desserts 5-10TL. Rakı 9TL.* ⓣ *Open daily noon-2am.*

PANDO KAYMAK

⊜⌂ BREAKFAST ❶

Mumcu Bakkal Sok. 5, Beşiktaş   ☎212 258 2616

This place has been open for over 100 years and is run by an elderly Bulgarian couple. Come here for bread with *kaymak* (cream) and honey, and have a cup of hot milk with it. It doesn't look like much at first, but Pando Kaymak is a very popular breakfast spot among students and expats.

➜ *Take the bus or ferry to Beşiktaş. Starting at the big eagle statue, walk in the opposite direction from the fish market. Pando Kaymak will be to your left (above the door it says "Kaymaklı kahvaltı burada"). Ⓢ Breakfast 5TL. ⏰ Open daily 8am-6pm.*

THE HOUSE CAFE 🏷 📶 🍸 🏠 CAFE [3]

Salhane Sok. 1, Ortaköy ☎212 227 2699 💻www.thehousecafe.com.tr

The House Cafe has a number of locations throughout the city, but this is probably the best-known one. The food is westernized and comes in large portions, which makes it a popular hangout for well-to-do local students, and which also allows the chain to keep expanding like the Lernaean hydra. The interior was designed with quite some care, and late-night the cafe turns into a bar with DJ performances.

➜ *Take the bus to Ortaköy. The cafe is right by the Ortaköy ferry dock.* **i** *Free Wi-Fi. Ⓢ Pizza 18.50-24TL. Burgers 25TL. Beer 10-13TL. Desserts 8.50-11TL. ⏰ Open daily 9am-1am. Kitchen closes earlier.*

YEDI-SEKIZ HASANPAŞA FIRINI 🏷 BAKERY [2]

Şehit Asim Cad. 12, Beşiktaş ☎212 261 9766

This unpretentious bakery makes many kinds of tea cookies, great as an afternoon snack. You might have to communicate in sign language to indicate which of the freshly baked cookies you want, but they'll understand what you want fast enough. The store's name is "7-8" because Hasanpaşa, the Ottoman *paşa* who started it, didn't know how to write and made these two numbers his signature.

➜ *Take the bus or ferry to Beşiktaş. From the big eagle statue, walk down Şehit Asim; the store will be to your left. Ⓢ Tea cookies 14TL per kg., coconut-flavored 18TL per kg. ⏰ Open daily 8am-9:30pm.*

KARADENIZ PIDE VE DÖNER SALONU 🏷 TURKISH [2]

Mumcu Bakkal Sok. 6, Beşiktaş ☎212 261 7693

Even though this part of town is generally associated with expensive dining, it is possible to find cheap, excellent kebabs. Karadeniz doesn't have a varied menu; instead, they have one enormous ball of lamb meat on a spit from which they cut off meat for individual portions. You can have it inside a *pide*, or simply on a plate. The eating area is nothing to write poems about, so focus on the taste.

➜ *take the bus or ferry to Beşiktaş. Karadeniz is near the big eagle statue, opposite from Pando Kaymak. Ⓢ Döner 12TL. Kskender 13TL. Pide 7-10TL.*

nightlife

Istanbul's bars and clubs are concentrated around **İstiklal Avenue,** so if you're staying in Sultanahmet, you should prepare yourself for a good amount of commuting. Sultanahmet does have a few bars, but these are generally looked down upon by the locals—that's why we listed a handful of *nargile* cafes instead. Another center of nighttime activity is **Muallim Naci Cad.,** the road running up from Ortaköy to Kuruçeşme, home to the city's most prestigious clubs. Note that during summer, many music venues close down and move to their summer locations (the famous **Babylon** is one of them). The English-laguage *Time Out Magazine* lists current performances as well as a very comprehensive list of GLBT-friendly bars and clubs. If you want to drink the infamous Turkish anise-flavored alcohol **rakı,** the best place to do so is a traditional *meyhane.* Whatever you do, don't fall for the **nighttime scams**—if a local speaking perfect English approaches you on the street and invites you for a beer after three lines of uninteresting dialogue, he's probably planning a scam of sorts on you (it usually involves you, an exorbitant bill, and coercion).

SULTANAHMET AND AROUND

🏵 SETÜSTÜ ÇAY BAHÇESİ

💨🍃 CAFE

Gülhane Park

On what is almost a cliff over the Bosphorus, this cafe offers an unbelievable, 180-degree view of the three parts of Istanbul and the water in between. With cascades upon cascades of small wooden tables, almost everyone gets Setüstü's best seats. The tea is pricy, but remember you're also paying for the monumental view. Make sure to order the heavy-looking stuffed potato (10TL). Especially suitable for couples and those people who catch more pics than the paparazzi.

‡ Ⓜ Gülhane. *Enter the park and continue all the way to its back gate, then follow the signs.* Ⓢ *Tea for 1-3 people 6-17TL.*

CHEERS BAR

◉🍸🍃 BAR

Akbıyık Cad. 20

🖥 www.cheerscafebar.com

One of the many drinking and socializing options on Akbıyık Cad., this bar has been around for a while and caters almost exclusively to tourists. The odds are it's right across the street from where you're staying, so unless you'd just rather stay on your hostel's terrace, come over for a beer and a bit of the old "Oh, you're from Australia? I'm from Austria!" thing. Your experience here really depends on whom you're with, as the bar itself is pretty standard.

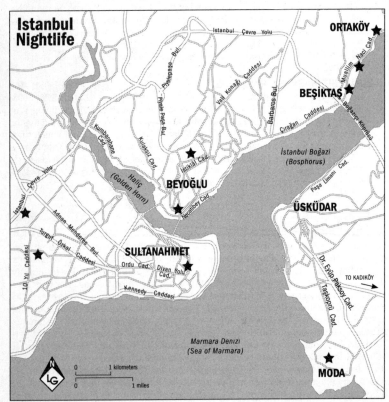

➜ [M]Sultanahmet. *In the middle of the hostel neighborhood.* $ *Small beer 5TL; large beer 6TL. Entrees 7-10TL. Nargile 10TL.* ⏰ *Open daily 11am-2am.*

ERENLER NARGILE ☕ CAFE

Çorlulu Ali Paşa Medresesi ☎212 511 8853

Çorlulu Ali Paşa Medresesi, a courtyard that formerly belonged to a *madrasa* (theological school), is famous among local students as the perfect place to come for a *nargile*. Erenler is the biggest of the three cafes here, and supplies visitors with waterpipes *(12TL)* and non-alcoholic drinks *(coffee and juice; 4TL)*. With plentiful seating and a 24hr. courtyard, the entire place smells of sweet fumes. While there is indoor seating, these rooms seem to be dominated solely by Turkish men playing backgammon.

➜ *From* [M]*Beyazır, follow the tram tracks in the direction of Hagia Sophia; the entrance to the courtyard will be on your left.* $ *Nargile 12TL.* ⏰ *Open 24hr.*

smoke and drink

For the indulgent type, Istanbul's hundreds of bars and hookah (refered to as "shisha") provide ample opportunity to destroy two relatively useless organs that start with the letter "l." For the less seasoned but curious traveler, this is how you avoid looking clueless or inadvertantly challenging somone to a fight.

Rakı is a must for your inner AA member. The anise-flavored liqueur will more closely resemble lighter fluid than its sweeter cousin, Absinthe. Drinking raki straight is considered macho, but if you're at a bar with a date, it's much classier to distill your glass with water before drinking.

Turkish Coffee: Don't look surprised to see a tiny cup of Joe served when you order coffee. Drink it slowly, since it's made to be savored, and also don't drink to the bottom, since you'll get a mouthful of coffee grounds.

Hookah: Probably one of the most enjoyed pastimes in Istanbul is smoking shisha, known as a *nargile*. Placed on the floor, the shisha sits in the center of a ring of people who pass the pipe around. It is meant to be inhaled, and it is considered rude to blow smoke in someone's direction. It is also rude to point the pipe at anyone as you pass it. Fold the pipe back and hand it to the next person with the mouthpeice facing you. And for God's sake, never place a shisha on a table when with locals, as this is a challenge to fight.

KAHVE DÜNYASI 💳📶❄ CAFE

Mollafenari Mahallesi, Nuruosmaniye Cad. 79 ☎212 527 3282 🖥www.kahvedunyasi.com

If after four days of kebabs, çay, and sütlaç you have a craving for something Western but aren't quite ready to cave in and go to Starbucks, come to Kahve Dünyası. In this Turkish coffee chain you can get sandwiches, cheesecake, bagels, and all kinds of coffee *(3.5-7.5TL)* in a very polished surrounding. Instead of the traditional sugar cubes, here you'll find brown sugar in small packets and plenty of small chocolates for sale—globalization at its finest.

➜ *From* [M]*Çemberlitaş, walk north from the Çemberlitaş Column and turn right at Nuruosmaniye Cad.; the cafe will be to your right.* $ *Coffee 3.50-7.5TL. Sandwiches, bagels, cheesecake 6.50TL.* ⏰ *Open daily 8am-8pm.*

GÜLHANE SUR CAFE ☕ CAFE

Soğukçeşme Sokağı 40/A ☎212 528 0986 🖥www.coskunbazaar.com

This small cafe on a historic cobblestone street between Aya Sofya and Topkapı

Palace is an excellent place to take a break from sightseeing. Have some tea or coffee while watching the other tourists trudge by and look at you enviously. To double their envy, order *nargile (10TL)*. The cafe is part of Coşkun Bazaar, a gift shop located right above it. Opposite the cafe is an unconventional "art exhibition" with paintings placed on the bare walls of a half-destroyed building, leading into a room that's full of stacked paintings—confused? So are we.

➔ From [M]Sultanahmet or [M]Gülhane, find the small street behind Hagia Sophia and continue down the hill. $ Tea and coffee 2-5TL. Nargile 10TL. 🕐 Open daily 9am-2am.

ARUNA CAFE
💳☀ CAFE [2]

Yeni Galata Köprüsü Altı ☎212 511 4770 💻www.arunacafe.com

Even if this place doesn't stick out shoulders above the rest of the competition on the Galata Bridge, coming here is a good compromise if you can't decide whether you want to spend your evening on the historic peninsula or the European side. It doesn't serve alcohol, but you can get *nargile*, tea, and some decent late-night eats (pizza, steak, sandwiches) while closely overlooking the intimidating waters of the Golden Horn. If you feel the urge to drink something a bit stronger, there are a few bars nearby on the bridge.

➔ [M]Eminönü. It's on the lower level of the bridge on the right side. $ Entrees 12-22TL. Tea 3-6TL. Nargile 15-17TL. 🕐 Open daily 8am-midnight.

FATIH

SARAY MUHALLEBICISI
💳📶❄ SWEETS

Fevzi Paşa Cad. 1, Fatih ☎212-521-0505 💻www.saraymuhallebicisi.com

Spending your Saturday night in Fatih is a bizarre idea, but if you insist on it, your best bet will be to go for a sugar high (restaurants here don't serve alcohol). Take the elevator to the terrace on Saray's top floor, where you can feed on kazandibis, muhallebis, profiterols, and baklavas while taking in a moderately interesting view of the city. It's also a good spot for breakfast (5-7 TL).

➔ Leave the Fatih Mosque grounds through the southeastern exit, turn right and walk to Fevzi Paşa. Saray will be right across the road. $ Desserts 5-6TL, pastries 4.50-7.50TL. Coffee 4TL. Sandwiches 6TL. 🕐 Open 6am-1am.

EYLÜL CAFE
🚫📶☀ CAFE

Macar Kardeşler Cad. 1, Fatih ☎212-621-3975

This is one of the few street cafes around where the seats aren't occupied solely by scowling middle-aged men. It's nothing exceptional, but you can have some tea or snacks here to take a break from walking around. It's at the beginning of a narrow street that has many small cafes with outdoor seating and backgammon.

*➔ It's a ten-minute walk down Fevzi Paşa from Fatih bus stop. **i** Free Wi-Fi. $ Tea 1.25TL, soft drinks 2.50TL. Snacks 2-5TL. 🕐 Open 7am-2am.*

KADIKÖY, MODA, AND ÜSKÜDAR

KÜP CAFE
💳🍸☀ GARDEN CAFE

Caferağa Mah. Güneşlibahçe Sok. 47, Kadıköy ☎216 347 8694 💻www.kupcafe.com

It's difficult to find for those who aren't searching for it, but Küp's atmospheric courtyard has everything you need for a quiet night out. There's a jungle of vegetation, some mood lighting, and a lot of corners to sit in. Come here when you're fed up with looking at the skyline, not too excited about people-watching, and just want to have a beer and discuss the more important things in life.

➔ Located toward the end of Güneşlibahçe Sok. If you're walking from Söğütlü Çeşme Cad., it will be on your left side. $ Tea 2-4TL. Beer 6TL. Entrees 8.50-15TL. 🕐 Open daily 9am-1am.

KARGA
💳🍸☀ BAR

Kadife Sok. 16, Kadıköy ☎216 449 1726 💻www.kargabar.org

One of the best known bars this side of the Bosphorus, Karga is so cool that it doesn't even need a name on its door. Thanks to its four stories, a garden, numerous balconies, and a top-floor art gallery, you can choose the decibel of your music and what kind of night you're going to have. Don't expect any Turkish music—Karga plays mostly alternative rock that fits its edgy atmosphere.

🧭 *On the bar street. Walking from Rexx Cinema it will be on your right, an unmarked wooden door with a raven drawn above it.* $ *Beer 6TL. Cocktails 6-16TL, Rakı 7.50TL, Food 4-9.50TL.* ⏰ *Open Sept-June noon-2am.*

ARKAODA 💵🍸⛅ BAR

Kadife Sok. 18, Kadıköy ☎216 418 0277 💻www.arkaoda.com

With red lighting and three different levels, Arkaoda tries to embody the alternative spirit of the Asian side of Istanbul. Usually playing minimalistic techno, ambient drone, or freak folk, Arkaoda also has frequent live concerts and DJ nights with internationally acclaimed acts. Try one of their alcoholic coffees *(7-10TL)*, which ingeniously manage to combine two vices at the same time.

🧭 *Walking from Rexx Cinema it will be on your right. It has an unmarked wooden door right next to Karga.* $ *Tea 4TL. Beer 7.50TL. Rakı 8.50TL. Whiskey 16TL.* ⏰ *Open daily 2pm-2am.*

LIMAN KAHVESI 💵🍸⛅ BAR

Kadife Sok. 37, Kadıköy ☎216 349 9818 💻www.limankahvesi.com.tr

This place will make you feel like you're on a boat—or at least surrounded by them. The drinks counter is in the shape of a boat, the bookshelf on the second floor is modeled after a barge, and there's a massive ship hanging from the ceiling. On the wall there are yellowed instructions for putting on an inflatable vest as well as a brick of an old ship transmitter—just make sure their various shots don't make you seasick. Liman Kahvesi brings in weekly DJs, presumably spinning nautically inspired sets.

🧭 *Toward the end of the bar street. Walking from Rexx Cinema it will be on your left.* $ *Beer 6TL. Rakı 8TL. Shots 9.50TL. Burgers and dürüms 8-9.5TL.* ⏰ *Open daily 10am-2am.*

BENZIN CAFE 💵🍸⛅ BAR

Faik Sözen Cad. 7, Kadıköy ☎216 450 5252

With neon signs saying "Big Yellow Taxi" and images of Western rock icons from floor to ceiling, Benzin is a shrine to American culture more than anything else. You'll soon realize all of this Bob Dylan and Rolling Stones stuff is more about admiration than about authenticity—the main beer here is still Efes and the staff doesn't speak a word in English. Instead of critiquing the faux-American ambience, have some pizza or a burger and enjoy this entertaining paradox.

🧭 *Across the street from the IETT bus parking lots. From the ferry terminal, cross the street and head southwest down Faik Sözen; Benzin will be on your left.* $ *Beer 6TL. Cocktails 12-17TL. Pizza 11-16TL.* ⏰ *Open daily 8am-2am.*

BOMONTI CAFE 🌸⛅ GARDEN

Kalamış Bomonti Çay Bahçesi, Moda ☎216 346 3430

Bomonti is not a cafe worth a long trek, but if you're in the area, it's a nice place to sit and relax. Despite the fact that a bunch of unruly trees can partially block your field of vision, many tables here offer a really nice view and overlook the sea. Have some tea or *nargile*, and then go pursue romance in the tiny park that's underneath.

🧭 *Get off the historic tram at the intersection of Cem Sok. and Moda Cad. Go down Moda until the road forks, then take a left. When you see the sea, take another left and continue straight for about 5min., past Moda Teras.* $ *Tea 1.50TL. Nargile 12TL. Food 5-14TL.* ⏰ *Open daily 8am-1am.*

BAST CAFE KITAP 💵🍸⛅ CAFE ❷

Moda Cad. Nesime 245/2, Moda ☎216 450 2640

This cafe exhibits some of the sterility that's typical of Moda, but the owners are doing what they can to give it some character with cheerfully colored chairs, bookshelves filled with Turkish and English books, and images of cats in all forms and sizes (including two enlarged *New Yorker* covers). Even if the staff doesn't speak English, this seems like the kind of place expats might like in Istanbul.

🧭 Get off the historic tram at the intersection of Cem Sok. and Moda Cad. Go down Moda until it forks, then take the left. The cafe will be to your left. Ⓢ Tea 2-5.50TL, coffee 5.50-7TL, beer 8TL, milkshakes 7TL. ⏰ Open daily 10am-midnight.

BEŞIKTAŞ AND ORTAKÖY

REINA — NIGHTCLUB, RESTAURANT

Muallim Naci Cad. 44, Ortaköy — ☎212 259 5919 💻www.reina.com.tr

If you're going to wallow in excess, do it big time. Probably the most famous club in the city, Reina is where local and international social elite come to spend unchristian amounts of money. The club has six different restaurants (Chinese, sushi, kebabs, Mediterranean, fish, and international) and a dance floor in the middle, all with the Bosphorus Bridge looming as a backdrop. Reina also owns two boats that will transport you here from your hotel, if you happen to be one of the VIP guests. Not sure if you qualify as a VIP or not? Then you probably don't. However, there are ways to enjoy the club for very little money—come on a weekday and then spend the night nursing a beer or two.

*🧭 Take the bus to Ortaköy. Then walk down Muallim Naci until you see it to your right. **i** Reservation for dinner required. Dress code is strictly enforced. Men need female company to enter the club. Ⓢ Cover F-Sa 50TL F and Sa; includes one drink. Beer 10TL. Cocktails 30TL. ⏰ Open daily for dinner 6pm-midnight. Club open daily midnight-4am.*

ANJELIQUE — NIGHTCLUB, RESTAURANT

Salhane Sok. 5, Ortaköy — ☎212 327 2844 💻www.istanbuldoors.com

Don't let the absence of cover charge at Anjelique on the weekends trick you: this is still one of the most prestigious clubs in the area. There are three floors, two restaurants (Asian and Mediterranean), and, during the club hours, two DJs at a time (one plays house, the other popular songs). The decor is stylish and simple (you won't find any of Reina's antlers-turned-lamps here) and the club's position over the Bosphorus is definitely an asset.

*🧭 Take the bus to Ortaköy. Anjelique is in a small street in the center of Ortaköy, opposite the Jazz Center and near a Hotel Radisson entrance. From the Ortaköy ferry jetty, head inland and take the first left, Anjelique will be to your left. **i** Reservation for dinner required. Dress code strictly enforced. Men need female company to enter the club. Ⓢ No cover. Beer 13TL. Cocktails 30TL. ⏰ Open daily for dinner 6pm-midnight. Club open Tu-F midnight-4am.*

SUPPERCLUB — NIGHTCLUB, RESTAURANT

Muallim Naci Cad. 65, Ortaköy — ☎212 261 1988 💻www.supperclub.com

This undeniably cool concept club has a number of branches in metropoles all over the world. There are no chairs; instead, there are huge beds covered with white satin. There is no menu either—if you order the surprise dinner *(80TL)*, the only thing you need to say before they bring it is whether you're vegetarian or not. The DJs are imported from the Netherlands and the club remains open till 7am, the latest among the Bosphorus' bling establishments. It is more compact than the other clubs, with the dancing section separated from the drinking section by a big glass wall.

*🧭 Take the bus to Ortaköy. Walk down Muallim Naci until you see it on your left. **i** Reservation for dinner and club required. Dress code strictly enforced. Men need female company to enter the club. Ⓢ Cover F-Sa 35TL; includes 1 drink. Beer 10TL. Cocktails 30TL. ⏰ Open daily for dinner 8-11:30pm. Club 11:30pm-7am.*

SORTIE — NIGHTCLUB, RESTAURANT

Muallim Naci Cad. 141, Ortaköy — ☎212 327 8585 💻www.sortie.com.tr

Sortie's cascades make this club a bit more confusing than Reina, but that's about where the differences between the two end. With many restaurants and bars on its grounds, the club caters to the elite and those who would like to be perceived as such. If you're male and want attention, show up alone, wearing shorts, sandals, and a straw hat, and try to charm your way past the humorless bouncers.

🧭 Take the bus to Ortaköy. Sortie is just a few dozen meters down from Reina. Walk down Muallim Naci until you see it to your right. ℹ Reservations for dinner required. Dress code strictly enforced. Men need female company to enter the club. $ Cover F-Sa 50TL; includes 1 drink. Beer 10TL. Cocktails from 20TL. ⏰ Open daily for dinner 8-11:30pm. Club open daily 11:30pm-6am.

JAZZ CENTER ISTANBUL

💳🍸 JAZZ CLUB

Salhane Sok. 10, Ortaköy ☎212 327 5050 💻www.istanbuljazz.com

If you're one of those people whose knees start to shake when they hear names like Mike Stern, Dave Weckl, or Stanley Clarke, you'll enjoy visiting this club. Outside of the summer months, the Jazz Center hosts jazz concerts five days a week, with two sets per night. The names that come to play here are relatively big, and so is the bill for food and alcohol at the end of the night. The small performance room gets crowded very easily, so come a bit earlier to catch a good spot.

🧭 Take the bus to Ortaköy. From the Ortaköy ferry jetty head inland and take the 1st left; Jazz Center will be to your right. $ Cover 15-50TL. Beer 15TL. Set menu 40-60TL. Entrees 25-36TL. ⏰ Open daily 7pm-4am. Music daily 9:30pm-midnight. Performances less frequent during the summer.

AŞŞK KAHVE

💳📶🍸🌳 CAFE

Muallim Naci Cad. 64/B, Kuruçeşme ☎212 265 4734 💻www.asskkahve.com

Aşşk really ought to mean "love" in Turkish, what with this cafe's romantic atmosphere. With a terrace right next to the water and plenty of vegetation, Aşşk is extremely popular with stunning young girls and passable young men. Some of the specialties you can get here include smoked veal tongue (Tongue of Aşşk) and burgers, but frankly it's more of a cocktail place.

🧭 Take the bus to Kuruçeşme. It's quite a hike up Muallim Naci from Ortaköy, so maybe you'll be better off taking one of the buses that run along the shore to Kuruçeşme. To get to the cafe, go down the unmarked steps that are near the Macrocenter. ℹ Free Wi-Fi. $ Beers 12-15TL. Cocktails 25-30TL. Sundaes 14-16TL. Burgers 20-24TL. ⏰ Open daily 9am-2am.

BEYOĞLU

👍 PAPILION INC.

💳📶🍸 BAR

Balo Sok. 31/4 ☎537 840 6359 💻papilioninc.blogspot.com

This place combines surprisingly cheap drinks with an elaborate decor (think aquariums, a crazy disco ball, and something that looks like a big spiderweb). It's run and manned by friendly young people, and you can choose between the louder lower level or the more intimate upper level with beanbags. If you're lucky, grab a seat on the coveted balcony.

🧭 Ⓜ Taksim. It's on the opposite side of the street as Araf. Find an unmarked black gate with two red alert lights (Machine Club), and then walk up the staircase that's to the left; Papilion is on the top floor. $ Happy hour beers 2.50-3.50TL. Tequila 3TL. Beer 4-5TL. Vodka 5TL. ⏰ Open M-F noon-3am, Sa-Su noon-6am. Happy hour noon-9pm.

PEYOTE

💳📶🍸 LIVE MUSIC

Kameriye Sok. 4 ☎212 251 4398 💻www.peyote.com.tr

Don't get discouraged by Peyote's first floor, which features some indifferent electronic music—the real places to be are the second floor (live music) and the third floor (a wonderful beer terrace). Peyote is a well-known venue where young bands perform before going big, and the place even has its own recording label. Even if you're not a big music fan, Peyote is worth checking out for its large terrace.

🧭 Ⓜ Taksim. Walk to Galatasaray, turn right onto Hamalbaşı Cad., and take the 4th right and walk until you see Peyote on the right. $ Cover varies. Sausages 8TL. Beer 6TL. Shots 9TL. ⏰ Open daily noon-4am. Live music W, F, Sa at 11:30pm.

LIMONLU BAHÇE
◆((•))♀⛱ CAFE

Yeni Çarşı Cad. 98   ☎212 252 1094 ✉www.limonlubahce.com

With its overgrown vegetation and apathetic-looking tortoises crawling amidst the table legs, this garden is great for an evening drink. The furniture and decor aren't glittering with newness, but perhaps that's part of its appeal. The food portions are big, so you can consider coming here for lunch when the prices are lowered by 10%. Fun game for erstwhile Pokemon fans: catch all the tortoises.

⚡ Ⓜ️Tünel or Ⓜ️Taksim. Walk to Galatasaray, go down the hill on Yeni Çarşı, and continue until you see its sign on the right. *i* Free Wi-Fi. Ⓢ Entrees 13-23TL. Coffee 5-6TL. Beer 7.50TL. Cocktails 13-19TL. ⚏ Open daily 9am-midnight.

BADEHANE
◆((•))♀⛱ CAFE

General Yazgan Sok. 5   ☎212 249 0550 ✉www.badehane.net

Everyone knows Badehane. It was one of the first cafes to open in the streets above Tünel Square, previously a shady area with drugs and porn cinemas, and a brief walk through the area today shows that Badehane got it right. Popular with expats and students, this cafe offers reasonably priced alcohol and a lot of outdoor tables that are perfect for people-watching.

⚡ Ⓜ️Tünel. Badehane is just a few dozen meters away from the funicular exit. It's to the north of Tünel Square, where the General Yazgan Sokak bends. *i* Free Wi-Fi. Ⓢ Beer 5-8TL. Shots 8-17TL. ⚏ Open daily 9am-4am.

LEB-İ DERYA
◆((•))♀ RESTAURANT/BAR

Kumbaracı Yok. 57/6   ☎212 243 9555 ✉www.lebiderya.com

Leb-i Derya is a posh place, widely acknowledged as having one of the best views of Istanbul in the city. Its open terrace is quite nice, but if you want the best view, reserve the tiny upper terrace in advance as the spots here go quickly. The cuisine is Mediterranean and international, but the cheapest way to enjoy the place is to come for a drink. Don't get this branch confused with the other Leb-i Derya branch in the Richmond Hotel, where the view isn't half as interesting.

⚡ Ⓜ️Tünel. Walking up İstiklal from Tünel take the second right. Walk down the hill for a while, until you see Leb-i Derya to your right. Ⓢ Beer 11-15TL. Cocktails 25-29TL. Entrees 32-40TL. Desserts 15-16TL. ⚏ Open M-F 4pm-2am, Sa 10am-3am, Su 10am-2am.

MOJO
◆♀ LIVE MUSIC

Büyükparmakappı Sok. 26/1   ☎212 243 2927 ✉www.mojomusic.org

Bars on İstiklal tend to have a very limited understanding of what "live music" means (one jangly guitar and an annoying singer), so this edgy club hosting performances of local underground bands (pop rock, alternative rock) is a refreshing change. There is no seating on nights when cover is charged, so you'll have to either dance, stand, or pretend you're dancing. The club isn't very big and can get quite crowded, but that's the problem with most good clubs anyway.

⚡ Ⓜ️Taksim. Walk down İstiklal and take the third left turn. The club is toward the end of that street, on the right side. Ⓢ Cover W 15TL, F 20TL, Sa 25TL. Beer 8-10TL. Vodka 10TL. ⚏ Open daily 10pm-4am. Live music M-Sa at midnight.

BALKON
◆((•))♀ BAR

Şehbender Sok. 5   ☎212 293 2052

One is tempted to call Balkon the poor man's Leb-i Derya, but that wouldn't be quite true—it's more like the I'm-too-lazy-to-dress-up man's Leb-i Derya. After taking the tiny elevator to the top of the building, you'll find two floors with a great view of Istanbul serving moderately priced beers and a lot of seating. It gets cold up there sometimes, but they have blankets in which you can wrap yourself. Music is not disruptive, and it graduates from jazz to electronic over the course of the night.

⚡ Ⓜ️Tünel. Walk north past Badehane, turn right onto Sofyalı Sokak, and walk straight. Take a left *turn at Şehbender Sokak; Balkon will be to your left.* $ *Beer 7-12TL. Shots 9-12TL. Desserts 7TL. Pizzas 11.50-17TL.* ⏰ *Open daily 11am-3am.*

MACHINE 🎫🍸 CLUB

Balo Sok. 31

This rather clandestine establishment has no phone number or website and is open only 12 hours per week, but if you're into dancing to loud electronic music, this could be your place. The interior is dark and simple, but there is an awesome cage that separates the DJs from the dance floor. Relaxed bouncers, no cover before 2am, and reasonably priced drinks.

➡ *Ⓜ Taksim. Walk toward Galatasaray, then turn right at Halkbank; Machine is behind an unmarked black gate.* $ *Free cover, after 2am 5TL. Beer 8TL. Vodka 8TL. Whiskey 10TL.* ⏰ *Open F-Sa 11pm-5am.*

KIKI 🎫🍸☕ BAR

Sıraselviler Cad. 42 ☎212 243 5373 💻www.kiki.com.tr

A place popular with Cihangir dwellers, Kiki is known for its brunches and low-pressure atmosphere. The beer isn't cheap, but the price is similar to what many places in Cihangir charge. In the back there's a small garden good for talking and smoking (if a bar in Istanbul doesn't have an outdoor space for smoking, it's doomed), while indoors some dancing takes place between its narrow walls.

➡ *From Ⓜ Taksim, walk down Sıraselviler. After a few blocks, Kiki will be on the right.* $ *Beer 10TL. Cocktails 20-22TL.* ⏰ *Open M-F 6pm-2am, Sa-Su 6pm-4am. Music W, F-Sa at 11:30pm.*

ARAF 🎫🍸 LIVE MUSIC

Balo Sok. 32 ☎212 244 8301 💻www.araf.com.tr

Some expats say Araf is an "Erasmus trap," attended mostly by exchange students and Turks who would like to hook up with them. On the other hand, the odds that you'll meet somebody who actually speaks English are quite high, which could be a refreshing change after every other place in Istanbul. The bands play loud world music, the drinks are relatively cheap, and the focus is on dancing.

➡ *Ⓜ Taksim. Walk down İstiklal toward Galatasaray, then turn right at Halkbank onto Balo Sokak. Continue down the street until you see Araf on the right.* **i** *Live music M-Th and Su; DJ performances F-Sa.* $ *No cover. Beer 6TL. Rakı and shots 8TL.* ⏰ *Open M-F 5pm-2am, Sa-Su 5pm-3am.*

arts and culture

THEATER AND CLASSICAL MUSIC

👍 GARAJ İSTANBUL BEYOĞLU

Kaymakam Reşat Bey Sok. 11/A ☎212 244 4499 💻www.garajistanbul.org

Many venues in Istanbul are restored hamams or ancient water cisterns or fancy things like that, so a restored parking garage seems kind of like a fresh idea. The space is used for all kinds of contemporary art performances, including theater, music, and dance. Despite the fact that it's so young, Garaj already takes part in many international artistic collaborations. Due to such worldly interaction, some of the events here are in English or have English subtitles, giving this place a distinct edge over all the small artsy places where you need to know Turkish to fit in with the crowd.

➡ *Ⓜ Taksim. Walk down İstiklal and turn left immediately after Yapikredi Kültür near Yeni Çarşi. Take a right turn, then a left turn, and you'll see it on the left side.* $ *25TL, students 15TL, art students 10TL.* ⏰ *Open Sept-June. Consult the online program for performance times.*

CEMAL REŞIT REY KONSER SALONU

✎ BEYOĞLU

Gümüs Sok., Harbiye ☎212 231 5497 💻www.crrks.org

When the renovation of Atatürk Culture Center on Taksim Square got stalemated because of political squabbles, the CRR Konser Salonu took over as the city's leading venue for classical music performances. Its 860-seat concert hall has hosted acts ranging from the Tchaikovsky Symphony Orchestra to Paco de Lucia, and with 25 concerts per month during the working season, it stays busy. There is no official programming by the management during the summer, but the concert hall is rented out for other performances.

🚶 [M]Osmanbey. Get out of the Metro station, take the left turn at Tekstilbank, then take the 1st right. Cross the street, enter the park, and go down the steps. The venue will be to your right, behind the Military Museum grounds. Alternatively, take the 1km hike from Taksim by going up Cumhuriyet Cad. $ 10-55TL. Check for 20% student discount on some events. ⏰ Box office open daily 10am-7pm; concerts start around 8pm.

AKBANK SANAT

BEYOĞLU

İstiklal Cad. 8 ☎212 252 3500 💻www.akbanksanat.com

It is very common in Istanbul for banks to run performance spaces like this one, and regardless of whether their motives are selfless, it's these places that host some of the best events around. Akbank Sanat is a site of weekly concerts during the year and hosts a jazz festival in the fall. The first two floors function as an exhibition space for contemporary art (with six or seven different exhibitions per year), while the upper floors hold a music archive, lithography workshops, and a dance studio.

🚶 [M]Taksim. It's very close to Taksim Sq., just a few meters down İstiklal on the right side. $ For prices, see their program online. Student discount is available, usually 50%. ⏰ Open 10:30am-7:30pm. Music archive open daily 2-7pm. For performance times check the program.

SÜREYYA OPERASI

Kadıköy

Bahariye Cad. 29 ☎216 346 1531 💻www.sureyyaoperasi.org

Even though it was built in 1927, operas weren't staged here until 2007 because the building didn't have the necessary facilities until the recent reconstruction. Today, it's home to the IDOB (Istanbul State Opera and Ballet), hosting almost 20 performances each month from September to June. If you're an opera fan and come here during the summer when the venue is closed, maybe you can catch the International Istanbul Opera Festival, which takes place in eccentric venues (Topkapı Palace and Rumeli Castle) in July.

🚶 Ferry to Kadıköy. Either walk there by going up Söğütlüçeşme, turning right onto Bahariye and then walking until you see the venue to your left, or take the nostalgic tram, which has a stop nearby. $ 13-30TL. ⏰ Open Sept-June. Box office open daily 10am-6pm; performances usually start at 8pm.

BATHHOUSES

ÇEMBERLITAŞ HAMAMI

✎ HAMAM

Vezirhan Cad. 8, Çemberlitaş ☎212 522 7974 💻www.cemberlitashamami.com.tr

This is one of the well-known hamams frequented mostly by tourists, and everything here corresponds to that—it's clean, aesthetically pleasing, and on the expensive side. Built in 1584 and based on plans created by Mimar Sinan, this hamam offers all the basics from body scrubs and bubble washes *(55TL)* to facial masks *(12TL)* and head massages *(40TL)*. Your experience here depends on the crowds, so try to come in outside the rush hours (generally 4-8pm). If you plan to go to a hamam only once, this place is one of the top contenders. Yes, it's touristy, but visiting a hamam seems to be turning into a tourist activity anyway.

🚶 [M]Çemberlitaş. The hamam is just across the street from the tram stop. ℹ Separate sections for men and women. $ Self-service 35TL; body scrub and bubble wash 55TL, with oil massage 95TL;

facial mask 12TL; reflexology 40TL; Indian head massage 40TL. ⏰ *Open daily 6am-midnight.*

SOFULAR HAMAMI — ☸ HAMAM

Sofular Cad. 28, Fatih ☎212 521 3759

If a local, "authentic" experience is what you're after, consider going to the Sofular hamam in Fatih. Don't expect much English from the staff or too much polish in the changing rooms (it looks a bit like a hospital here), but once you enter the *hararet* (hot room) and lie down under its pleasant dome, all of these amenities will not matter. Instead of other tourists there will be old, local men with enormous bellies (or their female equivalents), and you'll pay about half the price charged by touristy hamams.

➜ Take bus to Fatih. Head southeast down Fevzipaşa and turn right at Aslanhane. After one block get on the diagonal Sofular Cad. and continue down that street until you reach the hamam, which will be on the left near Sofular Mosque. ℹ *Separate sections for men and women.* $ *Self-service 20TL; bath with massage 28TL, with scrub 28TL, with scrub and massage 36TL.* ⏰ *Open daily for women 8am-8pm, for men 6am-10:30pm.*

CAĞALOĞLU HAMAMI — ☸ HAMAM

Cağaloğlu Hamamı Sok. 34, Cağaloğlu ☎212 522 2424 🖥www.cagalogluhamami.com.tr

For some reason, somebody decided to list this hamam in a book called"1001 Things To Do Before You Die," and the hamam has been unabashedly profiting from this citation ever since. With walls covered in photos of celebrities who have stopped by (yes, this includes Mr. Atatürk) and a few of Kate Moss engaging in some softcore posing, these guys surely know how to advertise themselves. If you keep in mind that few things that are well advertised in Sultanahmet live up to their image, your visit to this 270-year-old hamam could be very enjoyable.

➜ [M]Sultanahmet. It's a few blocks down the street from the entrance of Basilica Cistern, on the right side. ℹ *Separate sections for men and women.* $ *Self-service 38TL. Bath with scrub 57TL; with massage 62TL; with scrub and massage 75TL. Full service 95TL.* ⏰ *Open daily for women 8am-8pm; for men 8am-10pm.*

how to take a bath

The Turkish bath, or hamam, may be synonymous with homosexual activity in Western culture, but it's not what the Village People would have you think. It's actually a mainstream, important daily ritual for locals as clean water is not always readily available in the city.

Get Naked: Ok, now that we have your attention, you don't actually have to get totally naked. Oftentimes, you will be given a towel to wrap around yourself, but don't be surprised to see old people who just don't care if their junk is hanging out.

Get Steamy: You will be led into a large steam room, where there will be either a large raised marble slab in the middle, or seating areas around a central pool of boiling water. Sometimes you are provided with a bowl to dunk cold water on yourself in between steams. Now sit, sweat, and relax for as long as you want.

Get Scrubbed: If you pay for it, after your steaming, you will be led into a private room where you'll either lie on the floor, or on a bench and be scrubbed vigorously with soap and pumice stones, probably by a large, hairy attendant. Get ready to be felt up like you never have before.

Get Tea: After hosing you down, the attendant will leave you to steam for as long as you would like. After this, you will leave the steam room and be dried off by more attendants and given your choice of tea or coffee to finish the experience.

TARIHI GALATASARAY HAMAMI
HAMAM

Turnacıbaşı Sok. 24, Galatasaray

women ☎212 249 4342, men ☎212 252 4242
🖳www.galatasarayhamami.com

Another hamam focusing mostly on tourists. How do we know? Their brochure is filled with pictures of some pretty steamy heterosexual situations among young people, despite the fact that everyone who has been to a hamam before knows that genders have separate sections (an exception is the **Süleymaniye Hamamı**, near the Süleymaniye Mosque). This hamam is one of the priciest of the lot, but in exchange for its pricetag, it offers one of the loveliest interiors of all the local hamams. Not that you'll pay much attention to it when you're being massaged, but it's a nice touch.

✦ Ⓜ️*Taksim. Walk down İstiklal from Taksim and turn left at Turnacıbaşı, near Halk Bank. It's at the end of the street.* 𝒊 *Separate sections for men and women.* Ⓢ *Self-service 50TL. Bath with scrub 75TL; with massage 80TL; with scrub and massage 95TL. Full service 125TL.* Ⓩ *Open daily for women 8am-9pm; for men 7am-10pm.*

BÜYÜK HAMAMI
HAMAM

Potinciler Sok. 22, Kasımpaşa

☎212 253 4229 🖳www.buyukhamam.net

Serving mostly locals, this is one of the biggest hamams in town (as you probably figured out by your fourth day in Turkey, *büyük* means "big"). Although this hamam is not frequented by tons of tourists, it still holds historic value similar to that of its more popular brethren—it is the brainchild of Mimar Sinan, built in 1533. While its walls could use a fresh coat of paint, its swimming pool on the roof (only for men) and its cheap prices make Büyük a decent choice.

✦ Ⓜ️*Tünel. From Tünel go up İstiklal, then turn left at Kumbaracı Yokuşu. Go down the hill until you reach Bahriye. Cross the street, turn right and walk for one block. The hamam will on your left close to Kasımpaşa Mosque.* 𝒊 *Separate sections for men and women.* Ⓢ *Self-service 17.5TL. Bath with massage 25TL; with scrub 22.5TL; with massage and scrub 30TL.* Ⓩ *Open daily for women 8:30am-7:30pm; for men 5:30am-10:30pm.*

DANCE PERFORMANCES

HOCAPAŞA ART AND CULTURE CENTER
SIRKECI

Hocapaşa Hamamı Sok. 5-9D

☎212 511 4626 🖳www.hodjapasha.com

Sema is a religious ceremony that has become a popular tourist attraction—and very few people seem to find this strange. This practice is performed by dervishes of the Mevlevi Sufi order, a branch of Islam which was founded by Rumi, a 13th-century poet. The highpoint of the event is the activity that so many tourist brochures present as quintessentially Turkish—the whirling of dervishes. This act focuses on the dancer's arms, one palm pointing to the sky, the other to the ground, symbolizing the channeling of spiritual energy from God to the Earth. Since the Galata Mevlevihanesi closed for restoration, the 15th-century hamam inside the Hocapaşa Center has become the safest bet to see whirling dervishes perform.

✦ Ⓜ️*Sirkeci. After getting off the tram, walk north, away from the water. Take the 1st left after you pass the tram tracks; there will be signs pointing to the venue.* Ⓢ *Adults 40TL.* Ⓩ *Performances last 1hr. and start M, W, F-Su 7:30pm. Box office open daily 10am-9pm.*

GALATA TOWER
BEYOĞLU

Galata Kulesi

☎212 293 8180 🖳www.galatatower.net

If you're set on seeing belly dancing and other traditional dances in Istanbul, you're going to have a hard time finding something that's not expensive and touristy as hell. Dancing is usually packaged along with a set menu into a "Turkish night" that takes a few hours and can be thoroughly entertaining, provided that you're an overzealous European tourist. However, if you really want to experience it, head to the Galata Tower, another standard-bearer of Turkish culture. The tower dates back to the 14th century and allegedly served as a take-off point for Hezarfen Ahmet Çelebi, who is said to have used artificial wings to fly across the Bosphorus to Üsküdar sometime around 1630. If you don't want to come for the cultural night, you can take an elevator up during the day, even though the entry price is disproportionately high.

➡ [M]Tünel or [M]Karaköy. From [M]Tünel, head down Galipdede Cad. until you see the tower on the right side. $ 80€ per person; includes a set menu and unlimited local drinks. Entry during the day 10TL. ⏰ Shows 8pm-midnight. Galata Tower open daily 9am-4pm.

shopping

BAZAARS AND MARKETS

👍 GRAND BAZAAR — BEYAZIT

Kapalı Çarşı ☎212 519 1248 💻www.kapalicarsi.org.tr

No offense, but it is obligatory that you get lost here—this covered maze of 60 streets and 1200 shops is one of the largest bazaars in the world. It's been around for 550 years, first started in order to finance the conversion of Hagia Sophia into a mosque. Today, you can buy just about anything here, with the potential exception of love and happiness. With streets named after the specific trades that used to be centered in them (Fez-makers, slipper manufacturers, etc.), there is a central *bedesten* (market hall) where valuable jewelry and antiques are sold. We'll save you the trouble and won't recommend any specific shops within its walls—searching for particular places here is a harrowing experience.

➡ [M]Beyazıt. From the tram station, head north. ⏰ Open M-Sa 8:30am-7pm.

SPICE BAZAAR — EMINÖNÜ

Mısır Çarşısı ☎212 455 5900

Also called the Egyptian Bazaar, this market is easier to navigate than the Grand Bazaar—its layout is in the shape of the letter "L." Finished in 1663, it was built to provide funds for the upkeep of the New Mosque. The bazaar sells what it's named after (that's spices, not Egyptians), but there also are containers of dried fruit, herbs, nuts, sweets, and trinkets. Some merchants get more creative than others—you'll come across glued balls of dried fruit and mystery nuts called "Turkish Viagra." Live on the edge and smell a heap of spices from close up to encounter a true Turkish sneeze.

➡ [M]Eminönü. Right behind Yeni Cami, the New Mosque. ⏰ Open 8am-7:30pm.

ARASTA BAZAAR — SULTANAHMET

Arasta Çarşısı 107 ☎212 516 0733 💻www.arastabazaar.com

What's that? Your flight home's in four hours and you suddenly remember you forgot to buy an "I Love Turkey" T-shirt? Run to Arasta Bazaar, a conveniently located strip of shops right below the Blue Mosque. Apart from clothes, there's all kinds of souvenir stuff—fabrics, *nargile*, handmade pipes, tiles, and cheap bric-a-brac of all sorts. Here you can also find the small Great Palace Mosaic Museum showcasing a collection of old Byzantine mosaics.

➡ [M]Sultanahmet. It's behind the Blue Mosque. ⏰ Bazaar open daily 9am-7pm. Museum open M 9:30am-5pm, W-Su 9:30am-5pm.

SALI PAZARI (TUESDAY MARKET) — Kadıköy

Kent Meydanı, Tarihi Salı Pazarı ☎216 339 9819

Every Tuesday, this enormous marketplace in Kadıköy gets filled with locals selling and buying cheap clothes and fresh produce. Women outnumber men 10 to 1, but it's safe to assume that all genders are welcome. The bazaar is open on Fridays as well, but there tend to be fewer sellers. If your clothes have endured

some wear and tear during your travels, come here to refill your supplies.
➡ Walk down Söğütlü Çeşme Cad. away from the ferry terminal past the bull statue, and turn right onto Mahmut Baba Sok. There is a bus stop behind Wash Point, a carwash place. Get on the free shuttlebus that will take you to the bazaar. The ride takes 10min., and the shuttles leave approximately every 10min. 🕒 Open Tu, F 8am-7pm.

EKOLOJIK PAZARI ŞIŞLI

Feriköy Halk Pazarı, Lala Şahin Sok., Bomonti Cad. ☎212 252 5255 💻www.bugday.org/eng

The idea of "organic food" is slowly starting to penetrate Turkish society, and this market is proof. The first of its kind in Istanbul, Ekolojik Pazarı is organized by the Buğday Association and offers organic fruit, vegetables, and other food products.. A skeptic would say that all food in Turkey is organic, but here you can be sure that what you get qualifies as such.
➡ From ⓂOsmanbey, get on the other side of the cemetery and continue down Ergenekon Cad. until you reach Lala Şahin Sok. It's in parking lot number 6. $ Prices vary. 🕒 Open Sa 8am-5pm.

TARLABAŞI PAZARI TARLABAŞI

The streets around Tarlabaşı

First, we have to say that the Tarlabaşı neighborhood isn't the safest place to go if you look like a naive Western tourist. However, it's interesting for the same reason—this market is unlike the others we mention, offering low prices and a very authentic feel. It gets really crowded, so beware of pickpockets. Tarlabaşı, inhabited mostly by the Roma, Kurds, and African immigrants, is surprisingly close to Taksim, so it's not that hard to get back into a safer neighborhood.
➡ ⓂTaksim. Walking down İstiklal, take a right onto Ağa Camii, then cross Tarlabaşı Bul. Continue down the hill until you hit the market, which sprawls across many streets of that neighborhood. $ Prices vary. 🕒 Open Su 10am-dusk.

GIFTS

KARADENIZ ANTIK GALATASARAY

Çukurcuma Cad. 55 ☎212 251 9605 💻www.karadenizantik.com

This is a good place to start your search for all kinds of old junk that get lumped into the category of antiques. The objects on sale range from old gramophones and cameras to furniture and lamps to statuettes and vases. There are many other shops around, so make sure you compare prices elsewhere before buying here. The best places in Istanbul to buy antiques are here (on and around **Çukurcuma Cad.**), inside the **Grand Bazaar's** central bedesten, and in the huge **Horhor Flea Market** *(Kırık Tulumba Sokak 13 ➡ ⓂAksaray).* Just make sure you don't buy anything of real value—if it's more than 100 years old, taking it out of the country may be illegal.
➡ ⓂTophane. Walk up Boğazkesen Cad. until you reach Çukurcuma; turn right and continue straight until you see the shop to your right. Alternatively, walk down from Galatasaray. 🕒 Open daily 9am-7pm.

ASLIHAN PASAJI GALATASARAY

Located on the street opposite of Yeni Çarşı

This passage off İstiklal is stacked with shops selling all kinds of used books, so come here to buy your copy of Dan Brown's *Da Vinci Sifresi* or Mario Puzo's *Vaftiz Babası* (or their English equivalents). Secondhand bookstores are often concentrated in clusters, so apart from this one, there's also the **Sahaflar Bazaar** *(ⓂBeyazıt)* and the **Akmar Pasajı** (between Mühürdar Cad. and Neşet Ömer Sok). If you're looking for new books, try **Robinson Crusoe, Pandora,** or **Homer Kitabevi.**
➡ ⓂTünel or ⓂTaksim. From Galatasaray walk on the street opposite to Yeni Çarşı and you'll see the passage to your right. 🕒 Open M-Sa 8am-8pm.

PAŞABAHÇE 🚋 TÜNEL

İstiklal Cad. 314 ☎212 244 0544 💻www.pasabahce.com

If you went through all the glass in the Grand Bazaar and didn't find anything to satisfy your high demands, try Paşabahçe. This well-known glass chain offers all kinds of practical and impractical glass products. While more expensive than similar items at the bazaars, these pieces are of higher quality and better design. If you've picked up a bit of the Turkish superstitious bug, you can get one of their enormous glass evil eyes to ward off bad luck.

✦ ⓜTünel. Walk up İstiklal until you see the store on your left, opposite the Dutch consulate. ⓩ Open daily 10am-8pm.

a magic carpet ride

According to recent travel statistics, about 70% of visitors to Turkey leave with a carpet as their prized Turkish souvenir. Made of various materials such as wool, silk, rayon, or cotton, Turkish carpets are known for their superior handmade quality—an art that originated in other regions of the country but has now moved to the capital city Istanbul to appeal to the tourist demographic. The Turkish handmade carpet is recognizable by its detail and precision—the carpet is made by literally tying thousands of knots together, one by one. Thus, it stands to reason that the more knots in the carpet, the thicker the rug and the higher the price tag.

Color is another important factor in the quality of a Turkish rug. All of the colors used in the carpets signify something according to ancient Turkish tradition: red leads to good fortune, yellow and black offer protection from evil, blue indicates nobility, and green shows leisure and paradise. The best dyes are vegetable dyes that hold vibrant color for years afterwards. Chemical dyes are cheaper and may leave a large tie-dyed stain on your feet or precious white bichon frise.

As with any souvenir, navigating the Turkish carpet market is no joke. If you are not careful, you may get "tied up" in a rug scam and leave with an overpriced machine-made wreck that will be an embarrassment upon your grandma's next visit. If someone approaches you saying they have friends and family members with carpet shops, your best bet is to keep on walking. It's likely they are just touts being paid by shop owners on commission. Likewise, once in the carpet shop, the seller will undoubtedly throw around the adjectives "silk," "Persian," and "antique." Yet, "antique" might refer to the machine it was made on, and the "silk" is probably a fake rayon or wool blend. Lastly, don't let the seller ship it for you or you may never see the carpet you just bought. You'll undoubtedly have better luck wrapping and shipping it yourself (or having Aladdin give you a magic carpet ride home, but this has only worked for readers that are bug-eyed princesses.)

CLOTHING AND JEWELRY

▨ BY RETRO   ✦ TÜNEL

Suriye Pasajı 166/c   ☎212 245 6420 ▧ www.byretro.com

Descending down into this store is a bit like Alice going down the rabbit's hole. It sells and rents all kinds of clothes and props, ranging from the normal-looking to the preposterous, a favorite for film crews looking for costumes and sometimes even to shoot. Even though you might not be interested in the army uniforms and other things that are clearly there for film people, you might find a suitable sultan's outfit or just an eccentric garment for yourself.

✦ ⓜTünel. From Tünel walk up İstiklal for a few blocks; the Suriye passage will be to your left. By Retro is in the back of the passage. ⓩ Open daily 10am-10pm.

KANYON LEVENT

✦ LEVENT

Büyükdere Cad. 185 ☎212 317 5300 ☐www.kanyon.com.tr

When you think of Istanbul, you don't ordinarily think of shopping malls, but a number of these can be found and are becoming increasingly popular. The easiest one to go to is Kanyon, which has 160 shops and a multiplex cinema screening Hollywood hits (☎212 353 0853 ☐www.cinebonus.com.tr). You can find your usual McDonald's and Starbucks here, but you should try one of the Turkish chains, like the dessert palace Saray Muhallebicisi or the clothing store Vakko. If you aren't in the adventurous mood, your patriotic friend Tommy Hilfiger and Banana Republic can also be found.

✦ ⓂLevent. It is on the Taksim-4 Levent Metro line. After getting off the Metro, follow the signs to the mall. ☼ Open daily 10am-10pm.

AVANTGARDEAST

☺ GALATASARAY

Galatasaray İş Hanı, İstiklal 120/12 ☎212 245 1507 ☐www.avantgardeast.com

This store in **Galatasaray** passage is a good place to start your clothing hunt through İstiklal's passages. Head to Avantgardeast for cheap and moderately priced streetwear, and then get lost in the **Atlas** and **Halep** passages (opposite each other, north of Galatasaray), both of which have their share of clothing stores. **Avrupa** passage right next to the **Aslıhan** book passage (both across from Galatasaray) sells things that mostly conform to the "shiny bric-a-brac" category, while the **Aznavur** passage sells clothing, comic books, and CDs.

✦ ⓂTünel or ⓂTaksim. From Galatasaray walk toward Tünel; the Galatasaray passage will be to your right. ☼ Open daily 10am-10pm.

how much is that...thing?

Setting foot in the **Grand Bazaar** or the **Spice Bazaar** can be a tumultuous experience: not knowing what to get, what's real, and most importantly, why everyone considers you "my friend"? Here are some tips for what you should get, what's affordable, and what to steer clear of.

- **DO** keep your ground and don't let anyone push you into their shop. Play it cool and pretend to not be interested. Supply and demand never worked so well in negotiating.

- **DO** seriously look into buying **Iranian Saffron**. It's the most expensive spice in the world, and your mom or grandma will love you for getting it for her, even if she doesn't know what food it's used for. It costs around $100 an ounce, but Nana would be thrilled with a gram for $6.

- **DO** buy **Turkish Delight**. No skyrockets in flight, just a gooey, sweet candy made from starch and sugar. Often pistachios will be mixed in. It's best served cold and not melted in your backpack.

- **DON'T** buy into fakes. Everything from handbags, to Roman coins, and even carpets are offered by scrupulous street vendors. Be sure to lowball the price if you suspect that it's a forgery, or just avoid it all together.

- **DON'T** be convinced that the 50TL bill you handed your vendor was really a 5TL bill. This is a common practice with taxi cab drivers and shopkeepers alike. Make sure you inspect every bill before handing it over, or face the realization that you spent $100 on hookah coals.

istanbul

essentials

PRACTICALITIES

- **TOURIST OFFICES:** There are a number of offices in different districts, including **Sultanahmet** *(Divan Yolu Cad. 5* ☎*212 518 1802* ✪ *Open daily 9am-5pm)*, **Beyoğlu** *(Hilton Hotel* ☎*212 233 0592* ✪ *Open M-Sa 9am-5pm)*, **Sirkeci** *(Sirkeci Train Station* ☎*212 511 5888* ✪ *Open M-Sa 9:30am-5:30pm)*, **Beşiktaş** *(Süleyman Seba Cad.* ☎*212 258 7760)*, **Atatürk International Airport** *(*☎*212 465 3151* ✪ *Open daily 8am-11pm)* and **Karaköy** *(Karaköy Liman Yolcu Sarayi* ☎*212 249 5776)*. All provide free maps, brochures, and information in English.

- **BUDGET TRAVEL OFFICES:** Some of the biggest low-cost carriers are **Pegasus Airlines** *(*☎*444 0737* 🖳*www.flypgs.com)*, **Onur Air** *(*☎*212 663 2300* 🖳*www.onurair.com.tr)*, and **SunExpress** *(*☎*232 444 0797)*, operating both domestic and international flights. Virtually every hostel has a partnership with tour companies that run affordable tours.

- **CURRENCY EXCHANGE:** Exchange bureaus are called *döviz* and can be found on İstiklal and around Divan Yolu. Among the better ones are **Klas Döviz** *(Sıraselviler Cad. 6/F* ☎*212 249 3550* ✪ *Open daily 8:30am-10pm)* and **Çetin Döviz** *(İstiklal Cad. 39* ☎*212 252 6428* ✪ *Open daily 9am-10pm)*.

- **ATMS:** English-language **ATMs** *(bankamatik)* can be found on almost every corner. If your account is at a foreign bank, cash withdrawal will cost you extra (for precise amount, inquire at your bank). Most ATMs work with Turkish Lira. If you want to withdraw USD or Euros, try some of the banks around **Sirkeci Train Station.**

- **LUGGAGE STORAGE:** 24hr. **luggage storage** *(Emanet Bagaj)*, is available at the **Atatürk International Airport** *(*☎*212 465 3442* ⑤ *15TL per day)* and **Sirkeci Train Station** *(*☎*539 885 2105* ⑤ *4-7TL for the first 4hr.; 0.50 TL per hr. thereafter, 96 hr. max)*.

- **GLBT RESOURCES:** Istanbul's **GLBT resources** are rather decentralized, so your best bet will be an internet search. **Time Out Istanbul** magazine provides a good overview of the city's GLBT establishments. Some other organizations of interest are **Kaos GL** *(*☎*312 230 0358* 🖳*www.news.kaosgl.com)* and **Lambda** *(*☎*212 245 7068* 🖳*www.lambdaistanbul.org* ✪ *Open M-Tu 5-7pm, F-Su 5-7pm)*.

- **TICKET AGENCIES:** Tickets to most major cultural events are available through **Biletix** *(*☎*216 556 9800*🖳*www.biletix.com)*.

- **LAUNDROMAT:** Most hostels will do your laundry for a small fee. If you'd prefer a laundromat, some of the options are **Beybuz** *(Topçekenler Sok. 17* ☎*212 249 5900* ✪ *Open daily 9am-2:30am.* ⑤ *2.25TL per kg, dry cleaning 10TL)* and **Şık Çamaşır Yıkama** *(Güneşli Sok. 1/A* ☎*212 245 4375* ✪ *Open 8am-8pm.* ⑤ *15TL per load)*.

- **INTERNET ACCESS: Sultanahmet Square** offers free Wi-Fi. **Beyoğlu** has free Wi-Fi as well, but you'll need a cellphone to receive the access code. One of the best internet cafes in town is **Net Club** *(Büyükparmakkapı Sok. 8/6* ✪ *Open 24hr.* ⑤ *1.25TL per hr.)* off İstiklal Avenue, but there are many others around Istiklal and a few near the Sultanahmet tram stop. In most cafes, expect to pay 2TL per hr.

- **POST OFFICES:** You can send letters and make calls at any of the many **PTT booths** around the city. There's a central post office in **Eminönü** *(Büyük Postahane Cad. 25* ☎*212 511 3818)*, while some other offices are in **Taksim** *(Cumhuriyet Cad. 2* ☎*212 292 3650)*, **Galatasaray** *(Tosbağa Sok. 22* ☎*212 243 3343)*, and **Sultanahmet**

(Sultanahmet Meydanı ☎212 517 4966 ⏰ Open daily 8:30am-12:30pm and 1:30-5:30pm).

EMERGENCY!

- **EMERGENCY NUMBER:** ☎112.
- **POLICE:** (☎155; 212 527 4503)
- **LATE-NIGHT PHARMACIES:** Pharmacies are called *eczane* in Turkish. Some stay open overnight (*nöbetci*) on a rotating basis, and the closed pharmacies will list the nearest open pharmacy on their doors. For a list of all open pharmacies, go to 💻www.treczane.com.
- **HOSPITAL/MEDICAL SERVICES:** The best option for international travelers is to use a **private hospital.** They are clean, efficient, and have 24hr. emergency units and some English-speaking staff. Some of the options are **Alman Hastanesi** *(Sıraselviler Cad. 119 ☎212 293 2150 💻www.almanhastanesi.com.tr 💲 Consultation 160TL.)* and the **American Hospital** *(Güzelbahçe Sok. 20 ☎212 444 3777 💻www.americanhospitalistanbul.com 💲 Examinations 190TL).* **Public hospitals** are generally crowded, confusing, and without English-speaking staff, but they are an option if you want to save money. The most conveniently located one is **Taksim Hastanesi.** *(Sıraselviler Cad. 112 ☎212 252 4300 💻www.taksimhastanesi.com.tr.)*

GETTING THERE

By Air

ATATÜRK INTERNATIONAL AIRPORT AIRPORT

İstanbul Atatürk Havalimanı, Yeşilköy ☎212 465 5555 💻www.ataturkairport.com

The airport is 28km from central Istanbul and has an international and a domestic terminal. The easiest way to get from the airport to the center is to take the **metro** (LRT) and then the **tram.** At the airport, follow the "LRT" signs, get on the metro *(💲 One jeton costs 1.50TL),* and get off at Zeytinburnu. Here transfer to the tram going to ⓂKabataş, which passes through ⓂSultanahmet. You'll need to buy another 1.50TL *jeton* for the tram. You can also get off the metro at ⓂAksaray, but the transfer to tram here isn't as convenient. Alternative ways of getting to and from the airport include the express **Havaş bus** *(☎212 465 4700 💻www.havas.net 💲 10TL. ⏰ Around 40min., every 30min. 4am-1am)* and **taxis.** *(💲 Around 30TL for Sultanahmet, 35TL for Taksim.)* There is a **Lost and Found Office** *(☎212 465 5555, ext. 4690 ⏰ Open M-F 8am-5pm),* a **Tourist Information Office** *(In the international terminal ☎212 465 3451 ⏰ Open 9am-11pm),* and 24hr. **luggage storage.** *(☎212 465 3442 for the international terminal; 212 465 3000, ext. 2805 for the domestic terminal 💲 10-20TL per day.)* The airport serves almost 40 airlines, including Turkish Airlines *(☎212 444 0849),* British Airways *(☎212 317 6600),* and Air France *(☎212 465 5491).*

🧭 Metro to Havalimanı. 💲 Parking 7.50TL per hr., 9.75TL per 1-3hr. ⏰ Open 24hr.

SABIHA GÖKÇEN INTERNATIONAL AIRPORT AIRPORT

Sabiha Gökçen Uluslararası Havaalanı, Pendik ☎216 585 5000 💻www.sgairport.com

Located on the Asian side of Istanbul, this airport is 40km from Kadıköy and 50km from Taksim. The best way to get to central Istanbul is to take the **Havaş bus.** *(☎555 985 1051 💻www.havas.net 💲 13TL. ⏰ Around 1hr., every 30min. 4am-midnight.)* Alternatively, you can take the **public E10 bus** to Kadıköy *(💲 1.5TL. ⏰ 90min., every 10min.-1hr.)* and then transfer to a **ferry** to either Eminönü or Karaköy *(💲 1.50TL. ⏰ Around 20min.).* **Taxis** are rather expensive, charging around 75TL for the trip to Taksim. Among the facilities at the airport are **luggage storage** *(💲 10-20TL per day),* a **lost and found office,** and a **PTT booth.**

🧭 Bus to Sabiha Gökçen. ⏰ Open 24hr.

By Bus

Bus travel is concentrated at the **Büyük İstanbul Otogarı,** *(☎212 658 0505 🖳www.otogaristanbul.com)* known simply as the "Otogar." The Zeytinburnu-Havalimanı metro line has a stop here, so to get to the center, take the metro to Aksaray and then walk to the Yusufpaşa tram stop. Many bus companies have free shuttle service *(ücretsiz servis)* between the Otogar and Taksim. Among the major bus companies are **Metro** *(☎212 444 3455 🖳www.metroturizm.com.tr),* **Kamil Koç** *(☎212 658 2000 🖳www.kamilkoc.com.tr),* and **Ulusoy** *(☎212 444 1888 🖳www.ulusoy.com.tr).* Some of the most frequent bus routes go to **Ankara** *($ From 35TL. ⏰ 6-7hr.);* **Edirne** *($ From 10TL. ⏰ 2½ hr.);* **Çanakkale** *($ From 35TL. ⏰ 6hr.);* and **Izmir** *($ From 45TL. ⏰ 8½hr.),* often via **Bursa** *($ From 20TL. ⏰ 3hr.).*

By Train

Sirkeci Train Station *(☎212 520 6575)* is the final stop for all trains from Europe. The Bosphorus express from **Bucharest** *(⏰ 20½hr., daily at 10pm).* The Balkan Express goes to **Sofia** *(⏰ 12½hr.)* and **Belgrad** *(⏰ 21½hr., daily at 10pm),* and the Dostluk/Filia Express goes to **Thessalonica** *(⏰ 13hr., daily at 8:30pm).* Trains from the Asian side terminate at **Haydarpaşa Train Station** *(☎216 336 4470).* Six different trains connect Istanbul with Ankara *($ Daytime tickets from 16TL, overnight 85TL. ⏰ 8hr., 5 per day).* Information about train schedules and routes can be found on 🖳www.tcdd.gov.tr.

By Ferry

Apart from local ferries, **IDO** *(☎212 444 4436 🖳www.ido.com.tr)* operates intercity ferries from Istanbul's **Yenikapı Ferry Terminal** to **Yalova** *($ 14TL. ⏰ 6-7 per day),* **Bandırma** *($ 32TL ⏰ 4-6 daily),* and **Bursa** *($ 21TL. ⏰ 4-6 daily).* Over a dozen ferries per day on three different routes connect Yenikapı to **Bostancı.** To get to Yenikapı, take the suburban train from Sirkeci Train Station.

GETTING AROUND

The public transportation network in Istanbul is very reliable and easy to navigate. This applies especially to ferries, trams, and trains, because they don't suffer from Istanbul's traffic congestion. Rides on all of the following (apart from the dolmuşes and the funiculars) have a flat rate of 1.50 TL, but it's cheaper if you use Akbil or another transit pass.

By Tram and Funicular

Tram: The tram line that runs from **Zeytinburnu** to **Kabataş** is excellent for transportation on the European side, stopping in **Aksaray, Sultanahmet,** and **Karaköy** *(⏰ Every 10min., 6am-midnight).* There are two nostalgic tram lines. One runs along **İstiklal Cad.,** connecting **Tünel** and **Taksim,** while the other follows a circular route in **Kadıköy** on the Asian side.

In addition to the trams, Istanbul is also connected by underground funiculars. Since there is no direct tram connection between Taksim and Sultanahmet, the funicular connecting Kabataş and Taksim *($ 1 TL.)* is almost necessary for getting from one to the other. Another funicular connects **Karaköy** and **Tünel** *($ 1 TL).*

By Metro

There's a metro line running from the **Atatürk International Airport** through **Büyük Otogar** to **Aksaray.** [M]Aksaray is a 5min. walk away from the Yusufpaşa tram stop (there are signs showing the way). Another metro line runs from **Taksim** north to **4. Levent.** *(⏰ 6am-midnight.)*

Two suburban trains complement the tram service. One line starts at **Sirkeci Train Station** and goes west through **Kumkapı and Yenikapı,** while the other starts at **Haydarpaşa Train Station** in Kadıköy and runs east through **Göztepe** and **Bostancı.** *(⏰ Every 20min., 5:30am-midnight.)*

By Ferry

Commuter ferries are the best way to get to the Asian side or to access some of the more distant neighborhoods. The most useful lines are **Eminönü-Kadıköy, Karaköy-Haydarpaşa-Kadıköy, Kabataş-Üsküdar, Eminönü-Üsküdar, Kadıköy-Beşiktaş, Kabataş-Kadıköy-Prince's Islands,** and the **Golden Horn line** (stops include **Üsküdar, Eminönü, Fener,** and **Eyüp**). *(☎212 444 4436 💻www.ido.com.tr ⏰ Every 20min., consult website for departure times.)*

By Bus

There are many useful bus lines. See the table for a partial list of buses that connect major neighborhoods. For more specific information, contact IETT *(☎800 211 6068, 💻www.iett.gov.tr).*

The **dolmuş** is a shared minibus that runs on set routes, stopping every couple of blocks to take on and drop off passengers. The system is chaotic, but the destinations are always listed on the boards visible through the windows. Especially useful is the **Kadıköy-Taksim** dolmuş *($ 5TL),* which leaves every 20 minutes, even after ferries stop running.

BUS ROUTES	
Üsküdar-Kadıköy	12, 12A
Kadıköy-Taksim	110
Fatih-Taksim	87
Fatih-Eminönü	28, 31E, 32, 336E, 36KE, 37E, 38E, 90, 910
Fener-Taksim	55T
Fener-Eminönü	33ES, 36CE, 399B, 399C, 399D, 44B, 99, 99A
Beşiktaş-Taksim	110, 112, 129T, 25T, 40, 40T, 42T, 559C, DT1, DT2
Ortaköy-Taksim	40, 40T, 42T, DT1, DT2

By Taxi

The initial charge for cabs is 2.50TL, and every additional kilometer costs 1.40TL. The rates are the same for day and night. If you're taking a cab across the Bosphorus, you'll have to pay the bridge toll as well. Tipping is not necessary. Beware of common taxi scams like a "broken meter" or roundabout routes.

istanbul 101

HISTORY

A Head Start

Our story begins not in the misty shroud of lore and legend, but in the 21st century. Ambitious excavation was underway, but archaeologists weren't the ones at work: Istanbul's modern subway system was under construction. Fast forward to one worker's surprise of a lifetime. Peeking inside a nondescript brown bag found onsite, he was greeted not with a few misplaced construction implements, but by the grins of **nine human skulls**. Dating back to 6000 BCE, these remains, along with some pottery, shells, and enough horse skulls to make the Godfather proud, are the oldest evidence of human settlement in what is now Istanbul.

To Byzantion and Beyond!

Although the area had been dotted with small settlements for centuries, it wasn't until 667 BCE that it became home to a true city. Legend has it that a Greek named **Byzas** (see where this is going?) was looking for some prime real estate on which to found his very own metropolis. In the absence of ancient realtors, he paid a visit to the **Oracle at Delphi** for advice. In typical oracular ambiguity, he was told to set up shop "opposite the blind." Not having a clue what the oracle meant, he set off across the Aegean anyway, eventually reaching the Bosphorus, a narrow strait dividing the European and Asian landmasses. The Greek city of Chalcedon occupied the eastern shore, and Byzas decided that its inhabitants must have been totally blind not to notice the fabulous land lying only a half a mile away on the western shore. With one fanciful interpretation of prophecy under his belt, Byzas established a city on the western shore of the Bosphorus and named it **Byzantion** after its glorious founder.

Capture the Flag

For the next few hundred years, Byzantion's strategic location made it a hub for commerce, as well as an appealing prize for passing conquerors. In 512 BCE, it was captured by the **Persian Emperor Darius**, only to fall under Spartan rule in 479 BCE. The Athenians soon decided that they wanted a piece of the pie, and ruled until 334 BCE, when **Alexander the Great** rolled into town. After Alexander's death, Roman influence increased, and by 74 CE the region had become part of an official Roman state. Deciding that Byzantium sounded way better in Latin, the city underwent its first of many renamings. In 196 CE, **Byzantium** made the poor decision to side against the Roman Emperor Severus and was almost completely destroyed. However, Severus ultimately decided that Byzantium was worth more to him alive than dead, and rebuilt the city, complete with fancy new walls.

Capital Gains

With the Roman Empire fragmenting into East and West, the first Christian Emperor Constantine I chose Byzantium as the new capital in 324 CE. The seven hills of the city were a dead ringer for the Roman hills, and Constantine did his darndest to turn Byzantium into a fitting imperial residence. After he died, the city was renamed **Constantinople** in his honor and became the capital of the Eastern Roman (Byzantine) Empire after Rome fell in 476 CE. Constantinople, a bustling port city at the nexus of two continents and countless cultures, flourished during this period. Byzantine Emperor Junstinian (527–565 CE) extended the boundaries of the empire from Palestine to Spain, created an organized legal system called the **Codex**, and ordered the construction of the magnificent **Hagia Sophia** church.

Time to Split

Things took a turn for the worse in the seventh and eighth centuries, as Constantinople found itself under siege from Arab forces and the Byzantine and Roman churches squabbled endlessly over the role of icons. However, all was not lost: art forms like **stone carving** and **manuscript production** thrived, and architects meticulously designed dazzling monasteries. In 1054 CE, the **Greek Orthodox Church**, centered in Constantinople, split from the Roman papacy once and for all. By the beginning of the 13th century, the Crusades were in full swing, and Constantinople was in the middle of the war path. In 1204 CE, Western Crusaders came to town and ransacked the city against the Pope's wishes (Constantinople was Christian, after all).

State of the Art

In 1453 CE, Constantinople fell to the **Ottoman Turks**, who decided that the city was due for another name change and rechristened it **Istanbul**. As the new capital of the Ottoman Empire, the city was refurbished and thrived as a multicultural center for learning, art, and architecture. Under Sultan Suleiman I (1520–1566 CE), calligraphy and ceramics reached their height, and the famous architect Sinan designed numerous mosques. Following Suleiman's rule, the city began to wane as the fortunes of the Ottoman Empire fluctuated.

In This Day and Age

After nearly 1500 years as a capital city, Istanbul lost its title in 1923 when the Republic of Turkey, founded by **Mustafa Kemal Atatürk**, chose Ankara as the capital of the new nation. Istanbul began a campaign of modernization in the 1940s, with public squares and sweeping boulevards breathing new life into the city. The 1970s were a period of rapid industrialization and population growth as workers flocked to the city to find work in factories. The city swallowed up nearby towns and forests as demand for housing skyrocketed. If the urban sprawl seems unplanned, that's because it was; experts estimate that 65% of the city's buildings were constructed without proper planning. Istanbul's historic neighborhoods were added to the UNESCO World Heritage List in 1985, and the city was chosen as a **European Capital of Culture** for 2010.

CUSTOMS AND ETIQUETTE

When in Istanbul...

Istanbul is a modern, cosmopolitan city that has adopted many Western social customs, but for visitors who've never traveled to a Muslim country before, certain traditions may seem foreign. Public displays of affection are not as common or as widely accepted as in many other European countries, so even if you've found yourself a Turkish sweetheart (or brought one with you), keep your public canoodling to a minimum. Turkey's residents have a great deal of national pride, and insulting the Turkish nation, national flag, or founder Atatürk is both rude and illegal. Steer clear of touchy subjects; Islam is not an acceptable target for your latest rant or comedy routine. Turkish culture also places a high value on respect for elders. It is considered proper to make your greetings from eldest to youngest, regardless of how well you know each person.

At the Table

Invited to dine at someone's home? Welcome to Istanbul, land of legendary hospitality. Show your gratitude by bringing a small gift, such as flowers or a dessert. Play it safe and don't bring a bottle of wine for your host. Because Turkey is mostly Muslim, many residents don't drink alcohol. Enjoy your meal, and make sure to let your host know how good it tastes. They'll be sure to keep loading up your plate, so bring a hearty appetite. If you're invited to dine out at a restaurant, bear in mind that the host always pays (although an offer to pay is customary). Leaving a 10% tip in restaurants, cafes, and bars is expected.

Mosque Etiquette

Visitors are generally welcome in Istanbul's exquisite mosques, provided that they are courteous and respect local customs, but there are some mosques open only to Muslims. Remove your shoes before entering and wear modest clothing. Miniskirts, shorts, and tank tops are a definite no-no. Both men and women should make sure that their shoulders, upper arms, and thighs are completely covered. When entering, women will be provided with a headscarf to cover their hair—but feel free to bring your own to match your outfit! Once inside, pause for a moment to take in the splendor of your surroundings. Remember that this is a place of worship, so speaking loudly or taking pictures will likely not be appreciated. When you hear the call for prayer, clear out to make room for worshippers.

Body Language

Remember that body language isn't universal. Even something as simple as shaking your head might not mean what you expect. To say "yes," nod your head downward. "No" is nodding your head upwards, while shaking your head from side to side means that you don't understand. Making the "OK" sign with your hand has a much different meaning in Turkey, and is not appropriate for polite company. When you enter someone's home, take off your shoes and accept slippers if offered. Sitting cross-legged on the floor is common, but pay attention. Exposing the bottoms of your feet to another person is considered offensive, no matter how adorable your toesocks are. Blowing your nose is not something done in public, so take a quick trip to the bathroom instead.

ARCHITECTURE

Ancient Greek and Roman

The fascinating architecture of Istanbul is shaped by a long history of East-meets-West, Christianity-meets-Islam, and Crusaders-meet-city walls. Back in the days of the Greeks, architects valued both form and function. The famous **Maiden's Tower**, perched on a tiny island in the Bosporus, was built by a Greek general in 408 BCE as an ancient stoplight equivalent to direct ships passing through the strait. When the Romans rolled into town, Constantine decided that the new capital city of the Roman Empire wouldn't be complete without the **Column of Constantine**, which he erected in 330 BCE. The Romans also built two large aqueducts and the **Hippodrome of Constantinople**, which was more than a quarter of a mile long and could seat 100,000 spectators.

Byzantine

The Byzantine Empire fortified the city with impressive walls that included 55 gates, one of which was made of gold. But the greatest architectural masterpieces of the era were the city's churches and monasteries. The **Hagia Sophia**, built at the order of Justinian between 532 and 537 CE and widely known as the greatest work of Byzantine architecture, stood as the world's largest cathedral for more than a millennium. On the practical side, architects built massive cisterns to provide water to the palace, including the **Basilica Cistern**, a massive underground chamber supported by 336 ornately decorated columns. Another highlight is the six-domed **Chora Church**, first erected in the fifth century CE and later revamped from 1077-1081 CE, containing 45 unbelievably detailed mosaics depicting traditional religious scenes.

Ottoman

With the conquest of Constantinople, there was a new boss in town, with seriously different priorities. Churches were converted into mosques, and Sultan Mehmed II began an ambitious reconstruction plan. The first project was the **Eyüp Sultan Mosque** (1458 CE), followed by the even more impressive **Fatih Mosque** (1463-71 CE). But mosques weren't the only addition on the Ottoman agenda. The **Tokapi Palace**, begun in 1459 CE, was home to the Ottoman Sultans for 400 years and housed as many as 4000 residents. But amazing architecture wasn't restricted to rulers alone. The 58 covered streets of the **Grand Bazaar**, opened in 1461 CE, were the ancient equivalent of a megamall. More impressive mosques followed, including the famous **Sultan Ahmet** or **Blue Mosque** (1616 CE), with six minarets and a 10,000-worshipper capacity. The 18th and 19th centuries brought increased European influence, giving architects a chance to mix and match different styles with varying success. The late 19th and early 20th centuries saw Istanbul change direction once again and become a leader in the **Art Nouveau** movement.

FOOD AND DRINK

Fusion Food

With more than 2000 years of culinary history, Istanbul has had plenty of opportunity to refine its palate. Fish, fresh eggplant, fragrant herbs, and local olive oil will please your stomach and maintain your waistline. Modern cuisine is a delicious blend of Balkan, Central Asian, and Middle Eastern specialties, from spicy kebabs of chicken and beef to *baklava*, a deliciously flaky pastry. *Doner kebabs* are one popular Turkish dish, consisting of lamb roasted to perfection on an upright spit. Meat-lovers will also enjoy *kofta*, balls of ground beef or lamb mixed with onions and spices. For lighter fare, order *dolma*, vine leaves stuffed with anything from spiced rice (*zeytinyagli dolma*) to eggplant (*patlican dolma*) to mussels (*midye dolma*).

Another Turkish specialty is *pilav*, known to Westerners as pilaf, a rice dish cooked with an almost infinite variety of spices and ingredients. Carnivores should try *özbek pilav*, made with diced lamb, onions, tomatoes, and carrots, or *hamsili pilav*, cooked with anchovies. Vegetarians can order *domatesli pilav* (tomato pilaf) or *nohutlu pilav* (rice cooked with seasoned chickpeas). Turkish desserts are world-renowned and for good reason. Flaky pastries like *baklava* and *kadaif*, along with *sütlaç*, a fresh rice pudding, are sure to sate even the most die-hard sweet tooths.

Drink Up!

Caffeine-addicts should try a strong Turkish coffee on for size, then examine the dregs to test their skills at *kahve fali*, or coffee dreg fortune-telling. For less mystery and a stronger kick, sip *rakı*, an anise-flavored alcoholic drink often served with seafood. A common Turkish saying claims that if you want to get to know someone, you should either travel with them or drink *rakı* with them. If you're visiting Istanbul with friends, you can do both, and that effects of this famously strong drink will probably reveal more secrets about your friends than the *kahve fali* did earlier. Also called *aslan sütü* ("lion's milk"), *rakı* turns milky-white when diluted. Teetotalers can try another of Turkey's favorite drinks, *ayran*. An interesting mixture of yogurt, water, and salt, *aryan* is served chilled and provides the perfect concoction to accompany a steaming kebab.

ATHENS

In any history or philosophy class, chances are Athens came up more than a few times. Democracy, theater, and the foundations of Western thought all began in this beautiful *polis*. Socrates, Plato, and Herodotus called this city home, and architectural wonders like the Parthenon, Dionysus's Theater, and the Ancient Agora still stand after thousands of years. By all accounts, Athens is a city for the ages. However, even today life goes on in this capital. Athens' modern age has its own angsty populace, financial burdens, nightlife, and transit system. Though much of what is worth seeing in Athens is from thousands of years ago, getting to the ancient ruins requires navigating through a city of winding streets and tons of people living daily life. In fact, some of the modern aspects are worth appreciating in their own right. The metro system was redesigned for the 2004 Olympic Games, and it is among the cleanest subway systems in the world. The ubiquitous *souvlaki* stands on the street provide a taste of Greek fast food, and trendy bars serving warmed red wine sweetened with honey keep the 20-something crowd grooving to the newest Europop. Despite harboring its own Greek traditions, Athens is traveler-friendly, and almost everyone speaks some degree of English. Hipster bars and large warehouses converted into performance spaces crowd the streets among Byzantine churches, traditional *tavernas*, and toppled columns. In fact, it's almost like Athens is carrying Plato's Republic in one hand and a bottle of beer in the other, so join this city for a history lesson and stay for the fast-paced lifestyle.

greatest hits

- **BAKLAVA IS REALLY HEALTHY.** No, it's not. But it's delicious and you should eat it at Beneth (p. 101).
- **FRUITY COCKTAILS.** Go to Showroom, where they use all fresh juices to make tasty mixed drinks (p. 107).
- **ACROPOLIS MUSEUM.** You'll probably be disappointed by some of the ruins in Athens (understandable, since they've been around for almost 3000 years), but this museum has the best of the best—don't miss it (p. 96).

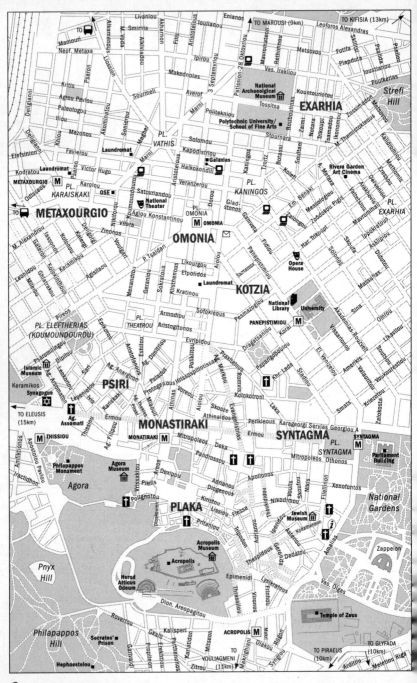

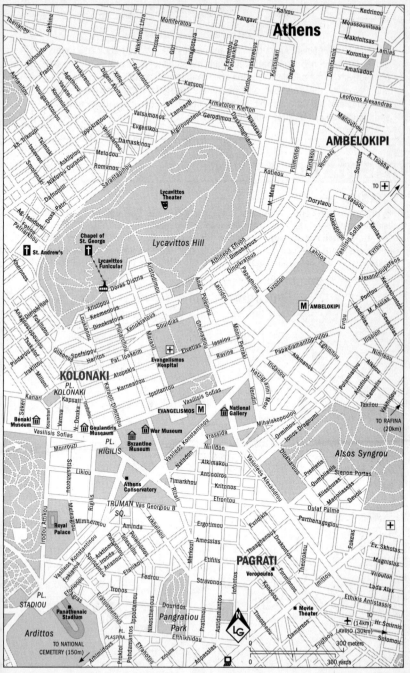

orientation

SYNTAGMA

Pl. Syntagma is the center of Athens' transportation hub. The stately, Neoclassical **Parliament building** and the **Tomb of the Unknown Soldier** mark the foot of the nature lovers' haven, the **National Gardens.** Looking in the opposite direction, the long stretch of Ermou teems with high fashion shops and trend-seeking teenagers on skateboards. The bustling square has gum spots blackening the white tile floor and is surrounded

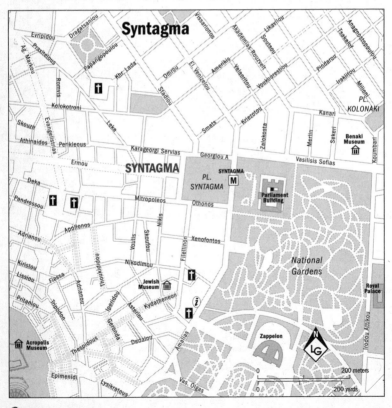

by roads crammed with public transport. Airport-bound buses leave from the right edge of the square, and the main metro entrance is across from the Parliament on **Amalias**. The trolley lets out on the top right corner of the square, and cabs are everywhere. **Georgiou**, **Filelinon**, and **Othonos** border the other three sides of the square. Step out of the main square and Syntagma quiets significantly. Streets wind along, cafe tables sit in wait, and shop owners attempt to lure in customers. **Mitropoleos**, **Ermou**, and **Karageorgi Servias** (which turns into Perikleous, then Athinados) start here and extend far into Monastiraki and Psiri. The occasional public concert, the changing of the guard at the Parliament Building, and the abundance of unlicensed vendors around the square add to Syntagma's status as an energetic center of human activity.

PLAKA

Situated in the middle of the triangle formed by **Syntagma Square**, **Monastiraki Square**, and the **Acropolis**, Plaka is a plush, touristy section of Athens that's surprisingly the best place for low-budget travelers to live while in the city. Many of the streets are pedestrian thoroughfares with only a few wayward motorbikes, and vendors take full advantage of this extra sidewalk space. While **Kydatheneon** and **Adrianou** have scores of tourist-oriented *tavernas* and souvenir shops, the smaller and quieter streets have retained an antique charm.

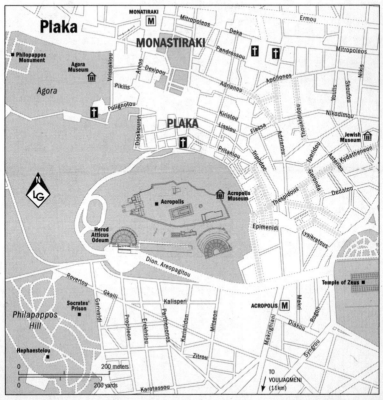

MONASTIRAKI

Behind the metro station, which borders on Hadrian's Library, and across Ermou, is a maze of streets speckled with bead shops, artisan's stores, scrumptious restaurants, and interesting nooks. Nowhere in Athens are pedestrians as stylish nor ice cream shops so picturesque. Sticking to the main straightaway of Athinas Street, perpendicular to Ermou at the square, is far more touristy but after a few blocks leads to the Meat Market, which is certainly worth a visit for those with strong stomachs.

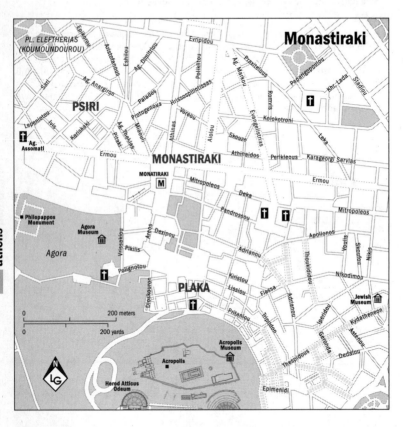

EXARHIA

In 1973, students in Exarhia participated in a powerful demonstration against the right-wing dictatorship that was then in control of the Athenian government. Today, this section of Athens is still a hotspot for youth culture and is filled with graffiti, coffeeshops, and shisha (think hookah, you westerners). Be wary of getting lost on the way to a destination in this sometimes desolate neighborhood, but don't let the difficulty stop you from seeing this anarchist-enclave-turned-bohemian-mecca in the flesh—especially for a hip dinner.

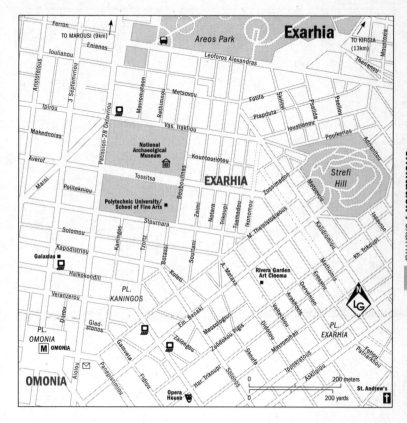

KOLONAKI

Sandwiched by Pl. Syntagma at the base of **Lycabettus Hill,** Kolonaki is the poshest area of Athens. Foreign designer boutiques line the streets, and those walking around the area are slender and decked out in perfectly tailored clothes. This area is also incredibly expensive, so with the exception of a few lunch places, it is best seen as a backpacker walk-through zone rather than a place to stay in Athens.

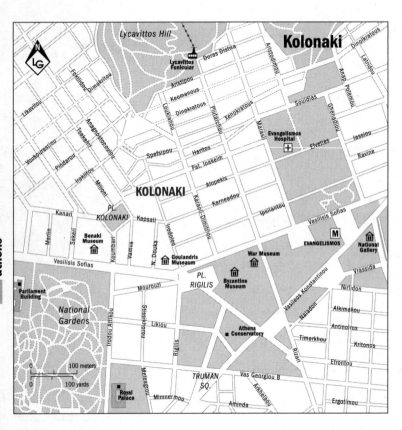

SYNTAGMA

"JOHN'S PLACE" GUEST HOUSE
HOTEL [3]

Patrou 5 ☎210 32 29 719

For a trip back to another era, stay in this parquet-floored, steep-staired yet somehow homey hotel. "John" seems to have forgotten all modern amenities when founding this hotel that lacks internet, television, elevator, and credit card capabilities. However, A/C is available in each fresh-linened room, and the white embroidered drapes let in a pleasing amount of afternoon sunlight. High ceilings and Tiffany blue walls add charm to each floor's common space. Make sure to lock valuables in the room's safe; it has been said that the woman at the front desk seems to be fond of her afternoon naps.

From Syntagma square, walk down Mitropoleos 4 blocks; Patrou is on the left. $ Singles €35, doubles €50, triples €60.

HOTEL KIMON
HOTEL [4]

Apollonos 27 ☎210 331 4658 🖳www.kimonhotelathens.com

Long and quiet hallways, a fire extinguisher on every landing, and an attentive man behind the desk make this is a well-tended hotel. Cantaloupe-colored walls and prismatic glass windows on the stairway landings add some pizzazz to the otherwise cramped space—including some rooms with balconies just large enough to cram two people—expertly magnified by full-length mirrors at the entrance. Not the cheapest hotel, Kimon might be saved by the diligence of its staff.

From Syntagma square, walk down Mitropoleos 3 blocks. i Request a room with a safe. Breakfast of eggs and juice can be added for €5 per person. ⏰ Late June-Sept doubles €60-€70; Oct-June doubles €50-€60.

HOTEL METROPOLIS
HOTEL [5]

Mitropoleos 46 ☎210 32 17 871 🖳www.hotelmetropolis.gr

Tiny seems to be the operative word here. Overpriced and not quite up to snuff, Metropolis' bathroom doors are chipped at the bottom and its balconies are miniscule. A few rooms have a nice view of the Acropolis, but you pay for it with smaller rooms offering little walking space.

Walk 5 blocks down from Pl. Syntagma. On Mitropoleos near Petraki. i Breakfast can be added for €5 per person. Luggage storage on request. $ Doubles €100.

HOTEL AMAZON
HOTEL [5]

Mitropoleos 19 and Pentelis Street ☎ 210 32 34 002 🖳wwww.amazonhotel.gr

A classy hotel for a decent price, Hotel Amazon is equipped with marble entrance stairs, two elevators, and guests of the blond-hair-big-bag-big-sunglasses variety. Its bathrooms come with soap and shampoo, a rare amenity in the hostel world. Though not a steal, the two elevators and fresh scent of the rooms make it worth the splurge for glamour.

i Internet cables in room, €3 per hour, €12 per day. Breakfast included. $ Doubles €80, prices vary seasonally.

PLAKA

STUDENT AND TRAVELLER'S INN
HOSTEL [1]

16 Kydathineon ☎210 32 44 808 🖳www.studenttravellersinn.com

Centrally located, full of friendly people, and constantly pulsing with a Top-40 playlist, Student and Traveller's Inn is a backpacker's dream come true. Every need is met in this no-frills establishment. This hostel is located right at the top of a street lined with restaurants in the heart of every sight worth seeing, so if there's room and you don't mind bunk beds, this is the place to go.

⚑ Ⓜ*Syntagma. Walk along Filelinon in the same direction as traffic. Turn right onto Kydatineon. Walk a few blocks and pass a church on your right.* *i* *Same-day laundry €8 for 2kg wash, dry, and fold. Daily happy hour 6:30pm. Breakfast options around €5. Quiet time starting at 10:30pm.* Ⓢ *June-Sept: 8-bed dorms €20; 4-bed €23, with bath €25. Singles €45, with bath €55; doubles €65, with bath €73; triples €81, with bath €90. From Oct-Mar prices drop by roughly €10.* ☒ *Reception 24hr. Quiet hours start 10:30pm. Happy hour daily 6:30pm.*

ATHENS BACKPACKERS
🛏(ᵥ)⚒❄☂ HOSTEL ❶
12 Makri, 3 Veikou ☎210 92 24 044 💻www.backpackers.gr

Stepping into Athens Backpackers is like stepping into Ikea. This 20-year-old's dreamland is the epitome of cool (with a rooftop bar and daily happy hour). Bright color schemes and extreme cleanliness highlight this accommodation's attention to detail, and amenities like communal soaps and shampoos, free walking tours, power outlets by every bed, and free breakfast make this hostel worthy of your stay. Check out the community white board in the lobby for the list of weekly activities.

⚑ Ⓜ*Syntagma. Walk down Amalias as it turns into Dionissiou Areopagitous. After one block turn left onto Makri.* *i* *Breakfast included. €5 lost card fee. Laundry in Veikou building, €5 for 8 kilos to wash, €2 to dry.* Ⓢ *3-, 4-, and 6-person dorms €23-28. 2-person studios €85-90; 4-person €90-95. 2-person apartments €93-95, 4-person €120; 6-person €140.* ☒ *Reception 24hr. Breakfast 7:30-9:30am. Happy hour daily 7-8pm.*

HOTEL ACROPOLIS HOUSE
🛏(ᵥ)❄ HOTEL ❺
6-8 Kondrou ☎210 32 22 344, 210 32 26 241 💻www.acropolishouse.gr

Located within an old mansion near Syntagma Square, this hotel offers a charming stay for travelers looking to find a taste of home in Greece. The cozy rooms, though not large, have all the amenities one could want, and the family staff is warm. From the third floor hallway there is a fabulous view of the Acropolis, and a few rooms have balconies that overlook the neighborhood. Potted greenery abounds.

✢ *At intersection of Iperidou and Kondrou just a few blocks from Syndagma.* **i** *TV and phone in all rooms. Wi-Fi included but works only on ground floor for most computers. Breakfast included.* Ⓢ *May-Oct singles €68; doubles for 1-2 nights €91, for over 2 nights €83; triples €119/108. Nov-Apr singles for 1-2 nights €56, for over 2 nights €51; doubles €70/64; triples €91/83.*

PHAEDRA HOTEL
✦❄(((•)))⍦ HOTEL ❹

Cherefondos 16 and Adrianou Street ☎210 32 38 461 ▨www.hotelphaedra.com

Located 5min. from the Acropolis and 3min. from a bunch of restaurants, Phaedra is an average but clean hotel with a working elevator. This unexciting hotel's staff is a bit fussy, but the rooms are kept clean. To make the halls more aesthetically pleasing, Phaedra hangs pictures of the Greek islands on its walls that make you wish you were somewhere more exciting.

✢ Ⓜ*Syndagma. Walk along Filelinon in the same direction as traffic. Turn right onto Kydatineon. Take a left after 3 blocks; the hotel will be to the left when you reach the cross-street.* **i** *Breakfast €5. Wi-Fi in lobby.* Ⓢ *Doubles €60, with bath €70; converted triples €90.*

MONASTIRAKI

▨ HOTEL PELLA INN
◉Ⓧ(((•)))⍦❄♨ HOTEL ❹

104 Ermou Street ☎210 32 50 598 ▨www.pella-inn.gr

This hostel reminiscent of a ski lodge is run by a maternal woman who cares for the hostel like it is her own offspring. Though the decor is a bit dated, everything is clean. Bring a drink or snack up to the roof—the view of Athens and the Acropolis is phenomenal.

✢ *From* Ⓜ*Monastiraki, walk down Ermou and take a right onto Karaiskaki; the hotel will be on the left.* **i** *Breakfast included. Laundry €6.* Ⓢ *Doubles €50-60; triples €120.*

HOTEL ARION
✦♿(((•)))⍦❄ HOTEL ❺

18 Ag. Dimitriou ☎210 32 40 412 ▨www.arionhotel.gr

Offering amenities like hairdryers and full-length mirrors to soap in a customized wrapper, this spacious hotel is for those who are willing to pay for the plush. Meticulously clean and in a very cool neighborhood, some rooms look out onto the Acropolis.

✢ *From* Ⓜ*Monastiraki, walk down Ermou street and turn right onto Georgiou Karaiskaki; Hotel Arion will be on the left.* **i** *Breakfast included. Free Wi-Fi on first floor. Rooftop garden. Laundry is €10 for a small bag.* Ⓢ *Singles €105; doubles €130; triples €150.*

CECIL HOTEL
✦♿(((•)))⍦❄ HOTEL ❺

Athinas 39 ☎210 32 17 079 ▨www.cecil.gr

Located in the heart of Monastiraki and graced with a metal grate elevator perfect for travelers schlepping huge bags around, this hotel is larger than most. The charming dining room has upholstered chairs that seat a well-dressed clientele.

✢ *From* Ⓜ*Monastiraki, cross Ermou street and walk down Athinas a few blocks; Cecil Hotel will be on the left.* **i** *Breakfast included.* Ⓢ *Singles €60; doubles €70; triples €120; family suits €160.*

EXARHIA

▨ HOTEL EXARCHION
✦♿(((•)))⍦❄ HOTEL ❹

55 Themistokleous ☎210 38 00 731; 210 38 01 256

Right in the middle of Pl. Exharia's hipster-zone, Exarchion is a convenient spot to get a taste of Athens' youth culture. This part of town is lively at night and close to plenty of coffeshops and *tavernas* that are popular with the locals. Very clean and wheelchair-accessible, Hotel Exarchion is the best sleeping option in the area.

✢ *Half a block down from the base of Pl. Exharia.* **i** *Breakfast €5.* Ⓢ *Singles €50; doubles €50; triples €70; family suite €90.*

Acropolis and Agora

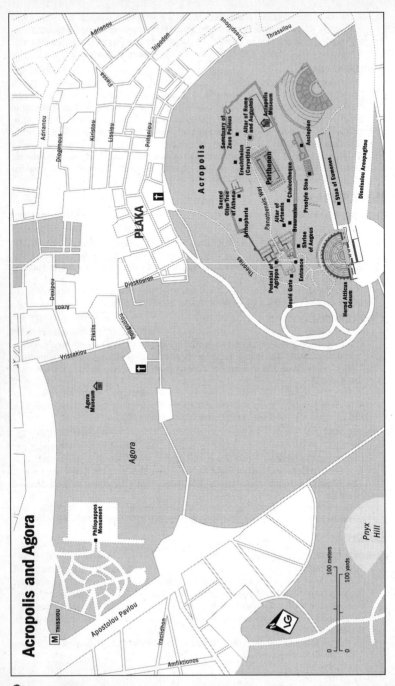

PLAKA

Acropolis

Sanctuary of
Zeus Polieus

Altar of Rome
and Augustus

Acropolis
Museum

Erechtheion
(Caryatids)

Parthenon

Sacred
Olive Tree
of Athens

Arrhephoria

Panathenaic Way

Altar of
Artemis

Chalcotheque

Asclepion

Brauronion

Shrine
of Aegeus

Prostyle Stoa

Stoa of Eumenes

Pedestal of
Agrippa

Theoreia

Entrance

Beulé Gate

Herod Atticus
Odeum

Dionissiou Areopagitou

Adrianou

Tripodon

Flessa

Kiristou

Lissiou

Pritaniou

Diogenous

Dexipou

Areos

Pikilis

Vrissakiou

Dioskouron

Ragkava

Agora
Museum

Agora

Philopappos
Monument

THISSIOU

Apostolou Pavlou

Iraklidhon

Amfiktionos

*Pnyx
Hill*

100 meters

100 yards

HOTEL ORION AND DRYADES

 HOTEL ❷

105 Em. Benaki and 4 Dryadon   ☎210 33 02 387 🖳www.orion-dryades.com

This hotel is an amalgamation of 2 hotels that used to exist side-by-side, and it's a bit scattered as a result. Located at the extremity of Exharia, Orion and Dryades is off the beaten track and houses dated decor and a creaky elevator. But with great prices and clean rooms, think of walking back to the hotel from the sights as a free daily workout.

🚌 *From Pl. Syntagma, take bus #230 to Kalidromiou. Or, walking from Pl. Syntagma, follow Panipistimiou and take a right onto Em. Benaki.* 🛈 *Breakast €6. Laundry €3 per load. Wi-Fi €10 per week.* ⓢ *Singles €25; doubles €35, with bath €60.*

sights

ACROPOLIS

Throughout its 2,500 year existence, the Acropolis has seen its fair share of action. Though somewhat worn for the wear (oh hey Lord Elgin), it is a fascinating and quintessentially Athenian site. The Acropolis began as a political center in the Mycenean period from the 15th to 12th centuries BC. The king lived atop the hill that now provides tourists a breathtaking view of the entirety of Athens, from the Aegean Sea to the mountains. But in the 8th century BC a temple was erected to honor **Athena**, the patron goddess of Athens, and ever since the story of the Acropolis has been one of construction, demolition and changing religious orders. Perhaps no site other than the Dome of the Rock rivals the Acropolis' multi-denominational appeal.

The first temple, called the **Hekatopmpedos** for its measly 100 foot length, was made of wood and probably was not much to look at. So, just under 50 years later, the Athenians decided to construct a more elaborate temple, now known as the **Old Temple**. In celebration of their victory in the battle of Marathon in 490 BC, the ancient Athenians decided that a third renovation was in order. But just 10 years later in 480 BC, **Xerxes** and his Persian army swept Sparta and in order to fight the intruder at sea (the Athenians' strong suit) rather than land (Xerxes' strength), the Athenians fled the city, abandoning the Acropolis. Xerxes and his crew vandalized the newest temple, smashing statues' heads and wreaking general havoc. Not until Pericles' heyday from 450 BC-429 BC did the Athenians decide to face the ruins and build yet again, and this reconstruction resulted in the Parthenon.

After its tumultuous, extended, and awkward growth spurt, the Acropolis went through an angsty, religiously unsound period. From the 4th century AD until Greece claimed independence in 1833, the Acropolis went from its original dedication to Athena to a Christian Orthodox church to a Catholic church under the Byzantine Empire to a center of Muslim faith under Ottoman occupation—if this doesn't confuse you, well done. During this phase **Lord Elgin**, a British ambassador to the Ottoman Empire, carried some of the Parthenon's remains with him back to Britain, where they now remain in the British Museum—much to the dismay of many Greeks.

Now, centuries after its founding, the Acropolis is a tourist site and is currently undergoing another renovation started in 1983. Even through the throngs of tourists, looking down on Athens from a vantage point that must be like that of Mount Olympus, it is possible to imagine why the Acropolis and its turf have been fought over for so long.

🛈 *Admission gets you into the archaeological site of the Acropolis, the archaeological site and museum of the Ancient Agora, the north and south slopes of the Acropolis, the Theatre of Dionysis, the Roman Agora, Kerameikos, the Temple of Olympian Zeus, and Hadrian's Library.* ⏰ *Open daily 8am-7:30pm.* ⓢ *€12, students and EU seniors €6, EU students and internationals under 19 free on Su.)*

sights • acropolis

Parthenon

The Parthenon is the pinnacle of the Acropolis—historically, geographically, and artistically. Designed at the height of Periclean democracy by Iktinos, the structure, though now only the remnants of what once stood, is commonly seen as a symbol of Western culture. It took only nine years to build the Parthenon, but many layers of design went into its construction. The temple, which consists of over 16,500 pieces of white marble, is Doric but has Ionic features, and eight columns line each of its narrow sides. Now only white, the Parthenon was formerly painted inside with friezes and a deep blue hue. There were three key design features to the Parthenon. First, the **metopes**, or relief slabs, depicted scenes from Greek mythology like the war between the gods and the giants and the fight the centaurs had over women. Second, the Parthenon had Ionic **friezes**. The last, and perhaps the most notable design feature is that of the **pediments**, which were mounted between 438 and 432 BC along the top of the columns. The East pediment, laid out in great detail on the third floor of the Acropolis museum, tells the story of the moment of Athena's birth when she sprung from Zeus' head. The West pediment shows the contest between Athena and Poseidon for Athens, when her olives won out over his salt water.

Erechtheum

Set to the left of the Parthenon, the Erechtheum is divided into two parts—the East portion to **Athena**, the West portion to her losing foe in the bid for Athens, **Poseidon**. The monument was built during the Peloponessian War between 421 BC and 409 BC. Work was paused while Athens went to war with Sicily and resumed at the completion of that battle, which did not go well for Athens. The Erechtheum is notable for the six **Carytid** statues—women standing in a horseshoe shape supporting the roof—and is named after a hero Poseidon supposedly smote in his losing bid for Athens.

church protocol

Byzantine Athens consists of a few churches scattered through the city, oddly but somehow beautifully set alongside the modern city. Kapnikaria Church, for example, is directly opposite an H and M on one of Athens' main shopping avenues. Unlike the Acropolis and temples to the gods of Greek mythology where worship died out ages ago, most of these churches are still fully functional houses of faith. As a result, appropriate dress is required. Women shouldn't wear anything that exposes their knees. Morning is generally the best time to visit.

Propylaea

The Propylaea is the gateway to the Acropolis. Once a majestic entryway through which all walked, it is now a somewhat haggard collection of columns. First constructed in 437 BC under Pericles' instruction, the Propylaea was never fully completed because of a series of wars that interrupted its construction. The same blast that damaged the Temple of Athena Nike in 1686 also damaged the structure, ambitious in its many tiers and mixed Doric and Ionic styles. A renovation project began in 1984 was recently completed, so enjoy the Propylaea in all its dilapidated splendor.

Theater of Dionysus

Down a path to the right of the main entrance to the Acropolis sits a giant, steep-stepped ancient theater that must strike fear in anyone who stands on its stage. Originally constructed in honor of **Dionysus**, the ancient Greek god of making merry

athens

through the aid of dance and wine, the theater became a place of celebration and artistic ecstasy. One ceremony led to another, and in 500 BC a contest for playwrights that had been in Athens' outskirts was moved to the city. It was in this theatre that Aeschylus', Sophocles', Euripides', and Aristophanes' plays were first performed in honor of the gods. Recently, the theatre was renovated, and it now serves as a fully functional performance space.

Temple of Athena Nike

As you and hundreds of other travelers ascend the steep, slippery steps toward the Parthenon and walk through the Proplyaea, glance to your right: you will see the Temple of Athena Nike. Designed in the Ionic style by the famed architect **Kallikrates** during the Peace of Nikias from 421-415 BC, the temple is now in its third iteration. Like the Parthenon, this temple has been ransacked many times throughout its history, primarily during the Turkish-Venetian War (1686-1687 AD). The temple initially had a frieze that was more than 25m long and depicted scenes of Athenian military success, but four parts of the initial 14 are now in the British Museum, and other portions have been destroyed. Make sure to check out some of the sections that are inside the Acropolis Museum on the second floor.

AGORA

If the Acropolis was the showpiece of the ancient capital, the Agora was its heart and soul. It served as the city's marketplace, administrative center, and focus of daily life from the sixth century BCE through the sixth century CE. Socrates, Demosthenes, Aristotle, and St. Paul all debated democracy in its hallowed stalls. The 500-person **Boule,** or senate of ancient times, met in the **Bouleuterion** to make decisions for this city, and the **Monument of the Eponymous Heroes** functioned as an ancient tabloid, where the government posted honors and lawsuits. Following its heyday, the Agora, like the Acropolis, passed through the hands of various conquerors. The ancient market emerged again in the 19th century, when a residential area built above it was razed for excavations. Today, the Agora is a peaceful respite from the bustling Athens around it.

TEMPLE OF HEPHAESTUS

The impressive temple atop Kolonos Agraraiso Hill is dedicated to Hephaestus, the Greek god of metal working. The temple is made mostly of Pentelic marble in the Doric style and has **friezes** that depict the battle between Athenian hero **Theseus** and the Pallantids along its ceiling. Built from 460-415 BCE, the temple was in use through 1834 but is now the best-preserved Classical temple in all of Greece.

SKIAS

Civic offices that held the polis' official **weights and measures** were managed in 35-day segments by each of Athens' different factions in the round building now known as the Tholos—Greek for "circle"—on the left side of the Agora beneath the Temple of Hephaestus. Next to the **altars to the gods** and across from the **gymnasium,** the Skias' location is a prime of example of what the Agora was in its heyday—a mix of everything Athenian.

STOA OF ATTALOS

This multi-purpose building was filled with shops and was home to informal philosophers' gatherings. Attalos II, King of Pergamon, built the Sota in the second century BCE as a gift to Athens. Reconstructed between 1053 and 1056, it now houses the **Agora Museum,** which contains relics form the site. The stars of the collection are the **black figure paintings** by Exekias and a calyx krater— a flower-like vase used to mix wine that depicts Trojans and Greeks quarreling over the body of Patroclus, Achilles' closest companion and possible lover.

🕐 *Open daily 8am-7:20pm.*

ODEION OF AGRIPPA

Designed for performances, this structure originally had a thatched roof, orchestra pit, and seating for nearly 1000 people—no small feat for a building in 15 BCE. Like many other structures in the Agora, the original was destroyed by the Herulian invasion of 267 CE.

CHURCH OF THE HOLY APOSTLES

On the left immediately after walking into the Agora, this church is the only remaining medieval monument in the Agora and was built in 1000 CE before being restored in 1954. Make sure to turn your **flash** off when taking photos of the 17th-century paintings in this gem.

ROMAN AGORA

When the Ancient Agora filled with administrative buildings and crowded out vendors, the shop owners picked up their commerce and moved to the Roman Agora. The structure was built from 19-11 BCE and had two **propyla,** or Doric vestibules at the entrance, one of which was given by Julius Caesar himself. Today, all that remains beyond the five imposing columns at the entrance is an open, grassy expanse ringed by white marble pieces. In the far end of the Agora stands the **Tower of the Winds,** built by Andronikos, an astronomer from Macedonia. Also, the far side of the Agora is the foundation of the Vespasianae, or public latrines, that showcase Greece's advanced sewage system.

⇟ Enter the Agora either off Pl. Thission, off Adrianou, or as you descend from the Acropolis. i For holiday schedule, call ☎210 32 16 690. Map kiosks are plentiful throughout the park, but it might be helpful to bring your own maps. $ €2, students and EU seniors €1. EU students and under 19 free. ⏰ Open daily 8am-8pm. Last entrance 7:30pm.

SYNTAGMA

ACROPOLIS MUSEUM — 🎓♿❄ MUSEUM

Dionyssiou Areopagitou Street 15 ☎210 32 10 185 💻www.theacropolismuseum.gr

A must-see—preferably before heading up the hill to the Acropolis—this modern museum has an astounding collection of ancient artifacts within its somewhat controversial modern design. Opened in 2007, it holds statues, terracotta wine vases, coins, and dioramas designated with placards that give great historical context in both Greek and English. 5 of the original 6 Caryatids from 420-415 BC are inside on the second floor; copies now stand in their stead on the Erechtheumn. Make sure to watch the video about the Parthenon on the 3rd floor for a great dose of information, and ask the archaeologists wandering the exhibits in black pants, white shirts, and nametags any pertinent questions.

⇟ Ⓜ Acropolis. Located 300m from the Acropolis itself. i The entrance to the museum has glass flooring, allowing visitors to see ruins beneath where they walk. Very cool and very reflective: make sure not to wear a skirt. Cafe on third floor. $ €5, students €3. ⏰ Open Tu-Su 8am-8pm, last admission 7:30pm.

NATIONAL GARDEN — 🌳 GARDEN

The land between Amalias, Vas. Olgas, Vas. Sofias, and Irodou Atikou

Step through the gates of the National Garden and the honks, heat, and general havoc of Athens fades into the shade, soft paths, and bird sounds within the park. This lush, expansive patch of peace has been public since 1923 and boasts, along with benches, marigolds, and winding pathways, a Botanical Garden, turtle pond, and cafe. In antiquity, the sacred grove of Cyceum stood in the same place.

⇟ From Syntagma facing the Parliament building, turn right. The many entrances to the park are behind the stalls and bus stops. i Don't go alone at night. $ Free. ⏰ Open 24hr.

PARLIAMENT BUILDING — PUBLIC BUILDING

Stadiou 13 ☎210 32 37 315 🖥www.nhmuseum.gr

Every hour on the hour, a small crowd of tourists assembles in front of the Parliament building to witness the changing of the guard, an absurd ritual that involves five men in tan colored shirts holding guns walking in a way that must resemble a loon mating dance. As part of the procedure for switching the soldiers need to touch their shoes' humongo pompoms. Between the hourly embarrassments, times two lucky men get to stand in the garb and get stared at by crowds without responding (a la Buckingham Palace). On Su at 11am there is an even more elaborate proceeding. All in all, the process takes about 5min.

➡ Yellow building at the head of Syndagma, along Amalias St. ℹ Changing of the guard every hour on the hour all day and night.

PANATHENAIC STADIUM — STADIUM

Renovated for the Athens Olympics in 2004, the stadium is a massive construction of marble with no hot dog vendors of the standard American stadium. Sadly, this stadium might be better appreciated through pictures—the angle that visitors are allowed does not provide much of a vantage point, and honking from the road 50m away undermine the structure's glory.

➡ On Vas. Konstantinou. From Sydagma, walk down Amalias 10 min. to Vas. Olgas and follow it to the left. Or take trolley #2, 4, or 11 from Syndagma. $ Free. ⏰ Open 24hr.

NATIONAL ARCHAEOLOGICAL MUSEUM — MUSEUM

Patision Street 144 ☎210 90 00 901

At home if you dig in the dirt, you find worms. In Athens, it seems, one finds ancient artifacts. The quantity of vases and statues in this museum, founded in 1892, is astounding, and to look at every exhibit would take days. Room after room is full of perfectly chiseled, nude forms, and the second floor is entirely pottery. Decide ahead of time how long you want to spend at the museum, but don't expect to breeze through. The placards are like textbooks, so read them like you do a textbook: skim.

➡ Walk 20 min. from Pl. Syndagma down Stadiou to Aiolou. Turn right onto Patission; or take trolley #2, 4, 5, 9, 11, 15, or 18 from the uphill side of Syndagma or trolley #3 or 13 from the north side of Vas. Sofias From Victoria, walk straight to the 1st street, 28 Oktuvriou; turn right and walk 5 blocks. Museum will be on the left ℹ Photos without flash permitted. $ General admission €7, Students and EU citizens over 65 €3. Free admission for EU students, those under 19, and disabled persons. ⏰ Apr-Oct M 1:30pm-8pm, Tu-Su 8am-8pm, Nov-Mar 1:30pm-3:00pm, Tu-Su 8:30am 3pm.

PLAKA

HADRIAN'S LIBRARY — RUINS

☎210 32 49 350

Built in 132 CE in the architectural style of the Roman Forum, this library was once the scene of a pool, a garden, and as the name suggests, a library with reading rooms. The books made of papyrus are long gone, but some columns still stand.

➡ [M]Monastiraki. Walk up the hill. ℹ Included in the €12 Acropolis ticket. $ Students and over 65 €2. EU students and under 19 free. ⏰ Open daily 8am-8pm.

ARCHAEOLOGICAL SITE OF KERAMEIKOS — RUINS

End of Ermou ☎210 346 3552

Come to this burial ground to walk on over 1000 years of ancient, rotting nobility. No markers indicate who lies where, but blooming flowers, huge funerary statues, and remains of the ancient walls of Athens dot the landscape, making this former cemetery a beautiful archaeologicalexcavation site. Look for the Dipylon gate, once the city's main entrance, where Pericles gave a memorable speech honoring those who perished during the first year of the Peloponnesian

War. Supposedly, the hill to the immediate right of the museum is where the most famous remains rest.

✷ Ⓜ*Monastiraki. Walk down Ermou street.* ⓘ *Included in the €12 Acropolis ticket.* Ⓢ *€2, with student ID €1.* ⏱ *Open daily 8:30am-3pm.*

NUMISMATIC MUSEUM

⬤&✻ MUSEUM

12 Panepistimiou ☎210 36 52 057 ▉www.nma.gr

It takes money to see money. More ▉**coins** than you could ever imagine are displayed in glass cases in this formal house of a German benefactor. As you walk through the displays, take note of the overzealous guards that watch your every move, almost assuming that you are going after one of these old pieces of change. With a huge variety of ancient currencies, this museum is worth your money—especially because it offers a complimentary hour-long audio tour of the first floor.

✷ Ⓜ*Syntagma. Go left down Panepistimiou, and the museum will be on the right.* ⓘ *Complimentary hour-long audio tour of the first floor.* Ⓢ *€3, students outside EU and over 65 €2, EU students and under 19 free.* ⏱ *Open Tu-Su 8:30am-3pm.*

MUSEUM OF GREEK POPULAR MUSIC

✻ MUSEUM

Diogenous 1-3 ☎210 32 54 119 ▉www.instruments-museum.gr

Although this museum is easy to miss while fighting your way up the hill past the Roman Agora, there is no excuse for skipping out on this fun and quick musical experience. Hear different instruments and music varieties through black headphones next to the display cases that play recordings of the music being showcased. While *Let's Go* doesn't know the first thing about Greek Popular Music, the chance to learn different ways to play the *defi* (tambourine) makes this museum music to our ears.

✷ *To the left of the hill beside the Roman Agora.* ⓘ *Check website for featured exhibits.* ⏱ *Open Tu 10am-2pm, W noon-6pm, Th-Su 10am-2pm.*

MONASTIRAKI

▉ MUSEUM OF CYCLADIC ART

⬤&✻ MUSEUM

4 Neophytou Douka ☎210 72 28 321 ▉www.cycladic.gr

This museum's informative and well-labeled contents highlight a style of Greek art different from the other museums of its caliber. The first floor holds prime examples of Cycladic art, which is defined by its violin-shaped figures that capture human form in extreme simplicity. The fourth floor also holds dioramas about life in seventh century Athens.

✷ *From* Ⓜ*Syntagma, walk to Pl. Konolaki; the museum is two blocks past the square.* ⓘ *Pictures without flash permitted.* Ⓢ *€7, over 65 €3.50, students €2.50 for students, under 18 free.* ⏱ *Open M 10am-5pm, W 10am-5pm, Th 10am-8pm, F-Sa 10am-5pm, Su 11am-5pm.*

BENAKI MUSEUM

⬤&✻ MUSEUM

1 Koumbari and Vas. Sofias ☎210 36 71 000 ▉www.benaki.gr

Founded in 1930 from a collection accumulated by Antony Benaki in his family's mansion, this museum—the central one of the Benaki museum network—houses an extensive collection of art from Greek history to the present. Pottery, busts, paintings, and a gold crown are shown behind glass in the museum that reopened in 2000.

✷ *From* Ⓜ*Syntagma, walk along Vas. Sofias; the museum is at the intersection of Vas. Sofias and Koumbari.* Ⓢ *€6, students and over 65 €3, EU students and under 19 free.* ⏱ *Open M 9am-5pm, W 9am-5pm, Th 9am-midnight, F-Sa 9am-5pm.*

NATIONAL GALLERY

⬤&✻ MUSEUM

Vas. Konstantinou 50 ☎210 72 35 937 ▉www.nationalgallery.gr

Greece is not renowned for its modern art, yet it seems the National Gallery showcases work mostly from the last few hundred years. The main collection holds a large number of Greek portraits, whose prominent moles have been immortalized forever, but lacks any artwork that really stands out.

✴ *Located on the intersection of Vas. Konstantinou and Vas. Sofias by the Hilton Hotel.* ℹ️ *Photos without flash permitted.* 💲 *€6.50; students, children, and over 65 €3.* 🕐 *Open M-Sa 9am-3pm, Su 10am-2pm.*

EXARHIA *(Byzantine Athens)*

KAPNIKARIA CHURCH
♿ CHURCH

Just below ground level on the intersection of Ermou and Kalamiotou   ☎210 32 24 462

Quaintly located in the heart of Athens, Kapnikaria Church is emblematic of the city's Byzantine structures. Set low in the street and surrounded by a short stone wall, this church's intricately shaped stone exterior is well-preserved despite the many decades that have passed since its construction in the 11th century. Inside, scaffolding from construction obstructs visitors' views of some wallpaintings, but those that are visible are golden and beautiful. If you only visit one church in Athens, this should be it.

✴ *Follow Ermou down from the base of Ⓜ️Syntagma.* ℹ️ *Make sure knees are covered before entering.* 💲 *Free.* 🕐 *Open daily 9am-3am.*

HOLY TRINITY
Ⓧ CHURCH

Fillelinon 21A   ☎210 32 31 090

Gilt-laden, the Holy Trinity is the largest of the Byzantine churches in Athens and easily accessible from Syntagma. With 1000 years of history, this church is still young relative to other sites of Athens. After being amazed by the giant chandelier in the church's center, don't miss a nook on the right that displays a fresco painted 850 years ago. Other than this piece, most of the paintings on the walls are from the 19th century.

✴ *Ⓜ️Syntagma. Follow Fillelinon at the base of the square. The church will be a few blocks down on the left.* 💲 *Free.* 🕐 *Open daily 8am-noon.*

sights . exarhia

KOLONAKI

FOLK ART MUSEUM
☉ MUSEUM

Kydatheneon 17 ☎210 32 29 031

Located at the top of one of Athens' most touristy streets, the Folk Art Museum is among the best collections of authentic Greek culture in Athens. Native garb, ancient tools, and beautiful photographs immortalize a culture that is less than evident among Plaka's many tourist shops. Be sure to stop on the second floor of the museum to see the Theofilos room, which showcases a mural that was formerly located in a house in Lesvos.

☈ MSyntagma. Follow Fillelinon at the base of the square and turn right onto Kydatheneon. The museum is 2 blocks down on the left. ⓒ €2, non-EU students and EU residents over 65 €1, under 19 and EU students free. ⏲ Open T-Su 9am-2pm.

THE JEWISH MUSEUM OF GREECE
☉ MUSEUM

Nikis 39 ☎210 32 25 582 ▣www.jewishmuseum.gr

Founded in 1977, this Jewish museum feels more like a religious education center than a history museum because it explains the different religious artifacts and their roles in services rather than just Jewish history. The spiral design allows visitors to move smoothly through the displays of old scrolls and kiddush cups as well as some very fermented wine.

☈ MSyntagma. Follow Fillelinon at the base of the square, and turn right onto Kydatheneon. Turn right onto Nikis two blocks down. ⓒ €6, non-EU students and EU residents over 65 €3, under 19 and EU students free. ⏲ Open M-F 9am-2:30pm, Su 10am-2pm.

BENAKI MUSEUM OF ISLAMIC ART
☉ MUSEUM

22 Ag. Asomaton and 12 Diylou ☎210 32 51 311 ▣www.benaki.gr

Designed with clean, grey marble for its opening in 2004, this spacious museum divides its many holdings by era, beginning with the oldest items on the first floor and ascending into more recent artifacts. Pressed for time? Don't miss the third floor, where an impressive reception room was transplanted from its original home in a 17th-century Cairo mansion.

☈ MMonastiraki. Follow Ermou to the big intersection and take a right. The museum is a few blocks down Ag. Asomaton on the right. i Pictures permitted without flash. ⓒ €5, students free. Free on W. ⏲ Open Tu 9am-3pm, W 9am-9pm, Th-Su 9am-3pm.

BYZANTINE MUSEUM
☉ MUSEUM

Vas. Sofias 22 ☎213 21 39 500 ▣www.byzantinemuseum.gr

This sandy-colored museum's design funnels visitors through the one-way exhibits that feature everything from gold earrings to knight's chain mail to old books hand-copied by monks. The collection of over 30,000 items from the 3rd to 20th century CE is extensive, making this museum long-winded. If you love Byzantine history, this museum is bound to impress; if not, the museum may be a slight bore—chain mail aside.

☈ MSyntagma. Follow Vas. Sofias. i Photos permitted without flash. ⓒ €4, non EU-students and EU citizens over 65 €2, under 19 and EU students free. ⏲ May-Oct M 1:30-8pm, Tu-Su 8am-8pm; Nov-Apr Tu-Su 8:30am-3pm.

food

SYNTAGMA

▦ PARADOSIAKO
☍✂★ GREEK ➊

Voulis 44 ☎210 321 4121

While many lunch places sit idle with empty chairs, this stop does not lack customers—and for good reason. The Greek salad (€6), though ubiquitous in

Athens (and oddly enough listed on menus as "Greek salad" rather than just... salad), is particularly scrumptious. Mop up the extra olive oil with the hearty, solid bread that comes the seat. Sitting either inside or outside on a quiet side street, meet the wonderful owners—a husband and wife team that has worked here since the restaurant's opening.

🪧 From Syndagma, walk along Filellinon, take a right down Nikodimou. Voulis St. is 3 blocks down. Paradosiako is on your right. $ €5-15 meals. ⏰ Open daily noon-midnight.

CAFE VOULIS 🌱🍸❄ CAFE [1]

Voulis 17 ☎210 32 34 333

Chat over a prosciutto and mozzarella sandwich *(€3.70)* along with some coffee *(€1.50-€3.20)* at this reasonably-priced coffee shop where customers smoke from their metal bar stools and relax for hours on end. Fairly crowded and just a few blocks from Syntagma Square, Cafe Voulis is not gourmet but is very convenient.

🪧 Behind hordes of motorcycles, set back on a corner just off Ermou street. ℹ Delivery available. $ Entrees €6. ⏰ Open M-F 7:30am-9pm, Sa 8am-5pm.

CAFE 21 🌱🍸⛅ CAFE [2]

Voulis 21 ☎210 322 3651

A small space manipulated with mirrors to look larger, Cafe 21 lacks a distinguishable decor. With slightly overpriced orange juices *(€4.50)* and club sandwiches *(€8)*, this cafe isn't the most bang for your buck.

🪧 Head down Voulis from Pl. Syntagma. $ Entrees €7-10. Drinks €4. ⏰ Open M-Sa 8am-8pm.

PETROS GRILL HOUSE 💳🍸 GRILL HOUSE [1]

Kidathineon 28 ☎201 32 46 229

Petros is a great place to grab a chicken or pork gyro *(€2)* for the road. While this restaurant does double as a locals' evening hangout, stick to their lunch menu and ask for the waiter from New York who moved to Greece to turn his life around after losing his job at Lehman Brothers.

🪧 Head 3 blocks down Kidathineon; it's on the right. $ Entrees €12. ⏰ Open daily 9am-2am.

MONO 💳🍸❄ GREEK [3]

Mnisikleous 4 ☎210 32 26 711 🖥www.mono.gr

Ultra-hip and staffed by incredibly friendly waitresses, Mono is not quite as bold as its red-orange paint, but it comes close. Try the "bread with three deeps" *(€7.50)* or tomato balls *(€8)*. Splurge on the salmon cooked in grease-proof paper *(€18)*, and try the orange pie *(€4)*—a cake covered in an orange flavored syrup.

🪧 Along Adrianou. ℹ Salads €6.50 9; seafood €7-15. ⏰ Open Tu-Su noon-midnight.

PLAKA

👍 YIASEMI 🌱♿🍸❄⛅ CAFE [1]

23 Mnisikleous ☎213 04 17 937 🖥www.yiasemi.gr

This cafe belongs by the sea rather than in the heart of Athens. With its adorable daisy-painted tables and stone staircases, it's a shame there's no view to go with this relaxed beach town vibe. The portions are small, but this cafe is better for sitting with a friend and catching up over coffee or tea *(€3.50)*. If hungry, try the lemon pie *(€5)* or meatballs *(€5)* that offer a hearty portion for their price.

🪧 Up the hill past the Roman Agora. To the right down the street with the red track paint and lanes drawn on the ground. $ Coffee €3.50. Entrees €5-10. ⏰ Open daily 10am-2am.

👍 BENETH 🌱♿🍸❄ BAKERY [1]

Adrianou 97 ☎210 32 38 822

If it's your birthday, if you want to pretend it's your birthday, or even if you just want to eat something delicious, go to Beneth. Pastries made on location and baklava that leaves you craving more even after eating your own body weight in these treats are well worth their pricetags *(€2)*. Packaged yogurt and beverages

food . plaka

are sold in a cooler on the left of the shop. Though Beneth offers no seating, try standing at the high metal tables out front.

Striaght down Adrianou. $ Pastries and fresh-baked bread €1-3. Cappuccino €1.50. Open daily 7am-10pm.

fatty yogurt

The majority of Greek food staples are made of veggies and milk products. But a note to the health fanatics: real Greek yogurt has incredibly high fat content and is not the health food mentioned in the United States—but it is still delicious—especially if accompanied by honey. For the diet-conscious, fat-free yogurt is sold in convenience stores and side shops for €2 or less.

SCHOLARHIO OUZERI KOUKLIS TAVERNA 2

Tripodon 14 ☎210 32 42 603 www.scholarhio.gr

This self-proclaimed traditional family restaurant is in actuality the neighborhood's restaurant best adapted to tourism. Waiters sneakily bring out bottled water before you can think to ask for tap and fill your table with platters of small plates whose prices add up quicker than you can eat. Keeping track of the tab aside, the food is pretty good, and green peppers in the Greek salad *(€4)* are a nice touch.

Up the hill past the Roman Agora. Down the street on the right with the red track paint and lanes drawn on the ground. $ Individual dishes €3, meal of two side plates, bread, beverage, and dessert €14. Open daily 11am-2am.

EAT AT MILTON'S FANCY 5

91 Adrianou ☎210 32 49 129 www.eatmiltons.gr

Perfect for the fanciest date of your life, this white-tiled restaurant serves fish so fresh that there's not even a freezer on-site. For those attempting to win over a heart—and willing to have a heart attack when the bill comes—there is a lobster special *(€50 per person)* that will impress the most gourmet of companions. If you're not trying to impress anybody, order one of the few modest options on the menu to save your wallet from extinction. Organic food fans will be pleased to learn that they serve a "BIO" Greek salad (€12) made with fresh local ingredients.

Up the hill past the Roman Agora. Take the street with red track paint and lanes drawn on the ground to the end, and then turn left at the next road. Milton's will be on the opposite corner at the end of the block. $ Salads and soups €9-12. Entrees €25-30. Lobster special €50. Open daily noon-5pm and 7:30pm-midnight.

STAMATOPOULOUS TAVERNA 3

26 Lyssiou ☎210 32 28 722; 210 32 18 549

Classy dining behind ivy-covered walls is executed perfectly at this swanky restaurant. Glasses are set on the table when the restaurant opens, and cloth napkins are folded at each seat—providing a welcome respite from the typical paper napkins found at the bottom of bread baskets. Forget about ice cubes in your white wine; here, glasses and bottles come chilled to help assuage your parched palate. The grilled chicken *(€10)* is juicy and a nice departure from the fried norm of Greek cuisine. Eat late and enjoy live music and dancing that gets started after 10pm.

Up the hill past the Roman Agora. Follow the street with the red track paint and lanes drawn on the ground to the corner. i Live music every night. $ Salads and appetizers €5-10; entrees €15-30. Open daily 6:30pm-1am.

MONASTIRAKI

⚜ MANDRAS
➤⊗♈❄☆ GREEK ❸
Ag. Anarguron 8 and Taki
☎210 32 13 765

Delicious food defines this classy establishment near a large square in the depths of Monastiraki. *Tzatziki* dip comes with olive oil drizzled on top and one regal olive perched in the center of the serving. Those craving a healthy serving of meat should try the lamb *(€16)* or grilled chicken *(€9.50)*.

✢ Ⓜ*Monastiraki. ⓘ Live music nightly after 8pm. ⓢ Appetizers €5; entrees €8-25. ⓩ Open daily 2pm-2am.*

SAVVAS
➤⊗♈☆ TAVERNA ❶
Mitropoleos 86
☎210 32 45 048

These gyros are cheap and delicious, and you'll almost feel like Pavlov's dog after eating your first. The cost of a gyro skyrockets to €8.50 if you eat at the restaurant, so grab a few to go and eat them in Pl. Monastiraki.

✢*Opposite* Ⓜ*Monastiraki. ⓢ Gyros from €1.80. ⓩ Open daily 9am-2am.*

IRIDANOS
➤⊗♈❄ TAVERNA ❷
Adrianou 9
☎210 32 79 678

A standard *taverna* at the base of the Agora, Iridanos serves Greek classics like lamb and potatoes *(€8)* to clients resting in wicker chairs with blue cushions. Steer clear of the fancy beverages—they may cost more than your meal.

✢ *Down Adrianou. ⓢ Entrees €6-12. Mixed drinks from €5. ⓩ Open daily 9am-2am.*

EXARHIA

⚜ BARBA YIANIS
⊛⊗♈❄ TAVERNA ❶
94 Em. Benaki
☎210 38 24 138

This *taverna* has been around for 90 years, and it hasn't lost any of its charm. Pale yellow walls, high ceilings, and a cafeteria-style food selection make this a cozy place to sit and enjoy some classic Greek "homefood," in the words of the manager. Try the beef in small pieces *(€8)*, roast pork in lemon sauce *(€8)*, and the green beans *(€5)*.

✢ *Straignt up Em. Benaki from Panepistimiou by Pl. Syntagma. ⓢ Entrees €5-€12. ⓩ Open M-Sa noon-1am, Su noon-7pm.*

BOE
⊛⊗⟨ᵗ⟩♈❄☆ CAFE ❶
Araxobis 56
☎210 38 35 811

A hipster coffee shop in a hipster area. In a giant corner venue with umbrellas and chairs out front, this cafe stays busy until closing every night. Settle in with a book or laptop and pass the afternoon away in the cool, marble-floored environment, then head outside with friends at night for some cappuccino and conversation. On a budget? Take your beverages to go—Boe, like many restaurants in Athens, has cheaper prices for takeout.

✢ *Opposite Club Creperie Xarchia in Pl. Exarhia. ⓢ Cappuccino freddo €3.80. Fresh orange juice €5, €3 if taken to go. ⓩ Open daily 9am-midnight.*

KAVOURAS
⊛♈❄ SOUVLAKI ❶
64 Themistokleous
☎210 38 38 010

Cheap *souvlaki* and beer in a great location make Kavouras a great spot for a quick lunch or dinner. Add a vegetarian *souvlaki* to any meal for just €0.90. Though variety isn't this place's forte—the menu consists entirely of *souvlaki* varieties—it does this Greek fast food staple well.

✢ *Half a block from the base of Pl. Exharia. ⓢ Souvlaki with meat €1.70; vegetarian €0.90. Beer €1.50-2.50. ⓩ Open daily 11am-3am.*

food . exarhia

CLUB CREPE XARCHIA

⬤♿️🍴❄️🅿️ FAST FOOD ❶

Corner of Ikonomou and M. Themistokleous on Pl. Exarhia ☎210 38 40 773

Delicious crepes right on Pl. Exarhia. Huge salads (€5) come with tons of ingredients, but the food is made to order and not as quick as the self-proclaimed "fast food" moniker would suggest. Fidgety people and late-night eaters beware: seating is on a bit of a slant and you may topple over on accident.

⚑ At the tip of Pl. Exarhia. *i* Food made to order. ⑤ Salads €5. Crepes €3. ⚇ Open daily noon-4am.

BARBARA'S FOOD COMPANY

⬤⊗🍴❄️🅿️ INTERNATIONAL ❸

Em. Benaki 63 ☎210 38 03 004 🖳www.bfoodcompany.gr

Wide, white-painted boards and metallic countertops give this spacious eatery an airy feel. Greek yuppies sit at tables and try the rigatoni with mozzarella (€6), the salmon with ginger and orange (€8.50), and fettuccini with swordfish and tomatoes (€7.50).

⚑ At the tip of Pl. Exarhia. ⑤ Entrees around €8. ⚇ Open M-Sa 12:30pm-12:30am, Su 1-11:30pm.

FASOLI

⬤♿️🍴❄️🅿️ TAVERNA ❷

Em. Benaki 45 ☎210 33 00 010

For food cooked with love and served under an obscene number of uber-hip, steel-encased lightbulbs, come to Fasoli to enjoy modern *taverna* food in their main room, downstairs, and outside. Every day brings new specials, and regulars boast about the great service.

⚑ At the tip of Pl. Exarhia. *i* Specials of the day. Vegetarian options. ⑤ Entrees €3.60-€12. ⚇ Open daily 12:30pm-12:30am.

KOLONAKI

DERLICIOUS

⬤♿️🍴🅿️ FAST FOOD ❶

Tsakalof 14 ☎219 36 30 284 🖳www.derlicious.gr

Delicious and inexpensive souvlaki from a pale blue eatery in the midst of Athens' most froufrou district seems unlikely, but Derlicious is as good as its name is misspelled. Their food is served on trays to the blue-painted, umbrella-covered tables outside. The staff's English is a bit rusty, so it may be best to point to the food you want when ordering.

⚑ Ⓜ Syntagma. Walk up Vas. Sofias to Neofytou Vamva, which turns into Tsakalof. ⑤ Chicken souvlaki €2.45; beef souvlaki €2.70. Beverages €1.20. Beer €1.50. ⚇ Open F-Sa noon-6am, Su-Th noon-4am.

JACKSON HALL

🍴♿️🍴❄️🅿️ AMERICAN ❸

Milioni 4 ☎210 36 16 098

This American-themed restaurant is a haven for tourists seeking a burger, Italian food, or something that comes inside an upside-down plastic baseball hat. Though we will never know whether Jackson Hall's name is a pun or a misspelling of America's wild west, the pricey filets are served in style in an stereotypically American-themed restaurant. Like a classier Hardrock Cafe, this is the antidote to too many meals of *souvlaki*.

⚑ Right off Pl. Kolonaki on Milioni St. ⑤ Missouri fillet €19.70. American chicken €11.20. ⚇ Open daily 10am-2:30am. Kitchen open 1pm-2am.

BIG APPLE

⬤⊗🍴❄️🅿️ RESTAURANT, BAR ❷

Skoufa 69 ☎210 364 3820 🖳www.bigapple.gr

Hip 20-somethings wanting to be 20, 16-year-olds wanting to be 20, and 32-year-olds wanting the same spill onto the street from Big Apple at lunchtime. This hot eatery is equally popular after dark, when it becomes a bar. Chairs are pulled back to open floor space for dancing, and the music that makes barstools rattle during the day is amped up even more at night. Hostesses and customers dress suavely, so don't just mosey in post-Acropolis.

⇥ From Panepistimiou, walk up Omirou to Skoufa. Big Apple will be a few blocks down on the left. $ Spaghetti with chicken €10. Mojitos, daiquiris, and cocktails €12. ⏰ Open in winter daily 9am-5am; in summer M-Th 9am-3am, F-Sa 9am-4am. Kitchen open daily noon-9pm.

PAGRATI

CUCINA POVERA — 💳♿🍸❄ RESTAURANT [5]

Eforionos 13 — ☎210 75 66 088 💻www.cucinapovera.gr

Though this restaurant's name translates to "poor man's kitchen," Cucina Povera is anything but cheap. Its menu is written daily based on market specials, and its sage green walls and pine wood tables create an atmosphere that is both earthy and classy. Some of the dishes are vegetable-based, like the green salad with beet root and warm goat cheese *(€9)*, and others might turn a sensitive stomach, like the assortment of cooked intestines on the menu. Regardless of preference, Cucina Povera is sure to satisfy; be forewarned that these rich panhandlers will take all your spare change and then some.

⇥ Walk east from the Panathenaic Stadium (away from the Acropolis) on Vas. Konstandinou, then turn right on Eratosthenous and left onto Eforionos. i Wine selection tops 350 choices. $ Meals €25, excluding wine. ⏰ Open in summer M-Sa 8pm-midnight; in winter, Tu-Sa 1-5pm.

POSTO CAFE — 🚭♿🍸❄⛱📶 CAFE [1]

Pl. Plastira 2 — ☎210 75 62 379

With red plastic chairs and lots of green plants around the patio area, this super-cheap cafe has a slight Gilligan's Island feel to it. Though they claim to be open 24/7, the cafe is closed for the brief window of 7am-9am on Monday mornings. Otherwise, though, this is a great spot to sit with a cheap *frappe*, crepe, or beer and take advantage of the free Wi-Fi.

⇥ In Pl. Plastira. Look for it behind the green potted plants. i Free Wi-Fi. $ Soda €1. Coffee €2. Orange juice €3. Small draft beer €2, large €3; bottle of beer €2.50. Crepes €2.50. ⏰ Open M midnight-7am and 9am-midnight, Tu-Su 24hr.

COYA — 🚭♿🍸❄⛱ CAFE [1]

Imitou 129 — ☎694 45 95 350

This unspectacular coffee, juice, and drink bar is just one in a row of similar stops. With a bar and wooden decor inside and seating under an extended umbrella across the street, it's a good place to stop if in the neighborhood and in need of an espresso. Otherwise, it's not worth the trek to the ubiquitous wicker seats for another average *frappe* (similar to an iced latte).

⇥ In the midst of a long line of similar cafes down Imitou. $ Coffees €3.50. Juices €4.00. Mixed drinks €6.00. ⏰ Open daily 9am-2am.

nightlife

PLAKA

CHANDELIER PLAKA — 💳🍸⛱ BAR

4 Benizelou — ☎210 331 6330 💻www.chandelier.gr

This quirky, ultra-modern bar is a hotspot Thursday through Saturday but quieter during the week. It serves up a variety of alcoholic concoctions, from standard beverages like strawberry daiquiris *(€9)* and mojitos *(€4.50)* to specialty drinks like the "Green Boy" that mixes cucumbers, lemon, and mustard with alcohol *(€4.50)* and the "Honey Love" that combines banana, lemon, honey, orange, and pineapple with a mixed drink to form a fruity frenzy *(€4.50)*. If alcohol isn't your thing, a plethora of booze-free drinks fill up two whole pages of the establishment's menu.

♯ ⓂSyntagma. Walk down Mitropoleos, take a left onto Evangelistrias after 7 blocks. Chandelier Plaka is 2 blocks down. Ⓢ €4-10. ♻ Open daily 7pm-2am.

BRETTOS
🍷❄ BAR
Kolonaki 41
☎210 33 17 793

In the mood to stomp on some 40-year-old's toes when fighting for a seat? Maybe brush up on someone else's fanny pack or jean shorts? Try Brettos, a bar in the heart of Tourist Land, Athens. With brightly colored bottles illuminating the high ceilings and functional barrels of beer lining the right wall, Brettos looks like fun, but its size and crowds make it almost too jam-packed to enjoy. With no room for dancing, conversation flows as freely as the wine or the ouzo (bottles from €19).

♯ ⓂSyntagma. Walk down Filelinon to Kidathineon. 4 blocks down on the left. Ⓢ Red wine by the glass from €2; ouzo from €2.50. ♻ Open M-F 10am-2am, Sa-Su 10am-3am.

CINE PARIS ROOF GARDEN CINEMA
🍷 OUTDOOR CINEMA
Kyd
☎210 32 22 071 ▪www.cineparis.gr

Want to get drunk and see a movie at the same time? Don't try to sneak that six pack of Natty into the nearby theater. Instead, head to Cine Paris Roof Garden Cinema to booze while you watch films in an ivy-laced rooftop garden in the middle of Plaka. Opened in the '20s by a Greek hairdresser who had lived in Paris, this cinema showcases thrillers like the "King of Mykonos" and recent blockbusters like *Knight and Day*.

♯ ⓂSyntagma. Walk down Filelinon to Kidathineon. 3 blocks down on the right. ⓘ All movies in English subtitled in Greek. Ⓢ €8, students €6. Drinks at the rooftop bar €2-6. ♻ Movies begin daily at 8:45pm.

sleepy syntagma

Syntagma is not known for its nightlife, and aside from the casual bar like **Brettos** (41 Kolonaki, ☎210 32 32 110), not much is happening. At night the square becomes a hangout for teenagers, and clubs are only open during the winter after midnight. A casual beer and walk around the neighborhood are the best bets for staying in Syndagma. Otherwise, venture into a nearby part of the city for some pulsing music.

MONASTIRAKI AND PSIRI

OINOPNEUMATA
🍷❄ BAR
Miaouli 21
☎210 32 39 370

Located on a street that is almost exclusively bars, Oinopneumata is the most crowded. Filled with teenagers unabashedly making out and others actively disputing the rules of soccer, this is a great place to come for some beers (from €4) in an unadorned, raucous environment.

♯From ⓂMonastiraki, cross Ermou street and walk down Miaouli 2 blocks. Ⓢ Beer €4-5.50. Rakomelo €8 for 8 shots. Shisha €10. ♻ Open daily 6pm-2am.

PSIRA
🍷❄ BAR
Miaouli 19
☎210 32 44 046

Order some *rakomelo*, Greece's local alcohol sweetened with honey, for €8 at this bar serviced by a friendly staff. Enjoy a slight breeze and good company in the outdoor seating, or head inside for a lively conversation.

✈ From Ⓜ Monastiraki, cross Ermou street and walk down Miaouli 2 blocks. ⑤ Beer €4. Ouzo €7. Rakomelo €8. ☪ Open M-Th noon-2am, F-Sa noon-4am, Su noon-3am.

KAZOZA
               ●⑤👍☕☼🍸 BAR
Miaouli 13   ☎210 32 16 469

The actual countertop to this bar is around the corner from Miaouli street in a hole in the wall, and customers only set foot inside to search for the bathroom. Most just sit down at a table outside along Miaouli proper and wait for the waiter to come take their order. With just plain chairs and tables and no real decoration, enjoy the free peanuts—what else do you need with your beer?

✈ From Ⓜ Monastiraki, cross Ermou street and walk down Miaouli 2 blocks. ⑤Beer €4-5. Wine €6. Ouzo €7. Honey and wine €12 per ½L. Shisha €10. ☪ Open daily 7:30pm-4am.

STYLE CAFE
               ●⊗👍☕☼🍸 BAR
Ag. Anargyron 12   ☎210 32 50373

As the revelers of Miaouliu St. aged they moved down the road to Style Cafe, where most of the crowd has passed 30 and wear a suit. Votive candles burn on the bar, and beer *(€5-6)* is more expensive than anywhere else in Psiri nightlife. Music blares to the hindrance of conversation, and the manager is less than friendly. Come here as a last resort.

✈From Ⓜ Monastiraki, cross Ermou street and walk down Miaouli 2 blocks; Style Cafe is 3 blocks down Ag. Anargyron. ⑤ Beer €5-€6. Whisky €8. ☪ Open daily 7am-2am.

EXARHIA

TRAIN CAFE
            ●⊗👍☼ CAFE, BAR
Em. Benaki 72   ☎210 38 44 355

A train carved into a slab of wood and painted with red and blue paint gives this well-lit wood bar its name. Though customers are sparse in the summer, crowds come in the wintertime to try the *psimeni raki (€4)*, a cocktail made of raki, honey, sugar, and herbs.

✈ Ⓜ Syntagma. Follow Panepistimiou to Em. Benaki. ⑤ Beer €3. Psimeni raki €4. ☪ Open daily 10am-3am.

UNDERGROUND
               ●⑤👍☕☼🍸 BAR
Metaxa 21   ☎210 38 22 019

If this bar could make a noise, it would be a gruff and sustained "grrr!" Black decor and bartenders wearing headbands and piercings give this bar a slight punk feel, and alternative music gives this place a truly underground feel.

✈ Ⓜ Syntagma. Follow Panepistimiou to Em. Benaki. Follow that for a few blocks, and take a left onto Andrea Metaxa. Underground is half a block down on the left side of the street. Look for the glass panel with the doorknob. ⑤ Draft beer €4. Special cocktails €7. ☪ Open M-Th 10am-2am, F-Sa 10am-4am, Su 10am-2am.

KOLONAKI

▨ SHOWROOM
             ✒👍☼ BAR
12 Milioni and 4 Iraklitou   ☎210 36 46 460 🖥 www.showroomcafe.gr

Settle into a comfortable white leather barstool at this local hangout not yet discovered by tourists. Although it's not cheap, Showroom is worth the splurge. As evidenced by the pineapple and bananas in the silver bowl prominently on display at the bar, its drinks are all made with fresh fruit. Soft, bongo-like background music gives the bar a relaxed feel, so order a drink and stay for a while.

✈ Ⓜ Syntagma. Follow Vas. Sofias past the Parliament Building to Sekeri. Take a left onto Sekeri and then a right onto Konstantinou Kanari. Milioni is one block down on the left side of the street. ⑤ Beer €7. Mixed drinks €12. ☪ Open daily 8am-2am.

TRIBECA 🍴♿🍸❄☁ BAR

Skoufa 46 ☎210 36 23 541

Hunter green walls and dark wood line this bar geared toward an older crew. Few under 30 can be seen at Tribeca, where most of the customers are graying. Dancing isn't the MO for this mature crew, but settle in at a standard outdoor table for a ginger mango daiquiri *(€9.50)* for a palette-confusing experience.

➡ [M]Syntagma. Follow Panepistimiou to Omirou. Turn left on Skoufa. $ Cocktails €9.50. ⏰ M-Sa 9:30am-3am, Su 10am-2am.

PASSEPARTOUT 🎟♿🍸❄☁ BAR

Skoufa 47-49 ☎210 36 45 546 💻www.passepartoucafe.com

Swanky, aesthetically pleasing, and easy to find, this bar was decorated with care. Honeycomb-shaped mirrors tile an expansive wall, and round lights hang from the high ceilings above the many barstools and tables decked out in candles. The clientele comes mainly from the surrounding neighborhood and includes few tourists, but some travelers filter in during the summer. Though customers keep it mellow during the week, weekend nights are danced away, sometimes with the help of a DJ.

➡ [M]Syntagma. Follow Panepistimiou to Omirou. Take that right and follow it for a few blocks. Turn right onto Skoufa. $ Beer €6. Martinis and cocktails €12. ⏰ Open M-Th 10am-2am, F-Sa 10am-4am, Su 10am-2am.

MAI-TAI 🍴♿🍸❄☁ BAR

Ploutarchou 18 and Kolonaki ☎210 72 58 306 💻www.mai-tai.gr

Inexplicably, this shabby bar is immensely popular with locals—so much so that elbow room is hard to come by on a Tuesday night. Smoky air masks a less-than-exciting wood paneling, but bright lights showcase the attractive 30+ crowd. Fight your way through the door to mix and mingle with the ritzy Kolonaki crowd any day of the week.

➡ [M]Syntagma. Follow Vas. Sofias past the Parliament Building to Ploutarchou, and take a left; Mai-Tai is a few blocks down on the right. $ Beers €5-7. Strawberry daiquiris €12. ⏰ Open daily 8am-2am.

THE DAILY CAFE 🍴🚫🍸❄☁ BAR

Xenokratous 47 ☎210 72 23 430

For a relaxed evening with a beer in front of a TV, settle in at the Daily Cafe, which serves mainly local old fogies who come out to watch the night's game. Decor is bland aside from the enlarged photo of a man in a jacuzzi on the inside wall, but the bartender is friendly and the atmosphere low-key.

➡ [M]Syntagma. Follow Vas. Sofias past the Parliament Building to Ploutarchou. Take a left and follow Ploutarchou to Xenokratous. The Daily Cafe is a long block down on the right. ℹ Outside tables are on a slant, so take a sip of your drink before putting it on the table. $ Beer €5. Mojitos €10. ⏰ Open M-F 8am-3am, Sa-Su 9am-3am.

arts and culture

FESTIVALS

ATHENS FESTIVAL 🎟🚫☁

Panepistimiou 39 ☎210 32 72 000 💻www.greekfestival.gr

Also known as the Hellenic Festival, this outpouring of the arts takes place from early June-July in a number of venues throughout Athens. Ranging from classical music concerts and dance recitals to plays and concerts by modern artists like Rufus Wainwright (of *Shrek* "Hallelujah" fame), performances are not so much insights into Athenian culture or tradition as a promise of a fun summer night in a beautiful city.

➜ To get to the box office from [M]Syntagma, follow Filelinon in the direction of traffic for two blocks to Nikodimou, which turns into Flessa. Make a slight right onto Kiristou; take Kiristou to Mnissikleous, and follow Mnissikleous to the end. ℹ See website for annual list of performances. $ Tickets from €15-50. ⏰ Open daily 9am-2pm and 6-9pm.

REVOLUTION DAYS

These holidays celebrate two battles that were monumental to Greek independence: the March 25, 1821 victory over the Ottoman Empire and the October 28, 1940 pronouncement by Metaxas that Mussolini may not occupy Greece. As with all Greek festivals, revelry ensues, including drinking, eating, dancing, and general merriment.

VIRGIN MARY DAY

Virgin Mary Day is actually a three-day-long festival beginning on August 15, the day Greeks celebrate the birth of Mary. With free foods, orchestras, dancing, partying and other things the Virgin Mary probably didn't partake in too much during her time, the Greeks enjoy themselves during this 72hr. holiday.

shopping

Athens' shopping can be divided into three categories: the touristy, the everyday necessities, and the posh. Shopping for tourist memorabilia is best done in the **Athens Flea Market,** located directly to the right of **[M]Monastiraki,** or in **Plaka** along Kydathineon. Amongst the *tavernas* there are a shocking number of shops selling exactly the same cotton dresses, keychains, magnets, packaged soaps, and T-shirts that will make great gifts for Aunt Darlene and Uncle Jim. For the everyday non-Greece specific shopping, head to **Ermou street.** Follow it from **Pl. Syntagma** down to **Pl. Monastiraki** and pass staples like H and M and Sephora, in addition to their Greek equivalents. This area is where most Athenian teenagers buy their wardrobes, and it's the place to look for that last-minute pair of shorts or bathing suit. The **posh shopping** is in **Kolonaki,** along **Tsakalof Street** or any street branching off of Panepistimiou up toward Pl. Kolonaki. Foreign designers from Theory to Lacoste to Longchamp have their stores here.

OUTDOOR MARKETS

👍 FISH AND MEAT MARKET — 🚫💳 🚫♿ 🍸 ⛅ SYNTAGMA

On Athinas between Armoudiou and Aristogeitonos

Squeamish beware: this place is not for the soft-hearted or for people who coo over pictures of kittens. Carcasses swing from behind glass encasements, and the thwack of butchers chopping their meat echoes through the concrete enclosure. Men in bloody aprons parade around as whole lambs stare with vacant eyes. The fish market smells horrendous but is a bit tamer.

➜ From [M]Syntagma, walk down Ermou street and turn left on Athinas. ⏰ Open daily 4am-6pm.

VARNAKIOS — 🚫💳 🚫♿ ⛅ SYNTAGMA

On Athinas between Armoudiou and Aristogeitonos

Like a supermarket with one aisle and a rougher crowd of check-out people, Varnakios has everything needed to stock an Athenian kitchen or cook a fresh meal. In fact, make it your one-stop shop for finding the makings of a fresh Greek meal. On the right side of this side-street-turned-grocery-store are tables invisible beneath cartons of tomatoes, cucumbers, peaches, cherries, and other varieties of fresh produce. On the left side of the "aisle" are shops with pre-packaged edibles and soaps as well as eggs and dairy.

🍴 Ⓜ*Syntagma. Walk down Ermou and turn left onto Athinas.* 💰 *Produce €1-3; shop prices vary.* 🕐 *Open M-Th 6am-7pm, F-Sa 5am-8pm.*

FLEA MARKET

⊛⊗⚘ MONASTIRAKI

Trinkets, knock-offs, and pottery form most of the main straightaway that is geared explicitly toward foreign tourists. In order to get the best deal, make sure to haggle with the vendors for your goods. As the market spreads into other alleyways, the merchandise becomes less touristy and more practical. Check out the antiques bazaar on Avyssinias St., where crowds of people try to find a diamond in the rough.

🍴 *Adjacent to Pl. Monastiraki.* 🕐 *Open M 8am-8pm, W 8am-8pm, Sa-Su 8am-8pm.*

essentials

PRACTICALITIES

Greece has had its fair share of economic strife lately, but aside from the weekly strikes, the city goes on buzzing as usual. Don't worry that you will step off the plane into an apocalyptic city: you won't. But one part of Athens is hellish, and that's the **sun**; don't underestimate its power. Carrying around a **water bottle** is something that locals, not only travelers, do. Everyone wears sunglasses—even in the shade—out of habit. Those not used to the bright lights of Greece should load up on some SPF in the morning, or you'll look like a beet next to the cool white marble of the Parthenon. **Comfortable shoes** are a must, but steer clear of the "I *am* a tourist" variety of Reeboks, which function as "steal from me" post-it notes on your traveling body. Besides some church conventions, there are no culturally mandated restrictions on what women may wear, so dress appropriately for the temperature. Athenians are friendly for the most part, so when in doubt, ask for directions—chances are they will point you toward **P. Syntagma** if you are looking for transportation. **Food** sold right by attractions is significantly more expensive than that sold in the back streets, so walk a few blocks away from the ticket booth before settling down for some fresh tomatoes and feta. Most important advice: think about the history. Amazing things happened where you stand right now.

- **TOURIST OFFICES:** The Information Office travel brochures are helpful and their **Athens map** indispensable. Ask for the lists of museums, embassies, and banks. Most up-to-date bus, train, and ferry schedules and prices also available. *(Amalias 26 ☎210 33 10 392* 🖥*www.visitgreece.gr* 🕐 *Open M-F 9am-7pm, Sa-Su 10am-4pm.)*

- **BUDGET TRAVEL OFFICES:** **Academy Travel** specializes in custom island-hopping routes. *(Iperidou 3 ☎210 32 45 071* 🖥*www.academytravelgreece.com* 🕐 *Open daily 9am-10pm.)* **STA Travel.** *(Voulis 43 ☎210 32 11 88* 🖥*www.e-travelshop. gr* 🕐 *Open M-F 9am-5pm, Sa 10am-2pm.)* **Adrianos Travel, Ltd.** *(Pandrossou 28 ☎210 32 20 702* 🖥*www.ticketgreece.gr* 🕐 *Open daily 9am-6pm.)* **Meliton Travel.** *(23b Apolonos ☎210 32 47235* 🖥*www.melitontravel.gr* 🕐 *Open summer M-F 9am-6pm, Sa 10am-2pm; winter M-F 9am-5pm.)*

- **CURRENCY EXCHANGE:** **National Bank**, Karageorgi Servias 2, in Pl. Syndagma. *(☎21033 40 500* 🕐 *Open M-Th 8am-2:30pm, F 8am-2pm.)* **Citibank**, the post office, some hotels, and other banks offer currency exchange. Commission is usually around 5%.

- **LUGGAGE STORAGE: Pacific Ltd.** is in El. Venizelos Airport's arrivals terminal, across from the large cafe. *(☎210 35 30 160 🖥www.pacifictravel.gr $ €2 per day. €30 per month. ⏰ Open 24hr.)* Main branch at 26 Nikis in Syndagma. *(☎210 32 41 007 $ €2 per day, €30 per month. ⏰ Open M-F 9am-6pm.)* Many **hotels** have free or inexpensive luggage storage. Lockers are also available at [M]Monastiraki, [M]Piraeus, and [M]Omonia.

- **LAUNDROMATS:** Most *plintirias* (launderers) have signs reading "Laundry." **National.** *(Apolonos 17 in Syntagma ☎210 32 32 226 🖥www.nationaldrycleaners.gr $ Wash, dry, and fold €4.50 per kg., min. 2 kg. Dry cleaning: men's shirt €3, dress pants €5. ⏰ Open M 8am-5pm, Tu 8am-8pm, W 8am-5pm, Th-F 8am-8pm.)* **Zenith.** *(Apolonos 12 and Pendelis 1 ☎210 32 38 533 $ Wash, dry, and fold €4 per kg. ⏰ Open M 8am-4pm, Tu 8am-8pm, W 8am-4pm, Th-F 8am-8pm.)*

- **INTERNET ACCESS:** Free Wi-Fi is now available through the athenswifi network in **Pl. Syntagma**, **Pl. Kotzia**, and **Thissio**. Athens also teems with Internet cafes. Expect to pay €3-6 per hr. **Bits and Bytes,** Kapnikareas 19 in Plaka *(☎210 32 53 142)* and Akadamias 78 in Exharia *(☎210 52 27 717)*, is the mother of new-age internet cafes with fast connections, and 2 floors with A/C and Internet 24hr. (*🖥www.bnb.gr* ***i*** *Cash only.* $ €2.50 per hr. min. charge €2 for 30min. ISIC cardholders €1.80 per hr. Black-and-white printing €0.30 per page; color €0.50 per page. ⏰ *Open 24hr.)* **Lobby Internet Cafe** is mainly a cafe with a few computers and a printer. *(Imittou 113 by Pl. Pangratiou, in Pagrati. ☎210 70 14 607 $ Internet €4 per hr. Printing €0.25 per page. ⏰ Open daily 9am-1am.)* **Quicknet Cafe** is extremely fancy with new flatscreen PCs, fast connections, espresso, and comfortable swivel chairs. *(Clathstonos 4 , just off Patission, in Exaria. ☎210 38 03 771 $ Internet €2.50 per hr. ⏰ Open 24 hr.)* **Arcade** has lots of computer services. (*5 Stadiou ☎210 32 21 808 $ Internet €1.80 for first 30min., every additional 10min. €0.60 . Printing black-and-white €0.30, color €0.60-€1.50. Scanning €1. ⏰ Open M-F 9am-11pm, Sa 10am-10pm, Su noon-8pm.)*

- **POST OFFICES:** For customer service inquiries call the **Greek National Post Office** (ELTA) *(☎210 32 43 311)*. For shipping abroad, try parcel post at the Syntagma ELTA branch at Mitropoleos 60 *(☎210 32 42 489 $ Stamps for postcards and letters up to 20g. €0.72, plus €3.22 for registered mail and €2.90 for express. ⏰ Open M-F 7:30am-8pm).* **Acropolis/Plaka** branch exchanges currency and accepts Poste Restante. Sends packages up to 2kg abroad. *(☎210 92 18 076 ⏰ Open M-F 7:30am-6pm.)* **Exharia** branch, at the corner of Zaimi and K. Deligiani, exchanges currency and accepts Poste Restante. *(⏰ Open M-F 7:30am-2pm.)* **Omonia** distributes stamps 24hr. and accepts Poste Restante and parcels up to 2kg to ship abroad. *(Aiolou 100 ☎210 32 53 586* ***i*** *Credit card required. ⏰ Open M-F 7:30am-8pm, Sa 7:30am-2pm.)* **Syntagma** branch is on the corner of Mitropoleos. Sells stamps, exchanges currency, and accepts Poste Restante *(☎210 33 19 500).*

- **POSTAL CODES: Acroplis and Plaka:** 11702. **Exharia:** 10022. **Omonia and Syntagma:** 10300.

EMERGENCY!

- **EMERGENCY:** ☎112. **Ambulance:** *☎106.* **SOS Doctors:** *☎1016.* **Poison Control:** *☎210 77 93 777.* **AIDS Help Line:** *☎210 72 22 222.* For medical information in Greek and English *(☎210 89 83 146).*

- **TOURIST POLICE: Airport Police** *(☎210 35 36 899).* **Athens Tourist Police** Station at 43-45 Veikou Str, Koukaki *(☎210 92 00 724).* **Athens Police Headquarters** 173, Alexandras Avenue *(☎100 on local phones, 210 64 76 000).*

- **LATE-NIGHT PHARMACIES:** Marked by a green cross. About 1 every 4 blocks is open 24hr.; they rotate. Once a pharmacy closes, it will list on its door the nearest ones that are open 24hr.

- **HOSPITALS:** Emergency hospitals or clinics on duty can be reached at ☎106. **KAT** (Nikis 2 ☎210 62 80 000) is located between Marousi and Kifisia. **Geniko Kratiko Nosokomio** is a public State Hospital at Mesogion 154 (☎210 77 78 901). State hospital **Aeginitio** (Vas. Sofias 72 ☎210 72 20 811) and (Vas. Sofias 80 ☎210 77 70 501) is closer to Athens' center. Near Kolonaki is the public hospital **Evangelismos** (Ypsilantou 45-47 ☎210 20 41 000).

GETTING THERE

By Air

Greece's international airport, **Eleftherios Venizelos** (ATH) (☎210 35 30 000 ■www.aia. gr), has 1 massive but navigable terminal. Arrivals are on the ground fl. **Metro Line 3** (blue) connects the airport to Ⓜ Syntagma in the Athens city center (Ⓢ €6). **Suburban Rail**, which serves the airport and runs along the Attiki Odos highway, connects with **Line 1** (green) at Ⓜ Neratziotissa and with the blue line at Ⓜ Doukissis Plakentias—the most central stations in Omonia and Syntagma, respectively (⚂ About 30min.). To get from **Plateia Syntagma** in the city center to the airport, take the X95 bus (Ⓢ €3.20. ⚂ 45min.-1hr. depending on traffic, every 10-15min.), which runs 24hr. Pick it up on Othonos near the top right corner of Pl. Syntagma. From Ⓜ **Ethniki Amyna**, take the X94 (Ⓢ €6, students €3. ⚂ Every 15min. 7:20am-8:40pm) or the X95, and from Ⓜ **Dafni** take the X97 (Ⓢ €6, students €3. ⚂ Every 30-60min.). From **Piraeus**, take the X96. (Ⓢ €6, students €3. ⚂ Every 20-25min.) Catch the bus in Pl. Karaiskaki on the waterfront, on Akti Tzelepi, across from Philippis Tours. From **Kifisia**, catch the X92 from Pl. Platanos. (Ⓢ €6, students €3. ⚂ Every 45min.-1hr.) If your travels have taken you to **Kifisos Intercity Bus Station**, take the X93. (Ⓢ €6, students €3. ⚂ Every 20-45min.) **KTEL** regional bus lines serve the airport as well. From **Rafinam**, a bus (Ⓢ €3) leaves every 30min. from the stop midway up the ramp from the waterfront, and stops at **Loutsa** (Artemis) along the way. Buses drop off at the 1 or the 4 departure entrances and wait outside the 5 arrival exits. You can catch the bus from Lavrio at Keratea, Kalivia Thorikou, and Markopoulo as well.

There are a number of ways to get from the airport to the center of town. From the **airport**, take the **X95 bus**. (Ⓢ €3. ⚂ 40-70 min., every 15min.) Bus tickets can be bought right outside the exit near baggage claim. The blue Metro line, **line 3**, is fast, clean, and also runs from the airport to Pl. Syndagma. (Ⓢ €6.) Signs for the metro are clearly marked by baggage claim. When in doubt, ask the **information booth** how to get to Syndagma and they will point you on the right path. Make sure to exchange a bit of currency to buy your bus or metro ticket to Syndagma. **Cabs** are also available, but they cost upwards of €40 and come with a €3.40 airport surcharge and additional baggage fees (Ⓢ €0.35 per bag). If sticking to a budget, the bus or the metro is the way to go.

By Train

Hellenic Railways (OSE) (Sina 6 ☎210 52 97 777 ■www. ose.gr). Contact the railway offices to confirm schedules before your trip. **Larisis Station** has trains that go to Northern Greece (☎210 52 98 829). Take trolley #1 from El. Venizelou (Panepistimou) in Pl. Syntagma (⚂ Every 10min. 5am-midnight) or take the metro to Sepolia. Trains depart for **Thessaloniki** (Ⓢ €14. ⚂ 7hr., 5 per day). To get to **Bratislava, Bucharest, Budapest, Istanbul, Prague, Sofia,** and other international destinations, take a train from Larisis Station to Thessaloniki and change there. **Peloponnese Train Station** has trains to **Albania, Bulgaria,** and **Turkey.** Ticket office open daily 5:45am-9pm. From Diligani, easiest entry is through Larisis Station; exit to your right and go over the footbridge. From El. Venizelou (Panepistimiou) in Syntagma, take blue bus #057 (Ⓢ €0.45. ⚂ Every 15min., 5am-11:30pm) to Nafplion (Ⓢ €5. ⚂ 3hr., 2 per day) and Patra (Ⓢ €5.30. ⚂ 4hr., 3 per day).

By Bus

Athens has 4 bus terminals, two of which serve the regional bus line and two of which serve the suburban bus lines. Check regional schedules *(☎210 51 14 505)* or suburban schedules *(🖳www.ktelattikis.gr)*.

Terminal A is located at Kifissou 100 *(☎210 51 24 910)*. Take blue bus #051 *($ €1. ⏰ Every 15min. 5am-midnight)* from the corner of Zinonos and Menandrou near Pl. Omonia. Don't mistake the private travel agency at Terminal A for an information booth. Buses from here run to various regional destinations; ask at information booth for schedule.

Terminal B is at Liossion 260 *(☎210 83 17 153)*. Take blue bus #024 from Pl. Syntagma on the National Garden side of Amalias, or from Panepistimiou *($ €1. ⏰ 45min., every 20min. 5:10am-11:40pm)*. Buses to Delphi leave from here.

Mavromateon 29 is in Exharia *(☎210 82 10 872)*. Walk up Patission from the National Archaeological Museum and turn right onto Enianos 9 Alexandras Av.; it's on the corner of Areos Park. Take trolley #2, 5, 9, 11, or 18. Buses from this stop go to the Rafina ferry stop, the Sounion Peninsula via Coast Road or Lavvio. Tickets are sold at two stands 50m apart.

Plateia Eleftherias has probably the fewest buses that will be of use to tourists. To get here from Pl. Syntagma, go west on Ermou, turn right onto Athinas, turn left onto Evripidou, and walk to the end of the street. From here, buses A16 or B16 will take you to Daphni Monastery and Eleusis *($ €1. ⏰ 10-20min., 5am-11pm)*.

By Ferry

Check schedules at the tourist office, in the Athens News, with the Port Authority of Piraeus, *(☎210 42 26 000; 210 41 47 800)*, over the phone *(☎185 from within Athens only)*, or at any travel agency. Most ferries dock at Piraeus; others stop at nearby Rafina. Ferry schedules are not regular and are formed at the beginning of each week, so checking ahead is very important.

Piraeus

Take the M1 (green) south to its terminus, or take bus #040 from Filellinon and Mitropoleos right off Pl. Syntagma. *(⏰ Every 15min.)* Ferries from Piraeus run to Tinos, Mykonos, Pyros, Naxos, Ios, Santorini, and Milos.

Rafina

From Athens, buses leave for Rafina from Mavromateon 29, 2 blocks up along Areos Park or a 15min. walk from Pl. Syntagma. *($ €2. ⏰ 1hr., every 30min. 5:40am-10:30pm.)* Ferries from here head to Andros, Mykonos, Naxos, Pyros, and Tinos. Flying Dolphoins sail to Andros, Mykonos, Naxos, Pyros, and Tinos.

GETTING AROUND

Buy **yellow tickets** at most **street kiosks** and validate them yourself at the purple machine on buses, trolleys, trams, and metros *($ €1. ⏰ 1½hr. of use)*. For those who plan to use public transportation frequently should opt for a 24hr. ticket *($ €3)*. which grants unlimited travel on city bus, trolley, tram, and metro after its validation. A weekly card *($ €10)* is also available. Hold on to your ticket: if you drop it or don't validate it, you can be **fined** up to €72 on the spot by police. Getting caught might not seem likely, but it's not worth the risk. As a general note, be wary of **public transit strikes**. If there is a general strike, chances are that **taxis** are still running, so even though the price will be far higher, you can get where you need to go.

By Metro

Most of the Athens **metro** *(⏰ M-Th 5:30am-midnight, F-Sa 5:30am-2am, Su 5:30am-midnight)* was rebuilt for the 2004 Olympics. It consists of three lines. **Metro Line 1** is green and runs from northern **Kifisia** to the port of **Piraeus,** connecting to **Suburban Rail** at **Neratziotissa. Metro Line 2** is red and currently runs from **Ag. Antonios** to **Ag. Dimitrios,** eventually continuing to **Anthoupoli** and **Helliniko** toward the **Saronic Gulf. Metro Line 3** is blue and now runs from **Egaleo,** west of the city center, to **Doukissis Plakentias,** where it intersects the Suburban Rail and the **airport.** After renovations it will continue northwest to **Haidari,** and ultimately may be extended to **Port Zea** in Piraeus. A new metro line is planned to run from **Alsos Veikou** to **Maroussi,** looping across both the red and blue lines.

By Foot

Aside from the heat, Athens is also a pedestrian-friendly city. Base your directions from central **Syntagma Square** and you'll be able to navigate almost anywhere in the city from this central location.

By Bus

Yellow **KTEL** buses leave from **Terminals A and B, Mvromateon 29,** and **Pl. Eleftherias,** and travel all over the Attic peninsula. Check schedules at Terminal A *(☎210 51 24 910 ⏰ M-Sa 5am-11:30pm, Su 5:30am-11:30pm)* or B. *(☎210 83 17 153 ⏰ M-Sa 5am-11:30pm, Su 5:30am-11:30pm.)* Certain buses like the **X95** from **Syntagma** to **El. Venizelou airport,** the **X96** from **Piraeus** to **El. Venizelou airport,** and **#40** from **Piraeus** to **Syntagma** run 24hr. Buy KTEL bus tickets on board or in the terminal. The other buses frequently visible around Athens and its suburbs are blue, designated by 3-digit numbers. Both are good for travel throughout the city and ideal for daytrips to **Daphni** and **Kesariani,** the northern suburbs, **Glyfada** and the coast, and other destinations in the greater Athens area. The Metro stations' and tourist offices' maps of Athens label all of the most frequented routes.

By Trolley

Yellow trolleys *($ €1. ⏰ M-Sa 5am-midnight, Su 5:30am-midnight)* can be differentiated from buses by their electrical antennae. Service is frequent and convenient for short hops within town. See the detailed Metro and tourist office map for routes and stops.

By Taxi

Meter rates start at €1.10, with an additional €0.60 per km within city limits and €1.10 outside city limits; min. fare €2.80. From midnight-5am everything beyond the start price is €1.10 per km. There's a €3.40 surcharge for trips from the airport, and a €0.95 surcharge for trips from port, bus, and railway terminals. Max 20min. waiting time would cost €9.60. Add €0.35 extra for each piece of luggage over 10kg. Pay what the meter shows, rounding it up to the next €0.20 for a tip. Hail your taxi by shouting the destination, not the street address (e.g. "Pangrati"). The driver will pick you up if he feels like heading that way. Get in the cab and tell the driver the exact address or site. Many drivers don't speak English, so write your destination down (in Greek if possible) and be prepared to try to type the address into the GPS system yourself. Include the area of the city, since streets in different parts of the city may share the same name. It's common to ride with other passengers going in the same direction. Schedule a pickup with Radio Taxi *($ €3-5 additional charge;* **Acropolis** *☎210 86 95 000 or 210 86 68 692;* **Ikaros** *☎210 51 52 800;* **Ermis** *☎210 41 15 200;* **Kosmost** *☎210 52 18 300).*

athens 101

HISTORY

Founding Feud

Legend has it that both **Athena** and **Poseidon** had their hearts set on naming Athens and bribed its residents in hopes of winning their favor. Poseidon struck the ground with his trident, producing a saltwater spring, while Athena planted the **first olive tree**. Ancient inhabitants, deciding that Athens rolled off the tongue more easily than Poseidonia, made their decision. Thousands of years and millions of delicious olives later, few Athenians seem to regret their choice.

A Long, Long Time Ago...

Athens' history begins more than 6000 years ago, when settlers decided that the **Acropolis** (literally "high city") would be the perfect spot for a hill fort. Athens has been continuously inhabited ever since, making it one of the oldest cities in Europe. By the eighth century BCE, the king of Athens, with the help of **archons** and a **polemarch** (city officials), had brought nearby towns under Athenian control.

Big Ideas

Athens soon decided that monarchies were "so 7th-century BCE," and appointed **Solon** to draft a new constitution. Solon forbade the enslavement of citizens, increased trade, and extended voting rights to the lower classes. Although **democracy** was born, it was crushed only 20 years later by a violent uprising. However, the seeds of democratic rule were sown, and by the fifth century BCE Athens had entered a **Golden Age** of democracy, philosophy, and art. Greek theater flourished under playwrights like Sophocles, Aeschylus, Aristophanes, and Euripides, although Greeks seemed to have some lingering mommy issues—*Medea* and *Oedipus Rex*, anyone? Philosophers like Socrates, Plato, and Aristotle had some excellent ideas, including **formal logic** and the **scientific method.** (They also had a few not-so-bright ideas: Aristotle believed that men had more teeth than women).

Collide and Conquer

Brilliant art and philosophy, however, were little defense from military attack. In 431 BCE, Athenians made the poor choice to go to war with Sparta, and the **Peloponnesian War** began. The pen proved not quite as mighty as the sword, and Sparta (six-pack abs included) defeated Athens in 404 BCE. The next century was little better. In 338 BCE, Athens became the latest victim of Alexander the Great's conquering spree. The second century BCE marked the beginning of five centuries of **Roman rule**, during which Athens remained a center of teaching and knowledge.

More Rulers, More Problems

In 529 CE, the Byzantine emperor **Justinian** decided that the pagan teachings of the Greeks were at odds with Christianity, and that the Parthenon would make an awesome church. Athens suffered repeated raids and fell into ruin, and 500 years passed before restoration began at the order of Byzantine Emperor Basil II. But prosperity was short-lived, and the **Fourth Crusade** overcame Athens in 1204 CE. The Ottoman Turks were next in line, converting the Parthenon into a mosque when they took power in 1458 CE, beginning 400 years of rule.

No Time Like the Present

Athens returned to Greek rule and was restored as the capital of Greece in 1832. Modern restoration began, and the population skyrocketed from 4000 to over half a million in less than a century. The mid-20th century brought German occupation during WWII and bloody civil war. Greece joined the **European Union** in 1981, but the ancient city soon fell victim to modern problems: gridlock and smog choked the metropolis, and air pollution proved even more effective than the Spartans at destroying millennia-old monuments. Recently, preparations for the **2004 Olympic Games**, including infrastructure improvements, a new airport, and a sleek new transportation system brought Athens into its own as a modern city.

CUSTOMS AND ETIQUETTE

Invitation Explanation

Don't know anyone in Greece? Don't worry. Greek culture puts a high value on warmth and hospitality. Don't be surprised if you wind up with multiple invitations to chat over lunch at a local cafe or join a family for a home-cooked meal. If you're invited out for dinner or a drink, keep in mind that the host usually pays the bill. If you are lucky enough to land an invitation to a Greek home, be prepared for VIP treatment! Arriving 30 minutes late is considered punctual, and it is customary to bring a small gift, like flowers or chocolate. Perplexed by an invitation to a "name-day" party? Greeks tend not to celebrate birthdays, but rather "namedays," the birth date of their namesake saint. Take note: gifts are expected–and don't forget a funny nameday card!

Mind Your Manners

Meals are a terrific time to socialize, gossip, and get to know the city better. Thank the giver by saying *yamas*, "cheers." Table manners are simple: allow your host to seat you, and wait to eat until the host starts. Bring a healthy appetite—finishing everything on your plate and accepting a second helping is considered a compliment to the host. Expect lively conversation, and feel free to offer a toast of *stinygiausou*, ("to your health"). At restaurants, a tip is sometimes included in the bill, but it is common to tip 10-15% for good service.

Godly Garments

Sightseers are welcome to visit Greek Orthodox churches, but conservative dress is expected, so leave your beachwear behind. For both men and women, this means covering up from shoulders to knees. Respect worshippers by refraining from photography and other disruptive behaviors.

Don't Ruin the Ruins

Inanimate objects deserve respect too: observe posted signs and avoid touching monuments so that visitors can appreciate the sights for another few thousand years. Found a broken shard of marble that bears a striking resemblance to Socrates? Leave him in his homeland for other visitors to enjoy—taking anything from historical or archaeological sights is not only disrespectful, it is grounds for arrest.

ART AND ARCHITECTURE

Geometric Period (1050-700 BCE)

Urn Your Stripes

Urn-lovers, rejoice! Emerging from the Dark Ages, Athens became the capital of a new ceramic art form during the Protogeometric Period (1050-900 BCE). Deciding that functional pottery would benefit from a little bit of sprucing up, craftsmen began adorning their wares with decorative **zigzags**, **arcs**, and **concentric circles**. During the eighth and ninth centuries BCE, painters began to depict little rows of marching geese, horses, and goats on parade among increasingly ornate geometric bands. Huge ceramic grave markers called **funeral amphora**, measuring up to six feet tall, were decorated with scenes of human stick figures lamenting the dead. Architecture was still in its infancy: most buildings were made of wood or brick, although small columned temples provided a convenient place to leave large numbers of bronze animal figurines.

Archaic Period (700-480 BCe)

Face to Vase

By the end of the Geometric Period, artists had come to the conclusion that stick figures just weren't going to cut it anymore. Vase painters adopted the Corinthian black figure style, painting more complex human forms. Increased contact with Syria and Phoenicia brought new motifs, such as **sphinxes**, **griffins**, and **lions**.

A Nude Mood

Perhaps the greatest leap forward occurred in the realm of sculpture. Around 650 BCE, life-size artistic sculptures called **kourai** came into vogue. Made from limestone and marble, kourai were statues of nude male youths, reflecting a newfound emphasis on the human figure. Each kouros was sculpted in an Egyptian-influenced style, complete with rigid posture, clenched fists, and a distinctive Archaic smile. These idealized forms were at once warriors, athletes, and gods, as the human form itself was considered sacred. Female public nudity was still a major no-no, so the female equivalent of the kouros, the **kore**, appeared draped in thick folds of the latest fashions, with elaborate braided hairdos. Representing priestesses, goddesses, and nymphs, korai were often painted vibrant colors and assumed more natural poses, with one hand at the side and the other outstretched, often carrying flowers or a piece of fruit. Sculptures lined the walkways of temples and sanctuaries, appeared on public memorials, and marked graves. As the Archaic Period progressed, understanding of anatomy and proportion improved, and statues became much more realistic: poses became more relaxed, and statues were no longer forced to fake overly exuberant grins, but could assume a subtle smile or even a sulky brooding expression as they stood baring it all.

A Tale of Two Columns

Archaic architects were also hard at work, crafting increasingly impressive temples from limestone. Columns not only provided vital structural support, but they did it with style. Beautiful examples of Archaic architecture include the Temple of Apollo at Corinth, built in the sixth century BCE, and the Temple of Aphaia at Aegina, built in the early fifth century BCE. But change was afoot, and soon came a split that haunts hapless art history student to this day. In the sixth century BCE, the **Doric** and **Ionic** orders diverged. Mainland architects favored simple, sturdy Doric designs, as seen in the extraordinarily well-preserved **Temple of Hephaestus** in Athens, built in 449 BCE. Ionic enthusiasts, residing mostly in coastal and island colonies, crafted slender, decorative columns capped with twin curlicues. The **Temple of Athena Nike** is a stunning example of Ionic architecture, so just do it and go there.

Classical Period (480-323 BCE)

Practice Makes Perfect

The Classical Period ushered in a Golden Age of art, architecture, literature, and philosophy. Sculptors sought perfection of the human form in their art, crafting figures in a variety of natural poses and expressions. From the magnificent bronze **Charioteer of Delphi** (474 BCE), complete with delicate copper eyelashes, to the famed *Discobolos* ("Discus Thrower") of Myron (c. 460 BCE), many of the most famous works of Ancient Greek art were produced in less than 200 years. Statues began to depict real people and events, including stunningly personal funeral scenes of grieving families. Near the end of the Classical Period, women were finally granted the right to appear as naked statues alongside their male counterparts: Praxiteles' **Aphrodite of Knidos** was called the greatest statue in the world by famed historian Pliny.

Ancient Bling

To this day, Athenian residents gaze up at the Acropolis, crowned by the magnificent **Parthenon**. Originally constructed in less than a decade as a monument to Athena, the Parthenon is notable for its incredible attention to detail. Intentionally containing no straight lines, its columns bulge slightly at the center to appear perfect to ground-based observers. The temple once housed the four-story-tall statue Athena Parthenos. This chryselephantine (made of ivory and gold) monolith was crafted by master sculptor Phidias using 2500 pounds of gold, a sizeable portion of the Athenian treasury.

Face Value

A new fad was established in the world of ceramics, as the **red-figure technique** allowed artists to paint detailed scenes directly onto pottery. Forget about stick figures and simple geometric shapes—vases now depicted detailed facial expressions, realistic anatomy, and a sense of perspective. From scenes of weddings and warriors to athletes and gods, Classical pottery gives a unique glimpse into the daily life and legends of ordinary Athenians.

Hellenistic Period (323–46 BCE)

Working Wonders

The Hellenistic Period was the last hurrah for ancient Greek art and architecture, but this period went out with a serious bang. Not only were some of the most world-renowned sculptures crafted, including the now-headless **Nike of Samothrace** (c. 190 BCE) and the **Venus de Milo** (c. 130 BCE), but the Greeks made sure to leave behind the **Colossus of Rhodes**, one of the Seven Wonders of the Ancient World. The monumental Colossus, a statue of the sun god Helios, stood over 30m (107 ft.) high and provided a model of design, posture, and dimension for architects designing the Statue of Liberty more than two millennia later. Unfortunately, the Colossus took a tumble 56 years after it was built, although the ruins were so impressive that it remained an ancient tourist hotspot for hundreds of years.

Routine Scenes

The Hellenistic Period released the restrained, idealized forms of Classical sculpture from the demands of perfection. Ordinary people (gasp!) were suddenly acceptable subjects for sculpture, and **domestic scenes** of women, children, and animals were the new must-have lawn ornaments for the wealthy. The ancient Greeks had had enough of restraint; now their statues were free to laugh, cry, and even relax.

FOOD AND DRINK

Eat Up!

After traveling through centuries of magnificent art and architecture and across miles of dazzling beaches, pause to give your hungry stomach some relief. If you're in the mood for a little bite to eat, stop for *meze*, small dishes that make an ideal snack. Vegetarians can choose from *meze* including *melitzanosalata*, eggplant salad, and *dolmades*, leaves stuffed with pine nuts, currants, and rice. For the carnivorous at heart, *bekrí-mezé*, diced pork stew, and savory meatballs like *keftédes* and *soutzoukákia smyrnéika* are sure to hit the spot. No trip to Athens is complete without sampling local olives, fresh feta, and authentic gyros made with rotisserie-coooked meat and *tzatziki* (garlic, yogurt, and cucumber sauce) served in pitas. Try specialties like *aïdakia*, seasoned lamb chops, or *chtapodi sti skhara*, grilled octopus.

For a budget-friendly option, stop for *souvlaki*, tender skewers of meat (choose from pork, chicken, beef or lamb) grilled to perfection. Enjoy *souvlaki* fresh off the skewer or in a pita sandwich with garnishes and sauces. Found your new favorite food? You're in good company – Aristotle, Aristophanes, and Homer all mentioned this tasty dish in their works. *Phyllo* pastry is another Greek favorite, used in dishes ranging from *spanakopita*, made from spinach, feta cheese, onions, and egg wrapped in delicate sheets of pastry, to *baklava*, a desert consisting of thin pastry layers filled with nuts and drenched in sweet syrup. Don't worry–they aren't too Greece-y!

Buy You a Drink?

Wet your whistle after climbing the Acropolis at local coffee shops serving sweet, strong Greek coffee, or try a *frappé*, foamy iced instant coffee. If you're in the mood for wine, you've come the right place–Greece has a 6500-year history of wine production. Even small *tavernas* often serve a wide variety of local wines. If you're in the mood for something stronger, take a sip of Greece's favorite alcoholic drink, *ouzo*. *Ouzo's* intense black-licorice flavor and powerful kick are not for everyone. *Ouzo* often accompanies *meze*, and is sometimes drunk diluted with water or ice, which causes the drink to turn an opaque white color.

EXCURSIONS

When the sprawling metropolises of Istanbul and Athens become old hat, get out of town. This chapter is devoted to trips, some possible as daytrips, that you can make from Athens and Istanbul. Head down for the day to Cape Sounion Peninsula from Athens and check out the Temple of Posiedon perched on the barren cliffside.

From Istanbul, a trip to Ephesus takes four to six hours, and you should consider making arrangements for an overnight trip. Ephesus is the site of the famous Temple of Artemis, one of the Ancient Wonders of the World, and also the puported site of Virgin Mary's house during the last years of her life and the burial site of St. John. Thus it is site for everyone from ancient Grecophiles to Christian pilgrims. The town near the ancient city of Ephesus is Selçuk, which is definitely worth a stay in a few days: the food is tastier and cheaper than in Istanbul, and the accommodatiuons are a fraction of the price as those you'lll find in Sultanahmet and twice as comfortable.

For a shorter trip, visit the shores of Gallipoli and Troy. Gallipoli was the site a disastrous British military campaign during World War I that resulted in 130,000 deaths, the majority of those Ottoman Empire casualties. Troy, located about 40mi southwest of Gallipoli in the Dardanelles, is where at least 6 different cities were built, from Hittite to Greek to Roman civilization. There's not much to see here, but the windswept terrain of the site is terrific.

greatest hits

- **HELEN OF TENNESSEE.** Imagine that you're the face that launched a hundred ships as you look out over the site of ancient Troy (p. 129).
- **REMEMBER THE FALLEN.** Take time to think about the thousands who lost their lives on the battlefields of Gallipoli (p. 128).
- **STAY AT HOMEROS PENSION.** This guesthouse is miles better than anything in Istanbul and so much cheaper, even with breakfast included (p. 122)!

ephesus ☎232

An unbelievable amount of history took place around these parts—the ruins of the Roman city of **Ephesus** are just a stone's throw away from the house where **Virgin Mary** supposedly spent the last years of her life, while the remnants of one of the **Seven Wonders of the Ancient World** are just a short walk away from the hill where **John the Apostle** wrote his part of the Gospel. Most people who come to Ephesus are here as part of a packaged tour—at night they stay at the resort port of Kuşadası, and during the day they are rushed through these places on a tour bus, one by one. This is a terrible way to do it. Independent travelers have it much better—stay at **Selçuk** and wander at ease through its sleepy streets, admiring the *chutzpah* of the storks who nest on top of every historically significant structure in this town. Selçuk is a rural paradise compared to Istanbul—the pensions offer a lot for little money, the food is always cheap and tasty, and the people are not very interested in ripping you off. And Selçuk is just the beginning: there are many small, interesting towns around that you can go explore on your own.

ORIENTATION

Selçuk is a small, easy-to-navigate town. The main thoroughfare is the **Atatürk Cad.,** which runs north to İzmir and south to Denizli. The town **center** runs parallel to this road, roughly between the **bus station** and the **train station,** with a small pedestrian zone around **Cengiz Topel Cad.** The **Ephesus** ruins are just 3km from the bus station, while **Meryemana** is almost 9km away. The other major sights, including **St. John's Basilica, Artemis Temple,** and **Ephesus Museum** are within walking distance from the center, across the **Atatürk Cad.** A number of cheap pensions are clustered above the Ephesus Museum, but there are also some around the bus and train stations. The sandy, 14km **Pamucak beach** is a few kilometers to the west, in the direction of Kuşadası.

ACCOMMODATIONS

HOMEROS PENSION — GUESTHOUSE ❶

1048 Sok. 3 ☎232 892 3995 www.homerospension.com

The rooms here look nothing like what you'd expect from a pension at this price—they are full of antique furniture, *kilims*, and other decorations that make them look like somebody's home. Add in the bikes that you can borrow for free, the terrace with a wonderful view, and the free glass of wine served every night at 8pm, and the result is one of the most charming budget accommodation options we've seen in the entire country. If all of this pension's 12 rooms are taken, try the **Australia and New Zealand Guesthouse** *(1064 Sok. 12 ☎232 892 6050 www.anzguesthouse.com)* nearby, which has similar prices and features a similar set of amenities.

From the bus station cross Atatürk Cad, walk across the park, walk up the street next to the Ephesus Museum, and then turn right. Look for signs. [i] Breakfast included. Bikes available. Some rooms have A/C. $ Singles 25TL, with bath 35TL; doubles 50TL/70TL. Dinner approx. 15TL. ⏰ Reception 24hr.

AUSTRALIA AND NEW ZEALAND GUESTHOUSE — GUESTHOUSE ❶

1064 Sok. 12 ☎232 892 6050 www.anzguesthouse.com

This guesthouse, run by Australian expatriates of Turkish descent, has similar prices and amenities to Homeros pension. Additionally, enjoy drinks on the rooftop terrace.

Just a 3 blocks south of Homeros Pension. [i] Breakfast included. Bikes available. A/C available for 9.50TL. Pick up available from the bus station or Kuşadası port. $ Dorms 15TL. Double 40TL; triple 45TL; quad 60TL. ⏰ Reception 24hr.

NUR PENSION

📶❄ GUESTHOUSE ❶

3004 Sok. 20 ☎232 892 6595 🖥www.nurpension.com

Tucked away across the railroad tracks, this pension might be a bit hard to find at first, but if that's a problem, the owners will pick you up from the bus station for free. These guys speak a lot of languages and will direct you to some of the better places in town. You can also join in on one of the many tours that they offer, which include a guided tour of Ephesus *(80TL)* or the more demanding tour of Miletos, Didyma, and Priene. The rooms are cheerful, and the outside courtyard is a pleasant place to sit and have some free tea.

From the train station, cross the train tracks on the white bridge. Continue straight, take the 2nd left, and continue straight until you see the pension to your right. ℹ *Breakfast included. Pick up available from the bus station or Kuşadası port.* $ *3-bed dorms 15TL; singles with bath 25TL; doubles 50TL; triples 75TL. 3-bed dorms 15TL.* 🕒 *Reception 24hr.*

KIWI PENSION

❄📶 GUESTHOUSE ❶

1038 Sok. 26 ☎232 892 4892 🖥www.kiwipension.com

Just a short walk from the bus station, Kiwi features clean, spacious rooms and a private swimming pool (the catch is that it's a bit of a hike away from the pension). An expat for over 20 years, the English owner Alison knows a lot about this region and can direct you to many places that aren't well known but are worth visiting—make sure you consult her before leaving for the day. Only ensuite rooms have A/C.

From the bus station, go to the taxi parking spot, then cross the road, walk toward the tennis court. Walk straight until you see the pension to your right. ℹ *Breakfast included. Swimming pool some 2.5km away.* $ *Basement dorms 15TL; singles 20TL, with bath 50TL; doubles 40TL, with bath 68TL; triples 84TL; quads 96TL.* 🕒 *Reception 24hr.*

SIGHTS

EPHESUS

RUINS

Efes ☎232 892 6010

In its heyday, Ephesus was one of the biggest and most prosperous cities in the world. It used to be a harbor town, but since then the sea has moved some six kilometers away, which has contributed to the city's decline. Today it's one of Turkey's best known tourist attractions, functioning as a showcase of Roman architecture and culture. The ruins have two entrances a few kilometers apart, one in the north and the other in the south. The southern exit is conveniently located for a trip to Virgin Mary's House. It gets unpleasantly hot during the day, so try to come early in the morning or toward the evening.

Ephesus was a Ionian city, and it was at various points under the rule of Lydians, Persians, Alexander the Great, Egyptians, Romans, and other powers. The city was famous as the site of the **cult of Artemis** (Diana during the Roman times), which had its main temple here. Its most famous iteration was the temple completed around 550BCE under the auspices of the Lydian King Croesus, which was one of the Seven Wonders of the Ancient World. However, the temple is closer to Selçuk than to this particular site—the location of the city kept changing over the centuries, due to the changing conditions of its harbor. The city's name was changing as well. Lysimachos, the general who took over the city after Alexander the Great's death, renamed it "Arsinoe," after his wife. Needless to say, the Ephesians were unhappy and eventually revolted. Ephesus prospered after the Romans took the helm, becoming the second largest city in the empire, second only to Rome. The city's decline was set off by a Gothic raid in the third century and was ended in the 15th century when the city was abandoned.

Starting at the northern entrance, almost right after entering, you can see the ruins of **Mary's Church,** which was presumably built on the site of a destroyed medical school. Further down Harbour Street you'll see the **Great Theater,** which could seat 24,000 people and was the largest outdoor theater of the ancient world. It's here that St. Paul delivered his speech against Artemis and was subsequently forced to leave the city by the townspeople. From the theater, walk down **Marble Street** to reach the **Library of Celsus**, built by Consul Gaius Julius Aquila in honor of his father. The four statues represent this fine man's qualities, which were allegedly wisdom, character, knowledge, and intelligence.

Next to the library is the **South Gate** leading to the **Agora**, a marketplace where monuments and statues of gods and significant people formerly stood. Up **Kurets Street** on the right you can see the **Terrace Houses** *(admission extra 15TL),* where you'll find mosaics (on floors) and frescoes (on walls) that once adorned the homes of well-off Ephesians. Opposite are the partition-less **communal latrines**, which don't seem to have provided much privacy to the patrons. The floors here were covered with mosaics, and there was a pool collecting rainwater in the center. Behind is the structure sometimes called the **brothel**, and the engravings that you can find in the center of Marble Street (a left foot, a woman's figure, a heart) supposedly advertised this place. Further up the street is the **Temple of Hadrianus**, completed in 138 AD, with the relief of Tyche, the Goddess of Cities and Luck. Yet further up the street is the **Traian Fountain**, the source of a number of sculptures that can now be found in the Ephesus Museum. Kurets Street ends at **Domitian Square** and the ruins of the **Domitian Temple**, which was re-dedicated to the Emperor's father Vespasian after Domitianus got killed by his servant with a *khanjar.* Further up is the rather anticlimactic **Odeon**, where concerts and council meetings took place. Some of the remaining structures near the southern gate are the **Magnesian Gate,** the **Prytaneion,** and the **Government Agora.**

⚑ *See the Getting Around section.* Ⓢ *20TL; only payments in Turkish Lira are accepted. Tours start at €30 per hr. Audio tours 10TL.* ⏱ *Open daily in summer 8am-6:30pm; in winter 8am-5pm.*

VIRGIN MARY'S HOUSE
Meryemana Evi

◉ SHRINE
☎232 894 1012

This is believed to be the place where Virgin Mary spent the last years of her life, after the crucifixion of Jesus. The story of how this building was discovered is quite unusual. Anne Catherine Emmerich (1774-1824) was a bedridden German nun who at various points in her life developed stigmata and had religious visions. Her visions were transcribed into two volumes, one about the life of Jesus Christ, the other about that of the Virgin Mary. Some 50 years after Emmerich's death, a French priest discovered this house using the descriptions in Emmerich's book, even though the nun had never left her country. Those who think Mary had lived here often mention two pieces of evidence: the basilica of St. John in Selçuk (Jesus supposedly entrusted his mother to this apostle) and an early church devoted to Virgin Mary that was found in Ephesus. Today, there isn't that much to see inside this reconstructed stone shrine, but the place has an undeniable mystical aura. In vitrines you can see objects that were left here by various popes, who have been paying visits to this site for over a century (most recently, it was Pope Benedict XVI in 2006). Below the shrine are water springs believed to have healing powers—make sure you bring a water bottle with you.

⚑ *See the "Getting Around" section.* ℹ *No photography or videotaping permitted. Appropriate dress requested.* Ⓢ *12.50TL. Cars 5TL; minibuses 15TL.* ⏱ *Open daily 8am-7pm.*

ST. JOHN'S BASILICA
St. Jean Cad.

✎ RUINS
☎232 892 6010

This is supposedly the burial site of St. John, an evangelist and Jesus Christ's disciple, who spent his last years on Ayasuluk Hill, writing his part of the Gospel. A simple basilica that was constructed here in the fifth century was later replaced with a much bigger church built on the orders of Emperor Justinian. After the

Turks took over Selçuk in 1304, the basilica was converted into a mosque, but it was leveled by earthquakes in the 14th century. Today, there's not much left of the basilica to observe, but the ruins gives some idea about how enormous the church was. The overall plan is cruciform (in the shape of a cross) and the one memorable structure here is the **baptistery,** a section of the church where baptisms took place inside the central pool. To the north you can see the **Ayasuluk Castle,** which is currently out of bounds for tourists. If you walk to the western side of the ruins, you'll see the **Isa Bey Mosque,** built in 1375 and recently renovated. To the south, some distance away you'll see a reconstructed pillar of the **Artemis Temple,** a building that counts among the Seven Wonders of the Ancient World. Unfortunately, probably the only ones who find it wondrous today are the storks nesting on top of it. The temple was destroyed a number of times, most famously by Herostratos, who set it on fire in 356BCE to achieve immortal fame. To prevent Herostratos from achieving his goal, the angry Ephesians tried to erase his name from the records and banish it to oblivion, but they obviously failed.

The ruins are across Atatürk Cad. from the pedestrian town center. Walk uphill on St. Jean Cad., past some aqueduct remnants, until you see the ruins entrance to your right. $ 5TL. ⏰ Open daily in summer 8am-6:30pm; in winter 8:30am-5pm.

EPHESUS MUSEUM — MUSEUM

Uğur Mumcu Sevgi Yolu ☎232 892 6010

This museum is home to many archaeological discoveries that were uncovered during the excavation of Ephesus and other ruins in the area. The most memorable exhibit is probably the **statuette of Bes,** the Egyptian god of fertility, which lurks inside a dark vitrine so that nobody's modesty gets accidentally offended. Press the "Light" button to see what Bes has to offer. In the **hall of Emperor Cults,** don't miss the opportunity to stand face-to-face with the busts of many Roman Emperors and the childlike head from an enormous statue of Emperor Domitianus. Don't forget that these people used to be some of the most powerful men on the planet. A number of times Ephesus was selected as a *neokoros* (a place which the Emperor allowed to build a temple devoted to him), which was considered an honor to the city. Also of interest are two quite impressive statues of **Ephesian Artemis** in the hall devoted to the cult of this goddess. Similar to the representations of Bes and Priapus, Artemis is sculpted with many egg-like breasts that symbolize her fertility.

The museum is located opposite the tourist office. To get here from the bus station, cross Atatürk Cad. and continue across the park; the museum will be in front of you. $ 5TL. ⏰ Open daily in summer 8:30am-6:30pm; in winter 8:30am-5pm.

FOOD

EJDER RESTAURANT — TURKISH [1]

Cengiz Topel Cad. 9/E ☎232 892 3296

This is a very touristy place, and for once we mean that in a good way. With outdoor seating directly below the stork-ridden ancient aqueduct, portions that are twice the size of what you can eat, and friendly service, the restaurant has been inciting loyalty in travelers for years. And it's not even expensive! Try the chicken şiş *(8TL)* or one of the many vegetarian dishes. The owner has 25 scrapbooks full of thank-you notes from satisfied customers.

From the bus station, walk north on Atatürk Cad., turn right at Cengiz Topel and continue until you see it to your right. The restaurant is near the train station, overlooking a Byzantine aqueduct and a fountain. $ Kebabs 8-10TL. Vegetarian entrees 4-10TL; meat entrees 9-17TL. ⏰ Open daily 9am-midnight.

EPHESUS RESTAURANT — TURKISH [1]

N. Kemal Cad. 2 ☎232 892 3267

In addition to meat, this relaxed restaurant has a great selection of vegetarian dishes—just point at those that you like and the owner will make a plate just for you. Try

the mushrooms with lightly toasted bread, or go for the excellent *mücver* (zucchini pancakes) with yogurt. The dishes here are filling, cheap, and surprisingly tasty.
This restaurant is in the pedestrian zone, 1 block north of the post office (with a partial view of the aqueduct. $ Vegetable entrees 4-6TL; meat entrees 6-10TL. Desserts 5TL. ⏰ Open daily 8am-2am.

CAFE CARPOUZA CAFE [1]
Argenta Cad. ☎232 892 2665
This building once housed the first hotel in Selçuk and later belonged to the director of the train station. More recently, the government took it over, renovated it, and put it to better use—today it's a cafe that serves cheap drinks and desserts in a nice small park. Sit outside in the shade of an enormous tree, or move indoors, where you can see some photos from the building's earlier history.
This cafe is opposite the train station, above the aqueduct ruins. $ Beer 4TL. Soft drinks 3TL. Rakı 6TL. Desserts 3TL. ⏰ Open daily 8am-midnight.

OKUMUŞ PIDE SALONU PIDE [1]
Şahabettın Dede Cad. 2 ☎ 232 892 6906
Most restaurants in Selçuk are above-average, and all have their ardent backers. According to some sources, this *pide* salon makes some of the best pides in town, and even if they weren't the best, they certainly are good. It's especially convenient for people waiting for a bus or *dolmuş*.
Okumuş is adjacent to the bus station, located on its southern side. $ Pide 3.50-5TL. Köfte 6.50-8TL. ⏰ Open daily 10am-11pm.

ESSENTIALS

Practicalities

- **TOURIST OFFICE:** Located opposite the Ephesus Museum at Agora Çarsisı 35. Free maps. *(☎232 892 6945 ⏰ Open daily in summer 8:30am-noon and 1-5:30pm; in winter 8am-5pm.)*
- **ATMS:** At Cengiz Topel, there's a cluster of 24hr. ATMs and **banks**.
- **POST OFFICE:** Located near the banks and ATMs at Cengiz Topel 13. *(i 2% commission on traveler's checks. ⏰ Open M-Sa 8:30am-5pm.)*
- **INTERNET:** Among the available **internet cafes** are the Han Cafe at 1005 Sok. *($ 3TL per hr.)* and Nutuk Cafe at 1040 Sok. *($1.5TL per hr.)*

Emergency!

- **TOURIST POLICE:** ☎232 892 8989.
- **PHARMACIES:** There are dozens–one of them is on 1006 Sok. 5/A in the center.
- **HOSPITAL:** The **Selçuk Hospital** is across the traffic circle from the bus station. *(☎232 892 7039 ⏰ Open 24hr.)*

Getting There

By Plane

The fastest way to get here from **Istanbul** is to take a plane to İzmir and then take a dolmuş or train to Selçuk. Cheap 1hr. flights are offered by **Pegasus Airlines** *(☎444 0 737 www.flypgs.com)*, **Atlas Jet** *(☎212 663 2000 www.atlasjet.com)*, **Onur Air** *(☎212 663 2300 www.onurair.com.tr)*, and other carriers. You can get a flight from either of Istanbul's two major airports, with the price very dependent on how early you're buying your ticket *($ 50-150TL)*. From İzmir Adnan Menderes Airport *(☎232 474 2009 ⏰ 24hr.)* you can take a **dolmuş** to Selçuk *(☎232 892 3979 ⏰ 1hr., every 40min. 6:55am-10:15pm. $ 8TL)*. Note that the dolmuşes don't leave directly from the airport, but from a stop on the highway some 3km away, so if you can, it's better to take one of the **trains** that stop right at the airport. *($ 4TL. Adnan Menderes to Selçuk ⏰ 1hr., daily at 8:31, 10:45am, 2:45, 3:54, 6:00, and 7:30pm.)*

By Train

Another way to get to İzmir is by bus *($ From 45TL ⏰ 8½hr.)* and after arriving at İzmir's otogar, you can take a dolmuş to Selçuk *(☎232 892 3979 $ 8TL ⏰ 1hr., every 40min. 7:20am-10pm; dolmuşes leave from the upper level)*. It's also possible to go to İzmir by train from Bandırma *(⏰ 9:50am, 4pm)* after taking the ferry here from Istanbul's Yenikapı. Finally, there are some slow **direct overnight buses** from Istanbul to Selçuk offered by **Metro** *($ From 58TL ⏰ 11hr., daily at 9:30pm)*. If you're coming **from the Greek Islands,** take a ferry to Samos, then a ferry to Kuşadası, and then a dolmuş to Selçuk *($ 4TL ⏰ 25 min., every 15min.)*.

Getting Around

Selçuk's **center** and sights can be easily covered on foot. **Taxis** *(☎232 892 3125)* can be found at the bus station and elsewhere. They often charge a lot for short drives, so ask at your hostel if they can arrange a cheap taxi. To get to the northern gate of **Ephesus,** you can take a **Pamucak dolmuş** from the bus station *($ 2TL⏰ 8min., every 30min. to Ephesus 7:30am-8pm, to Selçuk 8:15am-8:30pm. Erratic schedule in summer)*, take a taxi *($ officially 10TL, likely 15TL)* or walk *(⏰ 30min., from the traffic circle near the bus station head down Dr Sabrı Yayla Bulvarı, turn left at Tusan Restaurant, continue up the hill until you see it)*. Pensions used to provide free lifts to Ephesus, but the local government banned it recently, presumably under pressure from taxi companies. However, some pensions might still help you out. The southern gate doesn't have any public transport options, so you'll have to either take a taxi or walk *(3km)*. **Virgin Mary's House** isn't accessible by public transport, but you can get there by an overpriced taxi. *($ officially 50TL round-trip, but in reality around 35TL one way.)* Some travelers say that the best way to get there is to hitchhike from the southern gate of Ephesus and then to hitch a ride back to Selçuk, but *Let's Go* never recommends hitchhiking. To get to the **Pamucak beach,** take the same dolmuş as for Ephesus.

gallipoli and troy

Both Gallipoli and Troy are famous sites of war. The way **Homer** tells it, the Trojan War was actually pretty fun: Paris chooses the wrong goddess to receive his golden apple, Achilles is sensitive about his heel, and Odysseus outsmarts everyone in Troy with a **wooden horse,** only to get lost for ten years on his way home. These legends have little to do with what you'll see in the actual remains of Troy, but they do give it a mysterious spirit that draws crowds. Gallipoli, on the other hand, is the site of unambiguous tragedy—the military campaign that took place here in 1915 had over 400,000 casualties. The events became a defining event for some of the participating nations. It was the first independent military action for Australia and New Zealand and the moment of metaphorical birth for Turkey's national hero, **Kemal Atatürk.** Deceptively peaceful, the Gallipoli battlefields are among the most touching places you can find in Turkey. If you want to go to see Gallipoli and Troy, the easiest way to do it is by going to **Çanakkale**, a cheerful little seaside town on the Dardanelles. Çanakkale is no Istanbul, but maybe taking a short break from this metropolis is exactly what you need to appreciate it more fully.

ORIENTATION

It's difficult to get lost in Çanakkale's center. In the middle of town is the **Cumhuriyet Meydanı Square.** Just a few steps south you can find the **Clock Tower** (1897), a good point of orientation. Restaurants and bars run in both directions along the shore, and a few hundred meters north from the jetty you can find the **wooden horse** that was used as a prop in the 2004 movie **Troy.** The naval museum and the Çanakkale fortress are 500 m south from the jetty. The **bus station** is a ten-minute walk away from the center on Atatürk Cad., and the **dolmuş** stop is under a bridge over the Sarı River fifteen minutes away. The ruins of **Troy** are located 30km south of the town, while the **Gallipoli**

battlefields are on Gallipoli peninsula across the Dardanelles strait from Çanakkale. Most tours of cemeteries and monuments travel northwest to the town Eceabat, but there are other cemeteries and monuments in the south of the peninsula as well.

ACCOMMODATIONS

YELLOW ROSE PENSION — HOSTEL [1]

Kemalpaşa Mah. Aslan Abla Sok. 5 ☎286 217 3343 www.yellowrose.4mg.com

There's an Australian flag at the front door and jovial "G'day mate!" sign pointing you this way, so it's pretty obvious who the target customer group is at Yellow Rose Pension. This is one of the most appealing budget choices in the area—the rooms are clean, and many of them have fans. The reception desk also offers tours to Gallipoli and Troy *(60TL each).*

From the Clock Tower head down Kemal Yeri Sok. and turn right onto the 2nd street. It will be to your left. **i** *Breakfast included.* $ *Dorms 17TL; singles 25 TL, with bath 30TL; doubles 40TL, with bath 50 TL; triples 60TL, with bath 75TL; quads 80TL, with bath 100TL.* ⏰ *Reception 24hr.*

KONAK HOTEL — HOTEL [1]

Kemalpaşa Mah. Fetvane Sok. 12 ☎286 217 1150 www.konakhotelcanakkale.com

The amount of money that it takes to get a damp hostel room and a sleepy receptionist who spends most of his time in the hotel next door in Istanbul will get you much more in Çanakkale. Equipped with a minibar, A/C, and civilized-looking bathrooms, your lovely room might make you question going back to the bigger city. The prices here don't fluctuate with seasons, and it's one of the cheaper mid-range hotels in the area.

From the Clock Tower head down Fetvane Sok., it will be on your right. **i** *Breakfast included.* $ *Singles €19; doubles with bath €36.* ⏰ *Reception 24hr.*

ANZAC HOUSE YOUTH HOSTEL — HOSTEL [1]

Cumhuriyet Meydani 59 ☎286 213 5969 www.anzachouse.com

The walls seem to be made of paper and the beds of concrete. On the upside, it's as centrally located as it gets, and... yeah, it's centrally located. With no private bathrooms and a shaky Wi-Fi service, the amenities are pretty bare bones, but to get you excited about the battlefields to the north, every night there's a screening of the same two movies about Gallipoli—a documentary and a feature-length film with Mel Gibson.

A few meters away from the tourist information office near the docks. From the Clock Tower, backtrack to the square and go west; it's on your right. **i** *Houses the Hassle Free Travel Agency (guided tours are 60TL for Troy, 70TL for Gallipoli).* $ *Dorms 17TL; singles 25TL; doubles 40TL.* ⏰ *Reception 24hr.*

SIGHTS

GALLIPOLI BATTLEFIELDS — NATIONAL PARK

Almost one hundred years ago during WWI, the Gallipoli peninsula was the site of an eight-month-long military campaign that resulted in over 400,000 casualties and no military progress. These battlefields are now covered with shrubs and grass, but even today the soil here contains bones, pieces of shrapnel, and bullets. Cemeteries were built, monuments were erected, and the whole area is now a national park that commemorates the soldiers of this battle.

The objective for the **Allies** (British Empire, France) was to capture **Constantinople** (Istanbul) and thus knock the **Ottoman Empire** out of the war. They thought it would be an easy thing to do, but this takeover was actually very difficult. After failing to cross the **Dardanelles** by sea, the Allies decided to disembark on the Gallipoli peninsula and attack by land. Their progress was stalled early on, led to trench warfare, and ultimately ended with a withdrawal. This campaign has a special importance for the collective memory of Australians and New Zealanders because Gallipoli was the first major military operation for the Australia and New Zealand Armed Corps (ANZAC) since gaining independence. It was also important for Turkey, as the superhero lieutenant **Mustafa Kemal** made a name for himself as an extraordinarily capable leader in battle. This victory paved his way to becoming **Atatürk**, the father of modern Turkey.

The most commonly visited group of cemeteries and monuments lies near the **Anzac Cove**, the place where ANZAC forces disembarked. A few kilometers south is the **Kabatepe Museum** *(☎286 814 1297 $ 3TL, students 1.50TL 🕓 Open 9am-1pm, 2-6pm)*, where you can see a gruesome collection of objects from the campaign, including a soldier's skull embedded with a bullet, old shoes with pieces of foot bones still inside them, artificial teeth, detached mandibles, unexploded hand grenades, and bullets that hit each other midair. There are also letters written by soldiers during the campaign. Look for a letter written by a certain William, who wrote to his mother and referred to one of the military skirmishes as "rather a hot job!"

A few kilometers to the northwest of the museum on the road that lines the sea, you can find a number of cemeteries including the **Anzac Cove**, where the ANZAC forces landed on April 25, 1915. Today, there's a commemorative ceremony held every year on this day. One of the graves nearby supposedly belongs to John Simpson Kirkpatrick, a soldier whom Australians know under the moniker "the man with the donkey." Before he died, Simpson had been one of the people who transported wounded people from the front lines to the seashore.

If you walked from the museum, you'll need to backtrack and find the walking trail to the left that leads deeper inland and connects onto a different road. On this trail you'll find the **Lone Pine** cemetery, where almost 5000 soldiers who died in the span of a few days are buried. The pine standing in the center of the cemetery came from a seed that was produced by a pine tree in Australia, which in turn came from a cone that an Australian soldier sent from Gallipoli to his mother in 1915.

Continuing north up the road you will pass a number of cemeteries, including the Turkish **57th Regiment Cemetery.** In its graves are the people who received Atatürk's famous command: "Men, I'm not ordering you to attack. I'm ordering you to die. In the time it takes us to die, other forces and commanders can come and take our place." The soldiers obeyed the order, and in their honor, the Turkish army has never had a 57th regiment again.

Finally, a few kilometers up past some eroded trenches is **Chunuk Bair**, the only hill that the Allies captured during the whole campaign. Their success didn't last long, and the Turks regained the hill just a few days later. The New Zealand Memorial is here, along with a big statue of Atatürk.

We hate to admit it, but a **guided tour** might be the best way to see all of this, especially as most buses come equipped with air-conditioning. Your experience depends on the guide, so look for an enthusiastic one. Make sure to ask about the legend of Mustafa Kemal being shot in the heart, only to be saved by a pocket watch in his chest pocket. *$ Free. Tours around 60TL.*

TROY ✎ RUINS

Tevfikiye Köyü ☎286 283 0536

After visiting this place, many people complain that it's just a heap of stones. Perhaps there are a lot of stones, but these are some of the most interesting stones around. Troy wasn't just one city—the ruins go back to 2900 BCE and contain the remains of nine different cities, all built on top of another. Sundried mudbricks and trash from older periods weren't always removed but were actually paved over and used as foundation, creating the 15m mound on which the ruins are now located.

There are disputes about whether it was Troy VI or Troy VII that was the famed location of Homer's Iliad. Based on the signs of siege and fire that can be seen on the remnants of Troy VII, many believe this iteration was the subject of the myth. Troy VI seems to have been damaged by an earthquake, and even though there's no earthquake in Homer's version of the story, some think that the Trojan horse was in fact built to celebrate Poseidon, the god who possibly caused the earthquake that facilitated Troy's fall. These legends seem to be the main draw of the ruins today, and the tourist authorities know it—they recently built a big wooden horse near the entrance. Climb in and hope that the Trojans don't hear you sneeze.

Over the centuries, Troy was abandoned and forgotten. It was rediscovered for the Western world by German businessman Heinrich Schliemann in 1868, who excavated the ruins believing they were the site of the Homeric legend. More of a businessman than an archeologist, Schliemann believed Troy was only one city and destroyed many valuable buildings during the excavations. Notice the **Schliemann Trench,** which cuts through a number of settlement layers. Another subject on the list of grievances against this man is **Priam's Treasure,** a collection of valuable items that Schliemann found here, believing they originally belonged to the Trojan King Priam. Not only was he wrong about their origin (the artifacts come from Troy II, not Troy VII), but he smuggled the objects out of the Ottoman Empire. The ownership of Priam's Treasure remains problematic even today, as many of the objects were seized by the Russian Army after World War II and are now tucked away in the Pushkin Museum in Moscow, which refuses to return them to their country of origin.

Some of the more interesting heaps of stones include the Roman **Odeon** from Troy XI, where musical performances took place, the **sanctuary** dug into the remains of Troy VI and VII that was dedicated to unknown deities, and the **ramp** from Troy II close to where Schliemann discovered Priam's Treasure. Under a hideous white roof nearby, you can find the **megaron,** a house with a porch from the transitional period between Troy II and III. Down the hill, there's also a **water cave** that originated in the third millennium BCE and was associated with the god Kaskal.Kur (no, that's not a website).

⚑ *Near Tevfikye village. Also known as Truva, or Troia.* Ⓢ *15TL, ages 9 and under free.* Ⓒ *Open daily in summer 8am-7:30pm, in winter 8am-5:30pm.*

NAVAL MUSEUM (MILITARY MUSEUM) ⊛ MUSEUM

Fevzipaşa Mah. Çimenlik Sok.   ☎286 213 1730 🖳www.denizmuzeleri.tsk.tr

Just a simple walk through this museum's gardens yields WWI cannons and the giant carcass of a sunken German submarine UB-46. Perhaps the only sight in Çanakkale's center that's worth visiting, this museum consists of three parts—a picture and photograph **gallery,** a replica of the Turkish minelayer ship **Nusrat,** and the **Çimenlik fortress.** Nusrat played an important role in the naval confrontation between the Allies and the Ottoman Empire in 1915 by laying mines in the Dardanelles that destroyed or damaged three Allied ships. Inside the boat you can find maps and plans of the naval campaign as well as old air-dropped bombs and bits of the sunk German submarine. The Çimenlik fortress was built by Mehmet the Conqueror to protect the Dardanelles. Within its cavernous entrails you'll find some not-very-persuasive-looking figurines of soldiers at war as well as flasks and other historical objects from WWI. Outside the castle is a still-unexploded, 38cm shell from HMS Elizabeth that drilled its way into the fortifications.

⚑ *From the Clock Tower head south, parallel to the shore, down Rıhtım Cad. and Yalı Sok. After 500m you'll find the entrance to the museum's gardens.* **i** *A guide for groups of 3 or more can be arranged at the ticket booth.* Ⓢ *4TL, students 1TL.* Ⓒ *Open Tu-W 9am-noon and 1-5pm, F-Su 9am-noon and 1-5pm.*

FOOD ◳

▨ YALI HANI ⊛ Ⓨ ⌂ CAFE ❶

Fetvane Sok. 28   ☎286 212 4926 🖳www.yalihani.com

This is possibly the best down-to-earth hangout in town. Shaded by a huge wisteria tree and full of small wooden tables, this popular courtyard is an excellent place to come for some beer *(4TL)*, a few cigarettes or *nargile*, and friendly conversation. If you don't feel like sitting in the courtyard, there's always the darker, less spacious upper level.

➡ From the Clock Tower continue down Fetvane Sok.; the courtyard will be to your right. $ Beer 4TL. Nargile 7TL. Sandwiches 2-3TL. Tiramisu 3TL. ⏰ Open daily 11am-midnight.

GÜLEN PIDE
🍴 TURKISH [2]

Cumhuriyet Meydanı 27/A ☎286 214 0410

Competing with the nearby Doyum for the title of The Best Kebab Place Around, Gülen Pide offers a cheerful interior and tasty food. Watch cooks prepare dough in the open kitchen, and try the *halep işi kebab*—it's extra spicy, extra oily, and covered with tomato sauce.

➡ From the ferry jetty head inland 300 meters. It will be to your right. $ Kebabs 9.50-13.50TL, pides 5.50-8.50TL. ⏰ Open daily 11am-10:30pm.

YALOVA
🍴🍸☀ FISH [3]

Yalı Cad. Gümrük Sok. 7 ☎286 217 1045 🖥www.yalovarest.com

If you're in a celebratory mood or just want to eat fish with fewer risks than in Istanbul, come eat at Yalova. There's a display of fish to choose from, including fish that look harmless and fish that look like they could beat you up in a dark alley. The tables on the terrace offer a nice view of the Dardanelles, but the first-floor patio is the most popular option and stays crowded. Locals come here for special occasions, so come here to celebrate the fact that you finally stopped pronouncing Çanakkale as "Kanakkale."

➡ From the ferry jetty, head south by the shore, and you'll see the restaurant's name on top of a building to the left. ℹ Reservations not necessary, but will get you a better table. $ Appetizers 4-18TL; fish entrees 15-100TL. Desserts 5-6TL. ⏰ Open daily noon-midnight.

DAMAK TADI
🍴 FAST FOOD [1]

Yalı Cad. 20 ☎286 217 4590 🖥www.damaktadi.net.ms

To see what it's like to be a starving student in Çanakkale, have something at Damak Tadı. This place screams "fast food" from afar, but it's quite popular due to its menu ranging from the mundane (hamburgers) to the exotic (grilled sheep's intestines in a bread). The interior isn't too aesthetically pleasing, so get takeout and sit by the sea.

➡ It's right next to Yalova. From the Clock Tower take the Yalı Cad., and it will be to your right. $ Sandwiches 1.75-4.50TL. Pide 5.50-8.50TL. Fish 7.50-15TL. ⏰ Open daily 7:30am-12pm.

ESSENTIALS

Practicalities

- **TOURIST OFFICES:** The throbbing heart of all things practical is **Cumhuriyet Meydanı.** The **Tourism Information Office** has current schedules for ferries going to Eceabat and for dolmuşes going to Troy. *(☎286 217 1187. ℹ Call ahead for schedules. ⏰ Open daily in summer 8:30am-7pm; in winter 8:30am-5:30pm.)*
- **TOURS:** There are a number of companies offering tours of Gallipoli and Troy, including **TJs Tours** *(☎286 814 3121)*, and **Hassle Free Travel Agency** *(☎286 213 5969)*.
- **CURRENCY EXCHANGE:** Use the **PTT booth** *(☎286 212 6981)* to exchange money, send postcards, and make phone calls.
- **ATMS:** Can be found mostly near the ferry jetty.
- **INTERNET:** There are no public wireless hotspots, but many cafes and hostels provide their own networks.

- **POST OFFICE:** The post office is 10min. away from Cumhuriyet Meydanı. (*İnönü Cad. 78* ☎*286 217 1022* 🕓 *Open daily 8am-7pm.*)

Emergency!

- **EMERGENCY NUMBER:** ☎112.
- **POLICE:** ☎155.

Getting There

By Bus

The intercity bus companies have their offices both in this square and inside the bus station (☎*286 217 5653*). There are numerous direct buses running from Istanbul to Çanakkale (🅢 *35TL* 🕓 *6½hr., 5 per day*) operated by **Truva**, **Kamil Koç**, **Metro**, and **Ulusoy**. You can board these at the **Büyük Otogar**, but some of these companies have minibuses at **Taksim** that will take you to the otogar.

By Ferry

A more pleasant way to get to Çanakkale can be to take the **ferry** from Istanbul's Yenikapı Ferry Terminal (accessible by suburban train from Sirkeci) to **Bandırma** (💻*www.ido.com.tr* 🅢 *32TL* 🕓 *2hr., 3 per day*) and then transfer to a Çanakkale-bound **bus.** (🅢 *20TL* 🕓 *3hr.*) To get to Bandırma's bus station from the ferry terminal, take the **# 8 bus** (☎*286 217 5653* 🅢 *1.25TL* 🕓 *20 min.*) that's 50 meters to the right of the terminal's exit.

By Plane

Turkish Airlines offers direct flights between the Atatürk International Airport and Çanakkale Airport. (☎*286 212 3366* ✈ *Transportation between the center and Çanakkale Airport is supplied by a shuttle bus. Airlines have office under the Anafartalar Hotel.* 🅢 *Flights vary. Shuttles 2TL each way.* ℹ *Call for exact shuttle times.* 🕓 *1hr.; Tu, Th, Su at 4:15pm, return at 6:05pm.*)

Getting Around

In Çanakkale everything is within walking distance. To get from the bus station to the city center, leave through the main exit (there are silver letters *otogar* above it), turn left, and continue to the traffic light. Here, turn right and continue straight all the way to the ferry jetty. To get to the dolmuş stop from the jetty, walk inland toward the bus station, but instead of turning left at the second light, turn right and continue straight until you see a bridge (the dolmuşes stand is directly underneath). If circumstances require it, you can easily get a cab at Cumhuriyet Meydanı.

Troy

You can get around Troy with a guided tour or on your own. To get there by yourself, take a dolmuş from under the bridge. (🅢 *4TL.* ℹ *Call for weekend times.* 🕓 *40 min., weekdays hourly 9:30am-5:30pm, return hourly 7am-3pm.*)

Gallipoli

If you don't have your own transportation and don't want to take a tour, moving around Gallipoli on your own is a bit tricky. First, you'll need to take the ferry across the Dardanelles from Çanakkale to Eceabat. (🅢 *2TL.* 🕓 *20min., hourly during the summer.*) In **Eceabat** you can hop on a dolmuş going to **Kabatepe** (they aren't too frequent and run primarily to connect with ferries that go from Kabatepe to **Gökceada** three times a day). The dolmuş will let you off at **Kabatepe Museum**, where you can walk to catch a dolmuş back. The distances are in kilometers and the area is hilly, so don't be too optimistic when estimating the time it will take you to cover most of the sites. Sometimes it's possible to arrange transport with guided tours or hire a taxi to drive you around, but these tend to be expensive for a student traveler.

cape sounion peninsula

Far out at the end of Attica, the incessant noise, huge buildings, and heeled occupants of Athens seem but a faded memory. After winding around a coast that inevitably, it seems, will throw the **KTEL** bus over the edge, you reach the top of a hill where mountains, water, and a smattering of dried greenery dominate the scenery. Cape Sounion Peninsula, though not the most beautiful of destinations, is possibly the most tantalizing beach that can be reached from Athens by land. For those who've had too many days in the city, or simply for those thirsting for open air, this is a great daytrip. The **tip** of Cape Sounion Peninsula, which ends at an enormous cliff-face into the sea, was dedicated to Poseidon, the mythological God of the Seas. On the right of the bus stop is the incredibly impressive **Temple of Poseidon,** built in 600 BCE, and down the road from the bus stop is the **Temple of the Goddess Athena,** a bit less impressive. Even just for the chance to see water and not concrete on the mainland, Cape Sounion is worth the bus ride.

ORIENTATION

Cape Sounion Peninsula is at the end of the bus line, and buses loop back home after dropping off their passengers. Directly behind the bus stop is **Cafe Naos,** the best dining option in Sounion. Down the road 300m is the Temple of Athena's ruins, and across the road from those ruins and down another 600m is the beach. Venturing farther than the beach on foot is unadvisable, as destinations nearby are sparse, and the one-lane road is frequented with buses that take up the whole pavement.

SIGHTS

👍 TEMPLE OF POSEIDON — TEMPLE [1]

At the end of the peninsula — ☎229 20 38 363

At the end of Attica atop a cliff, this temple sits in surroundings that, other than perhaps being more weather-beaten, are exactly the same condition as when the temple was first constructed. As a result, the temple—a massive white marble structure of pillars that was attacked by the Persians in 480 BCE—seems ancient in a way that even the Acropolis doesn't. The sea and the winding coastline, all that one can see from beside the temple, are calm and still. From the top of the hill, it is clear why the ancient Athenians chose to construct the temple to the God of the Sea here in 600 BCE.

➔ Visible from the bus stop atop the hill to the right. $ €4, students and EU citizens over 65 €2, EU students and those under 18 free. Free on Su Nov 1-Mar 31. ⏰ Open daily 9am-sunset.

TEMPLE OF ATHENA — TEMPLE [1]

Down the hill from the Temple of Poseidon — ☎229 20 38 363

What was once a temple dedicated to the Goddess Athena, the patron of Athens, is now a pile of crumbling marble accessible only through weeds infested with crickets. No ticket booth guards the ruins. In fact, to get to this sketchy site, you must walk down the highway. Instead, check out the ruins from the bottom of the path to the Temple of Poseidon, as seeing these remnants from afar is just as satisfying as seeing them up close.

➔ Walk down the hill from the Temple of Poseidon; look for a rusty gate. $ Free. ⏰ Open daily 9:30am-sunset.

BEACHES

There are a few beaches along Cape Sounion, though the divisions are somewhat artificial and determined by which hotel the patch of pebbly sand is near. The €10 charge for two chairs and one umbrella and €5 charge for one chair by an umbrella is uniform for every beach, but feel free to lay your towel directly on the sand for free. The beaches are populated by few tourists, mostly Athenian families with parents who have a free day and wanted to get out of the city. The water has some seaweed floaters and the sand is coarse, but if the alternative is the streets of Athens, then this is a decent place to go. On the way to the end of the peninsula, the bus drives past a host of other small beaches set in small towns, so feel free to hop off the bus and check out any of those. They are all interchangeable, with the same pebbly sand, chair charges, and body of water.

FOOD

CAFE NAOS
🐽♿☼❄ TAVERNA ❷

Right behind the bus stop
☎229 20 39 190

Though the food here borders on bland and the decor is a nondescript mix of stone, this restaurant is just 100m from the ticket booth for the Temple of Poseidon and sits right behind the bus stop. Check out the incredible view from the tables on the perimeter, but stick to the basic Greek fundamentals of salad (€6.60) and bread with olive.

✠ *Up the steps directly behind the bus stop and to the left of the Temple of Poseidon.* ⓘ *Sit by the edge for a great view.* ⏰ *Open daily 9am-sunset.*

AEGEON
🐽♿☼⛅ BEACH BAR ❶

Behind the far left side of the beach
☎229 20 39 200

This beach bar serves soda, beer, coffee, and water and has a few tables out front, but is more like a human-run vending machine than bar: it's nothing to look at but provides what you need quickly. Come here for a beer (€3.50-5) or can of coke (€2) when parched on the beach.

✠ *Behind the chairs on the left-most edge of the beach.* ⓢ *Soda €2. Beer €3.50-5.* ⏰ *Open daily 9am-9pm.*

ESSENTIALS

Practicalities

Cape Sounion is sparse land. No pharmacy, office buildings, apartments, shops, or medical offices mark the beautiful landscape. Unfortunately, that means that travelers are out of luck when it comes to most essentials. Make sure to bring what you will need for the day, and do not plan on accessing the internet from the cape. It is also quite hot and no trees offer shade, so bring a hat and sunscreen and plan on returning to Athens a bit redder than when you left. Water can be purchased in the water vending machine at Cafe Naos (€0.50) or in any of the beachside bars that line the Cape Sounion beach.

Getting There

By Bus

Orange-striped and white-bodied **KTEL** buses travel from Athens to Cape Sounion. One leaves from the **Mavromateon 14 bus stop** (near Areos Park, on Alexandras and 28 Oktovriou-Patission), stops at all points on the Apollo Coast, and can be asked to stop wherever you would like to disembark. (ⓢ €5. ⏰ 2hr., every hr. 6:30am-6pm.) The other buses follow a less scenic inland route that also stops at the port of **Lavrio**. (ⓢ €4. ⏰ 2 hr., every hr. 6am-6pm.) The last coastal bus leaves Sounion at 9pm, and the last inland leaves at 9:30pm. Every 30min., a bus to **Athens** should arrive at the base of Cafe Naos to return to the city. Don't panic if a bus does not arrive exactly on time—one will eventually show up.

Getting Around

Transportation around Cape Sounion is basically by foot. To get from the **Temple of Poseidon** or **Cafe Naos** to the **beach,** walk down the road until you reach a parking lot on the left side of the road. In the back of the parking lot is a hole in the metal barrier. Walk through the hole (and make sure to step over the refuse and toilet paper strewn on the path) and follow the path downhill. Though there are no paved stones or railings, the path is well-worn and passable—just be careful of brambles and the spot with barbed wire to the left. Within 5min., you will be on the sand. It is also possible to walk along the main road, but the path is longer, indirect, and puts you close to oncoming traffic.

GREEK ISLANDS

Sun-drenched white houses, winding stone streets, and trellis-covered tavernas define the Greek islands as a whole, but subtle quirks make each island distinct. Orange and black sands coat the shoreline of Santorini, sun-fried bodies and expensive food populate Mykonos, Naxos offers peaceful mountain villages, and celebrated archaeological sites testify to the mythical and historical legengs surrounding Delos. Don't restrict yourself to just one island—see as many as you can with the comprehensive ferry system and soak up the unique flavor of each Greek island has to offer.

greatest hits

- **BUST OUT YOUR HIKING BOOTS.** Hike up the hill on the uninhabited island of Delos to see all of the excavated sights of this UNESCO World Heritage Site (p. 146).
- **SWIM THRU RUINS.** In Andros Town, you can swim in the ocean that has swallowed up ancient Venetian Ruins (p. 154).
- **SWEET LEMONS.** Go to M. G. Vallindras Distillery and get a free sip of citron alcohol (p. 166).

mykonos ☎22890

Mykonos is renowned as an island of hedonism where the sea glistens next to the equally sparkling sweaty bodies of the naked old men beside it. Here, brown netting passes as a shirt, beaches are clothing optional, and happy hours come three times a day. Island-revelers sleep from 7am-2pm and then head to the beach to bring the day in with a piña colada and a discussion of their alcohol intake the night before. But the Dionysian impulse is only one side of the island. Tourists less inclined to relax on the scantily-clad beaches or rage at the local club scene can wind through the intertwined streets of Mykonos Town. If the nudity and drunkenness is making you blush, take a water taxi and head to a more family-friendly beach. Expensive restaurants, creperies, and shops line the tourist-packed streets of the town. In the middle of the island between Mykonos Town and Paradise Beach, houses are as white as Crest models' teeth and jut out from the parched earth, disturbed only by the lizards scuttling amongst long forgotten (or never remembered) Red Bull cans. Along the roadside, donkeys and chickens nibble on hay from behind rusted wire fences. Mykonos' gay scene far surpasses that of other Greek islands, and here men or women walking holding hands or kissing does not elicit so much as a second glance. With this mix of grandparent-friendly town and adult-only clubs, Mykonos can be made to suit any traveler's desires—though those seeking nighttime extravagance are the most likely to be sated.

ORIENTATION

Mykonos Town is located on the western side of the 41mi. island. On the south side of the island, **Paradise Beach** neighbors **Paraga Beach.** If you're staying at one of the island's campgrounds, the day will likely involve passing from one side of the island to the other by way of winding pathways that count as roads: it's a miracle that bus drivers don't ram into every stone wall along their routes. Along these roads, goats, cows, and the occasional donkey can be seen behind pens, a dramatic shift in scenery from both the classy development of Mykonos Town and the seedy developments of Paradise Beach.

ACCOMMODATIONS

Housing on Mykonos is to prices like red and purple are to the rainbow: they fall on either end of the spectrum. Very expensive accommodations are easy to come by, as are beds that cost very little and feel like it. Interestingly, middle-range hostels and hotels are hard to find. Expect either to be in a nice hotel with internet and ensuite bathrooms with shampoo by the shower or to stay in a room with seven other people swatting mosquitos. There is much to do on Mykonos, so don't sweat the rough living if you're looking to live cheaply—think of the saved funds as an excuse to buy that next drink.

greek islands

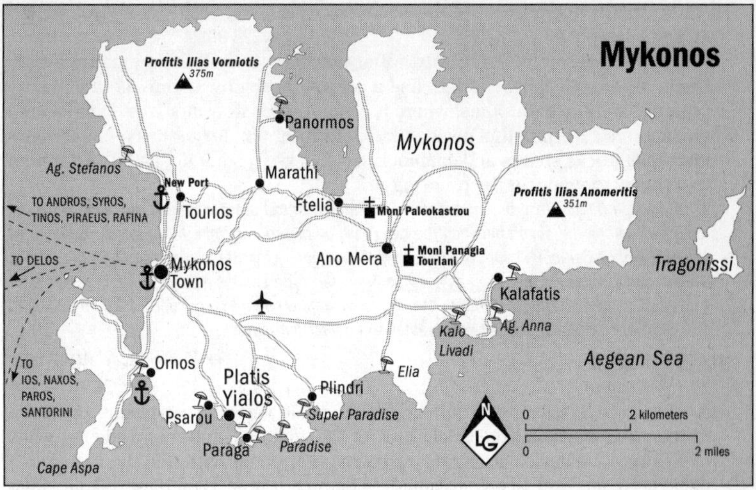

ZORZIS HOTEL
HOTEL [5]

30 Nik. Kalogera ☎228 90 22 167 💻www.zorzishotel.com

Elaborate wooden beds, mismatched cushions by the breakfast tables, and a community fridge are just a few of the special touches that make Zorzis Hotel feel homey. Located down a quiet street in Mykonos Town, this hotel has all the amenities that can be desired, including an eager-to-please staff. Highly visible security cameras will keep a watchful eye over your things while you are out at the beach or a nearby bar.

Down the street from Hotel Philippi. i Breakfast included. Laundry service, safety deposit box, and currency exchange available. Community fridge. Fans in every room. $ Singles €85; doubles €113. ⏰ Reception 24hr.

PARADISE HOSTEL
HOSTEL [2]

Behind Paradise Beach 💻www.paradiseclub-mykonos.com

Only 100m from the water and the site of some of the island's most advertised parties, Paradise Hostel is for those who want to pay as little as possible to be near the action. Cabins are cheap, tiny, and stripped of all but the basics, though the mattresses are plush. When filled to capacity in the summer months, nearly 800 beach-goers stay here, making this an agoraphobic's nightmare and a social butterfly's paradise.

Right behind Paradise Beach. i Breakfast included. Electrical outlet in each cabin. Luggage storage available. $ Singles €25-60; doubles €34-80. Motorbike rental €14 per day. ⏰ Reception 8am-11pm.

HOTEL APOLLON
HOTEL [4]

On the waterfront ☎228 90 22 223

With incredible views of Mykonos' waterfront from its porch, Hotel Apollon has the best real estate in town. Rooms are spacious and well-kept, but the entrance has accumulated knick-knacks and paintings through the years and is running low on usable wall space. Without many additional offerings beside bed and bath, Hotel Apollon is a convenient hotel—just don't expect to be able to check your email from the premises.

On the waterfront a few blocks to the left (when looking at the water) of Taxi Sq. Entrance is behind Yialos outside seating. i Refrigerator in every room. $ Doubles Sept-June €60, with bath €80; Jul-Aug €65/90. ⏰ Reception 8am-11pm.

PARAGA BEACH HOSTEL 🚌♿📶🍸☀ HOSTEL [1]

At Paraga Beach ☎228 90 24 578 💻www.mycamp.gr

Rustic and campy feeling, Paraga offers metal cots and skinny mattresses to tired partiers. Sleeping quarters line a central dirt pathway through the "campground," and the bathrooms, where hot water often does not work, are located on each end. Despite this decided lack of plush, this hostel has a clutch mini-mart that stocks snacks and sunblock, a self-serve restaurant, and a stellar pool that seems too nice for the price tag.

➔ At Paraga Beach. Take bus from Fabrika to Paraga, or to Paradise Beach, and walk along the rocky path along the ocean between the two (path takes around 7min. to walk). i Sometimes called Mykonos Camping. Laundry €5. Free Wi-Fi by pool. Computers with internet €1 per 10min. Groups can arrange for breakfast as early as 6am. $ 8-person mixed dorm €10; 2-person bungalow €30; 2-person TRB (tent with bed) €25. ⏰ Reception 8am-11pm. Pool open 9am-midnight. Mini-mart open 8am-10pm. Self-serve restaurant open 8am-10pm.

HOTEL PHILIPPI 🚌🚭📶🍸❄☀ HOTEL [5]

25. Nik. Kalogera ☎228 90 22 294

A central courtyard blooms with bright orange flowers that pop against the white of the hotel walls and the bright blue of the window shutters. Inside the walls of this perky exterior are standard rooms that come with a kettle and coffee packets to help you face your hangover in the morning. Health nuts should take note: while workout machinery is basically unheard of in Greece, this hotel has a treadmill. If running is for you, so is this hotel.

➔ Down the street from Hotel Zorzis i All rooms have shower, TV, refrigerator, and phone. Free Wi-Fi. $ Singles Sept-June €60, Jul-Aug €90; doubles €75/125. 3rd bed add 20% to price. ⏰ Reception 24hr.

SIGHTS 👁

Unlike most Greek sights, Mykonos' are not ancient ruins. Instead, welcome to a town of charmingly disorganized museums that specialize in the town's 18th-century incarnation.

LENA'S HOUSE 🏛♿ MUSEUM

On Matoyanni's extension ☎228 90 28 764

Originally an upper-middle-class home in 18th-century Mykonos, this house was donated as a museum by sibling-less resident Lena in 1970. The house stands as it did when she lived there and is notable for the amount of imported wood it contains, as no timber trees grow on Mykonos. As a result, only those with wealth could afford wooden tables, beds, and homes. Lena's father was a timber trader in the Black Sea, and he filled his house with this status symbol. The house provides an interesting glimpse into the island before it was a tourist destination.

➔ From Fabrika, walk down the main street, take the first right, and turn right at Jimmy's souvlaki shop. Continue down the street as it winds, and Lena's House will be on your left. i Walk only on the carpets. $ €2, students free. ⏰ Open daily 7-9pm.

FOLKLORE MUSEUM 🏛🚭 MUSEUM

The House of Kastro ☎228 90 22 591

Built in 1958, the Folklore Museum is the type of place that would never be built today: there are no ropes, placards explaining the rooms' contents, or plexiglass cases separating viewers from the displays. The disorganized explosion of plates, model ships, earrings, and votive offerings from the Mediteranean ports of the 18th and 19th centuries is a fun, quick walk through that feels like stepping into a really old treasure chest. Beware of the doll in the bedroom and the mannequin sitting at the table in the first room as their eyes creepily follow you as you explore the oldest house on the island.

⇟ *From Taxi Sq., walk along the waterfront to the left. Right before passing the port, take a left onto the street that has a visible upward slant; the Folklore Museum will be on the right before you reach the church.* $ *€2, students free.* ⏰ *Open M-Sa 5:30-8:30pm, Su 6:30-8:30pm.*

AEGEAN MARITIME MUSEUM — MUSEUM

Right next to Lena's House on Matoyanni's extension — ☎228 90 22 700

In the adapted kitchen and family room of Lena's House are a multitude of small model ships, framed maps, and other boat paraphernalia commemorating the old port town. Head out back to the garden to see a giant steering wheel from a long lost barge. While the museum is small, it's worth a stop if traveling near Lena's House.

⇟ *From Fabrika, walk down the main street, take the first right, and turn right at Jimmy's souvlaki shop. Continue down the street as it winds, and the museum will be on your left.* $ *€4, students €1.50.* ⏰ *Open Apr 1-Oct 31 10:30am-1pm and 6:30-9pm.*

ARCHAEOLOGICAL MUSEUM — MUSEUM

Kaminak — ☎22890 22325

Only one piece in the Archaeological Museum's collection actually comes from Mykonos—a giant urn in the back of the room straight from the door. This 7th-century pot displays a scene from the Trojan War already made immortal in Homer's epic—the Trojan horse. Aside from this pot, though, all the contents of the museum come from the nearby island of Renia, which functioned as Delos' burial ground after Pisistratus ordered that all dead bodies be expunged out of respect for the gods in the 6th century BCE.

⇟ *On the street above the Old Port where the road forks.* ℹ *The island where most of the collection comes from can be seen from the doorway of the museum.* $ *€2, non-EU students and EU residents over 64 €1, children and EU students free.* ⏰ *Open M-Sa 5:30-8:30pm, Su 6:30-8:30pm.*

THE GREAT OUTDOORS

SCUBA

MYKONOS DIVING CENTER — DIVE SHOP

Behind Tropicana Bar at Paradise Beach — ☎228 90 24 808 🖥www.dive.gr

Though your typical Mykonos tourist is known more for valuing what's on the surface than for looking beneath, the pale blue seas hold reefs and even a cement boat that sunk 30m that entertain divers of all abilities. At this official PADI dive center, beginners willing to dedicate three days to the activity can earn scuba certification, and those who already have a beginner license can take classes to become advanced. Those who want to try wearing the mask but don't want to sacrifice three days of tanning time to wear a wetsuit can try the "Discover Scuba Diving" course and dive to a depth of 12m.

⇟ *Set back behind Tropicana Bar on Paradise Beach.* ℹ *PADI dive center. All equipment included in prices. Minors need guardian signature. Make reservations 48hr. in advance and cancel more than 24hr. in advance; cancellation fee €60.* $ *Snorkeling €40. "Discover Scuba Diving" course €70. Full-day diving for certified divers €100. Night diver training €150.* ⏰ *Open daily 9am-7pm.*

Beaches

Mykonos is perimetered by beaches that give many a visitor a sun-kissed glow (or in the more dramatic cases, the appearance of having been submerged in a vat of tanning oil and then fried). Beaches fall into two categories—the pulsing music sort and the quieter, more family-friendly variety. The two main "pulsing music" beaches are **Paradise Beach** and **Paraga Beach,** which neighbor each other on the southern end of the island. Both have small rocks rather than sand and are harpooned with reed-covered umbrellas. Throughout the day both play top-40 dance tunes with added bass tracks, and at 5pm both beaches push the limits of the speakers' capacity and turn the volume way up. Many gaudy bathing suits make their debut here, and nudity is welcome though not so common among the younger set: those most willing to disrobe are the older men. The two beaches—which both accompany low-budget sleeping areas—can be distinguished by the number of supporting shops behind the sand. Paradise's number of eateries far outnumbers that of Paraga, which only has one main place to sit down for lunch or dinner.

Past these two beaches are **Super Paradise, B. Agrari,** and **B. Elia.** Super Paradise is a small but busy pebbly beach that lacks the pulsing soundtracks of its beach brethren. Most beachgoers here are in their mid-30s and still fit, though not buff enough to swim in the nude. **B. Agrari** is a quiet couples beach, and you probably need to ask the water taxi to stop here if it is your destination of choice. There are many open chairs and a floating wooden platform a bit out into the water for snuggling couples to lay on during sunsets. █**Elia,** (☎228 90 27 000) the last beach that water taxis hit on their usual route, is renowned as the gay beach, and a rainbow flag waves proudly above the sandy shore. From the view of the water taxi, the left side of the beach tends to be where gay couples settle. The water at Elia, though presumably the same as at all the other beaches, seems particularly turquoise blue and clear, and sand, not pebbles, is underfoot.

On the other side of Paraga and Paradise Beach are **Psarou** and **Ornos.** Ornos, the launching pad for many water taxis, is a family-friendly beach where an open space has been left open in the center of the beach for those who do not want to purchase chairs. Virtually no one opts out of swim trunks on this stretch of pebbly sand, where colorful straws mix with the stones. Psarou is also fairly quiet and family friendly. Off the water taxi route are two treasures of beaches, **B. Panormos** and **Ag. Sositis.** Both of these quiet beaches are on the northern side of the island and an ideal destination for those who do not want to be disturbed.

beaches in mykonos

All beaches charge for using their chairs and umbrellas (generally €12 for 2 chairs and umbrella). If staying on the beach for the day, the chair may be worth the investment, but if looking to be frugal, just plop down on the sand right next to a chair and use the umbrella's shade from the sun. Unless someone is fighting for that chaise, the fund-collectors don't seem to mind.

greek islands

FOOD

Mykonos is an expensive island, and finding dishes whose main ingredient isn't saturated fat for less than €10 requires some planning. Many visitors here sleep through breakfast and awake at lunchtime. For those who are up and want a not-so-pricey breakfast, try some packaged yogurt (€2) or fresh fruit from a mini-mart (€2). For lunch, Greek salads are a great pick—even in some of the more expensive restaurants, prices for these hover at just under €7. Crepes (€4), though not Atkins approved, are healthier than a gyro (€2) and can be found at just as many beach vendors. Dinner is the place to splurge on a gourmet meal. Food here, though expensive, is worth the cash.

█ **SUISSE CAFE** ●⊗♥❄❆ CAFE, CREPERIE ❶
End of Matoyani ☎228 90 27 462

Build your own salad of succulent tomatoes and cheeses topped with the cafe's special dressing or indulge in a powdered crepe in this Alice-in-Wonderland-esque cafe and dessert place. With pinks, blues, and greens accenting the white tablecloths, the fantasy decor makes every female feel like a princess. Well-priced and a welcome break from the ubiquitous *tavernas* and in-your-face Greekness of many other eateries in the same price bracket, Suisse Cafe is a treasure.

From the Fabrika bus station, take the 1st right and follow that road down to the left. Turn right when you reach the intersection with the gyro place with bright blue window shutters, and then make a left. $ Ice cream from €2.50. Crepes €3.50-6. Banana split €9. Fresh-squeezed orange juice €3.50. Cocktails €6. Sandwiches from €5. ⏰ Open daily 9:15am-midnight.

PASTA FRESCA ITALIAN ❸

Kouzi Georgouli 15 ☎228 90 22 563

For some good ol' Italian pasta come to...Mykonos? Down one of the main streets, a man in a white apron can be seen handmaking tortellini on a wooden table, with multicolored noodles spread out in front of him. Directly behind him, the products of his labor are served atop white tablecloths in the glow of candlelight and the sparkle of wine glasses. A variety of sauces are offered with these fresh pastas, and a wide selection of wines complement the course. This elaborate table is an ideal stage for romantic hand-holding.

On the main street from the bus station. $ Salads €11. Pasta dishes from €9. ⏰ Open daily 3pm-3am.

PICCOLO SANDWICH SHOP ❶

18 Drakopoulou ☎228 90 22 208 www.piccolo-mykonos.com

An adorable sandwich place just a few blocks from the waterfront, Piccolo offers up scrumptious bite-size concoctions with prices a bit out of proportion with the size but worth the splurge. Fresh ingredients like tomatoes, olives, and eggplant brighten the deli counter, and fresh oranges for juice adds a colorful splash. Order from the extensive menu right inside the door, or make your own sandwich combination from the displayed ingredients. Top off the meal with a pastry on display in the glass case at the end of the deli counter.

From the waterfront, walk straight up Drakopoulou for 2 blocks. $ Sandwiches from €4.90 ⏰ Open daily 9am-12:30am.

LA CASA RESTAURANT GREEK ❷

Matogianni 8 ☎228 90 24 994

For a middle-of-the-road meal at a midrange price, try La Casa. The food is average, as are portion sizes, but the classic decor of the restaurant somewhat makes up for the blandness of the food. Dishes are served on ivy-green-rimmed ceramic plates, adding a hint of charm to the usual Greek fare. Try the *moussaka (€4.90)* or Greek salad *(€6.90)* for a reasonably priced dinner in a pricey town.

Across from Suisse Cafe. $ Bread €2. Salads from €7. Entrees from €9. ⏰ Open daily 1:30pm-1am.

NAUTILUS GREEK ❹

Nik. Kalogera 6 ☎228 90 27 100

If the scent of cottonwood were made into a restaurant, the result would be Nautilus. Pale blue lacquer barely sets the chairs and tables off from the surrounding white buildings, giving the physical restaurant a peaceful feel. While diners are mostly happy families enjoying vacation, the candles and guitar-based music blow a romantic breeze through the tables. The food is intentionally light—on the presumption that after a day in the heat a greasy meal is less desirable than a finely-grilled fish or a sizable salad—but portions are still large and filling. Try the renowned grilled chicken with ginger, honey, and orange *(€18)*.

From Taxi Square, take a right onto the street in the middle of the square. Walk straight through the cluster of restaurants, and head to the right. $ Bread and dip €3. Salads €9-17. Entrees €15-80. ⏰ Open daily Mar-Oct 7pm-12:30am.

JIMMY'S GYRO ❶

Ipirou 1

Jimmy's opened 36 years ago, and for half of each of those years its doors have always been open. Or rather, its doorways have always been open. For the duration of Mykonos' main tourist season, the establishment takes the doors off their hinges and put them into storage. This eatery is the epitome of a greasy gyro *(€2.50)* place. Cheap, oily, and quick, this pita palace has its business down pat.

➜ On the main street from the bus station. $ Chicken and pork gyros €2.50. Kebab plates €8.50. ⏰ Open mid-Apr-mid-Oct 24hr.

SNACK BAR CAFE CAFE [1]

Mitropoleos 12 ☎228 90 24 895

Wooden signs outside advertise a host of cheap non-gyro options, and Snack Bar Cafe delivers on all fronts. Inside there's an ice cream counter, fruit section, crepe-making station, bar, and deli counter, and each refrigerated station can whip up a cheap snack or meal. For a small lunch, try the ham and cheese crepe *(€4.50)*, which is good, if you like pepper. Though it's nothing special, Snack Bar Cafe is a reliable place to go for a quick bite to eat.

➜ On the main street from the bus station. $ Frappes €2.80. Milkshakes €4. Mixed drinks €6-8. Sandwiches €2.50. Crepes €4. ⏰ Open daily 8:30am-6am.

NIGHTLIFE

Many travelers arrive at Mykonos with two goals: get drunk and stay drunk. Both of those goals are readily achievable on an island that has built a reputation for itself as party-until-dawn-and-maybe-a-bit-after central. All varieties of spandex and skimpy shirts and dresses make their appearance every night of the week, because on Mykonos, the weekend knows no bounds. From the beach clubs to the bars in Mykonos Town, everyone has a place to go to mix with other sweaty bodies. DJs from around the world come to the island to spin at the clubs, and events are well-advertised. Just don't make the mistake of going out too early: bars and clubs in town don't heat up until around 1am, and the beach clubs don't hit their full groove until 3am.

nightlife mykonos

Nightlife here, for better or for worse, spins on the wheels of intoxication. This beverage-centric habit can prove problematic for those traveling on a budget because bar concotions are often exorbitantly priced. To save a few euros (and after a couple of days, those few saved here and there will add up), do what college students do best: pregame. Head to Dimitris Likouris *(Koyzh Georgoyli 35 ☎228 90 24 384)* and buy a bottle of wine *(€3 and up)*, ouzo *(€6)*, or vodka *(from €10)* to enjoy while looking out on the boats tied for the night along the waterfront. *Let's Go* always recommends drinking responsibly (and cheaply!)

SKANDINAVIAN BAR AND DISCO BAR, DANCE CLUB [1]

Agios Ioauis, Barkia ☎22190 22 669 🖥www.skandinavianbar.com

If you go to one club in Mykonos, this should be it. While the beach clubs advertise heavily, their giant venues leave partygoers with too much room around them for the appropriate sweaty club feel. The Skandinavian is just the right size for clubgoers to feel packed in and still have room to shimmy. Rather than spin over-played Top-40s, classics to the tune of "I Will Survive" set the tone for the night (though Drake has his turn), and bartenders are incredibly friendly and willing to add some extra booze to a drink upon request. If you are going to run into that tantalizing guy or girl you saw on the beach earlier, it will be on top of the heart-tiled Skandinavian Bar dance floor.

➡ *From the waterfront, walk up 2 blocks by the Hotel Apollon.* $ *Wine and beer €5. Vodka €7. Cocktails €8.* ⏰ *Open daily 10pm-sunrise.*

★ PIERRO'S
💳⊘🍸❄☁▼ GLBT [1]

Ag. Kiriaki ☎228 90 22 177 💻www.pierrosbar.gr

At around 1am, the street outside Pierro's is filled with a throng of men—some in loafers, some in sneakers...and some in heels. This bar founded over 30 years ago has taken on the motto of "gay bar, straight friendly," according to the owner's wife, and every night the chocolate-colored decor is the backdrop for the heart of Mykonos' gay scene. Most of the socializing takes place outside in a night breeze that ruffles the feathers of drag-queen headdresses rather than in the extensive space indoors. Though the crowd tends toward 30-year-olds, and women are few and far between, all are welcome.

➡ *Next to Taxi Sq.* ℹ *Drag show nightly 1am.* $ *Beer €5. Whisky €8. Cocktails €10.* ⏰ *Open daily 10:30pm-4am.*

BAR DOWN UNDER
⊛♿🍸❄ BAR [1]

Ag. Ioanninou ☎687 46 82 554

This appropriately named bar is a magnet for the many Australians who for one reason or another find themselves in Mykonos. The clientele tends to be quite attractive, but under the flashing bright blue and red lights, even these attractive bar-hoppers seem to bob awkwardly in place like buoys in the ocean. In an attempt to reel people into the bar's dance space, a promoter stands by the door distributing cards worth a free shot. Take a card, take a free shot, and then move on for the rest of your night.

➡ *From the waterfront, walk up one block.* $ *Cocktails until midnight €5. Orgasm specialty drink €8. Mojitos €10. Buckets of each cocktail €25.* ⏰ *Open daily 9pm-2am or later.*

SPACE CLUB
💳♿🍸❄ CLUB [1]

Lakka ☎228 90 24 100 💻www.spacemykonos.com

There are three aisles outside the Space Club separated by metal railings and flashing lights. The left lane is for regular clubgoers who have to pay the fee, the right lane is for friends of the club who can enter without charge, and the middle aisle is for VIPs who, like their right lane counterparts, enter with a ton of money. Beyond the charming way the entrance scheme can make you feel like a serf, Space Club can offer a good time.

➡ *Walk down the main street from the bus stop and take the 1st right; Space Club is on the right.* $ *Cover €15, nights with guest DJs €20.* ⏰ *Open daily midnight-sunrise.*

CLUB CAVO PARADISO
⊛♿🍸❄☁ CLUB [2]

☎228 90 26 124 💻www.cavoparadiso.gr

Laid out with sequestering white fences that bring mini-golf courses to mind, Club Cavo has a reputation as one of Mykonos' hottest spots. Unfortunately, this reputation is lived up to only when enough people are in attendance to fill the club's space. Otherwise, the DJ's beats echo through a painfully empty arena, and the bouncer's tough guy stances seem farcical.

➡ *Located above Paradise Beach.* ℹ *Pool in the middle.* $ *Cover €15, includes 1 drink. Mixed drinks €10. Specialty drinks and drinks with Red Bull €12.* ⏰ *Open daily July-Aug midnight-7am.*

PARADISE CLUB
⊛♿🍸❄☁ CLUB [2]

In Paradise Beach, behind the sand ☎690 97 03 366 💻www.paradiseclubmykonos.com

Projectors, powerful speakers that send soundwaves several coves away, couches, and strobe lights make it evident that Paradise Beach has all the tools to host the most spectacular party of any given evening, and the hype that each event receives from the promoters imply that the tools will produce at capacity. But until around 5am, Paradise is void of sufficient angels to have earned its name, and the party is too spacious to be fun. Once it hits full throttle, though, it may not be paradise, but it sure is fun.

From Mykonos Town, take the bus to Paradise Beach from Fabrika station. Walk into the Paradise Beach campground and follow the music. $ *Cover, including 1 drink €15.* ⏰ *Open daily 11pm-sunrise.*

SHOPPING

Mykonos Town's streets are lined with the familiar names like **Hermes, Lacoste,** and **Sephora,** all of which sell their luxury goods without any discount in price. Interspersed with these big-name foreign imports are many boutiques selling cotton cover-ups or nightlife wear, most poorly made and justifying their cost with a few twinkling rhinestones or glittery additions. Sale items would only look good on the likes of Keira Knightly or Selma Hayek—and that's because they are stunning regardless of apparel. If you find yourself in dire need of a dress or heels or something appropriately revealing, your best bet is to spend 15min. wandering the streets, especially **Matoginni,** where one of the many shop windows will pop out. Closer down to the water are some shops selling small leather bags, scarves and, of course, **Mykonos T-shirts.** Expect haggling, and ask about credit cards, as not all shops accept them.

ESSENTIALS

Practicalities

- **TOURIST OFFICE: Sea and Sky Travel Agency.** *(Above Remezzo bus station. ☎228 90 28 240.)*
- **BUDGET TRAVEL OFFICES: Windmills Travel.** *(Next to South Station. ☎228 90 26 555 🖥www.windmillstravel.com).*
- **CURRENCY EXCHANGE: Alpha Bank** *(Matogianni 41 ☎228 90 23 180 ⏰ Open M-Th 8am-2:30pm, F 8am-2pm)* offers **currency exchange,** as does **Eurochange** in Taxi Sq.
- **LAUNDROMAT: Quick Clean** offers laundry services. *(☎228 90 27 323 $ Wash and dry €10.)*
- **INTERNET ACCESS:** Several cafes on the waterfront and by Fabrika station offer Wi-Fi with a food or beverage purchase. **Fast Internet** *(☎228 90 28 842 🖥www.fastinternetgreece.com ⏰ Open daily 10am-12:30am. $ €2.40 per hr.)* is immediately on the right by Fabrika and next to Quick Clean.
- **POST OFFICE:** The post office *(☎228 90 22 238 ⏰ Open M-F 7:30am-2pm)* is located across the street from Space Club.
- **POSTAL CODE:** 84600.

Emergency!

- **EMERGENCY NUMBER:** ☎108.
- **POLICE: Local police.** *(☎228 90 22 716 ⏰ Open 24hr.)* **Tourist police.** *(☎228 90 22 482 ⏰ Open daily 8am-9pm.)* Both are located by the airport.
- **HOSPITAL/MEDICAL SERVICES:** *(On the road leading from Fabrika station ☎228 90 23 994 ⏰ Emergency care 24hr.)*

Getting There

Mykonos is accessible from Athens by ferry *(4hr.)* and by plane *(20min.)*.

By Plane

Olympic Airways, *(☎228 90 22 490)* **Aegean Airlines,** *(☎228 90 28 720)* and **Athens Airways** all fly to Mykonos Airport (JMK).

By Ferry

Most boats dock at the New Port near Ag. Stefanos beach, 3km away from Mykonos Town, but some sea jets still dock at the Old Port. For information about which boats arrive where, call the **port authority** (☎228 90 22 218). Buy tickets at **Sea and Sky Travel Agency** (☎228 90 28 240), on the road above the Remezzo bus station and on the waterfront at Matogianni, where the latest ferry schedules are posted on its front porch. Ferries arrive from **Andros, Naxos, Paros, Rafina, Piraeus, Syros,** and **Tinos.**

Getting Around

Mykonos Town's main entrance is the **Fabrika bus station.** Streets are rarely labeled, and if they are labeled, buildings are not numbered. If looking for somewhere specific, know its name and ask for directions from shop owners along the way. The windy roads date back to when pirates claimed Mykonos' land and wanted to make their treasure chests as inaccessible as possible—and they succeeded. Be prepared to walk some as you find your destination. Though the town covers only a small geographic area, the paths loop around and you might get disoriented.

By Bus

Crossing from Mykonos Town to **Paradise Beach** or vice versa can be done by bus. (ⓢ €1.40 each way, €1.70 after midnight.) **KTEL** (☎228 90 23 360 ⓢ €1.40-1.70) has two stations on Mykonos. Tickets can be purchased on the bus from the driver, in the KTEL ticket station by the bus stop, or in many of the bodegas surrounding the bus stops. Bus stations are more like glorified parking lots than actual stations.

By Bike

Bikes are available for rent beside the **Fabrika bus station** in numerous and well-labeled shops and at Paradise Beach and Paraga Beach Camping. Bikes on Mykonos are full-throttle, and only some places require previous experience with the fast-moving two-wheelers in order to rent one for 24hr. But roads are hilly and windy, and it is often impossible to see oncoming traffic because of curvatures in the roads, so be careful. *Let's Go* does not condone drinking and driving—no matter what the vehicle.

By Taxi

Taxis (☎228 90 22 400 ⓢ €5-12, depending on destination) are an easy way to get around the island at any hour of the day. Wait for a cab at Taxi Sq., by the waterfront, or by the Fabrika bus station. Allow plenty of time, as there aren't usually enough taxis to meet demand.

By Water Taxi

Water Taxis run in a loop from **Ornas Beach** and scallop around the beaches on the southern side of the island, including **Super Paradise, Agrari, Ellia, Paranga,** and **Platy Gialos.** At Ornas, tickets can be purchased from the shack on the back of the sand in the middle of the beach or on the boat. Make sure to specify to the person steering where you would like to get off, and ask about the return schedule. Signs are unclear and faded, and the boats do not always run on whatever schedule does exist, so don't use water taxis if you are pressed for time.

By ATV or Motorbike:

ATV (ⓢ €15 per 24hr.) and **motorbikes** (ⓢ €10 per 24hr.) can be rented near the bus stops or at some hotels.

delos   ☎22890

Delos's history is rich—literally. On virtually every cultural and historical level, this island has been the stage for a notable occurrence. Let's start at the beginning, with the island's name. Delos translates to "seen." According to Greek mythology, this dollop of land just 40min. from Mykonos by ferry was brought to the surface from Poseidon's underwater kingdom. The god took pity on Leto, Zeus' most recent mortal crush, when she was ready to give birth to Zeus' godly children but could not find land on which to bear them. Supposedly Hera, the archetypal jealous wife, had forbidden all lands from hosting the roaming pregnant beauty. So who else but Zeus' brother to come to Leto's rescue? Bros before hos. Thus, the island, "seen," is the mythical birthplace of Apollo and Artemis, the God of the Sun and Goddess of the Moon, respectively. From 900 BCE to 100 CE the island was the site for cult worship of the two gods, as well as Dionysus.

In commerce, the island was also central. The Delian League—founded in 478 BCE and membered by 173 Greek city-states (Sparta not among them)—was based here, meaning that for about 400 years Delos was the closest thing to NATO or the World Bank until, well, NATO and the World Bank. Politically, the Delian League also had an agenda. Its member states paid a tribute to the league, funds which they could reclaim at any point in time, so long as the money was dedicated to defeating the Persians. Artistically, the island was home to marvelous, painstakingly thorough mosaics, frescoes, and architectural feats that, though now mostly washed away, can be glimpsed in the few remaining patches that have made it through the millenia. In terms of human rights, Delos' record is less stellar; the island was a former port city and had a busy slave trade. Delos had residents of Greek, Egypt, and other civilizations living side by side, and in that sense it was among the first cosmopolitan cities. But like most great things, this island civilization ended, and only one-fifth of the remains have been excavated. Fortunately, that one-fifth was impressive enough for the island to be made a World Heritage site in 1990.

SIGHTS   ◎

The ruins on Delos are so phenomenal that the island is now a World Heritage Site and has been for over two decades. Only one-fifth of the island is excavated, but that small fraction has unearthed an archaeological gold mine. Old mansions, a unique street design, and many temples devoted to the Greek gods still remain in some form on the multicultural island. Walk around; there will be no shortage of ancient marble on which to focus your camera.

🏛 HIKE UP THE HILL   ⊗ HIKE

Once you reach the top of this winding, heavy-breath-inducing path, you will never want to go down—not just because it's too steep, but because the view from the top is magical. Nearby islands are hazy in the distance, and the whole of excavated Delos is at your feet. When you are splayed on the smooth rocks at the peak of the hike, the sun god Apollo kissing you with abundant affection, the crowds and cacophonous Top-40 noise of Mykonos Town feel a lot more than a ferry ride away.

⚡ *Facing the museum, go right and follow the path. Roughly 15min. to the top.* ℹ *The terrain is steep in parts and the stones are not cemented together and sometimes wiggle underfoot. Be wary of where you step. Stable shoes advised. Bring water.*

🏛 THE THEATER QUARTER   ⊗ RUIN

Built in the 3rd century BCE with a seating capacity of over 5000 people, this theater is where the magnitude of ancient Delos is most tangible. The giant arch of seats bears down on the stage, which initially was home to only one actor but soon grew to a cast of three. In annual free performances funded by wealthy sponsors, ancient Delians would watch three tragedies, two comedies, and one satire in one rousing weekend of theater.

 # Number 95 on the free map by the ticket booth. Wind your way through the ancient homes inland from the agora.

TEMPLE OF ISIS — [R] RUIN

Reaching this Egyptian temple involves embarking on a beautiful 10min. hike on a path that leads to the highest point on Delos. The temple itself is fairly intact; a Doric-style marble structure with still-standing columns of impressive but not daunting height or breadth. It was erected in the beginning of the Roman period in honor of Isis, the Egyptian goddess of maternity.

 # Facing the museum, go right and follow the path. The temple will be on the left side and is marked Temple D'Isis.

DELOS MUSEUM — MUSEUM

Holding the real Lions of Naxians in a room to the back right, a number of pots and engravings, and a mosaic from the floor of a mansion from the town, this museum is absolutely worth a few minutes of your time. The labels are short and generally provide nothing more than a name and date, but the contents are self-evident.

 # On the right side of the island, inland from where the boat docks, behind the agora. i Photos permitted. $ Included in €5 admission fee to island. ⏰ Open Tu-Su when the first ferry arrives-2:40pm.

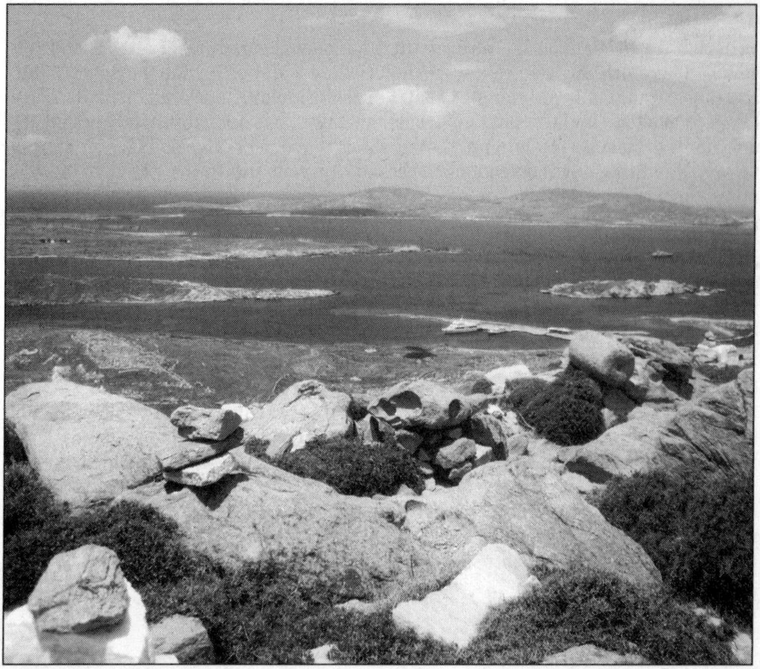

TERRACE OF THE LIONS
                                                                RUIN

Before 600 BCE, the Naxians gave between nine and 12 carved lions, squatting aggressively and facing directly forward, to Delos. Of the initial, dubious number, five now remain protected in the island's museum, and another was plundered by the Venetians and still snarls in Italy. Imitation lions now stand in the place of the originals, but the line-up is still a good photo op.

    On the left side, behind the agora.

TEMPLE OF APOLLO
    RUIN

Constructed in the 4th century BCE, the temple is now a giant 33-ton hunk of marble on the ground. The statues of Apollo and a giant building once stood on the slab, but now the base is empty. Although the current remains of the temple are not much to see, the fact that the Greeks could move so much marble to one place is impressive in itself.

    Close to the waterfront behind the agora.

HOUSE OF DIONYSUS
    RUIN

Step into this semi-restored mansion from ancient times and get a sense of the splendor that has dissolved into rock and weeds. The old plumbing aqueduct is still visible, as is the mosaic on the floor of the courtyard next to the giant columns. The house was initially for more than one family—think along the lines of a modern co-op—but no sign explains how many. On the right of the entrance are the beginnings of a flight of stairs that once led to upper levels of the house but now lead to the sky.

    In the back of the winding paths through the houses, on the left side of that part of the island.

ESSENTIALS

Practicalities

Delos is a World Heritage Site, so everything has been done to preserve the island as it stands. Therefore, the island allows no hotels, only one shop behind the ticket booth, and one restaurant. If you're a picky eater or really looking to scrimp on funds, bag a lunch. While food in the restaurant beside the museum is not exorbitantly priced, it's also not the cheapest. Make sure to wear shoes that can provide stability on a rocky terrain, and bring any medications necessary for your trip to the island as there is no pharmacy.

Getting There

Delos is accessible by ferry from **Mykonos.** Ferries dock at a port located on the far left side of the waterfront, and tickets can be purchased from the booth at the base of the dock or from a travel agency. Ferries *(⑨ €15 round trip. ⌚ 40min.)* depart for the island at 9am, 10am, and 11am, and ferries return to Mykonos from Delos at 12:15pm, 1:30pm, and 3pm. No one is permitted to stay on the island past the last ferry.

Getting Around

Delos is geographically small, but there is much to take in from that small patch of land. All moving about the island is done on foot. There are no roads on the island. It is best to grab a map from the booth you pass by when entering the island and where you pay the €5 entrance fee. In a stack to the right of the plexiglass window are maps that suggest different paths through the island's sights, each based on how much time the visitor will be on the island. Pressed for time? The blue arrows lead to a shorter path than the red arrows.

batsi ☎22820

Batsi is a small town where tourists are welcomed with a smile. A former fisherman's base snuggled into a cove at the base of Andros Island's mountainous terrain, Batsi is peaceful and tiny enough that sometimes the old men sitting in the shop doorways nod "kalimera," which means hello. Chances are the person whose *dormata* you stay in will be cousins with the shop owner who sold you a T-shirt yesterday or with your waiter from dinner the night before. Local kids run around the harbor's sand beach nude, burying things in the slightly silt-spoiled ground. Local businesses close for an afternoon siesta and any of the *tavernas* lining the harbor are great for an extended cup of coffee. The most central beach in Batsi is in the middle of the harbor. While this sandy area might not resemble the lavish beaches of other islands, it is still a great place to lounge and pick up some rays.

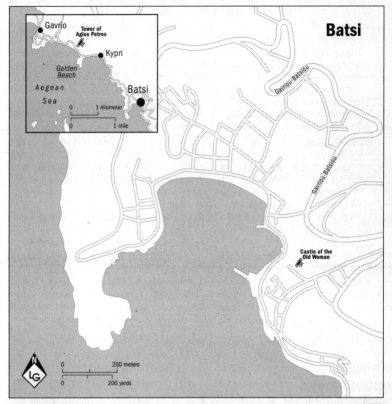

ORIENTATION

Batsi is set along a harbor, and everything fans out from the crescent of the waterfront. The harbor has two arcs and is shaped like a W when seen from the land looking toward the water. The left concave of the W is the **warf side.** Boats dock here, and the bank and tourist agency are along the main road near the water. The right concave of the W is a string of shops and buildings. The middle of the W is a row of *tavernas* and coffee shops, all fairly-priced. Other roads lead away from the town up the hill. When facing the waterfront, the main road, if followed to the right, leads to **Gavria** and **Golden Beach.** From the same perspective, the main road, if followed to the left, leads to **Chora,** also known as **Andros Town.**

The entirety of Batsi is not ideal for handicapped visitors. While it can be explored via car, most of the town is set up along a series of step risers to compensate for the enormous grade in the land that slopes down to the waterfront, making getting around in a wheelchair difficult. The main waterfront level would be passable but the next level of shops might be difficult to access.

ACCOMMODATIONS

Batsi is bursting at the seams with *dormatia,* or rooms to let. Even if you show up to the town without sleeping arrangements, chances are you will be able to find somewhere to sleep with little difficulty. Though there are no cheap hostels to soften the blow to your budget, most *dormatia* are worth the few extra euro. For a listing of *dormatia* in the town, call **Andros Information** (☎228 20 41 575).

VORONOFF'S ⊛⊗⁽ᵗ⁾ℽ⚲ DORMATIA ❷
Main Street ☎228 20 41 650

A powerful fan compensates for Voronoff's lack of A/C, and Voronoff himself only adds to the rest of this *dormatia's* appeal with his genuine kindness. Spacious rooms, good lighting with switches right above the clean-linened bed, a stone patio outside the rooms, and speedy Wi-Fi all over are just a few of the amenities that make Voronoff's go from a good place to stay to a great one.

� *Follow the main street uphill 5min.* **i** *Free Wi-Fi. Voronoff's also acts as Batsi's post office.* ⑤ *Singles and doubles €25.* ⏰ *Reception 9am-3pm.*

HOTEL SKOUNA ⊛⊗ℽ❈⚲ HOTEL ❸
Nik. Damianos ☎237 50 71 183

For a hotel that smells like your grandmother's attic, head to Hotel Skouna. Flower-patterned bathroom tiles and upholstered chairs straight from the '50s decorate a hotel that has scents from the same era. There are no computers or Wi-Fi, but the rooms are spacious and clean.

⧬ *On the right side of the waterfront.* **i** *Prices can be negotiated. Breakfast €6* ⑤ *Singles €35; doubles €45.* ⏰ *Reception 24hr.*

CAVO D'ORO ⬋⊗ℽ❈⚲ DORMATIA ❷
Right side of waterfront where road bends ☎228 20 41 776 ▤www.cavodoroandros.gr

An unspectacular *dormatia* in a spectacular location, Cavo D'oro is at the entrance of Batsi from Gavrio. A subtle fisherman theme is evidenced in a round blue mirror in each room that looks like a window on the lower deck of a ship and in the anchor-like coat hooks. Each room comes with a multitude of small amenities, so take advantage of the personal stovetop to cook some of your own Greek dishes.

⧬ *Where the road bends on the right side of the waterfront.* **i** *Laundry €10. Plug-in for ethernet cable available in every room. Stove top in every room.* ⑤ *Doubles €30-45.* ⏰ *Reception 24hr.*

SIGHTS ⦿

Batsi itself may not be the most historic of destinations, but within 45min. of the town by car or motorbike lie two old stone remains, and if possible, both are worth the trip. Beaches, of course, abound.

CASTLE OF THE OLD WOMAN ⊛ RUINS

If the difficulty of finding the parking lot didn't make it clear, it will be evident once you arrive at this castle that you are in the wilds of Andros Island. This gorgeous remoteness is the charm of the Castle of the Old Woman, now only rubble and a few scattered stone arches left over from its construction in medieval times when the island was occupied by the Venetians. No picture can accurately capture the full panorama of seeing mountain and sea in every direction. While the ruins of this castle are historically significant, the real gem here is the view.

Roughly 90min. from Batsi. Follow the road to Bay of Korthi. On the roundabout at the Bay of Korthi, take the road that runs perpendicular to the water out of town for about 8km. Turn right at the sign for Kohilu. From that road, there is a shoddily paved windy road on the left side. Follow the road to the end, and climb the stairs and follow the path to the top. ***i*** *Wear comfortable shoes. No signs.* $ *Free.* ⏰ *Open 24hr.*

TOWER OF AGIOS PETROS RUINS

Off the main road to Gavrio

In the crook of the mountain, this stone tower looks exactly like where Rapunzel let her hair down. Round and composed of grey stone, it's a relic of the Hellenistic period and was built to function as a lookout tower. The tower is amazingly well-preserved and located about 5min. past Golden Beach by car. Though it is impossible to climb the tower now, it once stood over five stories high.

About 15min. from Batsi on motorbike. $ *Free.* ⏰ *Open 24hr.*

GOLDEN BEACH ♿ BEACH

Along the road to Gavrio

Golden Beach, its name apt both for the color of the sand and the color it will turn your skin, is sure to turn after a few hours on the sand, is Batsi's most developed beach. Although a few other sandy patches speckle the coastline, this is the first one with an accompanying beach bar and advertisements. But even with this added attention, the beach stays clean and classy.

Along the road to Gavrio about 15min. by car or motorbike; 45min. by foot. $ *Two chairs and an umbrella €12.*

FOOD

Unlike on some of the other islands, Batsi's food is decently priced. Eat at one of the many *tavernas* along the waterfront, sip coffee from cushioned benches, or grab some fresh fruit from the centrally located fruit market. Don't expect to be amazed by the variety of food here, but chow down on the classic Greek cuisine.

TAVERNA STAMATIS 🍸 TAVERNA [1]

Wharf side of the harbor ☎228 20 41 975

For lack of a better word, Taverna Stamatis, open since 1965, is perfect. The lamb falls off the bone, the beetroot salad *(€5)* has just enough olive oil, and the waitstaff comes over three times a meal to ask about the food. Climb the steps to this *taverna*, claim a navy chair, and enjoy the sunset over the Batsi harbor with some fresh calamari. This is why life is worth living.

Opposite the wharf along the left side of the waterfront, up the flight of stairs. $ *Tzatziki €4, fried zucchini €3.50. Meatballs €5. Beetroot salad €5. Greek salad €6. Stuffed tomatoes €5.50. Fish €8-60.* ⏰ *Open daily noon-midnight.*

TOUNTA'S 🍸 BAKERY [1]

To the right of Taverna Stamatis ☎228 20 41 411

Loaves of freshly baked bread line the walls of Tounta's, while dishes of sugar-coated cookies and glimmering baklava sit along the shelf space. It is nearly impossible to leave the shop without a few calories in a bag or already in your belly. The offerings are simple—all things that are delicious and bad for you—and the woman behind the counter is generous. Even if you are not in the market for some *kourampies* (almond cookies with a powdered sugar coating), chances are she will give you a free taste.

On the second tier of shops on the left side of the waterfront, facing the water. Past the tavernas along the steps from Taverna Stmatis. $ *One big piece of baklava €1.50. Cookies 20 for €9. Fresh bread €1.80 per kg.* ⏰ *Open daily 7am-11pm.*

KOALA

●&♥※△ RESTAURANT ❷

On the left side of the waterfront　　　　　　　☎228 20 41696

Koala, whose mascot has absolutely no geographic integrity, advertises its om-elettes, but be forewarned: these cheesy dishes (€10) come soaked in grease, stingy on fillings, and look more like browned flat pancakes than eggs. A better breakfast option may be the classic and simple yogurt and honey (€4). Sand-wiches, like the yogurt, are a safe bet, but if you're in the mood for something that involves a skillet, it might be better to check out another *taverna*.

✤ *Along the main waterfront road on the left side of the shoreline, at the corner where the road curves.* ⑤ *Omelettes €10. Sandwiches €3-€7. Coffee from €1.50.* ☒ *Open daily Apr-Oct 8:30am-12:30am; Nov-Mar 9am-9pm.*

FRUIT MARKET

●&❄ MARKET ❶

Middle of the waterfront　　　　　　　☎228 20 41 254

This market is nothing but an undecorated space inhabited by a man selling fruit, but it is a gold mine for the palette. Find kiwis, bananas, oranges, pears, and tons of other fruits in the baskets outside the window, or head inside for your pick of vegetables. The designers at Whole Foods might be appalled by the aesthetic, but it doesn't take much in the way of decor to sell a delicious peach.

✤ *In the middle of the waterfront.* ☒ *Open daily in summer 8am-11pm.*

NIGHTLIFE

When it comes to nightlife, Batsi is no Mykonos. During the day the clubs moonlight as coffee shops, but at night the dance floors open up to willing patrons. Enjoy a leisurely drink looking out over the harbor early in the night, as dancing does not get started until around 2am.

NAMELESS

●Ⓧ⁽ᵗ⁾♥※△ BAR, DANCECLUB

In the corner on the wharf side of the waterfront　　　　☎228 20 41 488

The last stop of the night for locals and tourists alike, Nameless has earned itself a reputation as the best place to go in Batsi. In the midst of renovations, the inside combines an ultra-modern atmosphere—think white tea-cup barstools and black-tiled bathrooms—with chandeliers and brick walls that look like they are straight out of a dungeon. Try a late-night Juliet, a mojito with gin (€8), at the bar with the cheapest cocktails in Batsi.

✤ *In the corner on the left side of the waterfront, before the road rounds to Taverna Stamatis.* *i Newly designed garden behind the main entrance serves coffee during the day and cocktails at night. Free Wi-Fi with purchase.* ⑤ *Cocktails €8. Coffee €2.50-3.50.* ☒ *Open 24hr.*

CAPRICCIO

●♥△ BAR

Along the wharf side of the waterfront

Taglined "The Island Bar," Capriccio can be recognized by its white outdoor tables and the '90s music that plays from its speakers throughout the day. Inside the chairs are low to the ground, and playful marbles decorate the windowsills. Views of the harbor from the outdoor seating are beautiful, so feel free to make a night of this place with a post-dinner coffee (€2.50) and then a late-night cocktail (€11).

✤ *On the left side of the waterfront before you reach Taverna Stamatis.* ⑤ *Coffee from €2.50. Beer €5-8. Cocktails €11.* ☒ *Open daily 9am-3am.*

SKALA

●&♥※△ BAR

Yacht Club　　　　　　　☎228 20 41 656

Based on its size, it seems that Skala is an institution. The cafe-by-day and bar-by-night takes up the space of three eateries with its clover-colored seating and white-cushioned wooden benches. Though its cocktails and beers cost the same as those at most other bars in the town, each drink comes with a great view from of the wharf and beach.

✤ *In the middle of the waterfront under the sign that says yacht club.* ⑤ *Beer €5-8. Cocktails €11. Coffee from €2.50.* ☒ *Open daily 9:30am-2:30am.*

VRAXOS ⊗🍸❄ CLUB, BAR

In the middle of the waterfront ☎228 20 41 219

From school bus yellow seats, guests at Vraxos can enjoy the establishment's 8-scoop ice cream concoctions *(€8.50)*, strong coffee *(€3)*, or fancy cocktails *(€10)* on an elevated stone patio directly above the harbor. A DJ booth, dance floor, and pearlescent sofa wait inside to appease the sweaty masses. Though Vraxos is an average European club, it's sure to be a favorite with those who seek sunsets.

🧭 To the right of Skala, in front of the lone dock. Climb a flight of stairs to reach the patio. ***i*** *DJ daily July-Aug; in June F-Su.* $ *Red wine €6. Spirits €7. Cocktails €10. Ice cream €3.50-8.50. Coffee €3-4.* ⏰ *Open daily in June 4pm-4am; rest of summer 9:30am-4am.*

SHOPPING

Batsi is small, and though no major commerce takes place on the island, there are a few shops targeted toward tourists. Pick up your T-shirt and magnet at shops in the back left corner of the waterfront. For a more local specialty, look behind Taverna Stamatis for ceramics stores.

MELITA ⊗❄ CERAMICS [3]

To the left of Taverna Stamatis ☎228 20 42 005

If walking through museum after museum of cracked ceramics has made your heart ache for a bowl in one piece, this shop is for you. The handmade ceramics here are decorated with olives, pomegranates, and other identifiably Greek foodstuffs. A platter *(€35)* or plate *(€15)* makes for a classy gift for family and friends at home.

🧭 To the left of Taverna Stamatis on the left side of the waterfront, up the flight of stairs. ***i*** *Ask Sofia if she will put extra bubble-wrap around the items so they don't break.* $ *Small bowls from €7. Mugs €10. Big bowls and platters €35.* ⏰ *Open daily 10am-3pm and 6-10pm.*

ESSENTIALS

Practicalities

- **TOURIST OFFICE:** Batsi has no tourist office, but **Andros Information** has pamphlets and contact numbers for *dormatia*. *(☎228 20 41 575.)*
- **BUDGET TRAVEL OFFICES: Greek Sun Holidays** *(☎228 20 41 771)* is the only travel agency in the town.
- **CURRENCY EXCHANGE: National Bank** has a **24 hr. ATM** and offers currency exchange. *(☎228 20 41 400* ⏰ *Open Tu-W 9am-1pm, F 9am-1pm.)*
- **INTERNET ACCESS: Nameless** offers Wi-Fi. *(☎228 20 41 488* 🧭 *In the corner on the left side of the waterfront, before the road rounds to Taverna Stamatis.* ⏰ *Open 24hr.)*
- **POST OFFICE:** Mail letters and postcards at **Voronoff's** at the top of the hill above the harbor. *(☎228 20 41 650* ⏰ *Open M-F 9:30am-1:45pm.)* For packages, go to **Gavrio** *(☎228 20 71 254)* or **Andros Town** *(☎228 20 22 260)*.

Emergency!

- **POLICE:** Batsi's police station was closed, so **Gavrio's police station** *(☎228 20 71 220)* is the nearest one. You can also contact the Port Police. *(☎228 20 71 213.)*
- **LATE-NIGHT PHARMACIES:** The one **pharmacy** on the island is behind Dino's bike rental shop, around the block on the street that leads to Hotel Kaparesy. *(☎228 20 41 451* ⏰ *Open M-Sa 9am-1:30pm and 6:30-8:30pm.)*

- **HOSPITALS/MEDICAL SERVICES:** For medical emergencies, contact the **Medical Center** *(☎228 20 22 222; 228 20 22 333).* In Andros Town, to the left of the beach, behind a playground is a small **medical office** *(☎228 20 41 326 🕐 Doctor available daily 9am-1pm).*

Getting There

Batsi can be accessed by **ferries** from **Mykonos** *(🕐 2hr., 3 per day),* **Rafina** *(🕐 2hr., 3-4 per day),* and **Tinos** *(🕐 2½hrs., 3 per day),* all of which dock in **Gavrio.** To reach Batsi from Gavrio, board one of the **minibuses** that waits at the port for each incoming ferry and runs from Gavrio to Andros Town, stopping in Batsi on the way. You can also take the **bus** which runs from Gavrio to Andros Town and stops in Batsi on the way, or take a **taxi** *($ €20).*

Getting Around

Navigating Batsi is tricky. Walking up and down the slope of the town is not a small feat for the less athletically-inclined. Though it is possible to spend time in the town and never leave the main waterfront, the excursions to sights and distant beaches are worthwhile. To make such treks, it is hugely advantageous to rent a motorbike or car. If these aren't options, see if the bus or minibus will stop where you want to go; if not, there are always taxis, and some drivers will be willing to negotiate the meter price.

You can rent bikes at Dino's Bikes *(☎228 20 41 003 $ €16 per day),* on the right side of the waterfront.

andros town ☎22820

Andros Town, more commonly known as Chora (pronounced like the dance you did at your friend's bar mitzvah), is perhaps the least touristy place tourists frequent in the Cyclades. Though the town, comprised of one main stone-paved street, certainly has its dose of tourist-targeted *tavernas*, locals are seen breaking bread in these eateries as frequently as the foreigners. The three museums in Andros Town make it something of a cultural mecca for an island known for its sand and not its history. Be sure to take an hour and make the cultural rounds before settling down by the gentle waves.

ORIENTATION

The main road, **Georgios Embirikos,** is paved with stones and runs through the length of town to **Pl. Kairis** closer to the water. A 5min. walk past the arch at the far end of Pl. Kairis brings you to the outer edge of town, where those in the know **swim** among the ruins of a Venetian castle off the landing at the bottom of the steps. **Beaches** branch to the left and right of Pl. Kairis. Most *tavernas* and shops can be found along the main street. The port is about an hour away by bus, and Batsi is 20min. away by car.

ACCOMMODATIONS

Andros Town lacks cheap hostels so housing will be a bit of an expense. *Dormatia* are common though not over-abundant, so book in advance. Regular hotels are quite pricey, so try for a *dormatia* first.

KARAOULANIS ROOMS — DORMATIA [2]

3rd fl. of the Karaoulanis house ☎228 20 24 412; 697 44 60 330 www.androsrooms.gr

Brand new and sparklingly clean, these rooms are the color of cool water, and staying here is actually like sipping from a glass of ice water on a hot day. The owner, Yannis, has designed everything to be energy-efficient. Pouring lots of love into the premises, he has planted roses in the flowerbeds, bought the extensive variety of cushions for pull-out beds, and scrutinized every detail of his rooms' design. One warning: do not stay here if allergic to cats. Yannis and his wife are animal-lovers, and the kittens roam free.

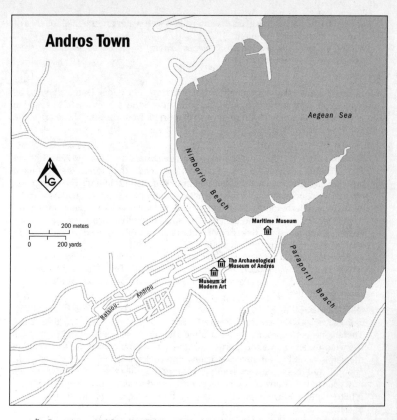

Andros Town

Aegean Sea

Nimborio Beach

Maritime Museum

The Archaeological Museum of Andros

Museum of Modern Art

Androu

Batsiou

Paraporti Beach

0   200 meters

0   200 yards

⚑ From the end of Georgios Ebirikos, bear right at the fork and continue in the same general direction away from the heart of town but do not take the road to the hard right. Follow this road until you pass the pet-mart, and head up the steep concrete steps on the corner with the nail salon. Karaoulanis is just over the cusp of that hill on the right-hand side with the stone driveway.
ⓘ Refrigerator, hot water, television in every room. Ⓢ High-season singles and doubles €50; low-season €30. 5-bed apartments €50-100.

NIKIS
On the beach near the port

⊛⊗❄ HOSTEL ❸
☎228 20 29 155

Location, location, location: Niki's is one step away from Pl. Kariris at the end of Georgios Ebirikos and 3min. from the beach. Though any rando from the street can waltz into the hostel, which has less than fabulous security, each sailboat-curtained room comes with a safe deposit box. Smelling like Dove soap and the fresh flowers that the soap is meant to imitate, Nikis is for those who like to be in the middle of the action and are willing to pay for it.
⚑ Between the Archaeological Museum and Navy Cafe beside Pl. Kariris on Georgios Ebirikos.
ⓘ All rooms come with safety deposit box and refrigerator. Ⓢ Doubles €65-90; triples €90-110.

AOXINTIKO ELENH HOTEL
On Georgios Ebirikos before it becomes pedestrian only

⬤⊗♈(ⁿ)❄⌂ HOTEL ❺
☎228 20 22 270

Far out of the student traveler's price range, this is where to stay when honey-mooning in Andros Town. Coral-colored walls and towering ceilings are offset with dark wood bookcases near balconies with wrought-iron railings. Marble-floored bathrooms and a glass decanter filled with water are the final touches of glamour in this establishment.

➤ Near the police station at the top of Georgios Ebirikos. i Laundry €8. $ Doubles €110; triples €150. 🕐 Reception 24hr.

SIGHTS 👁

Andros Town, somewhat surprisingly, is home to three museums. Don't expect to be wowed like you were at the Acropolis, but some interesting pieces are to be found in each of the cultural stops. If you're in need of a break from the sun, these are some entertaining escapes from the heat.

MUSEUM OF MODERN ART — MUSEUM

Down the stairs to the left in Pl. Kairis when facing the archway ☎228 20 22 444

This museum is divided into two parts: the special exhibition in the right-hand building and the permanent collection in the left-hand building. The permanent collection is lackluster, and the magnetic wall piece downstairs makes such an obnoxious reverberating clang that even the woman working there turns it off when visitors aren't in the gallery. The special exhibits are more interesting, however, and since the ticket covers both halves of the museum, you might as well go see (and hear) this magnetic wall for yourself.

➤ Down the stairs to the left from Pl. Karirisy. i No photos allowed. $ €6, students and soldiers €3, EU residents under 12 or over 65 free. 🕐 Open June-Sept M 10am-2pm and 6-8pm, W 10am-2pm and 6-8pm, Sa 10am-2pm and 6-8pm, Su 10am-2pm; Oct-May M 10am-2pm, Sa 10am-2pm, Su 10am-2pm.

MARITIME MUSEUM — MUSEUM

By the waterfront at the very end of Georgios Ebirikos ☎228 20 22 264

There is no better setting for a Maritime Museum. The ocean is visible through the window, and as visitors peruse the glass-encased model ships, the sound of the sea is audible as it splashes against the rocks. Old maps and model ships abound, and there is a very cool old compass on the table right by where you buy your ticket. Many of the items are crammed together in the tight space, so it takes some bodily maneuvering to get a good look, but this museum is worth a visit.

➤ Follow Georgios Ebirikos through the archway and all the way to the end. At the dead end turn left and then right down the first street you encounter. The museum is under the Greek flag right before the steps that lead down to the water. $ €2, students, children, and over 65 free. 🕐 Open daily 9am-9pm.

THE ARCHAEOLOGICAL MUSEUM OF ANDROS — MUSEUM

At the top right corner of Pl. Kairis ☎228 20 29 134

Dingy brick red tiles reminiscent of a drab high school adorn the floor of this museum. While the Statue of Hermes on the bottom floor of the museum—which was moved from Athens when the museum was founded—is worth a peek, the rest of the museum's contents are not that exciting.

➤ In the back left corner of the square. $ €3, students and over 65 €2, EU students free. 🕐 Open T-Su 8:30am-2:30pm.

BEACHES 🌊

Andros is home to two sand beaches, **Paraporti Beach** and **Nimborio Beach,** and one other beach that only locals know about. Facing Pl. Kairis from Georgios Ebirikos, Paraporti is to the right and Nimborio is to the left. Nimborio, which is backed with a beach bar and has chairs and umbrellas to rent already set up in the sand, is more developed than Paraporti, an open expanse of sand with a beautiful view of Andros' mountainous terrain. Both are sand, both are extensive, and both can be settled on free of charge so long as furniture is avoided. The third beach is down at the very end of Georgios Ebirikos at the end of Pl. Kaliris just past the Maritime Museum. Here, there is no sand, but there are rocks and a concrete platform to leave your belongings. Those who know Andros Town best—the old women and men who have lived here their entire lives—come here to swim. Immediately to the left are **Venetian ruins** left from when Italy occupied the island, and just a few hundred meters away is the still-functional **Andros lighthouse.** For a real treat, buy some goggles in one of the sand-bucket selling stores along Georgios Ebirikos to check out the fish of this hidden treasure.

FOOD

👍 PAREA — 🍴♿🍸❄☁ TAVERNA [1]

On the right side of the main square ☎228 20 23 721

Parea is the *taverna* most locals will recommend—and for good reason. Order any dish on their menu and you will be back the next day (or even possibly the next meal) for more of the same traditional flavor. Try the stuffed tomatoes *(€6)* to have your conception of cooking blown out of the water.

➜ On the right of the main square. Walk down Georgios Ebirikos; it's behind 7th Heaven Coffeeshop. ℹ Great view of the beach if you sit by the edge. $ Coffee from €2. Appetizers €1.50-5.50; entrees €6.50-8.70. ⏰ Open daily in summer noon-midnight; in winter noon-4pm and 7:30-11pm.

👍 OWEHSTIRIO — 🍴♿🍸❄☁ SOUVLAKI [1]

In the middle of Georgios Ebirikos ☎228 20 23 407

Owehstirio's menu is limited to souvlaki, salad, beer, and soda, but what more does a cheap-eats place really need? With incredibly thick *tzatziki* and pitas that taste as fresh as they are, this *souvlaki* place is high-quality fast food.

➜ Midway down Georgios Ebirikos on the right side when walking toward the main square. $ Souvlaki €2.50. Greek salad €5.50. Beer €2.70 ⏰ Open M-F 10am-3pm and 6pm-1am, Sa-Su 6pm-1am.

PLATANOS — 🍴♿📶🍸❄☁ TAVERNA [3]

In the back left corner of the main square ☎228 20 23 563

Nuzzled into the back right corner of the main square is this local favorite. Prices are steep—the Greek salad costs a whopping €8—but the food is worth the price tag. The Greek salad isn't just any old mix of tomato and cucumber, topped with wine-soaked grape leaves to give it a little kick. Make sure to try the *fortali*, an omelette with sausage, bacon, and other meats *(€10).*

➜ In the back left corner of the main square, opposite the Archaeological Museum and the rides. Look for the tree with the white paint on the trunk; that planter is in the middle of Platanos' seating. ℹ Free Wi-Fi. $ Greek salad €8. Entrees €10-30. ⏰ Open daily 9am-3pm and 6pm-1am.

7TH HEAVEN COFFEE SHOP — 🍴♿🍸❄☁ COFFEE SHOP [1]

On the right side of the main square ☎228 20 24 440

If you've had one too many Greek salads and want a break from the local cuisine, pull up one of the lime green seats and enjoy 7th Heaven's simple fare. Offering sweet and savory crepes *(€5.50-8)*, waffles, ice cream, and all sorts of coffee, the sugar high you are sure to enjoy here must be the inspiration for its name.

➜ On the right side of the main square at the end of Georgios Ebirikos. $ Coffee €2-4. Ice cream €4. ⏰ Open daily Apr-Sept 10am-2am.

GARYFALLOS — 🍴♿🍸❄ BAKERY [1]

Along Georgios Ebirikos ☎228 20 24 400

You just woke up and want a bagel, but you remember you're in Greece. Instead, go for the local substitute, a fresh pastry filled with apple or feta cheese from Garyfallos' bakery. If you're in the mood for something more weighty, try the dark bread with corn inside *(€0.65 for ¼ of a loaf).* While you're here, grab some *amydala* cookies *(€12.60 per kg)*, almond cookies so good that you won't mind having powdered sugar all over your face and shirt.

🪧 On the right side of Georgios Ebirikos when walking toward Pl. Karikis. $ Bottle of white wine €10. Cookies €12 per kg. Bread from €1 per loaf. ⏰ Open daily 7am-4pm and 6:30-10:30pm.

NIGHTLIFE

When the sun sets, so do happenings in Andros Town. No discos or raucous bars disrupt the town's peace and quiet, but some bars stay open until 2am. For a mellower evening, head to one of the bars along the main street Georgios Ebirikos like **Mickey's Bar** *(☎698 07 57 048)*, watch an English-language movie with Greek subtitles at the **outdoor movie theater** *(☎697 70 73 566)* at the 9:30 pm daily showing *(€7.50)*, or buy a bottle of wine and make your own party along the beach.

ARTS AND CULTURE

Andros is worth a visit for its sand, not its vibrant culture. For paintings of flowers and bees set against dark backdrops and interspersed with wire decorations, walk through the archway on Georgios Ebirikis to the **gallery** on the left side of the pedestrian-only street. *(⏰ Open daily 10am-2pm and 7-9pm.)*

ESSENTIALS

Practicalities

- **TOURIST OFFICE:** The tourist information kiosk is on the back right corner of the white marble square at the top of Georgios Ebirikos. Come here for *dormatia* listings or directions, but do not expect a computer; the kiosk is sparse. *(☎228 20 25 1620 ⏰ Open Jul-Aug daily 9am-10pm.)*
- **CURRENCY EXCHANGE:** The **ATE Bank** *(☎228 20 23 728)* is closest to Pl. Kariris; **National Bank of Greece** *(☎228 20 23 407)* is on Georgios Ebirikos; and **Euro Bank** *(☎228 20 29023)* all offer **currency exchange** and have **24hr. ATMs** out front. (*⏰ All open M-Th 8am-2:30pm and F 8am-2pm.)*
- **INTERNET:** **Mickey's Bar** has **Wi-Fi access** with a purchase. *(☎698 07 57 048 ⏰ Open daily 8:30am-4:30pm and 7:30pm-2am most of the year; July-Aug 8:30am-2am.)* Wi-Fi is also available at **Platanos** at the back of Pl. Kariris, where there is also a **computer** that can be used for free for up to an hour. *(☎228 20 23 563 ⏰ Open daily 9am-3pm and 6pm-midnight.)*
- **POST OFFICE:** The local post office offers stamps and mail service at the top of Georgios Ebirikos. *(☎228 20 22 260 ⏰ Open M-F 8am-2pm.)*
- **POSTAL CODE:** 84500.

Emergency!

- **POLICE:** The **Police Station** is on the inland end of Georgios Ebirikos on the left side of the street when walking away from Pl. Kariris. *(☎228 20 22 300 ⏰ Open 24hr.)*
- **LATE-NIGHT PHARMACIES:** A few pharmacies line Georgios Ebirikos, and they alternate on which one has extended hours. Call one of the pharmacies to know which has extended hours. *(☎228 20 23 203.)*
- **MEDICAL SERVICES:** The **health center** is in the back right of the white marble square at the top of Georgios Ebirikos and offers medical services emergencies *(☎228 20 22 222; 228 20 22 333)*.

Getting There

Andros Town can be accessed by **ferry** from **Mykonos** *(⏰ 2hr., 3 per day),* **Rafina** *(⏰ 2hr., 3-4 per day),* and **Tinos** *(⏰ 2½hr., 3 per day),* which all dock in **Gavrio.** To reach Andros Town from Gavrio, board one of the **minibuses** that waits at the port for each incoming ferry and runs from Gavrio; take the **bus,** which also runs from Gavrio; or take a **taxi** *(€40).*

Getting Around

The easiest way to get around Andros Town is to walk. The town's main street is pedestrian-only for most of its length, and to reach the beaches and museums from the town most quickly involves descending extended staircases. However, some of the hikes and more distant beaches are better reached by either motorbike or car. **Riva** rents out motorbikes and boats. *(☎697 44 60 330 ⏰ Open daily 9am-9pm. $ Bikes from €15 per day. Boats from €80 per day.)*

tinos town ☎22830

Tinos Town is far less touristy than might be imagined, though there are a few ill-conceived Barbie-emblazoned bags on the way up to the **Panagia Evangelistria Church,** the main church and attraction. The town is less sexualized than Mykonos but still quite vibrant, and as a result it has an active, relatively PG nighttime scene. Push past the town limits and into the countryside to see villages from another era and views of mountains like **Mount Exobourgo** that will make you gasp. The green shrubbery, hazy with purple flowers, is stunning, as is the sea from the high vantage point. Make sure to watch your hat—Tinos is incredibly windy, and the ancient Greeks thought the island was home to Aeolus, the god of wind. Also, plan your trips according to the local siesta times of 3-6pm. Businesses take a break, so don't plan on doing any shopping during those hours.

ORIENTATION

Tinos Town is located along the waterfront near its **central port** and **Old Port.** *Tavernas* line the main street **Akti Vasleos Konstantino,** and most other roads branch from it. The two other large streets are **Evangelistrias** and **Megalochares,** which run parallel to each other and both of which lead uphill to the **Panagia Evangelistria Church.** The back streets of Tinos Town are narrow and often nameless, so if you get lost in this area make your way back to the waterfront. The town slants downward toward the waterfront, so prepare for the hill-like streets by bringing comfortable shoes.

ACCOMMODATIONS

Make sure to book rooms in Tinos Town in advance.

NIKOLETA'S ROOMS TO LET ♿❄ HOTEL ❷

Kapodistriou 11 ☎228 30 24 719

Kept by Nikoleta, a woman whose enthusiasm when waving her hotel's placard by the ferry is so great that it's shocking to find that she's sincere, these rooms wouldn't win any design prizes with their painted wood beds or uncarpeted floors. However, they are spacious, clean, and equipped with a refrigerator and set of towels.

From the port, follow the waterfront to the left when facing the water to the end and then take the road to the traffic circle. Nikoleta's is on the road to the right, 2 blocks down on the left. ℹ Ask to be met at the port. Grocery store nearby. $ Singles €25-30; doubles €35-40; triples €45-50; quads €50-60; quints €50-60.

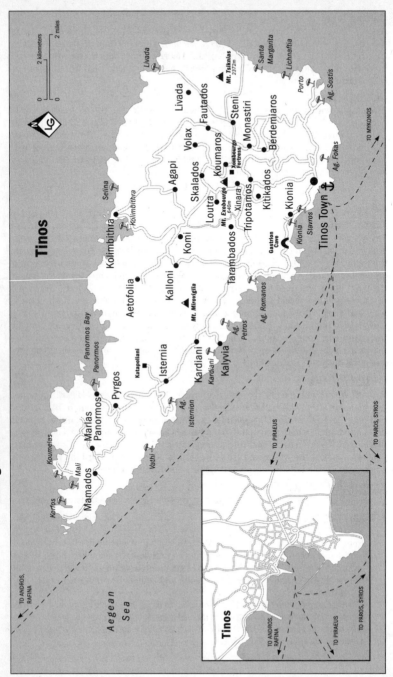

greek islands

Tinos

Aegean Sea

Panormos Bay

Mt. Tsiknias 2372m

Santa Margarita

Lichnaftia

Porto

Ag. Sostis

Livada

Livada

Fautados

Steni

Monastiri

Berdemiaros

Agapi

Volax

Koumaros

Skalados

Xomburgo Fortress

Loutra

Mt. Exobourgo 640m

Xinara

Kitikados

Kionia

Ag. Fokas

TO MYKONOS

Selina

Kolimbithra

Kolimbithra

Komi

Tripotamos

Kionia

Tarambados

Gastrion Cave

Stavros

Tinos Town

Kalloni

Mt. Miroviglia

Aetofolia

Ag. Romanos

Ag. Petros

Isternia

Kardiani

Kalyvia

Katapoliani

Kardiani

Pyrgos

Ag. Isternion

Marlas

Panormos

Panormos

Vathi

Koumelas

Mamados

Mali

Korfos

TO PIRAEUS

TO PAROS, SYROS

TO ANDROS, RAFINA

Tinos

TO ANDROS, RAFINA

TO PIRAEUS

TO PAROS, SYROS

0   2 kilometers

0   2 miles

TINOS CAMPING 🍴♿🍸 CAMPGROUND ❶

L. Sohou 5 ☎228 30 22 344

Grass sprouts in the middle of the pathways and the ripped-leather-on-the-chair decor is nothing to brag about, but Tinos Camping is certainly the cheapest housing on the island. The least expensive bungalows are furnished with a chair, outlet, folding table, bed, ashtray, and sheets—what more do you need?

➡ From the left end of the main waterfront when looking at the water, take the road up and take a right after 1 block. You will reach a roundabout that will have signs for Tinos Camping. Follow the sign down the street. Tinos Camping will be under the blue archway on your right about 3 blocks down. i If you want to use the communal kitchen, bring own gas. $ Singles €18; doubles €25-50; triples €65. ⏰ Reception 24hr.

HOTEL ALTANA 🛏♿📶🍸❄☀ HOTEL ❺

Stavrou Kionion ☎228 30 25 102; 693 27 24 253 💻www.altanahotel.gr

Established in 2007, Altana breathes cleanliness. The design is streamlined but homey, and every room comes with a stovetop, pots and pans, and a table graced with a candlestick. Prices are steep, even with breakfast included, so don't let yourself be wooed by the candles in the rooms unless it fits your budget.

➡ When looking inland, follow the road from the port along the waterfront to the left. It's about a 10min. walk. i Breakfast included. Laundry €7.50. Free Wi-Fi. Laptops can be borrowed from front desk. Pool. $ Doubles €100, junior doubles €145, superior doubles €200. ⏰ Reception 8am-midnight.

SIGHTS 👁

PANAGIA EVANGELISTRIA ♿ CHURCH

The top of Evangelistrias

On Sundays, pilgrims can be seen crawling on their knees from the port up the carpet along Megalochares to the church, an imposing structure of white marble and tall domes. Those who want to experience the tradition can wait in line at the top of the stairs, drop €1 into the slot, and take some candles to light in the church. In the right mindset, this can be a moving experience—even for an atheist.

i Modest dress required. $ Free. ⏰ Open daily 6:30am-8:30pm.

ARCHAEOLOGICAL MUSEUM 🍴⊗ MUSEUM

Megaloxatis ☎228 30 29 063

On the way back to the waterfront from the church, this museum is worth a peek. Items collected from the Sanctuary of Demeter and the Temple of Poseidon and Amphrite are gathered in this medium-sized museum. A courtyard in the middle has rose-pink walls and houses fragments of busts and pieces of the altar frieze from the Temple of Poseidon and Amphitrite, as well as decapitated Roman military torsos.

➡ Near the top of Megaloxatis on the left. $ €2, over 65 €1, students and children free. ⏰ Open Tu-Su 8:30am-3pm.

TEMPLE OF POSEIDON AND AMPHITRITE ♿ RUINS

Along the waterfront 3.5km

The ruins at the oft-discussed site are poorly preserved. What once was there is now just rubble, and only one placard explains its history. If you are going in this direction, check it out; otherwise, don't be tricked by the chatter—this sight is just a scattered pile of marble.

➡ To the right of the waterfront, 3.5km from the center of town. i Open daily 8:30am-2:30pm.

MUSEUM OF TINIAN ARTISTS ⊗ MUSEUM

In Panagia Evangelistria ☎228 30 22 256

Located in the premises of Panagia Evangelistria, this museum is readily

accessible, but these paintings and statues by Tinian artists are not that exciting. Aside from a random bust of Gladstone, the portraiture is of people lost to memory and whose busts are less than exciting (insert breast joke here).
➜ *In the church. Climb to the top of the bazaar street.* $ *Free.* ⏰ *Open M-Sa 8am-8pm, Su 10am-2pm.*

THE GREAT OUTDOORS

Beaches

Regardless of your interests, Tinos has a beach that will be perfect. Nudity isn't as fashionable on this island as on some of the others nearby, so don't plan on forgetting a swimsuit—you'll probably get some stares. Nearest to town is **Kionia** beach, which comes with beach chairs and is backed by a wooden boardwalk for most of its length. It is located directly across the street from the Temple of Poseidon and Amphitrite 3.5km from the town, so the efficient tourist can see a sight on their way to the beach. 12km from town is **Kolimbithra,** accessible by bus and by taxi *($ €15).* This one beach actually encompasses two sandy stretches divided by a big rock formation and reachable to each other only by climbing the stairs to the parking lot overpass. On the right side is the more developed and populated of the two beaches. Locals, with grandmothers and babies in tow, flock here to play paddle board and toss soccer balls (sand poses a problem when kicking). The environment is somewhat loud as a fair number of bikini-clad teenagers get tossed into the water by enterprising romancers and annoying brothers every hour, so don't come to this half of the sand if seeking a nap. Behind the chairs and umbrellas is a **taverna** with decent prices and hearty Greek cuisine. The other stretch of sand is far less developed and far more vast. While the tide ripples in on the right side, the undertow on the left is not a joke, so be sure to swim with a buddy and stay away from the rocks. Even though the current is more vivacious, the beach is almost deserted by people, and the crash of the waves make a great soundtrack for rest. Using the waves for fun is newly opened **Tinos Surf Lessons** *(☎697 24 04 628 💻www.tinossurflessons.com $ Soft surfboards €5 per hr.; hard surfboards €10 per hr. Lessons €15 per 1½hr. ⏰ Open June-Oct daily 10am-9pm),* at the far end of Kolimbithra Beach, where the waves are largest as a result of the cove and the wind's direction. If in the Pyrgos or Panormos area, **Panormos** beach is a sandy haven less frequented by tourists.

Hiking

Tinos's inland terrain is fairly mountainous, and walking along the roads would likely lead to breaking a sweat. For a longer and more difficult hike, trek to **Mount Exobourgo,** the highest point on the island. The fortress up top, **Xombourgo,** is Venetian and dates from the 13th century, offering tourists an excellent view of Santorini from the peak. Before your trip, make sure to check the weather, as sometimes the fort is closed off due to wind.

Another route takes hikers from Tinos Town to **Loutra** and back *(4hr.).* Wooden signposts point hikers in the right direction, but before setting out, consult the Tinos booklet which has hiking maps marked in different colors. Travel agents at **Kalypso Travel** *(☎228 30 25 407)* can also give some hiking tips.

FOOD

Food in Tinos Town is good virtually everywhere. As a general rule, the *tavernas* a row back from the main waterfront have better fare that the most prominent *tavernas.* For those trying to stick to a strict budget, Tinos Town is a great place to **cook for yourself.** Grocery stores abound, and some fresh vegetables and pasta go a long way. But even if you cook your own dinner, it's worth the €4.50 to try the **loukoumades,** or small, fried ringlets of puffed dough covered with honey and sprinkled with cinnamon. It will take all your willpower not to lick the honey-coated plate in public, so don't even try to resist.

AGIRA
💳♿🍸❄ TAVERNA [2]

Parada Sq. ☎22830 23 076

Perhaps the only restaurant in Greece where waiters wear uniforms, Agira, with its royal blue paint and furniture, somehow still maintains low prices and a real Greek vibe. It's restaurant of choice for local politicians and actors, but the staff says that patrons work to keep a low profile. So no matter how much you love the fried *courgette* balls made of zucchini and cheese, keep it on the DL.

➜ In Parada Sq., behind the playground by the bus station on the right side of the waterfront. $ Appetizers €3.50-4; entrees €8-20. ⏰ Open daily 10am-4pm and 7:30pm-2am.

PIGEON HOUSE
🚫🍸❄☀♿ TAVERNA [2]

Fragiskou Paximadi ☎228 30 23 425

On a quiet side street, Pigeon House is the type of *taverna* where grandmothers come to chat over watermelon and daughters sit on their fathers' laps after church. Serving all the Greek staples at reasonable prices, Pigeon House is a great place to come to escape the tourist atmosphere of the main *taverna* row along the waterfront.

➜ Pass the street with Häagen-Dazs on it and walk 2 more blocks, then turn right; look for pink-plaid table cloths. $ Appetizers €3.50-4; entrees €7-10. ⏰ Open daily 11am-4pm and 7pm-midnight.

SKOUNA
💳♿🍸❄☀ TAVERNA [2]

By the traffic circle ☎228 30 22 741

Though Skouna's decorations are the shade of green that people wish their grass would turn, vegetarians shouldn't be drawn in unwarned: the eatery specializes in carnivorous delights. The local dish *csisiro*, made from sausage, cheese, and fresh tomatoes, is meant to serve three, and the *fourtalia*, an omelet filled with different meats, is a local delicacy.

➜ At the end of the row of tavernas at the traffic circle at the base of Evangelistrias. $ Appetizers €4; entrees €8-15. ⏰ Open daily 10am-1am.

STAVROS
🚫♿🍸❄☀ CAFETERIA [1]

Evangelistrias 21 ☎228 30 23 287

This may be the only place along Evangelistrias that serves real food, but don't expect fancy service. Pick up your food on brown trays a la middle school and eat your Greek salad from a metal plate that seems more fitting to a hospital. The menu isn't in English (nor do the owners speak it), so whip out your best pointing skills.

➜ Up the bazaar street on the left side. $ Souvlaki €2-2.50. Greek salad €5.50. Entrees €6.50-7.50. ⏰ Open daily 11am-4pm and 6:30-11pm.

KAFENEIO KIRIAKATIKO
🚫♿🍸❄☀ CAFE [1]

Side street to the right of Evangelistrias ☎228 30 22 606

Like mint, a notoriously land-mongering plant, Kafenei Kiriakatiko has claimed all the available space for tables in the streets surrounding its official location. Entrees are not served here, and yogurt, honey, and toast (grilled cheese with ham and lots of butter) are the only things on which to nibble. Act like a local and just stop here for coffee.

➜ From Pl. Pantanasis, walk up Evangelistrias. Take the 1st right, and the cafe will be down the street. $ Toast €2.50. Yogurt with honey €4. Coffee €3. ⏰ Open daily 8am-midnight.

NIGHTLIFE

VILLAGE MUSIC CLUB
🚫🚭🍸❄ CLUB

Taxiarhon 24

The smell of lit cigarettes inundates your nostrils just one step into this club, but don't be afraid to breathe free: tonight's gonna be a good night at the village.

Music tends toward Top 40 and dance tunes until 3am, when the speakers start blasting out traditional Greek music. If you're here at 3am, you'll either love it or be too drunk to notice.

🧭 From waterfront taverna row, walk up Megalochares. It's in an alleyway right next to Sibylla. $ Beers €5-6. Cocktails €9. ⏰ Open in summer daily 10pm-4am, in winter F-Su 10pm-4am.

SIBYLLA 💳🍸🚭❄ CLUB

Taxiarhon 17

A black sign hangs above a white metal door, but don't take the black sign as a bad omen: Sibylla is where locals go to party year-round and where tourists only interrupt their groove in the summer months. For some late-night dancing under the gaze of the banana-holding stuffed monkey atop the DJ booth, enter this local dancing hub.

🧭 From the waterfront, walk up Megalochares. Right next to Village Music Club. i Doesn't fill up until late. $ Beers €5-6. Mixed drinks €6. Cocktails €8. ⏰ Open daily 9:30pm-3:30am.

KAKTOS BAR ♿🚭🍸❄⛅ BAR, CLUB

Along the highway behind Tinos Town ☎22830 25930 💻www.kaktos-bar.gr

Vaguely Mexican-themed with burnt orange walls and cactus decorations, Kaktos Bar exists solely for the benefit of tourists. Locals rarely frequent this distant stop that can be accessed only from the main highway. The view of Tinos Town from the outdoor seating is pleasant enough but not worth the cab ride, and the cactus theme is relevant only if Greece was your second choice destination to the Sierra Nevadas.

🧭 By cab, it's about 5min. away along a highway behind Tinos Town. $ Beer €5-6. Cocktails €9. ⏰ Open daily in summer 9pm-4am.

KOYPSAPOS ♿🍸❄⛅ BAR

Akti Ellis 1 ☎228 30 23 963

Seemingly popular with an older crowd, Koypsapos serves its cocktails *(€9)* under dimmed lights capped by perforated metal shades, and the bartop is covered in a stylistically vintage faded gold flower pattern. Flashing hot pink and blue lights in the back of the bar—jarring in their hipness—set up a visual anachronism. This bar is nothing to lust after, but it's conveniently located at the end of a row of *tavernas* with seaside seating.

🧭 At the end of the row of tavernas and cafes that starts at the base of Evangelistrias and wraps toward the waterfront. Directly in front of the taxi stand. $ Coffee €3-3.50. Beer €4-6. Cocktails €9. ⏰ Open daily 8:30am-3:30am.

PARADISE 🚭🍸❄ CLUB

Along Stavrou Kionion

A sunset of every color of the rainbow beckons from its sign, and broken Heineken bottles decorate the ground in front of the driveway. A faded stop sign faces the entrance to this late-night club, symbolically standing for the patrons of Paradise who don't want to call it quits when the rest of the clubs in town close down.

🧭 Along the road to the Temple of Poseidon and Amphitrite. i Let's Go recommends taking a cab. ⏰ Open daily 3-9am.

SHOPPING

The main shopping on Tinos is to be done along **Evangelistrias,** the street also known as the bazaar that leads uphill from the port to the church. Most of the shops, whose contents spill onto the pedestrian-only street, are open during the day except for the siesta between 3-6pm. This street is busiest at night when the bakeries' cookies shine under the lights, and everything from bracelets to Dora the Explorer paraphernalia can be bought from one of the vendors. Expect to haggle, and bring cash along with you.

Tinos' arts, though limited, are most evident in the ceramic shops that spot **Evangelistrias.** Here, artists show their handmade wares right along the main tourist walkway. Peruse the area for everything from small ceramic pieces to gigantic bowls.

ESSENTIALS

Practicalities

- **BUDGET TRAVEL OFFICE: Kalypso Travel** provides travel services. *(Taxiarhon 2 ☎228 30 25 407; 697 36 24 390 ⏰ Open daily Apr-Oct 9am-9pm; Nov-Mar 9am-2pm and 6-9pm.)*
- **CURRENCY EXCHANGE: National Bank** has **ATMs** and offers **currency exchange.** *(☎228 30 22 328 ⊕ Across the street from the bus stop along Akti Vasleos Konstantino, on the waterfront. ⏰ Open M-F 8am-2pm.)* **Piraeus Bank** also has ATMs and currency exchange. *(☎228 30 29 214 ⊕ Located along Akti Vasleos Konstantino, on the waterfront. ⏰ Open M-F 8am-2pm.)*
- **INTERNET: Cafe Antonello** has computers with internet access. *(☎228 30 24 510 ⏰ Open 10am-3pm and 6pm-midnight.)*
- **POST OFFICE:** Tinos Town has a post office on the far right end of the waterfront. *(☎228 30 22 247 ⏰ Open M-F 7:30am-2pm.)*
- **POSTAL CODE:** 84200.

Emergency!

- **POLICE:** The station is 5min. out of town on the road to Kionia. *(☎228 30 22 100 ⏰ Open daily 8am-10pm.)* **Tourist Police** *(☎228 30 23 670)* is in the same building as the police.
- **PHARMACY:** It's located just to the right of the base of Evangelistrias, next to a Hellas ferries ticket office. *(☎228 30 22 272 ⏰ Open M-F 8am-2pm and 6-9:20pm.)*
- **MEDICAL SERVICES:** For medical services, contact the Tinos Town hospital. *(☎228 33 60 000 ⏰ Open 24hr. for emergencies; daily 8:30am-2:30pm for regular inquiries.)*

Getting There

By Bus

A schedule is listed at the **KTEL ticket agency** *(☎228 30 22 440 ⏰ Open daily 8am-10pm)* across from the central port, next to the **Blue Star** ticket office. Buses depart from the **central port** and run to: **Agios Fokas** *(⏰ 5min., 5 per day);* **Kalloni/Kolimbithra** *($ €2.70. ⏰ 30min., 4 per day);* **Tripotamos** *($ €1.40);* **Chinara** *($ €1.40);* Loutra *($ €1.60);* **Komi** *($ €2.30);* and **Agapi** *($ €2.40);* **Kionia** *($ €1. ⏰ 7min.);* **Pyrgos/Panormos** *($ €4.20. ⏰ 45min., 4 per day);* via **Tripotamos, Kampos, Tarampados, Kardiani, Isternia, Pirgos,** and **Marlas/Porto** *($ €1. ⏰ 10min.);* **Skalados** *($ €2. ⏰ 20min.);* **Steni/Potamia** *($ €1.90. ⏰ 2 per day)* via **Trandaros, Dio Horia, Anados, Monastiri, Mesi, Falatados, Steni,** and **Mirsini.**

By Ferry

Ferry schedules vary, so check at the **port authority booth** *(☎228 30 22 220)* in the central port or at one of the many **Blue Star Ferry** ticket offices *(☎228 30 24 241)* along the waterfront. The largest one is directly across from the buses. Ferries run to: **Andros** *($ €8. ⏰ 1½hr., 3 per day);* **Mykonos** *($ €10.50. ⏰ 30min., 5 per day);* **Rafina** *($ €22. ⏰ 4hr., 5-6 per day);* **Syros** *($ €5.50. ⏰ 40min., 2 per week);* **Piraeus** *(⏰ 4hr., 3 per day);* **Rafina** *(⏰ 1hr., 4 per day);* and **Syros.** *(⏰ 20min., 3 per day)* There are two ferry ports in Tinos, so ask which you're leaving from when buying tickets.

Getting Around

Getting around Tinos Town is most easily done on foot. Evangelistrias is pedestrian only, and this uphill street is where most tourist activities are centered. But in order to see the sights or access any of the beaches, you'll need some public transportation. Buses are frequent and follow the schedule, and they present the cheapest option for getting around.

pyrgos ☎2621

Pyrgos is a small town 45min. away from Tinos Town by bus. White buildings line the stone paths of Pyrgos's streets, and potted flowers pop against the pale backdrop. Mountains dominate the distant skyline of this city renowned for its marble and the museum explaining the industry and the skill involved in this special art.

ORIENTATION

The **bus stop** is at the base of the town along the highway. To get to the **Marble Museum** or to the **School of Fine Arts,** follow the main street up and as it swings to the right. To reach the museum, pass through the main square, which is crowded with coffee tables, and up the stairs behind the church. Bear left and follow that stone road to reach the sights.

SIGHTS

MUSEUM OF MARBLE CRAFTS

MUSEUM

☎228 30 31 290 www.piop.gr

This museum opened in 2008 with funding from the European Union, and it's fabulous. More akin to the new Acropolis Museum than to any other museum

daytrip to halki

Head to Halki *(30min. by bus)* for a taste of authentic Greek food, a sip of free citron (a local alcohol sweetened with sugar and lemon leaves), and an hour-long walk through the back paths of the town. For lunch, bear left a block up from the bus stop and walk to the main plateia to find **Taverna Gannis.** *(☎228 50 31 214 Open daily 10am-5:50pm and 8pm-midnight.)* Try the local dishes in the big pans on the left when you step inside the restaurant *(€8),* or go classic with a particularly fresh Greek salad *(€5)* that comes with copious amoungs of crumbled feta cheese. For the local liquor, go to the **M. G. Vallindras Distillery** *(☎228 50 32 938 Open Apr-Nov daily 9am-6pm. $ English tours free)* along the same road that leads to Taverna Gannis. Right next to the distillery is a **handmade textile shop** *(☎228 50 32 938 Open daily 10am-7pm)* where Maria Marak has been weaving since 1960. For a hike to get your heart rate up, walk along the path that begins with the signs for the Church of Georgios Diasoritis on the left two blocks up the main road in town from the bus stop. Here, you'll encounter minor terrain and lots of local flora and fauna, including grape bunches hanging from a wall, yellow and purple plums, and flowers that smell like vanilla. The path has its moments of uphills and rocky ground, but do not expect rock scrambles; it will be nothing that dramatic. Continue up the town's main road for about 3km. *(20min. by foot)* and bear left at the fork to reach **Panagia Drosiani** *(M-F 10am-2:30pm),* a small, medieval round-topped church set in an olive grove.

in the Cyclades, the Museum of Marble Crafts walks visitors through all of the processes involved in marble sculpture—from extracting the substance from the earth to transporting it to the workshops to the process of planning to sculpt to actually carving the sculpture itself. Some parts are hands-on (visitors are invited to look at marble through a magnifying glass), others are high-tech (flatscreen TVs are spread through the museum), and others are just fun to look at (the display of over 20 different types of marble listing their origin).

🪧 From the School of Fine Arts, turn left and walk up the hill for about 30m until you see the next driveway on the left side. Turn in and follow the driveway to the museum doors. ℹ Photos permitted. $ €3, students, over 65, and under 18 free. ⏰ Open M 10am-6pm, W-Su 10am-6pm.

PETROS MARMARINOS

💳♿❄ MARBLE WORKSHOP

☎228 30 31 624 💻www.marmarinos.gr

Advertised as a workshop but actually just a gallery space, this is the place to come and see what marble sculptors are working on nowadays. The space is filled with carved doves, figurines modeled on the early Cycladic archetype, and round tabletops embellished with roses. Though there is no hands-on working to be seen, the selection of products is interesting to browse.

🪧 On the way to the main plateia from the bus stop. $ Figurines €40-73. Big plate €235. ⏰ Open daily 9am-9pm.

SCHOOL OF FINE ARTS

★♿ SCHOOL

☎228 30 31 225 💻www.tinosartschool.gr

The School of Fine Arts has the feel, as some places do, of a place where great things happen. The classrooms are fittingly marble and filled with desks where students, who forgo broader college education to pursue marble sculpture, have been taught their craft since the school opened in 1955. The windows of the classrooms are lined with busts and portraits for students to base their work upon. If you come during the school day, you can witness these artists in action. Acceptance to the school is highly competitive, and those you see carving marble are the rising greats in their field.

🪧 From the main plateia, walk up the stairs behind the church on the far side of the square. At the top, turn left and walk 2 blocks. On your right you will see the marble-covered cemetery through a gate. Immediately after this gate is a set of stairs up a short hill. The School of Fine Arts will be on your left at the top of the hill. Look for the flags. $ Free. ⏰ Open when school is in session.

MELICCOKOMIKA PROIONTA

💳♿🍸 HONEY SHOP

☎228 30 31 407

This honey house run by a mother, husband, and their son smells as sweet as you'd expect. All the honey is from their own hives in Pyrgos, and the glass jars of the sweet fluid, some with part of the beeswax still in the jar, are shelved beside jars of homegrown capers and bundles of homegrown and dried herbs for tea. The son makes and bottles his own *raki*, displayed in a basket in the back of the shop.

🪧 On the right-hand side of the main street as you walk from the bus station to the main square. $ Capers €5. Jars of honey €4.50-20. Bundles of herbs €1.50. ⏰ Open daily Aug 9am-9:30pm; daily Sept-July 11am-2pm.

YANNOULIS HALEPAS MUSEUM

★🚫 MUSEUM

Set in the artists' old house, this museum still showcases his bed and living room. Some plaster masks that he used when preparing to carve a bust decorate one of the two back rooms. It's on the way to the main *plateia*, so you might as well stop in—just don't expect anything mind-boggling.

🪧 Past the bus stop and the 1st museum on the left. $ €3, students free. ⏰ Open daily 10:30am-2:30pm and 5:30-8:30pm.

MUSEUM OF YANNOULIS HALEPAS

❄ MUSEUM
☎228 30 31 363

Burnt orange walls are the backdrop for the Tinian artwork spotlighted in this tiny museum. Though the island is known for its marble, this museum houses mainly the plaster casts used to figure out exactly what the artist wants to carve. Don't come here expecting gleaming white marble; for that, walk deeper into the town.

📍 *On the left as you step off the bus onto the main street.* $ *€3.* ⏰ *Open daily 10:30am-2:30pm and 5:30-8:30pm.*

MARBLE-COVERED CEMETERY

CEMETERY

Raised graves erected in honor of those buried wrap around three sides of a church, virtually covering the ground with white marble and elaborate tombstones. No sign explains who is buried here, but the impression is left not by the history of the people but by the sight of the marble-covered floor itself.

📍 *From the main plateia, walk up the stairs behind the church on the far side of the square. At the top, turn left and walk 2 blocks. Up the stairs and through the metal gate you will find the cemetery.* $ *Free.*

FOOD

Although coffee shops in Pyrgos abound, actual eateries are sparse. Either bring your own lunch or pick from the two below.

TA MERONIA

♿🍸❄ TAVERNA [2]

The entrance of the main square ☎228 30 31 229

At the mouth of the main square, Ta Meronia is the cluster of tables and brown chairs. This eatery serves local dishes like pigeon and pasta from Tinos, and the owner is a big fan of his cuttlefish with black lasagna. If you are hungry and in the main *plateia*, this is the place to eat.

📍 *In the main square up the main road.* $ *Salads €3-6. Entrees €8-15.* ⏰ *Open daily 11am-midnight.*

TAVERNA EIRINIS

♿🍸❄ TAVERNA [1]
☎228 30 31 165

This *taverna* might be at the bus stop, but don't think that means its food is oily or gross or anything bus-related. This place serves thick and creamy *tzatziki*, cooked meats, and omelettes, all in a spacious, ivy-roofed environment. Even the bread in the basket is thicker than usual.

📍 *At the bus stop. 2 entrances: one on the main road, the other off the side street.* $ *Appetizers €3.50-6; meat entrees €6-8, seafood €7.50-8.50. Beer from €1.80.* ⏰ *Open daily 11am-midnight.*

ESSENTIALS

Practicalities

- **POST OFFICE:** If you buy some marble and want to ship it home rather than lug it back to Tinos with you, head to the post office. *(☎228 30 31 882* 📍 *Located on the street on the way to the main plateia.* ⏰ *Open M-F 9am-1:30pm and 4-10pm.)*
- **POSTAL CODE:** 84200.

Getting There

Pyrgos can be accessed by **bus.** *($ €4.20.* ⏰ *45min.)* For schedules, check in the KTEL office by the far right side of the waterfront. For a map of Tinos, check **Kalypso Travel** *(Taxiarhon 2 ☎228 30 25 407; 697 36 24 390)* to the right of the marble traffic circle by the Old Port when looking at the water.

naxos ☎22850

Step off the ferry in Naxos and immediately look left to see what remains of the temple to Apollo, a beautiful marble archway that serves as a reminder of the island's past. Next, look right and you will see what the island has become: land cultivated for maximum tourist appeal. Luckily, even what has become of Naxos is wonderful in its own way. The beaches still rinse away the troubles, the food—particularly in the nearby town Halki—makes you want to stuff your face, and the nightlife is vivacious without the grimy feel of Mykonos. For a travel experience with all the resources at your disposal, head to Naxos.

ORIENTATION

Naxos centers on the **waterfront.** When facing inland, the port is on the left side of the waterfront. The **bus station** is directly in front of the port, and the **Temple of Apollo** is beyond the port all the way to the left. To the right is what is best referred to as *taverna* row. Interspersed with the *tavernas* are bars, cafes, and some tourist shops. Nightlife stretches all the way to the right on the waterfront and one street back from taverna row. **Kastro** is the area deeper into town, which can be accessed by turning left at the top of the street behind **OTE,** the telephone office.

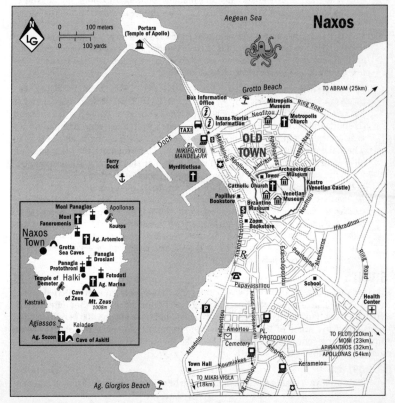

ACCOMMODATIONS

Naxos is a great place to sleep on budget. More expensive housing can be found along the waterfront, but the campgrounds are the best place to stay when on a budget.

MARAGAS CAMPING ♿ 📶 🍸 ❄ CAMPGROUND [1]

At Agia Anna beach ☎228 50 42 552 💻www.maragascamping.gr

If you came to Naxos to go to the beach, Maragas Camping is the place to stay. The road between the campground and the beach across the street sees so much foot traffic from the water to the campground and back that sand has been dragged across the pavement. Kids walk around the site barefoot, and four-wheelers sit under their cover ready for rental. The place is not fancy—the towels in the bathroom come frayed—but all is clean and family-friendly.

➜ From the port, take the bus headed to Agios Prokopios and get off at Maragas Camping 12km away. ℹ 30min. bus ride from town. Bus comes every 30min. Free Wi-Fi in the taverna. Motorbike and 4-wheeler rental. Safe box if requested. On-site supermarket. $ Doubles €20-45; studios and apartments €30-90. ⏰ Reception 8am-10pm.

GLARONISSI 1 ♿ ❄ HOTEL [4]

Past Maragas Camping along Agia Anna beach ☎228 50 41 201 💻www.glaronissi1.com

Somehow those who run Glaronissi 1 have coerced grass into growing from sand in front of their small establishment, which holds a few clean rooms decorated with shimmery blue bedspreads and metallic bunk-bed ladders. Located next door to Maragas Camping, Glaronissi 1 is just steps away from the mellow waves of the beach.

➜ From the port, take the bus headed to Agios Prokopios and get off at Maragas Camping, which is about 12km from town. Glaronissi 1 is just past Maragas; look for the grass on the ground out front. ℹ Refrigerator, coffee stovetop, and silverware in every room. $ High-season doubles €75; quads €90. Low-season doubles €30; quads €40.

NAXOS CAMPING ♿ 🍸 CAMPGROUND [1]

Middle of Agios Georgios beach ☎228 50 23 500 💻www.naxos-camping.gr

Naxos Camping's biggest appeal is its proximity to town. Though still 2km from the port, the public bus runs by the campsite's entrance every 20min., and it's easy to walk from town to the site by following Agios Giorgios all the way to where the windsurfers gather in the wide cove. Unfortunately, the premises lack all creature comforts. The shower faucet is so high that bathing is like shampooing in the rain, some mattresses have cigarette holes, beds come without sheets, and, when we visited, the bathrooms did not stock toilet paper.

➜ From the port, take the bus to Agios Prokopios and get off at Naxos Camping. By foot, walk along the main taverna row street by the waterfront, which leads to Agios Georgios beach. Walk along the beach past the main stretch of sand and around to the cove where windsurfers gather. At the back of that cove the highway is visible; cross the street and into the campground. It is 1.5km from town to the campground. ℹ Mini-mart, self-serve restaurant, pool, and refrigerators for communal use. $ €7 per person; huts €2 extra.

SIGHTS

Kastro is the area of town set back behind the first streets you see when stepping off the ferry. The area has winding, twisting, and confusing streets that date back to when the Venetians settled Naxos. The area used to house around 400 people in giant mansions. Now, some of the structures remain, but the luster of the place—which throughout the century has enticed guests like the Kennedys and Rockefellers—has somewhat diminished.

PORTARA RUINS

This archway, visible from basically anywhere along the waterfront, is a gem of a site. Dedicated to Apollo, the remains now lay scattered around the archway from their original construction in the fifth century BCE. On the far right of the waterfront when looking out on the water, the Portara is at the end of the island and looks out at an incredible view of ocean, mountains, and sky.

➡ On the far right of the waterfront when looking at the water. Up the steps. $ Free.

★ VENETIAN MUSEUM

⊗ MUSEUM
☎228 50 22 387

When as a boy the owner of the museum saw his neighborhood, the Kastro area, becoming commercialized and the old mansions being turned into shops and *dormatia*, he decided he wanted to preserve his home in its original state. He opened his doors to the public, and now all can wander through the rooms where he grew up to see the French couches where he sat with his parents and entertained movie stars and politicians decades ago. Make sure to find the piano where Leonard Bernstein once played.

➡ Pass the Byzantine Museum and walk under the archway. The Venetian Museum is under the arch. ℹ Nighttime concerts during the summer. $ €5, students and over 65 €3. ⏰ Open daily in summer 10am-3pm and 7-10pm.

CATHOLIC CHURCH

♿ CHURCH
At the top of the hill
☎228 50 22 725

A flood in 1915 destroyed the decorative tombstones of the ancient families of the Kastro area, but the tall white dome is still impressive inside. Behind the altar is supposedly one of the oldest examples of the Virgin Mary standing alone, without Jesus in her arms. Unless Catholic churches are your passion, this is just as well enjoyed in passing from outside as when stepping into the silent dome.

➡ At the top of the hill by the Archaeology Museum in Kastro. To get there, turn from the main waterfront road aroud the corner of OTE; walk uphill along the street until it branches 3 ways at the top of the hill. A pharmacy will be on the corner. Turn onto the left most street and follow it until you reach another fork; bear left and follow the street as it winds. Pass Taverna Kastro on your right and continue following the main street as it winds up. ℹ Modest dress required. $ Free. ⏰ Open daily 10am-7pm.

ARCHAEOLOGICAL MUSEUM

⊛⊗ MUSEUM
☎228 50 22 725

This museum houses the most extensive collection of early Cycladic figurines, including stylized models of humans and carvings that date from 2800-2300 BCE. The collection of pots is extensive, and the museum is larger than it may first appear.

➡ Around the bend from the Catholic church. ℹ No photos permitted. $ €3, students €2. ⏰ Open Tu-Su 8:30am-2:30pm.

BYZANTINE MUSEUM

⊛⊗ MUSEUM
☎228 50 22 525

The Glezos Tower in which the museum is contained was built in 1207 CE, and it's worth taking advantage of the free ticket price just to be inside the structure. The actual contents of the museum are sparse and consist of some maps on the wall and a few old ruins on the ground. Step out onto the porch of the tower; the view of the sea is breathtaking.

➡ From the Catholic church, orient yourself so that you are facing the church while standing on the main street. Look to your left and take the street that runs parallel to the one you just ascended down about a block. The Byzantine Museum will be up a flight of steps on your right.

THE GREAT OUTDOORS

Beaches

Naxos is chock-full of beaches: if there are two things the island is not short on, it's sand and sun. For the beach nearest to town, walk along the waterfront past OTE and the post-office playground to the far right of the port (when facing inland) to reach **Agios Giorgios,** where people play actively with paddle balls, toddlers splash in the shallow water, and European men rock swimsuits close to Speedos. Expect crowds and convenience. For a little more space on the sand, head to **Agios Prokopios, Agioa Anna,** and the nude beach **Plaka** just north of Maragas Camping. On this stretch of sand you will find gentle waves and a crew with fewer kids. All can be accessed by bus from Naxos Town. Check a map for more secluded beaches farther from town. Cabs are ready to take beachgoers nearly anywhere. For waterskiing, windsurfing, tubing, wakeboarding, and basically any watersport you can think of, head to Plaka beach for **Plaka Watersports** *(☎694 46 33 194 🖥www.plaka-watersports.com ℹ Cash only. $ €15-40. ⏰ Open daily 10am-7pm),* located right across the highway from the beach a few minutes walk from Maragas Camping.

FOOD

Beware of bland, touristy *tavernas* here; there are plenty of them. A key to identifying a more touristy establishment from a less touristy one is how prevalent English is in the menu. If dishes are listed in English second and the translation seems to have been made from a menu originally written in Greek, the restaurant is a go. If the menu is only in English or predominantly in English, steer clear.

BOSSA — ♿ 🍸 ❄ ☀ BAR, CAFE ❶

On the waterfront

The light fixtures here hang like giant, white dandelions about to blow away with a puff of wind from the sea. Many tables and chairs fill the extensive outdoor seating area, and even more chairs fill the modern, inside space as well. Popular with a crew of younger, more stylish foreigners, Bossa has both great views and great people-watching.

🧭 Follow the waterfront street to the end and turn right when you reach OTE. Walk toward the water past the cluster of cafes, and Bossa will be there on the left. Look for the light fixtures. ℹ At night it becomes a happening bar. $ Coffee €3.50. Beer €4. Cocktails €7. ⏰ Open daily 9am-2am.

TAVERNA KASTRO — ♿ 🍸 ❄ ☀ TAVERNA ❷

In Kastro ☎228 50 22 005

A traditional eatery with dishes like rabbit stew *(€9.50)* and *choriatiko*, veal baked in a clay pot with cheese and vegetables *(€12)*, this *taverna* is the place to go to experience the culinary culture of Kastro. The stone patio seating area awards diners here with views of the sea from the heights of the old, Venetian part of the city.

🧭 Turn from the main waterfront road aroud the corner of OTE; walk uphill along the street until it branches 3 ways at the top of the hill. Turn onto the leftmost street and follow it until you reach another fork; bear left and follow the street as it winds. The taverna will be on your right. $ Salads €3.50-5. Entrees €7-15. Coffee €1.50-2.50. Beer €2.50. ⏰ Open daily 6:30pm-1am.

DIOGENES CAFE — ♿ 🍸 ❄ ☀ CAFE ❶

Right by the port ☎228 50 26 617

Nothing like fresh fruit juice to quench your tourist thirst! Try an original mix of fresh fruit juices taken to go or one of their cocktails *(€4)* served during Diogenes Cafe's all-day happy hour. All-day happy hour, you ask? The manager says it's because they are very happy.

🧭 On the left a few doors down the street to the right of the port when looking inland. $ Coffee €3.50-5. Cocktails €4. Sandwiches €4.50. Greek salad €5. ⏰ Open daily 7am-2am.

MANOLIS' GARDEN TAVERNA ⊛♿🍸☁ TAVERNA [3]

End of Market St. ☎228 50 25 168

This *taverna* is about as far from the main tourist stretch as you can get within Naxos, and its food is equally far from the competition. Try the fresh fish served with lemon to remember the best thing about being on an island.

➜ *Old street can be accessed from a sidestreet on the left in the main taverna row along the waterfront by turning left when you see the sign for the secondhand bookstore. Follow this street to the end, then follow sign to Manolis' Garden and walk through the archway.* $ *Salads €3.50-6. Seafood €6.50-17.* ⏰ *Open daily 6pm-midnight.*

CAFE LOTTO 💳♿🍸❄☁ RESTAURANT [2]

Along the waterfront street ☎22850 23386

The fried calamari, Greek salad, *tzatziki*, and fries for €7.50 advertised on the chalkboard out front sounds like a steal, but really it's an advertisement for the lowest-quality "Greek" food around. The Greek salad is topped with an embarrassing square inch of feta cheese, and the idea of calamari is greater in theory than execution. The waterfront view might be beautiful, but the food is not worth even the admittedly low price.

➜ *On the right side along the waterfont, in taverna row.* $ *Salads €3.50-5. Entrees €7-€12.* ⏰ *Open daily 8am-1am.*

NIGHTLIFE

Naxos's nightlife centers on the outer edges of the waterfront. The dancing doesn't get started in earnest until around 1:30am, but beers and cocktails are consumed by the dozens earlier in the evening. Nightlife here ranges from the casual guitar-jamming bar to the full-on club with a bouncer, so nearly any sort of fun can be had. If you don't want to wait until 1:30am to start dancing, bring an iPod to the beach and have a silent rager. Who cares what the others think? You're in Naxos!

👍 **JAM BAR** ⊛⊘🍸❄☁ BAR

The street behind taverna row ☎698 85 08 024

The enterprising singer, guitarist, or drummer can find an audience here, where bands set in the corner play for the lively crowd. A British flag with the Rolling Stones' mouth emblazoned in the center flies high above the wood tables and bartop, and Red Hot Chilli Peppers and soul music croon from the speakers. Beer is the most popular drink of the somewhat older clientele, but cocktails are served up as well at this music-lovers' bar.

➜ *Take the 1st left after Krik Cafe when walking along taverna row away from the port. It is on the right opposite Waffle House.* $ *Beer €3-5. Cocktails €7.* ⏰ *Open Apr-Oct daily 8pm-3am.*

👍 **MOJO** ⊛♿🍸❄☁ BAR

On the waterfront ☎228 50 26766

The bartender here works magic, so watch him splash liquor and fruit juices into glasses. Just as there's no doubt that Yo-Yo Ma was born to play the cello, this man was born to make cocktails. Perhaps this art is less valued, but show your appreciation by paying the steep price of a pomegranate martini, a Hollywood-lipstick-red concoction that he creates with real pomegranate juice and serves with fresh pomegranate seeds in a martini glass. You will not regret it, even if the price means you forgo lunch tomorrow.

➜ *Follow the waterfront street to the end and turn right when you reach OTE. Walk toward the water past the cluster of cafes and turn left. Pass Bossa and you will see the sign for Mojo on the left.* **i** *The outdoor seating is in high demand, so get there on the early side or ask to reserve a table.* $ *Beer €5. Cocktails from €7.* ⏰ *Open in summer daily 7pm-5am.*

ON THE ROCKS ⊛⊘📶🍸❄☁ BAR, CLUB

The street behind taverna row ☎228 50 29 224 🖥www.naxosontherocks.com

With an absurdly large bar selection that counts 12 varieties of absinthe and many

dozens more types of rum, On the Rocks smells like *shisha* and will probably be able to serve up whatever your liver fears most. Havana cigars are also available, so smoke one of those and cue up "Guantanamera" for a Wednesday-night karaoke debut.
*➔ Take the 1st left after Krik Cafe when walking along taverna row away from the port. It is on the right opposite Waffle House. **i** Karaoke on W night in English and German. $ Beer €5. Cocktails €7. Absinthe €8. Cuban cigars €6-39. ⏰ Open Apr-Oct daily 6pm-4am, though it often closes earlier during the week.*

OCEAN CLUB

On the waterfront past Mojo

Glittery walls, a sizeable DJ booth, flashing lights, and a huge bouncer in a tiny white T-shirt pretty much explain why this is the Naxos hot spot. All of the well-dressed under-30 crowd on the island make their way here by 2am. The scene is far from mellow, so if seeking a casual evening, head to one of the bars by Waffle House.
*➔ Follow the waterfront street to the end and turn right when you reach OTE. Walk toward the water past the cluster of cafes and turn left. Pass Bossa and you will see the sign for Ocean on the left. **i** Same owner as Mojo. $ Cover €10. ⏰ Open in summer daily midnight-7am.*

ESSENTIALS

Practicalities

- **BUDGET TRAVEL: Zas Travel** provides ferry and airplane booking services and can answer questions about the island. Find the location two doors down from the tourist center and another 50m away from the port, both on the waterfront. *(☎228 50 23 330 💻www.zastravel.com ⏰ Open daily 8:30am-noon.)*
- **POST OFFICE:** *(☎228 50 22 211 ⏰ Open M-F 7:30am-2pm.)*
- **POSTAL CODE:** 84300.
- **TELEPHONE: OTE** offers phones and calling cards as well as help with broken phones. *(☎228 50 23 333 ⏰ Open M-F 8am-2pm.)*
- **INTERNET ACCESS: Citron Cafe and Cocktail Bar** provides free Wi-Fi and great beverages in a super hip, clean environment. *(☎228 50 27 055 ⏰ Open daily 8am-2am.)*

Emergency!

- **POLICE: Police** station is located on Amortou, the main road heading toward Ag. Giorgios beach from Pl. Prodikiou, 1km out of town. *(☎228 50 22 100, 228 5023 039 ⏰ Open 24hr.)*
- **PORT POLICE:** *(☎228 50 22 300)*
- **PHARMACY:** It's located right before the OTE on the far right of the waterfront street when looking inland. *(☎228 50 24 946 ⏰ Open M-Tu 8:30am-2:30pm and 6-10pm, W 8:30am-2:30pm, Th-F 8:30am-2:30pm and 6-10pm, Sa 8:30am-2:30pm.)*
- **MEDICAL SERVICES:** Health care for routine health questions as well as emergencies. To get there, turn inland at the fork in the road past the OTE, at the right end of the waterfront when looking inland. It is 500m farther on the left. *(☎228 50 23 333, 228 53 60 500 **i** Helicopter to Athens available in emergencies. ⏰ Open 24hr.)*

Getting There

Getting to Naxos can be done by ferry or by plane. If planning to fly from Athens, book tickets far in advance. Ferry tickets are easier to come by last-minute.

By Plane

Flights leave from **Naxos Airport (JNX). Olympic Airways** *(☎228 50 23 292)* has a desk in **Naxos Tours** *(☎228 50 22 095 💻www.naxostours.gr)*, on the left end of the waterfront. Air tickets also sold at **Zas Travel** *(☎228 50 24 330 💻www.zastravel.com)*. Flights go to **Athens**

($ €80) and come in from Athens *($ €95)*. Book tickets months in advance; planes seat only 40 people and fill quickly.

By Ferry

All ferries from Naxos leave from Naxos Town. Two docks are at the left end of town, one for large ferries and the other for smaller ferries and daily cruises. For updated schedules and prices, consult travel agencies. To: **Amorgos** *($ €14. ⏰ 2-6hr., depending on stops; 2-5 per day)*; **Astypalea** *($ €23. ⏰ 3hr., 1 per week)*; **Donousa** *($ €8.50. ⏰ 1-4hr., 4 per week)*; **Ios** *($ €9.30. ⏰ 1½hr., 6 per week F-Su)*; **Koufonisia** *($ €7.50. ⏰ 3hr., 1-2 per day)*; **Paros** *($ €7.50. ⏰ 1hr., 4 per day)*; and **Santorini** *($ €15.50. ⏰ 2-6hr., 1-3 per day)*.

By Boat

High-speed boats go to: **Ios** *($ €20.50. ⏰ 45min., 1 per week)*; **Mykonos** *($ €18.50. ⏰ 45min., 1 per day)*; and **Santorini** *($ €27.50. ⏰ 30min., 1-2 per day)*.

Getting Around

Getting around Naxos Town is best done on foot, and most of the streets other than the main waterfront one on the outside of the *tavernas* are pedestrian-only. Naxos's streets are particularly windy and mostly unnamed, so working your way through town can be complicated. Don't be shy about asking for directions from people in shops and on the street, particularly in Kastro. To reach distant beaches, buses or cabs are best. Buses head to Maragas Camping until 2:30am, so even those out late don't need to spend the extra money on cabs unless it's a really late night.

By Bus

Tickets for all buses *(☎228 50 22 291 $ €1.40-5.50)* must be purchased before boarding the bus. Sometimes drivers will let you board and then purchase tickets at the next open station, but be prepared just in case. Current schedules are available at the station, located across from the largest dock and at tourist offices. Buses to **Apollon** *(⏰ 2 per day 9:30am-1:30pm)* and **Filoti-Chalki-Sagri** *(⏰ 6 per day 9:30am-3pm)* are often packed. Buses also run to: **Ampram** *(⏰ Tu and Th 2:30pm)*; **Apiranthos** *(⏰ 5 per day 7:15am-3pm)*; **Apollon** *(⏰ Tu and Th 2:30pm)* via the coast; **Engares** *(⏰ Tu and Th 2:30pm)*; **Glynado-Tripodes** *(⏰ 4 per day 7:30am-3pm)*; **Kastraki** *(⏰ 3 per day 7:30am-3pm)*; **Korono-Skado** *(⏰ 2 per day 9:30am-1:30pm)*; **Melanes-Miloi** *(⏰ 2 per day 12pm-3pm)*; **Mikri Vigla** *(⏰ 3 per day 7:30am-3pm)*; and **Pyrgaki Beach** *(⏰ 3 per day 7:30am-3pm)*.

By Taxi

Taxis are located on the waterfront next to the bus depot *(☎228 50 22 444)*.

koufonisia ☎22850

Koufonisia is like a tater tot—golden, perfectly sized, and good even without ketchup. Most importantly, like tater tots, you can never get enough of this postcard-worthy and postage-stamped sized island. The sea is crystal clear, and even the beach immediately beside the port is sandy and splashing with naked two-year-olds. Koufonisia's roads are predominantly pedestrian-only, and only one of them is paved. No motorbikes rip through the streets, and no aggressive cab drivers honk. The island lacks a bank, a phone store, a laundromat, or any semblance of Dionysian nightlife, opting instead for peace of mind. Perhaps most conveniently, no archaeological sites or museums loom in the distance to remind you of Greece's ancient culture or heritage—here you can worship the sun god with peace of mind. White buildings with blue shutters spot the coastline, and fine sand wraps around the island's entirety.

Koufonisia
Koufonisia
Kato
Koufonisia
N
LG
0
0.5 kilometers
0
0.5 miles

ORIENTATION

The town of Koufonisia can be walked end to end in 5min.—that is, this island and its town are small. Looking out on the water, Koufonisia's **port** is on the far right. The road that runs from the port behind the centrally located sand beach of **Ammos** runs all the way to the left (when looking at the water) and continues on to many other beaches. The island's **main street** is on the right side of Ammos' sand. The stone road is spotted with *tavernas* and cafes, and it curves up to the left toward even more hotels and restaurants. To reach **Pori beach,** follow the paved road in the middle of Ammos beach away from the water, and turn right when the road stops perpendicular to another street. Follow the winding road, and you'll reach the beach.

ACCOMMODATIONS

SOFIA SOULTANIA — ROOMS TO LET ❸

On the waterfront — ☎228 50 71 452

If your room is on the side by the waterfront, prepare to be stunned each morning when you pull back the curtain. With exclamation-point-worthy views and a flower garden in front of the white, blue-shuttered building, Sofia Soultania is a family establishment in every sense: Sofia's grandkids play with Skype downstairs and Sofia's daughter mans the rooms when Sofia heads into town.

Along the waterfront street that runs behind the port beach; walk to the left side of the sand when looking out at the water. Sofia Soultania is the 3rd door down. $ *High-season doubles €65; triples €65. Low-season doubles €25; triples €45.*

KEROS ICONS HOTEL

✦♿((⅋))🍴❄♨ HOTEL❺

By the port on the left of main street ☎228 50 71 601 📧www.akeroshotel.gr

If saltwater isn't your thing, you should reconsider having made a trip to the beach. That lapse in judgment aside, Keros Icons Hotel is where the sodium-spurner should stay. A beautiful (non-salty) pool shines in front of the entrance where modern chairs provide a refuge for fresh water enthusiasts. Rooms are spacious, and most have balconies.

🍴 *Take the left fork that branches from the main street as soon as you turn onto it. Up a short hill on the right.* ℹ *Pool closes at 8pm. Buffet breakfast included.* 💲 *High-season doubles €130; triples €160; quads €185. Low-season doubles €100; triples €135; quads €165.*

AKROGIALI ROOMS

♨♿❄♨ ROOMS TO LET ❹

Along the waterfront to the left of the port beach ☎228 50 71 685

Wooden beds, white sheets, and tiled floors make up the uninspired decor of this somewhat overpriced but convenient place to stay. One warning about the doubles with two beds rather than one: the two beds are placed directly next to each other such that they might as well form one bed, so don't come here with any overzealous spooners unless you're prepared for some cuddling.

🍴 *Along the waterfront street that runs behind the port beach; walk to the left side of the sand when looking out at the water. Right past Sofia Soultania.* 💲 *Singles €40-50; doubles €45-65; triples €50-75.*

BEACHES

Koufonisia is lined with beaches, all of which are quiet, small, and look out onto distant islands' mountains. **Ammos** is closest to town and is directly to the right of the port when looking inland. Fortunately, even though the beach is right next to the port, it's not polluted. The sand on Ammos is fine, and the water is so clear that you can see the sea urchins beneath you while you wade. Continuing 10min. down the road behind the sand, past clusters of *dormatia*, leads you to **Porta** and the long stretch of fine sand at **Harakopou.** Quieter and smaller **Fanos** waits on the other side of the ridge. A 3km walk or a bike ride up some serious hills along the main inland road takes you to ⬛**Pori.** There are gorgeous, cavernous cliffs of sheet rock by Pori that, though stunning and endowed with natural ridges, are highly dangerous to climb down. A fair distance from the eateries in town is **Pori Cafe** (🕑 *open daily 9am-9pm).* The one downside to Koufonisia's beaches is their windiness; the gusts can blow the sand pretty aggressively—either embrace the natural exfoliation or position your towel such that you are protected from the pelting sand.

To reach the beaches, a boat can take you on a scenic coastal ride to **Kato Koufonisia** (🕑 *20min., 5 per day at 11am, 1pm, 5pm, 8:15pm, and 11pm from the port* 💲 *Round-trip €5).* Another boat (🕑 *5 per day at 10am, noon, 2pm, 4pm, and 6pm)* can take you to the mainland beaches. It stops at **Finikas** (🕑 *10min.),* **Italida** (🕑 *15min.),* and **Pori** (🕑 *20min.).*

FOOD

Food here is cheap relative to other islands, so eat up!

⬛ BAKERY

♨⊘🍴❄♨ BAKERY ❶

On main street ☎228 50 71 441

Pick any one of the bakery's flakey, sugar-sprinkled pastries—you can't go wrong. The breakfast offerings here are far better than an oily omelette elsewhere, and the seating outside, though nothing fancy, is entirely functional. With fresh food baked daily on the premises, it makes sense why this shop sells out of its crowd favorites quickly. In fact, this is where the locals get their breakfast, dessert, and everything in between.

🍴 *Up the steps past Music Cafe to the left on the 1st main straightaway.* 💲 *Pastries €1-2.50.* 🕑 *Open daily 7:30am-3:30pm and 6-9:30pm.*

👍 LEFTERIS
💳♿🍸❄⛅ TAVERNA [2]

Right behind the port beach ☎228 50 71 458

With tables that basically sit on the sand of the port, Lefteris is the most centrally located restaurant on Koufonisia. All sorts of Greek food is served here in flavorful dishes, and the service is so attentive that if you drop your fork, another one appears before you can bend down and pick up the casualty.

➔ Directly behind the port beach. [$] Greek salad €4.50. Grilled meats €6-7. Beer €2.50. ⏰ Open daily 7am-1:30am.

MELISSA FISH TAVERN
💳♿🍸❄⛅ SEAFOOD TAVERNA [2]

On mainstreet ☎228 50 71 454 💻www.melissanet.gr

The gentle vibe of the periwinkle tablecloths at this fish tavern are offset by the less sophisticated fingerpainted wooden chairs. Fresh fish and fried calamari are the specialties, though the long hours mean that breakfast food is also in high demand throughout the day. Sitting outside, the breeze feels nice, but this tavern is set back in town so don't expect any ocean views.

➔ Follow main street. When it wraps left, the tavern will be on right side about 3min. up. [$] Appetizers €2.50-€4. Calamari €3. ⏰ Open daily 6am-2am.

FNS FANARI
💳♿🍸❄⛅ GREEK [2]

On main street past Kalima Music Cafe ☎22850 71796

Though the food at this main street restaurant is passable, the menu has some unfortunate translations that are disturbing on any number of levels: the local *giourbasi*, made of goat, is translated as "kid in the oven" *(€7.50)*, and the spicy meatball dish is translated as "stewed meatball faggot" *(€6)*. Tough translations.

➔ Follow main street. The restaurant will be on the right past Kalima Music Cafe. [$] Salads €2.50-4. Pies €3.50. Pizzas €6.50-8. Beer €2.50. ⏰ Open daily 1pm-midnight.

koufonisia fish

Fish is listed on the menu in prices per kilo. Rather than be deterred from eating fresh seafood because the number on the menu is shockingly high, ask to see the fish and pick one whose weight corresponds to a reasonable price. A meal-sized fish generally can be purchased for €8 and up.

NIGHTLIFE

Nightlife in the club sense is nonexistent on this quiet island. But for a late night beer or cocktail, head to one of the cafes below. Don't expect any pulsing music, and definitely don't rock your new heels.

👍 KALAMIA MUSIC CAFE
💳♿📶🍸❄⛅ CAFE

On the main street opposite the bakery ☎22850 74444 💻www.kalamia.com

The place to go to hang with friends in the shade after a long day soaking up sun, Kalamia Cafe serves great cold chocolate *(€4)* in a very chill atmosphere. Round tables and side benches provide seating for customers who routinely come and stay for hours. Fun music that generally veers from the Top-40 plays non-stop, and waiters can sometimes be caught getting their groove on when not serving.

➔ Walk along main street from the waterfront; it will be on your right. ℹ Also great during day. Free Wi-Fi. [$] Omelettes €5. Coffee €2.50-5. Cocktails €6-8 ⏰ Open daily 8am-4am.

KALHMERA KRISTOFOROS CAFE
💳♿🍸❄⛅ CAFE

Along the main street ☎694 27 83 887

Little mint green couches outside this cafe stretch across Koufonisia's quiet, pedestrian-only main street. With extremely long hours, this place is perfect for an early morning coffee or a late night beer with the guys. The food isn't anything special, but it is cheap. Smoke is heavy inside the cafe, so if you're after some fresh air head outside and enjoy the breeze.

Just past the bakery. $ Sandwiches €3.50. Coffee €1.20. Beer €2. Mixed drinks €5. ⏰ Open June-mid-July daily 6am-2am; in high season 24hr.

TOKYMA CAFE

To the left of the port beach ☎697 290 0038

Though it's overpriced if you're purchasing anything other than coffee or cocktails, Tokyma has unparalleled views and the unbeatable advantage of a deck overhanging the water. While sitting here, you feel like you're on the water, sans the inconvenient rocking of being on a boat. For a late night cocktail, this should be the cafe of choice.

To the left of the port beach when looking out at the water. Look for the yellow chairs. $ Pastries €3.50-4. Breakfast €9. Coffee €2-3.50. Cocktails €7. ⏰ Open daily 9am-3pm and 7pm-3am.

ESSENTIALS

Practicalities

Koufonisia lacks a bank, laundromat, and full internet cafe, so make sure you are covered on those fronts before heading to the island.

- **INTERNET: Kalamia Music Cafe** offers free Wi-Fi to customers. *(☎228 50 71 741 ⏰ Open daily 8am-4am.)*
- **POST OFFICE:** Provides mail and stamps, as well as a **24hr. ATM** out front because there's no full bank on the island. **Currency exchange** also offered. *(☎228 50 74 214 It's located up the shorter left fork in the main road next to the Keros hotel. ⏰ Open M-F 10:30am-1:30pm.)*
- **POSTAL CODE:** 84300.

Emergency!

- **POLICE:** The station is located on the right fork leading inland from the port. *(☎228 50 71 375 ⏰ Open 24hr.)*
- **MEDICAL SERVICES:** The **Medical Center** provides healthcare. *(☎228 50 71 370 Located right next to the police station. ⏰ Open M 9am-2pm and 6-8pm, Tu 9am-2pm, W 9am-2pm and 6-8pm, Th 9am-2pm, F 9am-2pm and 6-8pm. 24hr. emergency service.)*

Getting There

Koufonisia is accessible by ferry from Aegiali, Iraklia; Katapola, Donousa, Naxos, Schinousa, Paros, and Piraeus.

Getting Around

Walking is the simplest and surest way to get around an island so small that there's no bus or cab service offered. **Bikes** (of the two-wheel and no-motor variety) can be rented on the far left side of Ammos beach when looking at the water, and they can speed up the process of reaching the more distant beaches. But on wheels or not, be prepared for hills when reaching the distant sand.

ios   ☎22860

If you aren't drunk when you arrive, you will be when you leave—sobriety is the antithesis of Ios' ethos. The most bodacious, juiced-up, accented, and horny travelers find their way here, where boxed wine is passed around on the public bus and phone calls home include gems like: "We're staying in a really beautiful place, but I don't know how long we're going to be there because we've vomited on everything." And, "Anus? No it's Ios." The most intrepid game-spitters find themselves at Mylopotas beach by day and the town clubs by night. The literati can escape the broey bacchanalia by driving about 30min. to Homer's burial site on the far side of the island, bearing down on the sea and mountains which he immortalized in his epics. Beaches galore dot the coastline and range from the silent cove-type to the girls-seeking-ass-while-drunk type, so know where you are headed before you board the bus.

ORIENTATION

Ios is a sizable island with beaches spread along its coast, but the two main hubs of activity are the town and Mylopotas Beach. The main road from the port passes through town on its way to Mylopotas. Ios Town and Mylopotas Beach are under 10min. apart by bus and about 25min. apart by foot. To get to Mylopotas Beach from town, follow the main road to the right when looking at the big blue-roofed church in town. Town itself is set up like a piece of terraced land; streets run parallel to each other along its slope. The main nightlife stretch—most easily found by following the music and crowds at 1:30am—is three terraces in the depths of town. To get to the first terrace, walk toward the church through the big parking lot in front, and bear right.

ACCOMMODATIONS

FRANCESCO'S

In town

♥♿(((ア))♥✤♨☂ HOTEL ❷
☎228 60 91 223 ▣www.francescos.net

This complex of buildings, a pool, cafe, and bar is a student traveler's ultimate destination. The complex forms a social world unto itself in the sparkling white buildings, and at night the crew rallies together when they hit **Blue Note.** The rooms are quite clean, though sparsely decorated. Breakfast is served for the extended morning of 8am-2:30pm on a patio that overlooks the ocean, and the fully stocked bar opens at 6pm for those who need only a few hours awake before beginning the party circuit again.

➜ In the village. With your back to the bank in the main plateia, take the steps up from the left corner of the platei, then take the 1st left. ℹ Safety deposit boxes and luggage storage. Free pick-up at port. Free Wi-Fi. Computers €1 per 15min. $ Singles €28-55; doubles €33-70; triples €48-75; quads €60-80. 🕐 Reception open 9am-2pm and 6-10pm.

FAR OUT BEACH CLUB ⊗♿📶🍸🏕 CAMPGROUND ❶

End of Mylopotas Beach ☎228 60 91 468 💻www.faroutclub.com

Far Out is the epicenter of Ios' daytime revelry. If you want to wake up in the early afternoon and head to the beach to be hit on by foreigners already on their third piña colada, this is the place to stay. Accommodations range from the bring-your-own-tent area to the "bed tent" (which looks like a giant dog house and holds two small, sheetless cots) to the bungalow (which comes with electricity, beds with sheets, and a fan). All the sleeping quarters are set up along a very steep hill, so be prepared to lug your backpack up. Bathrooms dot the ascent and are clean, though it's best to check for toilet paper in the stall before sitting down.

➜ At the end of Mylopotas beach. Take the public bus to Mylopotas beach. ℹ Laundry service available. Movies nightly 9pm. Computer station with internet €1 per 15min. Self-serve restaurant. Mini-mart. Connected to the Far Out Village, which has rooms from €12-55 per person. $ €5-11. Tents €6-15 per person. Bungalows €8-22 per person. 🕐 Reception 24hr. Mini-mart open daily 8am-11pm. Restaurant open daily 8am-10pm. Pool open daily 11am-8pm.

HOTEL GEORGE AND IRENE 💳⊗🍸❄🏕 HOTEL ❷

3 blocks up from the main road ☎228 60 91 927 💻www.irene.gr

If you can make it to the top of the beastly hill that leads to the hotel, you will have earned the A/C and stone patio that await. This hotel is nothing fancy—no pool, no Wi-Fi—but it's quiet, located in town, and lacks the crazy, sexually charged youth culture of Far Out Club and Francesco's.

➜ From the bus stop, cross the street away from the church and head toward the supermarket. Take the road to the right of the supermarket and walk uphill. The hotel is at the top of the hill. ℹ Laundry €3 per kg. Computers with internet €1 per 15min. $ 6-person apartments €10-30; 5-person dorms €5-25; doubles €30-80. 🕐 Reception 24hr.

SIGHTS 👁

👍HOMER'S TOMB ⊗ TOMB

Plakatos

For those who like mountains or heroes or honor or beauty or harrowing death, those forced to read *The Odyssey* in high school and secretly loved it, or those just amazed by the idea that a blind man 2000 years ago was able to dictate two epic tales that are still around today, this grave will feel like holy ground. At the end of a dirt path, the tomb is a stone platform with a stunning view that looks down on a tiny island that is reminiscent of the Sirens' island.

➜ On the northern tip of the island. ℹ Wear comfortable shoes. $ Free.

SKARKOS ⊗ RUIN

Main Road

A ruin from the Early Bronze Age, the middle of Ios' height as a Cycladic civilization, the site was first excavated in 1986 and is where most of the contents of the Ios Archeology Museum were found.

➜ About 5min. outside town on the way to Homer's Tomb. $ Free. 🕐 Open Tu-Su 8:30am-3pm.

IOS ARCHAEOLOGICAL MUSEUM ⊗♿🍸 MUSEUM

Opposite the bus stop ☎22860 91246

The museum is a testament to Ios' cultural height in the 3rd century BCE. The sand-colored exhibits showcase marble figurines in the stylized, simplistic Cycladic style and clay pots that held goods traded in the routes to which Ios was central.

➡ Opposite the bus stop. $ €2, students and over 65 €1, EU students and under 18 free. ⏰ Open Tu-Su 8:30am-3pm.

BEACHES

Ios is a beach and party island (if you didn't already get the gist); there's little to do here but eat, sleep, and copulate. Appropriately, there's no shortage of sand. **Mylopotas Beach** is a 25min. walk from town and can also be reached by public bus, which leaves from the town center every 20min. Here, the music's as loud as it can be and the bikinis are as small as they come. 👍**Saint Theodotis Beach,** on the northeast side of the island, is the quietest of the beaches and remains impeccably clean. Lounge by the pool at the debaucherous **Far Out Beach Club** at the end of the stretch of sand to start your daydrinking early. This is the place to go if seeking scantily clad, young Aussies. **Koumbara,** just under 2km down the road that follows Gialos beach, draws a much smaller crowd to its large cove, which is a popular place for windsurfing. For those who want quiet and natural beauty, check out **Manganari,** accessible by bus. Locals head to **Kolitsani,** a crystal pool of water at the little bay. Those who want to forgo all pretense of bathing suits should head to **Psathi,** the nude beach on the eastern coast. The port beach Gialos, Mylopotas, and Manganari all offer **watersports** ranging from paddleboats to windsurfing and tubing.

FOOD

👍 POMODORO

💳🚭🍸❄☁ RESTAURANT ❷

South of the main plateia ☎22860 91387; 697 978 0613

Walk up the marble stairs into Pomodoro—which means pomegranate in Greek—and you're face-to-face with the restaurant's Italian pizza chef. The food is out-of-this-world delicious, made with fresh ingredients and cooked by a diligent and smiling staff. The Halloumi salad *(appetizer €5; entree €9)* is made with a cheese from Crete that has been grilled, placed on a bed of lettuce, oranges, and hazelnuts, and topped with a honey-based dressing. Once you eat it, there's no way you will be able to resist coming back the next night for another. The decor is equally irresistible, a classy concoction of stone archways, sparkling glasses, and a scenic rooftop garden.

➡ From the main plateia, when facing the bank, walk down the street to the right and look for the Pomodoro sign above a side street. The entrance is about 20m up on the left side. ℹ Head upstairs to enjoy views of Ios's town from the rooftop garden. $ Salads €5-9. Pizzas €12. Gnocchi €12. Brownies €7. ⏰ Open May-Oct daily 6pm-1am.

ALI BABA'S

💳♿🍸❄ ASIAN FOOD, COMFORT FOOD ❷

On the north side of town ☎228 60 91 558

Want to get 12L of cocktails served in two goldfish bowls with neon-colored straws for €35? Really craving that *pad thai* even though you're in Greece? If so, Ali Baba's is the place for you. The owner takes meticulous care of his restaurant, which started as an Asian food place but has recently expanded to include basic comfort food like meat and potato pie. Despite its location, make sure to try the Thai fare prepared by the chef straight from Thailand. And a brief warning: don't do anything particularly embarrassing while you eat. When it gets late and the restaurant fills up, the waitstaff takes covert pictures and then flashes them up on the restaurant's big screen.

➡ From the bus stop, walk alongside the church into the archway by the Ios Gym. Take a right, and Ali Baba's will be 2 blocks up on your left. From other parts of town, look at the maps posted around; Ali Baba's has a star on the map. $ Most entrees from €9.50. ⏰ Open daily May-Oct 6pm-2am.

MAESTRO

🌐🚭🍸❄☁ PIZZERIA, CAFE, RESTAURANT ❷

The street above Ali Baba's ☎228 60 91 316

For a break from the beach bonanza and a seat in perhaps the only restaurant on

Ios where you don't need to worry about secondhand smoke, dine over calzones or salad at Maestro. The roast chicken, Frenchfries, and salad special is quite the steal *(€7.50)*.

➡ From the bus stop, walk through the parking lot and into town. Bear right. When you see the sign for Ali Baba's, turn left and walk uphill 2 blocks deeper into town. It will be on the corner. ℹ No smoking inside. $ Calzones €6-8. Pizza €7-8. Beer €2.50-3. ⏰ Open daily 6pm-2am.

IOS BAKERY

⊛♿🍸❄ BAKERY ❶

Front street in town ☎228 60 91 031

For a morning or late-night croissant, head to Ios Bakery, where delicious pastries are on sale at any hour during the summer. Although the apple pastries are perpetually sold out, the chocolate croissant is a standard crowd pleaser. Those avoiding carbs should probably steer clear of this place—it will make you rethink your diet.

➡ From the bus stop, walk through the parking lot and look for the green pharmacy plus sign; the bakery is just beyond the sign. $ Most baked goods €1.50-3. ⏰ Open in summer 24hr.

NIGHTLIFE

At night, Ios Town erupts into a giant, cacophonous party. Any street is likely to have at least two full bars by 1am. Because everything is so close, there's bound to be a bar just for you nearby.

👍 BLUE NOTE

⊛⊗🍸❄ CLUB

Off the main plateia ☎228 60 92 271

Because Francesco, of Francesco's, owns this club, it fills up every night with people from his hotel at around midnight. Dark with unexciting decor, this bar collects the liveliest group of partiers around. The doormen are chatty and announce entrances with seemingly genuine excitement. Smoke hangs in the air above the crowd, punctured only by fist-pumping dance moves.

➡ Past the main plateia walking away from Disco 69, past the fast food joints. ℹ Scandinavian music after 2am. $ Shots €3. Cocktails €5. Long Island Iced Tea special 2 for €5. ⏰ Open daily 11pm-3am.

👍 JÄGER BAR

⊛⊗🍸❄ BAR

Off the main plateia ☎693 77 94 324

Jägerbombs—Jäger Bar—Jäger Bar. Hop on the Blue Note bandwagon when that bar's early night crew swings around to Jäger Bar at around 1am. When they come the disco ball spins, the pine wood decor reflects light, and bodies pack in so tightly that you can't help but find your arms wrapped around that beautiful girl or guy to your right. It's not the best place to get your most elaborate dance moves on, but the bar is exciting and perfect for some sweaty dancing.

➡ Walk through the main plateia away from Disco 69 and continue down the street to the right past Rock Bar; it'll be on the left. ℹ Busiest from 1am-3am. $ Jägerbombs €5, 4 for €10. Cocktails 2 for €5. ⏰ Open daily 11pm-4:30am.

DISCO 69

⊛⊗🍸❄ CLUB

Main plateia ☎228 60 91 064 💻www.disco69club.com

With the ever-subtle name of Disco 69, this place draws hordes of girls to its bartop and dance floor. While girls get in free all night long, guys need to pay a €6 cover charge, the result being that until late the girl-to-guy ratio is very favorable for the heterosexual males willing to pay the entrance price. The bartenders promote their "sex on the beach" cocktails with a two for €5 special during the extended happy hour.

➡ In the main plateia. $ Cover men €6; includes 2 shots and 2 drinks. Shots €3. Cocktails €5. ⏰ Open daily 11pm-6am. Happy hour 11pm-2am.

CIRCUS BAR

⊛⊗🍸❄⛱ BAR

Off the main plateia ☎698 20 63 864

For real clowning around and a break from the top-40 and aggressively loud speakers of the rest of Ios' nightlife, head to this bar, where there is a bubble machine that goes off sporadically throughout the night, live music (11pm-2am), and a fire show (2am-3am). Cocktails have names like Pazzazz and Clown Juice, served by a vivacious bartender. Don't expect bumping and grinding here, but do expect a good time.

Up the street past Disco 69 by the main plateia. Look for the sign for Pomodoro, and once on the street, look for the giant clown face on the side of the building. ℹ *Fire show 2am-3am.* $ *Shots €3. Cocktails €6.* ⏰ *Open daily 11pm-4:30am. Live music 11am-2am.*

THE ORANGE BAR — BAR

Past the main plateia

The Orange Bar specializes in shots that taste like anything but booze, flavored with everything from Snickers and Twix to Malteasers and cappuccino. The rock music precludes dancing, but it's great background music for the main event at this bar—drinking. A shot from Orange Bar is, if you will, the cherry on top of the night's alcohol intake.

Walk through the main plateia away from Disco 69 and down the street past Club Sandwich. When you see No Name, turn left and walk straight; Orange Bar will be a bit on the right when you hit the cross street. ℹ *Buy 7 shots and get a free T-shirt.* $ *Shots €3. Cocktails €5-7.* ⏰ *Open daily 10pm-4:30am.*

REHAB — BAR,CLUB

Off the main plateia

What Rehab claims to be rehabilitation from is highly unclear, but the ambiguously named establishment make no moves to stop drunken revelers from reveling at all hours of the night. Though crowds don't peak at this Jägerbomb-heavy bar until 3am, the space is comfortably full at 1:30am when the DJ whips out the blacklight and strobe. Cold air somehow circulates around the crowd, so this wouldn't be the worst place to dance in that brand new grey T-shirt.

From the bus stop, walk through the parking lot in front of the church and then turn right and walk parallel to the big road. Pass the bakery and walk another block, and then turn left. Rehab will be on your right. $ *2 Jägerbombs for €5. Buy 7 shots and get a free t-shirt.* ⏰ *Open daily 11pm-6am.*

ARTS AND CULTURE

OPEN THEATER FESTIVAL PROGRAM — CULTURAL EVENTS

Theater of Odysseus Elytis

Every summer, a series of events take place at the Theater of Odysseus Elytis, a modern venue designed to look like an ancient theater. Events range from concerts to plays, and informational pamphlets with the schedule are available at the Ios Archaeological Museum and tourism offices.

By Scorpios Bar on the right on the way to Mylopotas. $ *Some events free. Price varies.*

ESSENTIALS

Practicalities

- **BUDGET TRAVEL OFFICE: Acteon Travel** provides ferry and flight booking. *(☎228 60 91 343 by the port; 228 60 91 004 in town; 228 60 91 005 by the supermarket. 💻www.acteon.gr* ℹ *Also has a branch by the port and across the street from the bus stop.* ⏰ *Main port office open daily 8am-11pm. Town office open daily 9am-11:30pm. Supermarket office open daily 9:30am-10pm.)*
- **CURRENCY EXCHANGE AND ATM: National Bank** provides **currency exchange** and a **24hr. ATM** in the main plateia. *(☎228 60 91 565* ℹ *Bring a passport for currency exchange.* ⏰ *Open M-Th 8am-2:30pm, F 8am-2pm.)*
- **LAUNDROMAT: Sweet Irish Dream Laundry** provides wash and dry by the club with

calder-what?

If you're asking what the hell is a caldera, here's a brief rundown: when a volcano erupts, the magma chamber underneath is emptied. Since the volcano is heavy (duh), the top can sometimes collapse into the magma chamber, creating a structure shaped like a cooking pot (caldera, in Spanish). This happened to Santorini in 17th century BCE—an enormous eruption covered the island with lava and then the center collapsed. This created a seawater lagoon in the middle (that's where the volcano island is today) and gave the present-day's Santorini its bean-like shape. The steep cliff on which Fira is located is the border between the part of land that collapsed and the part that remained standing.

the same name on the main road from the port. *(☎228 60 91 584 ℹ Cash only. ⏰ Open daily 10am-9pm.)*

- **INTERNET: Acteon Travel, Francesco's,** and **Far Out Beach Club** provide Wi-Fi and computers with internet access in the port, at the end of Mylopotas, and in the town, respectively. *(☎228 60 91 343 in the port; 228 60 91 468 at the end of Mylopotas; 228 60 91 223 in the town. $ All charge €1 per 15min. of computer use. Cash only.)*
- **POST OFFICE:** The post office provides mail service and stamps on the main road coming from the port. *(☎228 91 235 ⏰ Open M-F 7:30am-2pm.)*
- **POSTAL CODE:** 84001.

Emergency!

- **POLICE:** The police station is on the road to Kolitsani beach. *(☎228 60 91 222 ⏰ Open 24hr.)*
- **HOSPITAL/MEDICAL SERVICES:** The **Medical Center** provides routine health care and emergency services, located about 200m from the dock. *(☎228 60 28 611 ℹ Specializes in drunken mishaps. ⏰ Open M-F 8:30am-2:30pm and 6-8pm for emergencies only.)* The local doctor provides emergency and routine medical help on the main road next to Fun Pub opposite the bus stop. *(☎228 60 91 137; 693 24 20 200 ℹ If the door is closed, bang loudly in an emergency; Yiannis sleeps inside. ⏰ Open 24hr.)*

Getting There

By Ferry

Ios is accessible by ferry. The price and time ranges vary according to ferry line and type of boat. Inquire at travel agencies throughout the port and town for specific timetables and prices. To: **Mykonos** *($ €35. ⏰ 2hr., 1 per day)*; **Naxos** *($ €12-22. ⏰ 1-1½hr., 1-4 per day)*; and **Santorini** *($ €7-16. ⏰ 1½hr., 2-4 per day)*.

Getting Around

While in Ios Town, the best and only way to navigate the twisty streets, often narrow and fraught with steps, is by foot. To get from Mylopotas beach to the town, or to reach some of the more distant beaches, board the bus at Mylopotas beach, the port, or the parking lot in town. Tickets are purchased once on board. To get to Homer's tomb and a few of the farther beaches, rent a car or four-wheeler, or shell out the cash for a cab. To get back to Far Out Camping late at night, wait opposite the bus stop in town by the 24hr. food shops and hail a cab.

Frequent buses shuttle between port, village, and beach. (☏ *Every 10-20 min. 8am-midnight* Ⓢ *€1.40.*) There are clearly marked stops in all three locations: near the square of the port, along the main road in town, and all along the beach road in Mylopotas. Bus schedules are posted outside the bus stand in town along the main road in front of the church.

By Taxi

Taxis can take you where you need to go at any time during your stay on Ios. *(☎697 87 34 491; ☎697 70 31 708; or ☎697 77 60 570* Ⓢ *Cash only.)*

santorini ☎22860

Santorini has had its share of catastrophes—it acquired its present shape in one of the biggest volcanic eruptions in recorded history, and an earthquake in 1956 razed many of the island's buildings. Since then, tourism has allowed for Santorini to rebuild itself; in fact, most of the island's annual income is still earned during its high season. Many establishments close for the winter, and people have to live off money earned in August—partially explaining why Santorini is one of the most expensive islands in Greece.

Today, Santorini is close on the heels of Mykonos and Ios in its popularity with partiers, who come to revel nights away on the steep cliffs of the *caldera* in Fira. The island is also popular with honeymooners who come to gaze at sunsets in Oia and window-shop in the town's jewelry stores and art galleries. The island's black sand beaches are perfect places to tan the day away, while hiking trails up to the ruins of Ancient Thira and boat tours to active volcanoes elevate any adventure seeker's heart rate. Due to this versatility, armies of tourists pour into Santorini from across the world. Due to this popularity and the cost of importing its water and produce from the mainland, however, the prices of the island are about as steep as the cliffs of the *caldera*.

ORIENTATION

Fira is Santorini's principal town, set against a steep *caldera*, or volcanic cliff. Its center is **Plateia Theotokopoulou**, a small square with plenty of travel agencies, banks, and cafes. To get here from the bus station, walk uphill through the taxi park and then turn right. **25 Martiou** is the main road, running through the *plateia* and toward the town of Oia. Above the *plateia* is a web of small streets that connect to the **Golden Street**, which is parallel to the cliff and is home to many pay-us-for-the-magnificent-view restaurants and hotels. **Ethnikis Stavrou** (or simply the "bar street") can be found above the *plateia* and is home to some of Fira's liveliest restaurants and bars. A **cable car** further up the *caldera* connects the town with its port.

Oia is a town in the very north of the island. The central *plateia* is just above the town's beautiful main church. To get here from the **bus station,** turn away from the sea and zigzag your way uphill to the right. The **main street** runs both ways from the *plateia* along the cliffs—westward toward the **Ammoudi Beach** and eastward toward the small village of **Finikia.**

ACCOMMODATIONS

Official road names are pretty rare on Santorini, so the addresses for the following accommodations are actually the towns they are located within. For more specifics, look to the direction section of each listing, and be sure to ask around—when there aren't road names locals are more likely to know where landmarks like hostels and hotels are.

LETA HOTEL &⬩(ᵖ)❄ PENSION ❸
Fira ☎22540 🖳www.leta-santorini.gr

An alluring swimming pool is in the center of this colorful pension. The rooms are big and clean, and while they may get rather pricey during the high season,

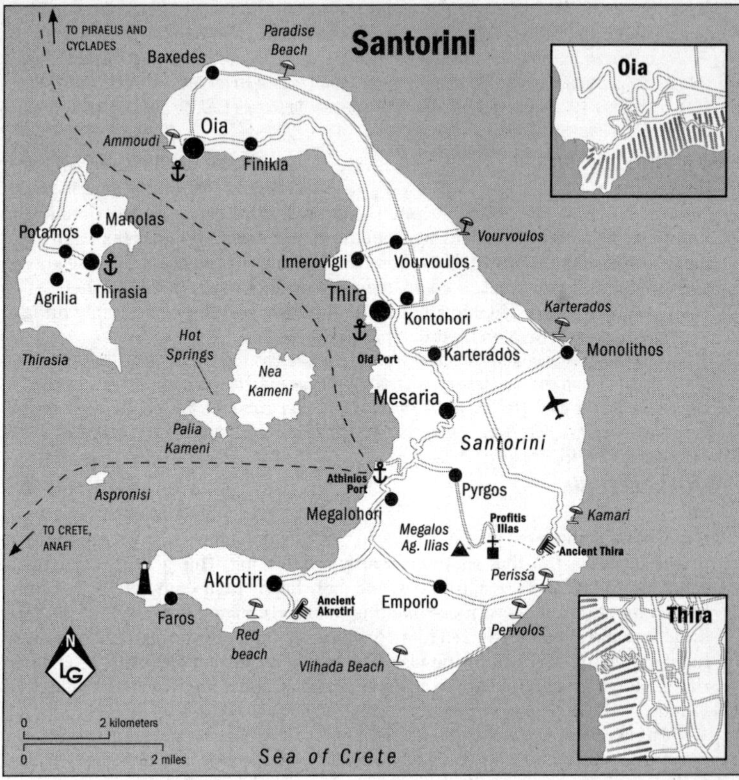

they are a safe bet for a comfortable stay. Enjoy the view of the Aegean from some of the balconies, or head down to the *plateia* to join the crowds.

*➜ To get here from the plateia, walk along the main road in the direction of Oia, past Pelican Tours and the food court; the pension will be to your right. **i** Breakfast included. Swimming pool. Shuttle service to and from the port/airport. $ High-season doubles €70. Low-season singles €35-45. ⏰ Reception 24hr.*

PENSION PETROS 🚐📶❄ PENSION [3]

Fira ☎22573 💻www.villapetros-santorini.gr

With its convenient location and glittery-clean interiors, Pension Petros is one of the best accommodation options in Fira. Try to stay here outside of the month-long high season, when the price doubles. The pension's small swimming pool isn't the liveliest spot on the island, but you probably didn't come all the way to Greece to spend time in a pension's pool.

*➜ From Pelican Tours in the plateia head downhill. When you reach the end, make a left and then an immediate right; Petros is further down the hill on the left. **i** Breakfast included. Swimming pool. Shuttle service to and from the port. $ High-season doubles €60; low-season €30-45. ⏰ Reception 24hr.*

SUMMERTIME PENSION 📶❄ PENSION [3]

Fira ☎24313 💻www.summertime-santorini.gr

Summertime Pension has lower prices and fewer perks than the pensions next to it, but it's still a very comfortable place. The charming rooms come with amenities (A/C, fridges, and TVs), and the top terrace with jacuzzi is an added bonus that most other establishments on the island lack.

🧭 From Pelican Tours in the plateia head downhill. When you reach the end, make a left and then an immediately right; Summertime is further down the hill on the left. ℹ Jacuzzi. $ High-season singles €40; doubles €50; triples €70. Low-season singles €30; doubles €40; triples €60. ⏰ Reception 8am-midnight.

SANTORINI CAMPING ⊛📶❄ CAMPING, HOSTEL ❶

Fira ☎22944 💻www.santorinicamping.gr

One of the most affordable accommodations in Fira is the no-frills Santorini Camping. It's a bit of a walk away from the center, but its popular pool and loud party music make it pretty lively. You can find better private rooms elsewhere, so come here if you want to camp, stay in a dorm, or stay in one of their tents equipped with a bed. The most hardcore of budget travelers can simply bring a sleeping bag and crash on their campgrounds *(€6-10)*.

🧭 The camping is about 400m from the plateia. From Pelican Tours, walk downhill until the end of the road, turn left ,and then take the first right; continue down the hill until you reach the camping. ℹ Swimming pool. Free shuttles to and from the port. Locks €2. Internet €3 per hr. Double rooms have free A/C, Wi-Fi. $ Bed tents €8-20; dorms €10-20. Doubles with bath €30-45; in high-season €70. ⏰ Reception 24hr.

YOUTH HOSTEL OIA ⊛ HOSTEL ❶

Oia ☎71465 💻www.santorinihostel.gr

If you're on a budget and want to stay in Oia, you don't have many more options that this place—but that isn't necessarily a bad thing. This hostel's courtyard, spacious and clean dorms, roof bar, and daily happy hour complete with a tombola competition make it more exciting than most island hostels, and the free breakfast and cheap organized tours of volcanoes and hot springs *(€20)* put most hotel concierge services to the test. The hotels on the *caldera* start at €80 per room, but you might find some cheaper pensions and *domatias* in the village of Finikia.

🧭 From Oia's bus station, walk uphill tot he right. Instead of going up the steps to the plateia, turn right and go straight; the entrance will be in a narrow street to your left. ℹ Breakfast included. $ Dorms €16; in high season €18. Internet €2 per hour. ⏰ Reception May-Oct 24hr.

YOUTH HOSTEL ANNA ⊛📶❄ HOSTEL ❶

Perissa ☎82182

Everything in Perissa is a bit cheaper than in Fira or Oia. Among the perks of this youth hostel are free Wi-Fi and A/C, something you rarely find in dorm rooms on Santorini. However, the more finicky types might object to the small, stuffy bathrooms. The hostel is close to Perissa beach and across the street from the Atlas restaurant (hostel guests get a 15% discount here). If you're not keen on staying in a bigger town (whatever that means on Santorini), this is a great option.

🧭 If you're taking a bus here from Fira, exit near the Matrix Internet Cafe. It's a 15min. walk from Perissa's main bus stop, down the main road. ℹ Internet €2 per hour. $ Dorms €7-12; 4-bed €9-15. ⏰ Check-in 8:30am-midnight.

CARLOS PANSION ⊛📶 PENSION ❸

Akrotiri ☎81370 💻www.carlospansion.gr

Located in the sleepy village of Akrotiri, Carlos Pension is a good place to escape the crowds and enjoy reasonably priced rooms and balconies with views of the sea. The owner makes all kinds of preserves (figs, tomatoes, capari) that are proudly exhibited in the neat dining room, so feel free to buy some if you like how they taste during the breakfast. The place is especially popular with French tourists, but that seems to be the case with the entire island.

🧭 From the bus stop of Akrotiri, walk down the main road away from the Red Beach and the

SIGHTS

▨ MUSEUM OF PREHISTORIC THYRA
Fira

⊛ MUSEUM
☎23217

"A masterpiece by an avant-garde painter" which combines "restraint in color and drawing with freedom of composition, intense movement, varied poses, and a registering of the momentary." No, that's not a description of a modern painting—it's the Bronze Age wall painting of monkeys that was recovered from the ruins of Akrotiri. This Minoan village was completely blanketed by lava after a volcano eruption in the 17th century BC and wasn't excavated until 1967. The museum exhibits many objects that were found during the excavations, offering an insight into the lives of people living here during the Minoan civilization (apparently, they had a "consumer society" back then). Among the most interesting exhibits here are a gold ibex figurine which was discovered hidden inside of a wooden box in 1999 and the miniature 3-D model of what the city looked like before the eruption. There are a few samples of Minoan jewelry as well—it is thought that since so little of it was found, people must have anticipated the eruption and collected their valuables before leaving the city.

✦ *From the plateia, walk toward the bus station; the museum's entrance will be to your right.*
ⓢ *Adults €3, students free.* ⓩ *Open in summer M 1:30-8pm, Tu-Su 8am-8pm; in winter M 1:30-3pm, Tu-Su 8am-3pm.*

▨ PYRGOS AND ANCIENT THIRA
Pyrgos, Kamari, Perissa

HIKING

If you're a mountain goat in your heart of hearts, we know just the hike for you (and maybe the psychiatrist as well). Start in **Pyrgos,** a beautiful little town that used to be the capital of the island and is the site of a Venetian fortress. Wander through its labyrinthine, sloping streets and discover tiny blue-domed churches (there are over 30 of these). If you continue up past Franco's Cafe and the large church, you'll discover a small set of steps that leads to a rooftop offering a panoramic view of the island. From Pyrgos, it's a 45min. walk up to **Profitis Ilias Monastery** *(☎31812).* The monastery was built in 1711, and for some reason, it now shares its site with a military radar station. The old monastery is open only for formal liturgies *(usually between 6:00-6:30am, modest clothes required),* but there's a smaller, newer church which is easier to visit. The unmarked entrance can be found by walking to the left of the final path, and you might be greeted by a friendly, multilingual monk who will answer your questions *(10am-1pm, free).* From here, it's a 1hr. hike over slippery gravel and craggy rocks which demand good footwear to the ruins of **Ancient Thira** *(ⓩ Open Tu-Su, 8:30am-2:30pm ⓢ €3, students free).* Be on a lookout for stacks of rocks, red spots, and views of the path ahead to navigate the poorly marked first part of the trail. At Ancient Thira, you'll see the ruins of an ancient theater, a church, various baths, and even a forum, most of which date back to the Hellenic period. Look out for carved dolphins and ruined columns, and don't forget to take in the magnificent view.

✦ *To get to Pyrgos, take a local bus going to Perissa or any bus that goes to Vlichada. If you want to reach the ruins of Ancient Thyra directly, you can hike from Kamari or Perissa—the former has a paved road leading up the hill, while the latter has only a footpath. Hikes from both places should take about an hour.*

MEGARO GYZI MUSEUM
Fira

⊛ MUSEUM
☎23077 🖳www.megarogyzi.gr

Housed in a 17th-century mansion, this museum holds a hodgepodge collection of objects and documents related to Santorini's history. The series of black-and-

santorini ⋅ sights

white photographs which portray the destruction caused by the devastating earthquake of 1956 may seem like the most interesting part of the museum, but there's much more. The upper floor has paintings of Santorini by local artists which vary in their artistic styles, media, and amount of talent, and on the lower floors, you'll find Venetian maps, engravings, and manuscripts (including some issued by the Ottoman Sultans) dating from between the 15th and the 19th centuries.

⚑ *From the cable car, head inland, turn left at the end of the road, and take the 2nd left.* Ⓢ *€3, students €1.50.* Ⓙ *Open May-Oct M-Sa 10am-4pm.*

PETROS M. NOMIKOS CONFERENCE CENTER
Fira

◉ MUSEUM

☎23016 🖳www.therafoundation.org

In this conference center you'll find life-size reproductions of the excavated Akrotiri wall paintings (the real artifacts can be found in the National Archaeological Museum in Athens and in Fira's Museum of Prehistoric Thyra), but these still feel quite realistic, and a copy of the iconic "Fisherman" painting can be found here as well. The explanatory tags in English are quite informative. If you don't feel like paying the entrance fee, just come for the free photo exhibit that documents the archaeological work at Akrotiri, or simply come for the view.

⚑ *From the cable car, walk along the caldera up the hill; it's the red house on the highest point of the cliff overlooking Fira.* Ⓢ *€4. Photo exhibition is free.* Ⓙ *Open daily 10am-7pm.*

VOLCANO, THIRASIA, AND HOT SPRINGS
Santorini, Caldera Rim

ISLANDS

If you feel a burning desire to experience the volcano and other parts of Santorini's *caldera* rim first-hand, you should take one of the many tours. Excursions typically go to the volcano first, where guides lead hikes up the black rocks to the active crater. After a 30min. up-close look at lava, the tours move on to the waters around Palea Kameni or Nea Kameni, where you can jump off the boat and swim to the (rather lukewarm) sulfur hot springs. Some excursions continue on to the small island of Thirasia, where tourists get a few hours to wander up to explore the towns above the port. The sleepy villages of Manolas and Potamos offer some decent views of Santorini's western coast and have quite an authentic feel. The most complete tour packages also include a sunset dinner at Oia.

Ⓢ *Tours start at around €13 (just the volcano) and go up to €35 and higher. Ask around at multiple agencies to find the right tour.*

AKROTIRI RUINS
Akrotiri

RUINS

The famous fate of Pompeii is just an imitation of an earlier disaster—in the 17th century BCE, a volcanic eruption destroyed Santorini and covered the maritime Minoan city of Akrotiri with lava. As a result, Akrotiri was preserved in time better than almost any other Minoan site. Only around three to five percent of the entire city has been excavated so far, but what's been found has been enough to show the sophistication of this Bronze Age culture. Akrotiri had multi-story houses and extensive sanitation, drainage, and sewage systems. Each house had at least one room decorated with wall paintings (which are now exhibited in Athens and Fira). No skeletons were found in the ruins, one more piece of evidence suggesting that the inhabitants escaped before the eruption. The site has been closed for a while now due to reconstruction and "technical reasons" involving a lawsuit, but ask around whether it's open when you come to Santorini. A (non)visit to the ruins can be conveniently combined with a visit to the **Red Beach,** which is a 15min. walk away.

✽ Take a bus from Fira to Akrotiri. The ruins are a 15min. walk from the village of Akrotiri, down the main road that continues toward the Red Beach.

BEACHES

The best-known beach on Santorini is ◪**Red Beach,** a small strip of pebbles and black sand under towering red-brick cliffs. You'll have to climb a small ridge to get here, but the beach, overflowing with umbrellas and beach chairs, is worth the 15min. walk from the Akrotiri ruins bus stop or the 30min. walk from Akrotiri village.

The island's most popular beach is **Kamari,** a large expanse of fine black sand with hordes of sunbathers, but locals love the festive beach towns of **Perissa** and **Perivolos,** which lie on a 9km stretch of black sand just south from the Ancient Thira mountain. In fact, beaches in Kamari and Perissa were awarded a Blue Flag for their beauty. While beach chair and umbrella rentals can be expensive *(from €7),* some restaurants in Perissa will let you stay on their beach beds without charge if you buy a drink.

To get away from the crowds, try ◪**Vlihada,** a pleasant, medium-sized beach near some impressive white cliffs. There are only a few buses per day to Vlihada from Fira, so either come with your own transport, or carefully check the bus schedule before your trip. When you're in Oia, don't miss the **Ammoudi Beach,** a small, rocky affair that's more of a dock than anything else. The cheap, infrequent boats for Thirasia leave from here as well. The closest beach to Fira is **Monolithos,** with thin, yellow sand and shallow water. All of these harder-to-find beaches can be reached by bus from Fira *(€1.40-2),* but some of the best and most peaceful beaches on the island are only accessible by car.

thirasia island

Take the dirt-cheap boat from Ammoudi Beach to the ◪Thirasia Island (boats leave at 8am, noon, or 4:30pm) and spend the day getting lost there, away from the crowds. This is one of the few opportunities to get to this island outside of a guided tour. Just make sure you ask when the last boat leaves back for Oia.

FOOD

◪ CAFE NRG
Ethnikis Stavrou, Fira

☀ CREPES ❶
☎24997

NRG (read: energy) has got some of the biggest and best crepes around. The menu items are more like suggestions than anything binding, so feel free to build your own monster crepe from the listed ingredients. Our suggestion: go for the simple but unbeatable combination of Nutella, chopped bananas, and Chantilly cream *(€4.50).* NRG has long opening hours, so it's a good place for late-night takeout.

✽ Located on the bar street, right next to the Koo Club. From Pelican Tours on the plateia's corner, walk uphill, take the 1st right, and walk until you see it on your left. Ⓢ *Crepes €3.20-6.60.* ☼ *Open daily 9:30am-4am.*

◪ POLSKI LOKAL
Oia

⊛(ᵗ)⌄⏚ POLISH/GREEK ❷
☎72083

This is the go-to place in Oia if you're a budget-conscious traveler (assuming that a budget-conscious traveler goes to Oia at all). Run by good-natured Polish immigrants and seasonal migrants, it offers some traditional Polish dishes (gulash, pirogi, bigos) paired with a *Zywiec* beer. If you're not feeling like Polish food, go for their gyros that harbor a delectable special sauce.

🧭 *From the plateia, walk down the main street in the direction of Ammoudi until you reach public toilets. Turn left, walk under the archway, and head downhill. Pass the parking lot and continue until you see the restaurant to your left.* ℹ *Free Wi-Fi.* $ *Pita €2.50-2.70. Greek dishes €7.50-9.50. Polish dishes €6.50-9. Beer €2.80-4.50.* ⏰ *Open M-Sa 1-11pm, Su 5-11pm.*

MAMA'S HOUSE 💳📶☀ GREEK [2]

Fira ☎21577

The warm, inimitable Mama will call you "darling" or "handsome" and then give you more food than you're able to eat. She's been running this place for almost 20 years, and it's become a tourist favorite due to its reasonable prices and great food. Come for the American breakfast *(2 eggs, 2 pancakes, bacon, toast, and coffee; €6.50)* or a dinner under the palm trees. The *moussaka* is literally enough to feed two people.

🧭 *From the plateia, walk toward the bus station past the tourist information booth; you'll see the restaurant to your left.* ℹ *Free Wi-Fi.* $ *Moussaka €7. Entrees €6-12.* ⏰ *Open in summer daily 8am-midnight; in winter 8am-11pm.*

CHINA RESTAURANT 💳🍸 CHINESE [2]

Fira ☎24760

If *souvlaki* and other Greek favorites have lost their charm for you, try coming here for a meal. Popular with Asian tour groups, this family-run place serves Chinese dishes with local and imported ingredients. Sit on one of their lantern-lit terraces for decent food at a better price than the *caldera* has to offer.

🧭 *The restaurant is close to the cable cars on bar street.* $ *Chicken chow mein €9. Pork and chicken dishes €10-13.* ⏰ *Open daily noon-midnight.*

NIKOLAS ⊗🍸 GREEK [2]

Fira ☎24550

For whatever it's worth, Nikolas Restaurant is the local supplier of authenticity. Set in the middle of the bar street, this traditional, unassuming restaurant contrasts sharply with the touristy establishments around it and on the *caldera*. It's got a good selection of Greek dishes, with the menu changing according to the season. Make sure to have the charismatic boss Nikolas recommend something to you that isn't on the English-language menu.

🧭 *Walking from the plateia, the restaurant will be on your right side next to the Town Club.* $ *Entrees €5-13. Stuffed zucchini €8.* ⏰ *Open M-Sa noon-10:30pm, Su noon-11pm.*

KRINAKI 💳📶🍸☀ GREEK [2]

Finikia ☎71993 🖥www.krinaki-santorini.gr

If you don't plan to eat in one of Oia's rather expensive restaurants, you can take a 30min. ramble to the nearby village of Finikia. Here you'll find Krinaki, a traditional tavern with some cool, old-fashioned decoration—an old, Greek, brick of a jukebox, dried herbs and garlic, and all kinds of junk you'd expect to find in a barn. The fare is all Greek food, and even though it's a bit tourist-oriented, at least it's the right kind of tourists who come here.

🧭 *From Oia's plateia, walk down the main street toward the Finikia village. Continue after the path changes into a tarmac road for 15min. Take a left turn at the road going down the hill, just before Finikia starts. Pass a mini-market and turn right at a small parking lot. Walk through the parking lot straight down a narrow path that will lead you to the restaurant.* $ *Entrees €8-10. Beer €3.* ⏰ *Open daily 12:30pm-1am.*

DOLPHINS FISH TAVERN 💳🍸☀ FISH [3]

Akrotiri ☎81151

Customers can sit on one of the two piers that extend onto the sea and eat amongst dolphins—hence the name. If you're feeling audacious, try the fresh swordfish—just remember that each fish is sold by the kg and can get outrageously expensive if you aren't paying attention. What you don't finish should be thrown to Paki, the restaurant's small but fierce-looking dog.

The restaurant is a 10min. walk from the Akrotiri ruins bus stop in the direction of the Red Beach. $ Seafood €6.50-13. Fish dishes with salad and potatoes €20-22 per person. ⏰ Open daily 11am-midnight.

NIGHTLIFE

There's a reason Ethnikis Stavrou in Fira is also known as simply the "bar street." You're not likely to find nightlife anywhere else.

KOO CLUB — NIGHTCLUB

Ethnikis Stavrou, Fira ☎22025 www.kooclub.gr

There's both an indoor bar and a luxurious, open-air garden, which together provide plenty of space for both talking and dancing. Head to the crowded dance floor for some loud music and flashing lights, just make sure to keep your sandals in your room—the bouncers are quite serious about the dress code.

On the bar street next to NRG Cafe. i No beachwear. $ Cover €10; includes 1 drink. Beer from €6. Cocktails €10. ⏰ Open daily 11pm-6am.

MURPHY'S — IRISH BAR

Ethnikis Stavrou, Fira ☎22248 www.murphys-bar.eu

Supposedly the first Irish bar in Greece, Murphy's is a reliable spot to do some social mingling. The traditional bar decoration is rather invisible in the nighttime hours, but you won't care much. There are a few very similar competitors on and around bar street like Highlander and 2 Brothers, so pick based on your aesthetic preferences.

It's on the bar street next to Enigma. $ Cover charge F-Sa €10; includes 1 drink and 1 shot. Beer from €5. Cocktails €9. ⏰ Open daily noon-6am. Happy hour 9:30-10:30pm.

TROPICAL BAR — BAR

Fira ☎23089

A cafe by day and bar by night, this place offers a great view of the surrounding islands and the sea—provided that it's not too dark to see anything. Come at sunset and get a seat on the balcony for the full spectacle. At night, Tropical Bar plays very recognizable and very loud American music, so get indoors and try to bust a move or two if there's any space on the cramped dance floor.

From Pelican Tours keep walking up until you reach the steps to the Old Port. Walk down the steps and Tropical Bar will be on the left. $ Cover in Aug €5, includes 1 beer. Beer from €5. Cocktails €8. ⏰ Open daily 4pm-4am.

KIRA THIRA JAZZ — JAZZ BAR

Ethnikis Stavrou, Fira ☎22770

With musical instruments hanging from the walls and a mellower mood than the rest of the frenetic establishments on Ethnikis Stavrou, Kira Thira can be a good option for a quieter night out. Come for a glass of sangria and a mix of reggae, jazz, and funk played by an elderly DJ. Alternately, come on one of the live jazz nights when this small bar is anything but quiet.

It's on the bar street across from the Nikolas restaurant. i Live jazz music 2-3 times per week. $ Beer €5. Cocktails €9. ⏰ Open daily 9pm-3:30am.

ARTS AND CULTURE

CINE VILLAGGIO
Kamari

(((•))) CINEMA

☎32800 🖳www.villaggiocinema.gr

If you can't get by without seeing Hollywood flicks every now and then, come here for your fix—the films are in their original language, with Greek subtitles. The cinema has A/C, snacks, and stays open year round.

✦ Take a bus to Kamari; the cinema can be found inside the Kamari Shopping Center. Ⓢ €7. 🕒 Check the schedules online, by phone, or on the notice board on Fira's plateia.

OPEN AIR CINEMA KAMARI
Kamari

⛺ CINEMA

☎31874 🖳www.cinekamari.gr

This cinema's open-air amphitheater is perfect for a romantic date. Make sure you check the posted schedule—sometimes there are live music concerts as well. If you don't feel like going all the way to Kamari, there's another open-air cinema in Fira (☎28881).

✦ Take a bus to Kamari, then walk inland on the road which leads back to Fira; the cinema will be on your left, right after the campgrounds. Ⓢ Tickets €7. 🕒 Check the schedules online, by phone, or on the notice board on Fira's plateia.

ESSENTIALS

🛈

Practicalities

- **TOURIST OFFICE: Tourist Information Booth** provides maps and general information. *(Fira, in the plateia ☎25940 🕒 Open 8am-10pm.)*

- **TOURS: Pelican Tours** sells ferry tickets and organizes boat trips to the volcano, hot springs, and Thirasia. Assists with airline tickets, helicopter or plane chartering, and currency exchange. *(Fira, in the plateia. ☎22220 🖳www.pelican.gr 🕒 Open daily 8am-11pm.)* In Oia, similar services are provided by **Ecorama Holidays.** *(At the bus station ☎71508 i Free internet for customers. 🕒 Open 8am-10pm.)*

- **CURRENCY EXCHANGE: National Bank** exchanges currency, traveler cheques, and has **24hr. ATM.** *(Fira, near the plateia. ☎23318 🖳www.nbg.gr. 🕒 Open M-Th 8am-2:30pm, F 8am-2pm.)* In Oia, there's a **24hr. ATM** on the main road, near the *plateia.*

- **LAUNDROMAT: AD Laundry Station** in Fira does washing, drying, folding. *(Below the plateia. ☎23533 i €10 per basket. 🕒 Open M-Sa 9am-2pm and 5-8pm.)*

- **INTERNET ACCESS: PC World.** *(Fira, in the plateia. ☎25551 i Internet €2.50 per hr., Wi-Fi €4 per hr. 🕒 Open M-Sa 10am-10pm, Su 11am-7pm.)*

- **POST OFFICE: Post Office.** *(Fira, main road ☎22238 🕒 Open M-F 7:30am-2pm.)*

- **POSTAL CODE:** 84700.

Emergency!

- **EMERGENCY NUMBERS: Medical Emergency:** ☎166. **Local Medical Emergency:** ☎22863 60300. **Police:** ☎100. **Local Police:** ☎22649. **Port Police:** ☎22239.

- **POLICE:** The local **police station** is in the nearby village of Karterados. It can be reached at ☎22659 or ☎22649.

- **LATE-NIGHT PHARMACIES: Pharmacy.** *(Fira, plateia ☎23444 🕒 Open 8am-11pm.)*

- **MEDICAL SERVICES: Santorini Hospital** in Fira provides 24hr. emergency care. *(☎22863 i Note that the phone code for the hospital is "22863" and not "22860" like the rest of the island. 🕒 Open 24hr.)*

Getting There

By Air

Flights (**$** *From €80.* ⏰ *1hr., 8 per day)* between **Athens** and Santorini National Airport (**JTR**) (*☎28405)* are operated by Olympic Airways *(☎28400)*, Aegean Airlines *(☎28500)*, and Athens Airways *(☎32020)*. There are also flights from Thessaloniki. *($ From €120.* ⏰ *1hr., 1-2 per day.)* From the airport there are public buses to Fira *($ €1.40)*, but hotels and pensions often provide free transport.

By Ferry

Ferries *($ €8-34)* and **Flying Dolphins** *($ €16-56)* connect Santorini with Piraeus and other islands—the latter are much faster and about twice as expensive. Note that ferry schedules often list Santorini as **Thira.** Ferries travel to: **Ios** *(⏰ 30min.-1½hr., 3-5 per day);* **Mykonos** *(⏰ 3hr., 2 per day);* **Milos** *(⏰ 1½-3hr., 1-3 per day);* **Naxos** *(⏰ 1½-2½hr., 3-4 per day)*. To check current schedules, ask at Pelican Tours or any other travel agency. If you're arriving by ferry, you'll be dropped off at one of the three ports (Fira, Oia, Athinios), but most likely at **Athinios** (even if your ticket says Thira). There are public buses from here to Fira *($ €2.* ⏰ *20min.)* meeting the ferries, but hotels often provide free transport from here as well. To get to and from Fira's port, either walk down the 588-step footpath, take the **cable car** *(☎22977 $ €4, children and luggage €2.* ⏰ *Every 20min. 6:30am-10:40pm)*, or hire a donkey *($ €5)* at the red donkey station.

Getting Around

By Bus

Local buses *(☎25404 💻www.ktel-santorini.gr)* connect most towns on Santorini. From the Fira bus station, buses head to: **Akrotiri** *(⏰ 30min., 10 per day. $ €1.70);* **Athinios** *($ €2.* ⏰ *25min., 4 per day);* **Kamari** *($ €1.40.* ⏰ *20min., every 30min. 7:30am-12am);* **Monolithos** *($ €1.40.* ⏰ *30min., 8 per day);* **Oia** *($ €1.40.* ⏰ *30min., every 30min. 6:50am-11pm)* via the airport; **Perissa** *($ €2.* ⏰ *30min., every 30min. 7:10am-12am);* **Vlihada** *(⏰ 5 per day €1.40)*. Transferring in small towns isn't very convenient, as the waiting times can be quite long. You can get a **taxi** at Fira's taxi park *(☎22555 ⏰ 24hr.)*, just above the bus station.

By Moped and ATV

Many **moped and ATV rental** agencies can be found in the streets around Fira's *plateia*. In mid-season, expect to pay around €10-20 per day for a moped and €15-25 for an ATV, with higher prices in August. Most car rental companies are open between 8am and 8pm, and you'll need a driver's license. Ask around for the best price, and make sure they give you a helmet.

milos ☎22870

Milos is pretty much the opposite of a party island—it's slow-paced and not excessively popular with foreign tourists. Instead, it's a collection of natural wonders dotting a bowtie-shaped shoreline. From volcanic beaches amidst colorful cliffs to sea caves and strange rock formations, almost the entire island is visually exceptional. You can go lie down on the moon-like beach of Sarakiniko, or take a boat cruise to the pirate hideouts of Kleftiko. Even if you abandon the dramatic shoreline and head inland, you can find the remnants of early Christian catacombs, a smattering of tiny museums, and a ton of Orthodox churches. The island's hilltop capital, **Plaka,** offers some great views of the island's entirety, while the port of **Adamos** is where you'll find some semblance of nightlife (there were around five bars last time we counted). There are no hostels on the island, but there are plenty of *domatia* and some reasonably cheap hotels to accommodate the budget traveler. Even though the island isn't exactly a whirlwind of activity, the tourist infrastructure is very developed—Milos maintains several websites that give a good overview of the main attractions and direct you to many interesting places. Sift through all the information, and then explore the winding shoreline by yourself: there are plenty of new discoveries to be made.

ORIENTATION

The best place to stay in Milos is probably **Adamos,** the port city with a lot of tourist-oriented infrastructure. Most activity is concentrated on the **waterfront,** where you'll find many restaurants and tourist agencies. The **bus stop** is opposite the ATE Bank, where the Plaka-bound **main road** adjoins the waterfront. Plenty of cheap *domatias* can be found in the labyrinthine streets directly behind the waterfront. The island's capital is **Plaka,** a hilltop city some 6km north of Adamos. Its upper part is a maze of narrow streets with many cafes that offers many unexpected scenic views, while down the hill you'll find the Archaeological Museum, the hospital, and the road that will lead you to Trypiti's **catacombs.** While you're in Plaka, don't forget to climb the hill to **Panagia Thalassitra Monastery,** where you can see the entire island.

ACCOMMODATIONS

HOTEL SEMIRAMIS

HOTEL [2]

Adamas ☎22117 💻www.semiramishotel-milos.com

This place may be one of the cheapest hotels on the island, but you wouldn't be able to guess that from the cozy, clean, and spacious rooms. The genuine owner will be happy to give you local advice on what to see on the island, while the leafy backyard is an excellent place to wait through the midday sun. For the most frugal of travelers, there are two rooms that share a bathroom and go for an even lower price.

From ATE Bank, walk down the main road for 30m; on the left you'll see a sign pointing you to the hotel. ℹ *Airport transportation available.* [$] *High-season doubles €55-65; low-season €28. Triples 20% extra.* ⏰ *Reception 9am-4pm and 7:30-9pm.*

ANEZINA

HOTEL [3]

Adamas ☎24009 💻www.anezinahotel.com

Anezina and Iliopetra are two actual sister hotels (as in, run by two sisters) that provide a very similar standard of services. The rooms are big, clean, and feature drawings of old ships. The mutually supportive system of these hotels can be quite helpful—if at some point there's nobody at one reception, you can always go talk to somebody in the hotel next door.

Walk down the main road past the pharmacy, take the 1st left turn, and then another left; you'll see the two hotels across the street on your right. ℹ *Laundry service available.* [$] *Doubles €30-90; triples €40-100. Studio apartments with kitchens €50-120.* ⏰ *Reception 24hr.*

ELENI HOTEL

HOTEL [3]

Adamas ☎21972 💻www.hoteleleni.com

A bit of a walk away from the hustle and bustle of the waterfront, this 15-room hotel is among the cheaper options, offering competent rooms with A/C and balconies and a very personable owner.

From the dock, continue down the waterfront away from the restaurants and tourist agencies. After you reach the Lagada beach, walk 50m inland, take a left turn, and walk until you see the hotel to your right. [$] *Doubles €30-70.* ⏰ *Reception 8am-midnight.*

SANTORINI CAMPING

CAMPING [1]

Achivadolimni ☎31410 💻www.miloscamping.gr

If you don't have your own transportation, staying here can be a bit inconvenient (it's some 6km away from Adamas, and buses run infrequently), but there are many advantages. The camping site is just a few minutes away from Hivadolimni, the island's most popular beach, and there's a swimming pool and

open-air cafeteria, both on a steep cliff overlooking the beach. You'll also be able to use the communal kitchen, mini-mart, and cheap laundry service *(€5).*
➜ Take the bus from Adamas. ℹ Free airport and port transportation. $ 2-person bungalows €30-98; 3-person bungalows €60-116; 4-person bungalows €70-131. ⏰ Reception 8am-12am.

MACHI'S HOUSE ♿📶❄ APARTMENTS [4]

Plaka ☎22129 💻www.milos-island.gr/rooms-apartments/machi

If the idea of staying in a historically significant place appeals to you, try Machi's House in Plaka. This house is where the current owner's great-great-great-grandfather supposedly hid the statue of Venus de Milo after finding it in a field near Trypiti. In the yard, look for the well that is speculated to be the original base of the statue. There are three apartments and one double room, and guests have access to a private parking lot (there aren't many parking options in upper Plaka). Make reservations in advance.
➜ From the upper bus stop in Plaka, walk down the main road. ℹ Apartments have kitchens. $ Doubles €35-75. Apartments €75-130. ⏰ Reception 10am-2am.

SIGHTS 👁

👍 CATACOMBS AND ROMAN THEATER ♿ RUINS

Trypiti ☎21625

Among the first Christian places of worship in the world, the **catacombs** at Milos were used for secret religious ceremonies and burying the dead in the days when Christians had to worship in secrecy to avoid persecution. A Christian community was on the island as early as the first century, and it grew considerably in the following centuries. Carved in soft volcanic rock, the catacombs were pillaged in the 19th century, and not much remains to see today. Still, the place remains strangely fascinating. Vaults in the sides contain graves which accommodated anywhere from one to seven bodies, and it's estimated that thousands of people were buried here. Only one of the three galleries can be accessed today, and that only on a guided tour. The guides don't speak much English, so don't expect thorough explanations. Notice the primitive inscriptions on the walls—no, these weren't made by early Christians; it's vandalism from a few years back when the catacombs didn't have a night guard. The **ancient Roman theater** is a few minutes on foot away from the catacombs. It is quite well-preserved and used to host musical performances. If you continue further up the hill, you'll come across the site where **Venus de Milo** was found, and further up is a small hill topped by a tiny chapel—the view from here is worth the climb.
➜ Trypiti is 1km away from the lower bus stop in Plaka. To get to the catacombs, follow the downhill road that adjoins the square above the lower bus stop. Pass the Ancient Theater sign but stay on the road, and the catacombs will be further down at the end of the winding road. To get to the theater, backtrack from the catacombs and turn left (just before the flight of steps) onto a path that will lead you there. ℹ Guided tours of catacombs every 20min. $ Catacombs €2, reduced ticket €1, EU students free. ⏰ Open Tu-Sa 8:30am-6:30pm, Su 8:30am-3pm.

👍 KIMOLOS ISLAND

Kimolos Island, north of Milos

Kimolos is an island stuck in time—some say the precise date is 1955, but decide for yourself. When you arrive by ferry at the port of **Psathi,** you might be awaited by the island's single bus *(☎6973 700 033 $ €1.5),* and bus driver, who's allegedly the only person on Kimolos who speaks some English. The bus will take you to **Chorio,** the island's capital, where you can find a number of small museums—the **Folk and Maritime Museum** (☎51118, €1) run by a friendly doctor, the **Archaeological Museum** where you can walk on a glass floor over tombs from the Archaic period, and a volunteer office dedicated to the **monk seal** (*Monachus monachus*), which is one of the most endangered mammals in the world and which lives on this island. Don't forget to wander around Chorio's **kastro**, the town's castle center. The opening times of these sights vary, but if you come outside of the visiting hours, you can always try banging on the door to win a personalized visit. If you have your own transport, you can go see **Skiadi**, an enormous mushroom-like rock structure in the northwest of the island—it can be reached by driving down a road from Chorio and then walking for some additional 30 minutes on an arrow-marked path. If you don't have a car, you can call the island's sole **taxi** (*☎51552*). Finally, south of Kimolos is the uninhabited island of **Polyaigos** (fittingly, the name means "many goats") which has some interesting volcanic caves. **Delphini Sea Taxi** (*☎51437*) organizes boat trips to this island from Psathi (these generally leave at 9am and cost €25). Since Kimolos is a small, untouristy island, things do not always run on fixed schedules - before going there, always get advice from local sources.

🧭 To get to Kimolos, drive or take a bus from Adamas to Pollonia, and then take one of the ferries to Kimolos (there are 2 per day in winter, 4 per day in middle season, 5-6 per day in July and August. Check the current schedules at a travel agency. The ferry can carry road vehicles as well. Tickets cost €2). There are ferries from Adamas as well, but these are more expensive and run only about once a week.

ECCLESIASTIC MUSEUM — 🏛 MUSEUM

Adamas, main road — ☎23956

With free entry, there's really no excuse good excuse for passing up this tiny museum crammed wall-to-wall with Orthodox icons. Housed in the small church of the Holy Trinity that was first built some 1150 years ago, it has been through various renovations but keeps its old world charm. Inside, you'll see paintings, lecterns, *epitaphios* icons, silver chalices, procession crosses, 17th-century books of saints, and much more. From this museum, walk uphill to reach the **church of St. Haralambos,** which dominates this part of Adamos. It's newer (inaugurated in 1870), but it's also larger and generously decorated.

🧭 From the fork at Artemis bakery, follow the signs into the small street that adjoins the main road. $ Free. ⏰ Open daily 9:15am-1:15pm and 6:15-10:15pm.

MINING MUSEUM — 🏛 MUSEUM

Adamas, main road — ☎22481 💻www.milosminingmuseum.gr

This museum is more modern in its feel than the Ecclesiastic Museum and celebrates the island's mining history. When you're in Milos, check the subject of their current temporary exhibition—this might be the most interesting part of the museum.

🧭 Follow the waterfront for some 200m in the direction of the airport, the museum will be to your left. $ €3, students €2. ⏰ Open daily in high-season 9am-2pm and 5:30-10pm; in low-season Sa 9am-2pm.

FOLK MUSEUM — 🏛 MUSEUM

Plaka, upper part — ☎21292

This tiny museum tries to show what life on Milos was like at the turn of the 20th century through a collection of old objects of daily use, most donated by inhabitants of the island. The exhibition is divided into rooms based on their function—bedroom, winepress room, kitchen, loom room—and features a couple of interesting objects, including a pirate-era trunk, bridal underwear (looks like something Lady Gaga might enjoy wearing), and some old beekeeping tools. If there aren't many people, ask the ticket person to show you around.

🧭 From the upper bus stop in Plaka, walk into the maze of small streets. The museum is in the same square as the Church of Panagia Korfiatissa. $ €3, students €1.50. ⏰ Open M 7-10pm, Tu-Sa 10am-1pm, Su 7-10pm.

MILOS (ARCHAEOLOGICAL) MUSEUM MUSEUM

Plaka ☎21620

Upon entering this museum, you'll be greeted by a plaster cast of **Venus de Milo,** the iconic, armless statue that was discovered in the nearby village of Trypiti and today is exhibited in Louvre. The statue was found in 1820 by a young farmer, who later sold it to the French for 400 *grosi* (about €1000 today), supposedly to prevent it from falling into the hands of Ottoman Turks. The French ambassador to Constantinople gave the statue to King Louis XVIII, who subsequently gave it to the famed museum. The remaining items on exhibit in the Milos Museum are originals, but decidedly less famous. The settlements on the island go back over 5000 years, and the exhibits' origins range from the Early Bronze Age and the Phylakopi period (2300-1400BCE) to Hellenistic and Roman periods. Be on the lookout for bovine figures, obsidian stones, and the statuette of "Lady of Phylakopi."

*Downhill from upper Plaka.* *$* *€3, reduced €2, EU students free.* *⏰* *Open Tu-Su 8:30am-3pm.*

KLIMA TRADITIONAL VILLAGE

Klima

If you're coming over to see the catacombs, you should pay a visit to the small fishing village of Klima as well. One of the island's most photographed landmarks, its colorful houses form a single row along the waterfront. The houses here have two floors. In winter, the lower floor is used for keeping the boats, while in summer the boats are on water and the inhabitants find themselves with an extra room. Come here to take photos and watch the sunset.

*Follow the road from Plaka to Trypiti, and keep to the right. After the village of Trypiti becomes less dense, take a right turn and follow the road down to Klima, which ends with 280 stairs going down to the village. The distance to Trypiti is about 1-2km. There's a footpath between the catacombs and the village, but it might be difficult to navigate, so we recommend that you backtrack to the village and then follow the paved road.*

KLEFTIKO AND GLARONISSIA ROCK FORMATIONS

Milos shores

Some of the best-known structures on Milos can't be accessed without a boat. One of these is Kleftiko, an impressive rock formation on the southwest shore of the island. It is said that the Ottoman pirate Barbarossa used to hide his boats in the marine caves of Kleftiko to avoid his pursuers. If you're lucky, you might glimpse an old cannon still lying on the seafloor. Glaronissia islands are home to 20m basalt blocks protruding out of the water. Composed of small crystals, they are shaped like hexagons and are often compared to organ pipes. To get to either of these rock formations, you'll have to join in on one of the many cruises organized around the Milos shoreline *(€20-60),* take part in a kayaking excursion, or do some rather audacious long-distance swimming.

THE GREAT OUTDOORS

MILOS KAYAKING KAYAKING

Triovasalos ☎23597 🖥www.seakayakgreece.com

If you feel like having a firsthand experience of the caves, arches, and cliffs that line the uneven shoreline of Milos, you'll be interested in some of the five different beginner-friendly **kayak** routes offered by Milos Kayaking. Among the major draws are the daytrips to Kleftiko and Glaronisia, but Klima, Gerakas, and the sulfur mines are interesting as well. The price includes a picnic lunch, snorkeling equipment, and transport to and from the paddle site.

*For information about trips and bookings, go to a travel agency in Adamas or contact the company directly.* *i* *Availability of trips depends on weather.* *$* *€65 per person.* *⏰* *Trips are usually 10am-5pm and involve 3hr. (7½-10 mi.) of paddling.*

MILOS DIVING CENTER DIVING

Pollonia ☎28077 🖳www.milosdiving.gr

For fans of sea anemones and shipwrecks from WWII, the Pollonia-based Milos Diving Center organizes diving trips and awards diving certificates (CMAS, PADI, IAHD). Southwest Aegean Milos Sea Club *(☎6977 288 847)* based in Adamas offers diving trips as well.

ℹ For information about trips and bookings, go to a travel agency in Adamas or contact the companies directly. $ Self-equipped dive €35; dive with equipment provided €50; ten dives €400.

FOOD

👍 ARTEMIS ⊛ BAKERY ❶

Adamas ☎22998

Artemis has an unbelievable selection of freshly baked croissants, cookies, breads, and pies, all very suitable for a fast breakfast or a picnic at a secluded beach. Try the big slice of watermelon pie *(€2)*, or supply yourself with the traditional Milos dessert, *koufeto*, made of pumpkin, honey, and almonds *(€3-8)*. Pizza, cheese buns, and other savory baked goods are also available.

➔ The bakery is on the fork opposite ATE Bank and the bus stop. $ Bread €1 per kg. Croissants €2. Cookies €9 per kg. ⏰ Open daily 5am-midnight.

👍 FORAS ⊛🍸☁ TAVERNA ❷

Plaka ☎23954

This traditional taverna in Plaka serves cheap, fresh food in generous portions. In fact, if you ask the boss Nikolas about which menu items are good, he'll pat his well-nourished belly and tell you that everything is good. Try their tasty rabbit with bread and onions *(€8)* or the swordfish *(€8)*—especially the more exotic meals come at good prices. Foras also serves white wine produced in Milos, so order half a carafe *(€2.50)* and get your drink on.

➔ From the upper bus stop in Plaka, head downhill on the main road; it will be on your right. $ Salads €2.50-5.50. Entrees €4.50-8. Beer €2.20-2.50. ⏰ Open daily 8am-1am.

NAVAGIO ⊛🍸☁ TAVERNA ❷

Adamas ☎24124

This popular fish taverna differs from the other, more central waterfront restaurants not only in that it offers seating closer to the water but also in its local reputation. Customers here usually come for the spaghetti or the fish dishes, so those are the safest bet. It has reasonably interesting food (try the garlicky *soutzoukakia*), but be warned that taxes are not included in the posted prices.

➔ Walk down the waterfront in the direction of the Mining Museum; Navagio's terrace will be on the right. $ Beer €2-3. Grilled fish €7-9. Swordfish €11.50. ⏰ Open daily 1pm-1am.

PITSOUNAKIA ⊛🍸☁ GRILL ❶

Adamas ☎21739

Less expensive than most restaurants down on the waterfront, Pitsounakia is especially good for a quick gyro or *souvlaki*. Coming later in the day seems to be more common than coming here for lunch. If you want a proper meal, go linger in the asphalt garden in the back of the restaurant. The gyros line gets quite long sometimes, so if you're running for a ferry or something, you may have to hit up somewhere with a higher price but shorter line.

➔ Pitsounakia is some 20m from ATE bank down the main road, on the left. $ Souvlaki €1.80. Entrees €5.50-7. Beer €2.50. ⏰ Open daily 1pm-1am.

BARKO ⊛🍸☁ TAVERNA ❷

Adamas ☎22660

If you want to eat meat, this traditional taverna is a very good choice. With its leafy, roofed garden and a nice view of the countryside, Barko caters to dinner-time crowds. Vegetarians (and everyone else!), try the excellent *immam* (eggplant stuffed with onions and tomatoes) with bread, which is a Greek take on the Turkish dish *imam bayildi* ("the Imam fainted").

🧭 Walk down the main road in the direction of Plaka; Barko will be on the left. $ Entrees €5.50-9.50. Beer €3.20-3.50. ⏰ Open daily May-July 5pm-1am; Aug 1pm-1am; Sept-Apr 5pm-1am.

PALAIOS 🌐⛅ DESSERTS [1]

Plaka ☎22548

This local landmark serves all kinds of cakes, pastries, and desserts, all produced daily in the basement of the building. If you're getting one of their tempting products, don't forget to have it with a scoop of their homemade ice cream *(€2 extra).* Perfect for when you're waiting for the Adamas-bound bus back home.

🧭 It's the big building opposite the upper bus stop. $ Desserts €4.50-7. Coffee €2-5.50. ⏰ Open daily 8am-1am.

NIGHTLIFE

AKRI 🌐🍸⛅ BAR

Adamas ☎22604

Akri ("edge") has a more laid-back feel and a nicer view than its neighbors down the hill. The sprawling terraces have many tables and stools from which you can observe the green-lit waters of Adamos harbor. The two levels of slick interiors are suitable for dancing, but Akri is also a good place to come for an evening coffee. This is not a place for you if you hoped to listen to Greek music, but they play just about everything else.

🧭 Continue up the hill beyond Vipera Lebetina and Aragosta cafe, Akri will be to your left. $ Coffee €2-3.5. Small beer €5-6. Cocktails €8-9. ⏰ Open daily 8pm-4am.

ARAGOSTA 🍸⛅ BAR

Adamas ☎22292 🖥www.aragosta.gr

One of the few nightlife establishments in Adamas, Aragosta gets very lively at night. The laid-back, white-and-red terrace overlooks the pedestrian zone of the waterfront, so this is the place to go if you want to be seen partying it up. A few meters up the hill, Aragosta has a small open-air cafe that has an excellent view of the harbor that serves as a refuge from the loud music inside the bar.

🧭 Climb up the stairs near Milos Travel, it's the bar on the right. $ Small beer €5-5.50. Cocktails €10. Desserts €5-7. ⏰ Open daily 7pm-5:30am. Cafe open daily 9am-2pm and 7pm-3am.

VIPERA LEBETINA 🌐🍸⛅ BAR

Adamas

This bar is named after the island's famous venomous snake, but let's hope none of that stuff made its way into their drinks. With a dock-facing terrace outside and a small dance floor inside, Vipera is one of the more compact bars here, but that doesn't make its charisma any smaller at night when rock music is playing at full volume.

🧭 Find it a few meters above Aragosta. $ Shots €3. Beer €5-6. Cocktails €9. ⏰ Open daily 9pm-5:30am.

UTOPIA 🌐🍸⛅ CAFE/BAR

Plaka ☎23678

This cafe in Plaka offers possibly the best view from among the many cafes in town. Sit on the stylish chessboard-checkered terrace and take in the view of the sea, the surrounding islands, and the setting sun (provided that you come at the right time). The interior has some interesting posters and jazz music blaring from the speakers, but it's the terrace that's the main attraction.

🧭 From the upper bus stop, walk toward the Folk Museum; soon you should see signs on the left pointing you to the bar. $ Small beer €4.50-6. Drinks €6.50. Coffee €2-6. ⏰ Open daily 9am-5pm and 6pm-2am.

BEACHES

Beaches in Milos are a cut above any other beach—they are natural works of art. After years of volcanic eruptions, mineral deposits, and aquatic erosion, the shoreline of Milos is a wonderland of multicolored sand, steep cliffs, and fascinating caves and arches. One of the most remarkable beaches is 👍**Sarakiniko,** a shallow pool of water in the middle of white volcanic moonscape. **Papafragas,** close to the ruins of Fylakopi, is a long, water-filled canyon ending in a small sandy beach. **Hivadolimni** is the longest beach on the island, named after the small saltwater lake behind it, while 👍**Paliochori** is known for its colorful cliffs and turquoise water. Out of the 60-something beaches on Milos, around 30 are accessible only by car, while the best-known ones have infrequent bus connections running from Adamas. Boats will take you to beaches that are hard to access by road, including the sea cavern of **Sykia.** For more information about individual beaches, ask for a brochure at the tourist office.

ESSENTIALS

Practicalities

- **TOURIST OFFICES: Tourist Information** provides maps, brochures, ferry and bus timetables, and has a complete list of the island's hotels. *(Adamas, waterfront ☎22445 💻www.milos.gr 🕐 Open M 8:30am-midnight, Tu-Sa 8:30am-11pm.)*
- **TOURIST AGENCIES: Brau Kat Travel** has very helpful staff and sells ferry tickets, rents cars, and arranges tours. *(Adamas, waterfront ☎23000 💻www.milosisland.gr 🕐 Open daily 8:30am-1am.)* **Sophia Travels** provides similar services. *(Adamas, waterfront ☎21994 💻www.milosferries.gr 🕐 Open daily 8:30am-1am.)*
- **CURRENCY EXCHANGE: National Bank** provides currency exchange. *(Adamas, waterfront ☎22332 🕐 Open M-Th 8:30am-2pm, F 8:30am-1:30pm.)*
- **ATM: ATE Bank.** *(☎22330, near the bus stop.)*
- **LAUNDROMAT: Smart and Fast Clean.** *(Adamas, main road ☎23271 ℹ €8 for 5-6kg of laundry. 🕐 Open M-Sa 8am-10pm, Su 11am-10pm.)*
- **INTERNET:** The municipality of Adamas has a **free Wi-Fi hotspot** on the waterfront. **Internet Info**. *(Adamas, main road ℹ €3 per hr., €0.50 per 5min. 🕐 Open daily 9am-3pm and 4pm-12:30am.)*
- **POST OFFICE: Hellenic Post** provides Poste Restante and express mail services. *(Adamas, waterfront ☎22345 🕐 Open M-F 9am-1pm.)*
- **POSTAL CODE:** 84800.

Emergency!

- **EMERGENCY NUMBERS:** ☎166. **Local Emergency:** ☎22700 or 22701. **Police:** ☎100. **Local Port Police:** ☎23360. **Local Tourist Police:** ☎21378.
- **POLICE: Police Station**. *(Plaka, main road ☎21378 🕐 Open 24hr.)*
- **LATE-NIGHT PHARMACIES: Pharmacy.** *(Adamas, main road ☎22178 🕐 Open daily 8:30am-3pm and 6pm-midnight.)*
- **MEDICAL SERVICES: Health Center** in Plaka provides 24hr. emergency care. *(Plaka, lower square ☎22700 or 22701 🕐 Open 24hr.)*

Getting There

By Plane

About twice a day there are government-subsidized **flights** between Athens and Milos Airport (**MLO**) (*☎22381*) operated by Olympic Airways *(Adamas, waterfront ☎22380).* Flights are cheap *($ €45-50)* and get sold out easily, so book in advance. There is no public transportation from the airport, so you'll have to take a taxi or arrange it with your hotel.

By Ferry

Ferry and **fast ferry** schedules change very often (three or four times just in June), but at the time of writing, the following connections were available: **Piraeus** *(4-7 per day, 2½-7hr.),* **Amorgos, Anafi, Folegandros, Heraklion, Ios, Karpathos, Kimolos, Kithnos, Koufonisi, Mykonos, Naxos, Rhodos, Santorini, Serifos, Sifnos, Sikinos, Sitia,** and **Syros.** Check the current schedules at any travel agency. Ferries travel to and from Adamas.

Getting Around

By Bus

Local transportation is provided by **buses** *($ €1.50-1.70)* which run from Adamas to different parts of the island. Among the destinations are **Plaka** *(via Triovassalos and Tripiti ⏰ Every hr. 7:30am-12:30am),* **Pollonia** *(via Pahena and Filakopi ⏰ 9 per day 6:45am-10:15pm),* **Paleochori** *(via Zefiria ⏰ 7 per day 10:30am-7:15pm),* **Achivadolimni** and **Provata** *(⏰ 8 per day 10:15am-6:20pm),* **Milos Camping** *(⏰ 11 per day 8am-11:15pm),* and **Sarakiniko** *(⏰ 11am, 1pm, 3pm).*

By Taxi

Taxis line up by the waterfront in Adamas *(☎22219 for Adamas; ☎21306 for Triovassalos).* Check the taxi price list at the tourist office. The best way to explore the island is with your own transport, since many beaches aren't accessible by bus.

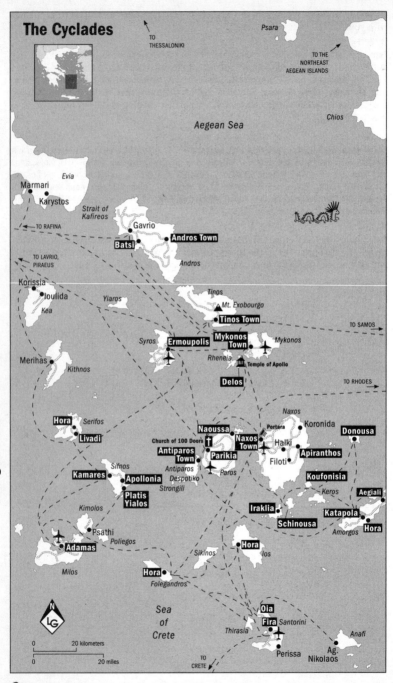

The Cyclades

Aegean Sea

TO THESSALONIKI

Psara

TO THE NORTHEAST AEGEAN ISLANDS

Chios

Evia

Marmari

Karystos

Strait of Kafireos

TO RAFINA

Gavrio

Batsi

Andros Town

Andros

TO LAVRIO, PIRAEUS

Korissia

Ioulida

Kea

Yiaros

Merihas

Kithnos

Tinos

Mt. Exobourgo

Tinos Town

TO SAMOS

Syros

Ermoupolis

Mykonos Town

Mykonos

Rheneia

Temple of Apollo

Delos

TO RHODES

Naxos

Hora

Serifos

Livadi

Church of 100 Doors

Naoussa

Portara

Naxos Town

Koronida

Donousa

Antiparos Town

Parikia

Halki

Apiranthos

Antiparos

Filoti

Kamares

Sifnos

Despotiko

Paros

Strongili

Apollonia

Koufonisia

Platis Yialos

Kimolos

Keros

Aegiali

Psathi

Iraklia

Katapola

Adamas

Poliegos

Schinousa

Amorgos

Hora

Milos

Sikinos

Hora

Ios

Hora

Folegandros

Sea of Crete

Oia

Fira

Santorini

Thirasia

Anafi

Perissa

Ag. Nikolaos

TO CRETE

N

LG

0   20 kilometers

0   20 miles

greek islands

204 | www.letsgo.com

ESSENTIALS

You don't have to be a rocket scientist to plan a good trip. (It might help, but it's not required.) You do, however, need to be well prepared, and that's what we can do for you. Essentials is the chapter that gives you all the nitty-gritty you need to know for your trip: the hard information gleaned from 50 years of collective wisdom (and that phone call to Greece the other day that put us on hold for an hour). Planning your trip? Check. Staying safe and healthy? Check. The dirt on transportation? Check. We've also thrown in communications info, meteorological charts, and a ▓phrasebook, just for good measure. Plus, for overall trip-planning advice from what to pack (money and as little underwear as possible) to how to take a good passport photo (it's physically impossible; consider airbrushing), you can also check out the Essentials section of ▣www.letsgo.com.

We're not going to lie—this chapter is tough for us to write, and you might not find it as fun of a read as 101 or Discover. But please, for the love of all that is good, read it! It's super helpful, and, most importantly, it means we didn't compile all this technical info and put it in one place for you (yes YOU) for nothing.

greatest hits

- **FERRY ME AWAY.** I'm on a boat (p. 217)!

- **GET A VISA.** Put it on your spring-cleaning list, since you'll need to apply six to eight weeks in advance (p. 206).

- **DON'T SMUGGLE IN ANY DRUGS.** Turkey's Kurdish rebels have already got that covered. And the police is covering them. You don't want Turkish police covering you (p. 212).

- **IT'S ALL GREEK TO THE POOR SAPS WHO DON'T HAVE THIS BOOK.** No Roman alphabet, no problem. Our phonetic phrasebook has got you covered (p. 221).

- **SHIP SOUVENIRS HOME BY SURFACE MAIL.** Our scintillating "By Snail Mail" section will tell you how. You'll laugh, you'll cry (p. 219).

planning your trip

- **PASSPORT:** Required for citizens of all countries. Must be valid for 90 days after the period of intended stay.

- **VISA: Greece:** Not required for citizens of Australia, Canada, Ireland, New Zealand, the UK, and the US. **Turkey:** Citizens of Australia, Canada, Ireland, New Zealand, the UK and the US all require sticker visas which can be purchased at entry points (the fee varies based on nationality).

- **WORK PERMIT:** Required for all foreigners planning to work in Greece or Turkey.

DOCUMENTS AND FORMALITIES

You've got your visa, your invitation, and your work permit, just like Let's Go told you to, and then you realize you've forgotten the most important thing: your passport. Well, we're not going to let that happen. **Don't forget your passport!**

Visas

Citizens of Australia, Canada, Ireland, New Zealand, the UK, and the US need a visa in addition to a valid passport for entrance into Turkey. Visas cost as much as €45 and depend on you nationality allow you to spend up to 90 days in Turkey. Visas are purchased at entry points in Turkey, airports, train stations, and bus terminals. It's technically a "tourist visa," but it's pretty much a cash grab and some travelers report that the officials seem to change the rates at will. EU citizens do not need a passport to globetrot through Greece or Turkey, but they do need a national ID card.

essentials

Citizens of Australia, Canada, New Zealand, and the US do not need a visa for stays of up to 90 days in Greece, but this three-month period begins upon entry into any of the countries that belong to the EU's **freedom of movement zone.** For more information, see **One Europe** (below). Those staying longer than 90 days may purchase a visa ($20-45) at a local Greek consular office.

one europe

The EU's policy of freedom of movement means that most border controls have been abolished and visa policies harmonized. Under this treaty, formally known as the Schengen Agreement, you're still required to carry a passport (or government-issued ID card for EU citizens) when crossing an internal border, but, once you've been admitted into one country, you're free to travel to other participating states. Most EU states are already members of Schengen (excluding Cyprus), as are Iceland and Norway.

Double-check entrance requirements at the nearest embassy or consulate of Greece and Turkey for up-to-date information before departure. US citizens can also consult █http://travel.state.gov.

planning your trip · documents and formalities

turkish embassies and consulates

- **TURKISH EMBASSY IN AUSTRALIA:** *(6 Moonah Place, Yarralumla A.C.T. Australia 2600* ☎+61 2 6234 0000 ▥*http://canberra.emb.mfa.gov.tr* ⏰ *Open M-F 9am-12:30pm and 1:30-4:30pm.)*

- **AUSTRALIAN CONSULATE GENERAL IN TURKEY:** *(Ritz Carlton residences, Asker Ocagi Cad. No. 15, Elmadag Sisli 34367, Istanbul, Turkey* ☎90 212 243 12 33 ▥*www.turkey.embassy.gov.au* ⏰ *Open M-F 8:30am-5pm.)*

- **TURKISH EMBASSY IN CANADA:** *(196 Wurtemburg St., Ottawa, Ontario K1N 8L9* ☎+61 2 6234 0000 ▥*http://ottava.be.mfa.gov.tr* ⏰ *Open M-F 9am-5pm.)*

- **CANADIAN CONSULATE GENERAL IN TURKEY:** *(Istikal Cad., 189/5, Beyoğlu, 34433 Istanbul* ☎90 212 251 98 38 ▥*www.turkey.embassy.gov.au* ⏰ *Open M-Th 9:30am-12:30pm and 1:30-5:30pm, F 9:30am-12:30pm.)*

- **TURKISH EMBASSY IN IRELAND:** *(11 Clyde Road ballsbridge, Dublin 4. Ireland* ☎+353 1 668 52 40 ▥*http://ottava.be.mfa.gov.tr* ⏰ *Open M-F 9am-12:30pm and 2-5pm.)*

- **IRISH CONSULATE GENERAL IN TURKEY:** *(Ali Riza Gürcan Cad., Meridyen İş Merkezi kat: 4 No: 417, Merter, Istanbul, Turkey* ☎0212 482 1862 ▥*www. embassyofireland.org.tr* ⏰ *Open M-F 9:30am-1pm and 2-5pm.)*

- **TURKISH EMBASSY IN NEW ZEALAND:** *(14-17 Murphy Street Level 8, Thorndon, Wellington, New Zealand* ☎64 4 472 12 90 92 ▥*http:// wellington.be.mfa.gov.tr* ⏰ *Open M-F 9am-5pm.)*

- **NEW ZEALAND CONSULATE GENERAL IN TURKEY:** *(Inonu Cad. No:48/3, Taksim, Istanbul 34437, Turkey* ☎0212 482 1862 ▥*www.nzembassy.com/ turkey* ⏰ *Open M-F 9:30am-1pm and 2-5pm.)*

- **TURKISH CONSULATE IN THE UNITED KINGDOM** *(Rutland Lodge Rutland Gardens, Knightsbridge, London SW7 1BW, United Kingdom* ☎020 7591 6900 ▥*www.turkishconsulate.org.uk/en* ⏰ *Open M-F 9am-1pm.)*

- **BRITISH CONSULATE GENERAL IN TURKEY:** *(Mesrutiyet Cad. No. 34, Tepe-basi Beyoğlu 34435, Istanbul, Turkey* ☎212 334 6400 ▥*http://ukinturkey. fco.gov.uk/en* ⏰ *Open M-F 8:30am-1pm and 1:45-4:45pm.)*

- **TURKISH EMBASSY IN THE UNITED STATES:** *(2525 Massachusetts Avenue Northwest, Washington DC 20008* ☎202 612 6700 ▥*www.turkish-embassy.org* ⏰ *Open M-F 9am-6pm.)*

- **USA CONSULATE GENERAL IN TURKEY:** *(İstinya Mahallesi, Kaplıcalar Mevkii No. 2, 34460 Istanbul, Turkey* ☎212 335 9000 ▥*http://istanbul. usconsulate.gov* ⏰ *Open M-F 8am-4:30pm.)*

essentials

Work Permits

Admittance to a country as a traveler does not include the right to work, which is authorized only by a work permit. For more information, see the **Beyond Tourism** chapter.

- **GREEK CONSULATE GENERAL IN AUSTRALIA:** *(Level 2, 216-223 Castleraugh Street, Sydney N.S.W. 2000 ☎612 926 49 130 ▄www.mfa.gr/sydney ⌚ Open M-F 9am-6pm.)*

- **AUSTRALIAN EMBASSY IN GREECE:** *(Level 6, Thon Building, Cnr Kifisias & Alexandras Ave, Ambelokipi, Athens, Greece ☎210 870 4000 ▄www.greece.embassy.gov.au ⌚ Open M-F 8:30am-3:30pm.)*

- **GREEK EMBASSY IN CANADA:** *(80 MacLaren St., Ottawa, Ontario K2P 0K6 ☎613 238 6271 ▄www.greekembassy.ca ⌚ Open M-F 9am-4pm.)*

- **CANADIAN EMBASSY IN GREECE:** *(4 Ioannou Ghennadiou Street, 115 21 Athens, Greece ☎210 870 4000 ▄www.canadainternational.gc.ca/greece-grece ⌚ Open M-Th 8am-3:30pm, F 8am-1:30pm.)*

- **GREEK EMBASSY IN IRELAND:** *(1 Upper Pembroke Street, Dublin 2 ☎01 676 7254 ▄www.mfa.gr/dublin)*

- **IRISH EMBASSY IN GREECE:** *(7 Leoforos Vasileos, Konstantinou, Athens, Greece 218111 ☎210 723 2771 ▄www.greece.embassy.gov.au)*

- **GREEK EMBASSY IN NEW ZEALAND:** *(38-42 Waring Taylor, Ptherick Tower, Wellington, P.O. Box 24066 ☎644 473 7775 ⌚ Open M-F 9am-6pm.)*

- **NEW ZEALAND EMBASSY IN ROME (SERVES GREECE):** *(Via Clitunno 44, Rome 00198, Italy ☎06 853 7501 ▄www.nzembassy.com/italy ⌚ Open M-F 8:30am-12:30pm and 1:30-5pm.)*

- **GREEK EMBASSY IN UNITED KINGDOM:** *(1A Holland Park W11 3TP London ☎20 731 35 600 ▄www.greekembassy.org.uk ⌚ Open M-F 9am-5pm.)*

- **BRITISH EMBASSY IN GREECE:** *(1 Ploutarchou Street, 106 75 Athens ☎210 7272 600 ▄http://ukingreece.fco.gov.uk/en ⌚ Open M-F 8:30am-3:30pm.)*

- **GREEK CONSULATE GENERAL IN UNITED STATES:** *(2217 Massachusetts Ave., N.W., Washington, DC 20008 ☎202 939 1306 ▄www.mfa.gr ⌚ Open M 9:30am-1pm and 2-5pm, Tu-W 9:30am-1pm, Th 9:30am-1pm and 2-5pm, F 9:30am-1pm.)*

- **USA EMBASSY IN GREECE:** *(91 Vasilisis Sophias Ave., 10160 Athens ☎210 721 2951 ▄http://athens.usembassy.gov ⌚ Open M-F 8:30am-5pm.)*

planning your trip · time differences

TIME DIFFERENCES

Both Greece and Turkey are 2hr. ahead of Greenwich Mean Time (GMT), and both observe Daylight Saving Time. This means that they are 7hr. ahead of New York City, 10hr. ahead Los Angeles, 2hr. ahead of the British Isles, 7hr. behind Sydney, and 9hr. behind New Zealand.

money

GETTING MONEY FROM HOME

Stuff happens. When stuff happens, you might need some money. When you need some money, the easiest and cheapest solution is to have someone back home make a deposit to your bank account. Otherwise, consider one of the following options.

Wiring Money

Arranging a **bank money transfer** means asking a bank back home to wire money to a bank in Greece or Turkey. This is the cheapest way to transfer cash, but it's also the slowest and most agonizing, usually taking several days or more. Note that some banks may only release your funds in local currency, potentially sticking you with a poor exchange rate; inquire about this in advance. Like most things in Greece and Turkey, bank transfers often take longer than they might in another country, possibly up to a week. Money transfer services like **Western Union** are faster and more convenient than bank transfers—but also much pricier. Western Union has many locations worldwide. To find one, visit ◙www.westernunion.com or call the appropriate number: in Australia ☎1800 173 833, in Canada and the US ☎800 325 6000, in the UK ☎0800 735 1815, in Greece ☎800 100 2020, and in Turkey ☎1 720 332 1000. To wire money using a credit card in the US, call ☎800-CALL-CASH; in the UK, ☎0800 731 1815; in Canada, ☎800-235-0000. Money transfer services are also available to **American Express** cardholders in Greece.

US State Department (US Citizens Only)

In serious emergencies only, the US State Department will forward money within hours to the nearest consular office, which will then disburse it according to instructions for a US$30 fee. If you wish to use this service, you must contact the Overseas Citizens Services division of the US State Department. *(☎+1-202-501-4444, from US 888-407-4747.)*

pins and atms

To use a debit or credit card to withdraw money from a cash machine (ATM) in Europe, you must have a four-digit Personal Identification Number (PIN). If your PIN is longer than four digits, ask your bank whether you can just use the first four or whether you'll need a new one. Credit cards don't usually come with PINs, so if you intend to hit up ATMs in Europe with a credit card to get cash advances, call your credit card company before leaving to request one.

Travelers with alphabetic rather than numeric PINs may also be thrown off by the absence of letters on European cash machines. Here are the corresponding numbers to use: 1 = QZ; 2 = ABC; 3 = DEF; 4 = GHI; 5 = JKL; 6 = MNO; 7 = PRS; 8 = TUV; 9 = WXY. Note that if you mistakenly punch the wrong code into the machine multiple (often three) times, it can swallow (gulp!) your card for good.

TIPPING AND BARGAINING

In Turkey, you should tip 5-10% in fancier restaurants. Tips aren't expected in inexpensive restaurants, but will definitely be appreciated. It is not customary to tip taxi drivers, but often people will "round up" the fare. For example if the fare is 4.5TL, then customers will give the driver 5TL. At hammams, attendants will line up to "bid you goodbye" when you leave, meaning that they expect tips—distribute 10-15% of the total cost amongst them. Porters generally expect a few liras, and generally if anyone ever helps you, they are likely to smile and ask for a *baksheesh*, or tip.

In Greece, law requires that restaurant and cafe prices include a 13% gratuity. Additional tipping is unnecessary, unless you are particularly pleased with the service, in which case leave 5%.

In both countries, bargaining in a street market or bazaar is life skill, but trying to get a cheaper price in an established shop can be considered disrespectful. The price tends to be more flexible in informal venues. If it's unclear whether bargaining is appropriate in a situation, hang back and watch someone else buy first. Be warned, merchants with any pride in their wares will refuse to sell to someone who has offended them in the negotiations, so don't lowball too much.

TAXES

Currently, Greece's value-added tax (VAT) is 21%; however, in return for the EU bailing them out of their tar pit of debt, the VAT will increase to 23%. Also, Greece will introduce a 10% excise tax on tobacco, fuel, and alcohol.

In Turkey, there is a 10-20% VAT, known as the KDV, that is included in the price of most goods and services (including meals, lodging, and car rentals). Before you buy, check if the KDV is included in the price to avoid paying it twice. Theoretically, the KDV and Greece's VAT that you pay on your trip can be reclaimed at most points of departure, but this requires much persistence and hassle. An airport tax of $15 in Turkey is levied only on international travelers, but it is usually included in the cost of the ticket.

the euro

Despite what many dollar-possessing Americans might want to hear, the official currency of 16 members of the European Union—Austria, Belgium, Cyprus, Finland, France, Germany, Greece, Ireland, Italy, Luxembourg, Malta, the Netherlands, Portugal, Slovakia, Slovenia, and Spain—is the euro.

Still, the currency has some important—and positive—consequences for travelers hitting more than one eurozone country. For one thing, money-changers across the eurozone are obliged to exchange money at the official, fixed rate and at no commission (though they may still charge a small service fee). Second, euro-denominated traveler's checks allow you to pay for goods and services across the eurozone, again at the official rate and commission-free. For more info, check a currency converter (such as ◪www.xe.com) or www.europa.eu.int.

safety and health

GENERAL ADVICE

In any type of crisis, the most important thing to do is **stay calm.** Your country's embassy abroad is usually your best resource in an emergency; registering with that embassy upon arrival in the country is a good idea. The government offices listed in the **Travel Advisories** feature at the end of this section can provide information on the services they offer their citizens in case of emergencies abroad.

Local Laws and Police

Greek police are used to having foreigners around, but that does not mean they allow them to break the law. Photographs and notes cannot be taken near military establishments (including docks). The purchase of pirated goods (including CDs and DVDs) is illegal; keep your receipts for proof of purchase. Taking objects or rocks from ancient sites is forbidden and can lead to fines or prison sentences. Drunk driving and indecent behavior also can result in heavy fines, arrest, and imprisonment. Although legal in Greece since 1951, homosexuality is still frowned upon socially. GLBT individuals are not legally protected from discrimination. That said, destinations like Athens, Thessaloniki, Lesvos, Rhodes, Ios, and especially Mykonos offer gay and lesbian hotels, bars, and clubs.

The General Directorate of Security *(Emniyet Genel Müdüdlüğü)* is the civilian police force in Turkey. Police officers wear navy blue uniforms and caps. Police cars are blue and white and have "Polis" written on the side doors and hood. Police violence is a problem in Turkey, especially at protests and demonstrations, so exercise caution when near these event. According to Human Rights Watch, police routinely use firearms during arrests without exhausting non-violent means and also when there is not an apparent threat of death or injury. Always be respectful and compliant when dealing with the police, and make it clear that you are a tourist. Homosexuality is not illegal in Turkey, but GLBT travelers should exercise caution when traveling due to the conservative values embedded in Muslim-majority Turkish society.

travel advisories

The following government offices provide travel information and advisories by telephone, by fax, or via the web:

- **AUSTRALIA: Department of Foreign Affairs and Trade.** *(☎+61 2 6261 1111 🖳www.dfat.gov.au)*
- **CANADA: Department of Foreign Affairs and International Trade (DFAIT).** Call or visit the website for the free booklet *Bon Voyage...But.* *(☎+1-800-267-8376 🖳www.dfait-maeci.gc.ca)*
- **NEW ZEALAND: Ministry of Foreign Affairs.** *(☎+64 4 439 8000 🖳www.mfat.govt.nz)*
- **UK: Foreign and Commonwealth Office.** *(☎+44 20 7008 1500 🖳www.fco.gov.uk)*
- **US: Department of State.** *(☎888-407-4747 from the US, +1-202-501-4444 elsewhere 🖳http://travel.state.gov)*

Drugs and Alcohol

Visitors of all ages generally have very little difficulty obtaining alcohol in Greece. In contrast, drug laws are very strict. Conviction for possession, use, or trafficking of drugs, including marijuana, will result in imprisonment and fines. If you use prescription drugs, have a copy of the prescriptions and a note from the doctor, if possible. Authorities are particularly vigilant at the Turkish and Albanian borders.

Turkey is a huge locus of drug trafficking coming in from Afghanistan and Iran into Europe. It is estimated that as much as 80% of heroin in Britain comes from Turkey. In recent years, the Interior Ministry has boasted a 149% increase in seizures of opium and opium derivatives, so the government takes drug trafficking

essentials

very seriously. The Turkish government has adopted a harsh policy (including fines and jail time) against those caught with drugs. If caught, a meek "I didn't know it was illegal" will not suffice. Remember that you are subject to Turkey's laws while within its borders, not those of your home country. Like in Greece, if you carry prescription drugs, have the prescription and if possible a note from the doctor. **Avoid public drunkenness.** Islam prohibits the consumption of alcohol, even though it is legal in Turkey. Do not drink during the holy month of Ramadan.

SPECIFIC CONCERNS

Natural Disasters

Located in one of the world's most seismically active areas, Greece and Turkey experience frequent and occasionally large **earthquakes.** The most recent serious quake in 1999 wreaked an estimated US$3 billion worth of damage and caused nearly 1,800 casualties in Athens and 45,000 casualties in Turkey. Earthquakes are unpredictable and can occur at any time of day. If a strong earthquake does occur, it will probably only last one or two minutes. Protect yourself by moving a sturdy doorway, table, or desk, and open a doorway to provide an escape route. In mountainous regions, landslides may follow quakes.

Demonstrations and Political Gatherings

Strikes and demonstrations occur frequently in Greece, especially now during the current economic crisis. Although generally orderly and lawful, they can spiral out of control: most recently, in December 2008, riots and violent demonstrations involving destructive vandalism and forceful clashes between civilians and the police rocked Athens and other major cities across the country. Disruption of public services, such as public transportation and air traffic control, can occur unexpectedly due to union strikes. Common areas for protest include the Polytechnic University area, Exharia, Omonia, Syntagma Square and Mavii Square in Athens.

Terrorism

Terrorism is a serious concern for travelers to Greece and Turkey. Terrorist activity has been on the rise in Greece because of domestic terrorist groups with marxist-anarchist leanings and anti-globalization agendas. **Revolutionary Struggle,** an extreme leftist paramilitary organization, launched a rocket at the US Embassy in Athens in early 2007. Its successor organization, **Revolutionary Nuclei,** has claimed responsibility for numerous attacks since, involving the use of Molotov cocktails, small-scale arms, and homemade explosives. The best thing you can do to be safe is to be aware of your surroundings, especially in crowded areas and tourist sites.

In Turkey, a number of terrorist groups remain active, though mostly in southeastern Turkey, where the separatist Kurdistan Workers' Party (PKK) regularly attacks national security forces. *Let's Go* does not recommend travel in the southeastern provinces of Hakkari, Sirnak, Siirt, or Tunceli due to the instability and terrorism in these provinces. However, the PKK has bombed government and civilian targets in Ankara, Istanbul, Izmir and tourist resorts of the Mediterranean and Aegean. Bombs are normally planted in crowded areas in trashcans, outside banks, or on mini-buses and trains. Bombings occur a few times a year but are generally not deadly and target the police and the government.

PRE-DEPARTURE HEALTH

Matching a prescription to a foreign equivalent is not always easy, safe, or possible, so if you take **prescription drugs,** carry up-to-date prescriptions or a statement from your doctor stating the medications' trade names, manufacturers, chemical names, and dosages. Be sure to keep all medication with you in your carry-on luggage.

Pharmacists often speak English reasonably well and can help you find common

Istanbul

YOUR GATEWAY TO TURKEY

LEADING LOCAL TOUR OPERATOR SINCE 1997

ISTANBUL MINI-STAY

DURATION
3 OR 4 DAYS
ACCOMMODATION
3 STAR HOTELS
ESCORTED BY
PROFESSIONAL TOUR GUIDE
TRANSPORTATION
NON-SMOKING A/C TOUR BUS
HIGHLIGHTS
ISTANBUL OLD CITY
HAGIA SOPHIA - BLUE MOSQUE
TOPKAPI PALACE - GRAND BAZAAR
SPICE MARKET - BOSPHORUS
BASILICA CISTERN

ESCORTED TURKEY TOURS

DURATION
TOURS FROM 2 TO 15 DAYS
ACCOMMODATION
4 & 5 STAR HOTELS
ESCORTED BY
PROFESSIONAL TOUR GUIDE
TRANSPORTATION
NON-SMOKING A/C TOUR BUS
HIGHLIGHTS
ISTANBUL - GALLIPOLI - TROY
PERGAMUM - KUSADASI - EPHESUS
PAMUKKALE - FETHIYE - MARMARIS
KAS - ANTALYA - KONYA
CAPPADOCIA - ANKARA

BUDGET TURKEY TOURS

DURATION
TOURS FROM 11 TO 14 DAYS
ACCOMMODATION
HOSTELS & GUESTHOUSES
ESCORTED BY
TOUR LEADER
TRANSPORTATION
NON-SMOKING A/C TOUR BUS
HIGHLIGHTS
ISTANBUL - GALLIPOLI - TROY
PERGAMUM - KUSADASI - EPHESUS
PAMUKKALE - FETHIYE - MARMARIS
KAS - ANTALYA - KONYA
CAPPADOCIA - ANKARA

FEZ TRAVEL
EXPERIENCE TURKEY

Hocapasa Mah. Tayahatun Sokak No:44 Sirkeci 34412 Istanbul Turkey
Tel: +90 212 520 04 34 Fax: +90 212 520 04 35 feztravel@feztravel.com

www.feztravel.com

over-the-counter drugs like aspirin in the pharmacy.

Immunizations and Precautions

You should consult with your doctor before traveling to Greece or Turkey, and she or he may recommend getting Hepatitis A, typhoid and rabies vaccinations, especially if you are traveling to rural areas.

Travelers over two years old should make sure that the following vaccines are up to date: MMR (for measles, mumps, and rubella); DTaP or Td (for diphtheria, tetanus, and pertussis); IPV (for polio); Hib (for *Haemophilus influenzae* B); and HepB (for Hepatitis B). For recommendations on immunizations and prophylaxis, check with a doctor and consult the **Centers for Disease Control and Prevention (CDC)** in the US or the equivalent in your home country *(☎+1-800-CDC-INFO/232-4636 💻www.cdc.gov/travel).*

STAYING HEALTHY

Diseases and Environmental Hazards

In Turkey, be wary of food- and water-borne illnesses, like traveler's diarrhea, dysentery, cholera, Hepatitis A, Giardia, and typhoid fever. The best cure is prevention. Be sure that everything you eat is cooked properly. Never drink unbottled water unless you have treated it yourself. Bottled water is very cheap, and a large bottle typically sells for less than an American dollar. To purify your own water, bring it to a roiling boil or treat it with iodine tablets. Don't use untreated water even to brush your teeth, and don't open your mouth when in the shower. Ice cubes are just as dangerous as impure liquid water, so enjoy that gin and tonic off the rocks! Salads and uncooked vegetables (including lettuce) are chock full of untreated water. Other culprits include raw shellfish, unpasteurized milk and sauces containing raw eggs. Peel all fruits and vegetables yourself, and watch out for street food that may have been washed in dirty water.

In Greece, water is safe to drink, except in certain isolated areas. In both countries, wear plenty of sunscreen and always have a bottle of water to avoid dehydration.

getting around

For information on how to get to Turkey and Greece and save a bundle while doing so, check out the Essentials section of **💻www.letsgo.com.** (In case you can't tell, we think our website's the bomb.)

BY PLANE

Commercial Airlines

For small-scale travel on the continent, *Let's Go* suggests **💻budget airlines** for budget travelers, but more traditional carriers have made efforts to keep up with the revolution. The **Star Alliance Europe Airpass** offers low economy-class fares for travel within Europe to 220 destinations in 45 countries. The pass is available to non-European passengers on Star Alliance carriers, including Turkish Airlines *(💻www.staralliance.com).* **EuropebyAir's** snazzy FlightPass also allows you to hop between hundreds of cities in Europe and North Africa. *(☎+1-888-321-4737 💻www.europebyair.com $ Most flights US$99.)*

In addition, a number of European airlines offer discount coupon packets. Most are only available as tack-ons for transatlantic passengers, but some are standalone offers. Most must be purchased before departure, so research in advance. For example, **oneworld,** a coalition of 10 major international airlines, offers deals and cheap connections all over the world, including within Europe *(💻www.oneworld.com).*

budget airlines

The recent emergence of no-frills airlines has made hopscotching around Europe by air increasingly affordable. Though these flights often feature inconvenient hours or serve less popular regional airports, with ticket prices often dipping into single digits, it's never been faster or easier to jet across the continent. The following resources will be useful not only for crisscrossing Turkey and Greece but also for those ever-popular weekend trips to nearby international destinations.

- **BMIBABY:** *(☎0871 224 0224 for the UK, +44 870 126 6726 elsewhere 💻www.bmibaby.com)*
- **EASYJET:** *(☎+44 871 244 2366, 10p per min. 💻www.easyjet.com $ UK£50-150.)*
- **RYANAIR:** *(☎0818 30 30 30 for Ireland, 0871 246 0000 for the UK 💻www.ryanair.com)*
- **STERLING:** *(☎70 10 84 84 for Denmark, 0870 787 8038 for the UK 💻www.sterling.dk)*
- **TRANSAVIA:** *(☎020 7365 4997 for the UK 💻www.transavia.com $ From €49 one-way.)*
- **WIZZ AIR:** *(☎0904 475 9500 for the UK, 65p per min. 💻www.wizzair.com)*

BY TRAIN

Trains in Turkey are generally comfortable, convenient, and reasonably swift with a new, high-speed train connecting Ankara and Istanbul. Trains cover much of the Anatolian peninsula. The Greek railway system is the OSE, but as one of the oldest systems in Europe, it is also one of the slowest. Trains connect to central Europe and into Turkey. Make sure you are on the correct car as trains sometimes split at crossroads. Towns listed in parentheses on European train schedules require a train switch at the town listed immediately before the parentheses.

You can either buy a **railpass,** which allows you unlimited travel within a particular region for a given period of time, or rely on buying individual **point-to-point** tickets as you go. Almost all countries give students or youths (under 26, usually) direct discounts on regular domestic rail tickets, and many also sell a student or youth card that provides 20-50% off all fares for up to a year.

rail resources

- **WWW.RAILEUROPE.COM:** Info on rail travel and railpasses.
- **POINT-TO-POINT FARES AND SCHEDULES:** 💻www.raileurope.com/us/rail/fares_schedules/index.htm allows you to calculate whether buying a railpass would save you money.
- **WWW.RAILSAVER.COM:** Uses your itinerary to calculate the best railpass for your trip.
- **WWW.RAILFANEUROPE.NET:** Links to rail servers throughout Europe.
- **WWW.LETSGO.COM:** Check out the Essentials section for more details.

BY BUS

Though European trains and railpasses are extremely popular, in some cases buses prove a better option, especially since Greece's trains are so slow and most tourist trips within Turkey are short distances. Often cheaper than railpasses, **international bus passes** allow unlimited travel on a hop-on, hop-off basis between major European cities. **Busabout,** for instance, offers three interconnecting bus circuits covering 29 of Europe's best bus hubs. *(☎+44 8450 267 514 💻www.busabout.com $ 1 circuit in high season starts at US$579, students US$549.)* **Eurolines,** meanwhile, is the largest operator of Europe-wide coach services. We get misty-eyed just thinking about their unlimited 15- and 30-day passes to 41 major European cities. *(☎90 444 18 88 Turkey 💻www.eurolines.com $ High season 15-day pass €345, 30-day pass €455; under 26 €290/375. Mid-season €240/330; under 26 €205/270. Low season €205/310; under 26 €175/240.)*

BY FERRY

Ferries are the best and sometimes only way to get to the islands in Greece. The Greek ferry schedule is available online *(💻www.greekferries.gr)*, but be aware that the schedule can change unexpectedly. Be sure to check at the port. Ferries are available to Italy and some Turkish islands in the Aegean Sea, but unfortunately there is no ferry that goes from Athens to Istanbul. Fares jump sharply in July and August. You'll occasionally have to pay a port tax (under US$10). Ask for discounts; ISIC and Eurail Pass holders get many reductions and free trips.

BY BICYCLE

Some youth hostels rent bicycles for low prices, and in Greece a number of outfitters offer bikes in Athens and on some islands. Istanbul also has a number of bike rental stores. In addition to panniers *(US$40-150)* to hold your luggage, you'll need a good **helmet** *(US$10-40)* and a sturdy **lock** *(from US$30).*

keeping in touch

BY EMAIL AND INTERNET

Hello and welcome to the 21st century, where you can check your email in most major European cities, though sometimes you'll have to pay a few bucks or buy a drink for internet access. Although in some places it's possible to forge a remote link with your home server, in most cases this is a much slower (and thus more expensive) option than taking advantage of free **web-based email accounts** (e.g., **💻www.gmail.com**). **Internet cafes** and the occasional free internet terminal at a public library or university are listed in the **Practicalities** sections of cities that we cover. For lists of additional cybercafes in Greece and Istanbul, check out **💻www.worldembassyinformation.com/world-cyber-cafe/cyber-cafe-in-greece.html** and **💻www.world66.com/asia/middleeast/turkey/istanbul/internetcafes.**

Wireless hot spots make internet access possible in public and remote places. Unfortunately, they also pose security risks. Hot spots are public, open networks that use unencrypted, unsecured connections. They are susceptible to hacks and "packet sniffing"—the theft of passwords and other private information. To prevent problems, disable "ad hoc" mode, turn off file sharing and network discovery, encrypt your email, turn on your firewall, beware of phony networks, and watch for over-the-shoulder creeps.

BY TELEPHONE

Calling Home from Greece and Turkey

Prepaid phone cards are a common and relatively inexpensive means of calling abroad. Each one comes with a Personal Identification Number (PIN) and a toll-free access number. You call the access number and then follow the directions for dialing your PIN. To purchase prepaid phone cards, check online for the best rates; 🖥www.callingcards.com is a good place to start. Online providers generally send your access number and PIN via email, with no actual "card" involved. You can also call home with prepaid phone cards purchased in Greece and Turkey.

If you have internet access, your best—i.e., cheapest, most convenient, and most tech-savvy—bet is probably our good friend **Skype** (🖥www.skype.com). You can even videochat if you have one of those new-fangled webcams. Calls to other Skype users are free; calls to landlines and mobiles worldwide start at US$0.021 per minute, depending on where you're calling.

Another option is a **calling card,** linked to a major national telecommunications service in your home country. Calls are billed collect or to your account. Cards generally come with instructions for dialing both domestically and internationally.

Placing a collect call through an international operator can be expensive but may be necessary in case of an emergency. You can frequently call collect without even possessing a company's calling card just by calling its access number and following the instructions.

international calls

To call Turkey or Greece from home or to call home from Turkey or Greece, dial:

1. THE INTERNATIONAL DIALING PREFIX. To call from Australia, dial ☎0011; Canada or the US, ☎011; Ireland, New Zealand, or the UK, ☎00; Turkey, ☎00; Greece, ☎00.

2. THE COUNTRY CODE OF THE COUNTRY YOU WANT TO CALL. To call Australia, dial ☎61; Canada or the US, ☎1; Ireland, ☎353; New Zealand, ☎64; the UK, ☎44; Greece, ☎30; Turkey, ☎90.

3. THE CITY/AREA CODE. *Let's Go* lists the city/area codes for cities and towns in Greece and Turkey opposite the city or town name, next to a ☎, as well as in every phone number. If the first digit is a zero (e.g., ☎0286 for Santorini), omit the zero when calling from abroad (e.g., dial ☎286 from Canada to reach Santorini).

4. THE LOCAL NUMBER.

essentials

Cellular Phones

The international standard for cell phones is **Global System for Mobile Communication (GSM).** To make and receive calls in Turkey and Greece, you will need a GSM-compatible phone and a **SIM (Subscriber Identity Module) card,** a country-specific, thumbnail-size chip that gives you a local phone number and plugs you into the local network. Many SIM cards are prepaid, and incoming calls are frequently free. You can buy additional cards or vouchers (usually available at convenience stores) to "top up" your phone. For more information on GSM phones, check out 🖥www.telestial.com. Companies like **Cellular Abroad** (🖥www.cellularabroad.com) and **OneSimCard** (🖥www.onesimcard.com) rent cell phones and SIM cards that work in a variety of destinations around the world.

BY SNAIL MAIL

Sending Mail Home from Turkey and Greece

Airmail is the best way to send mail home from Turkey and Greece. **Aerogrammes,** printed sheets that fold into envelopes and travel via airmail, are available at post offices. Write "airmail," or *"uçakla"* in Turkish or *"αεροπορικώς"* in Greek on the front. Note that most post offices will charge exorbitant fees or simply refuse to send aerogrammes with enclosures. Surface mail is by far the cheapest and slowest way to send mail. It takes one to two months to cross the Atlantic and one to three to cross the Pacific—good for heavy items you won't need for a while, like souvenirs that you've acquired along the way.

Sending Mail to Turkey and Greece

In addition to the standard postage system whose rates are listed below, **Federal Express** handles express mail services from most countries to Greece and Turkey (☎+1-800-463-3339 🖳www.fedex.com). Sending a letter within Turkey requires 0.80TL. Sending a postcard from Greece costs €0.72, while sending letters domestically requires €0.75.

There are several ways to arrange pickup of letters sent to you while you are abroad. Mail can be sent via **Poste Restante** (General Delivery) to almost any city or town in Greece or Turkey with a post office, and it is pretty reliable. Address Poste Restante letters like so:

Mustafa Kemal ATATÜRK	Plato
Postrestant, Merkez Postanesi	Poste restante.
City, Türkiye	City, Ελλάδα

The mail will go to a special desk in the central post office unless you specify a post office by street address or postal code. It's best to use the largest post office, since mail may be sent there regardless. It is usually safer and quicker but more expensive to send mail express or registered. Bring your passport (or other photo ID) for pickup; there may be a small fee. If the clerks insist that there is nothing for you, ask them to check under your first name as well. *Let's Go* lists post offices in the **Practicalities** section of each city.

American Express has travel offices throughout the world, including Turkey, but not Greece, that offer a free **Client Letter Service** (mail held up to 30 days and forwarded upon request) for cardholders who contact them in advance. Some offices provide these services to non-cardholders (especially AmEx Travelers Cheque holders), but call ahead to make sure. For a complete list of AmEx locations, call ☎+1-800-528-4800 or visit 🖳www.americanexpress.com/travel.

climate

Greece and Istanbul have very similar Mediterranean climates with mild winters and hot, dry summers, though Istanbul gets more rainfall overall. During the summer in both locales, you should worry less about your day sightseeing getting rained out and worry more about passing out from heat exhaustion. The names of the game are hydration, hats, sunblock, and aiming for the shade whenever possible.

ISTANBUL

MONTH	AVG. HIGH TEMP.		AVG. LOW TEMP.		AVG. RAINFALL		AVG. NUMBER OF WET DAYS
January	4°C	47°F	-1°C	39°F	79mm	1.8 in.	12
February	6°C	47°F	-1°C	38°F	43mm	1.9 in.	11
March	9°C	52°F	1°C	41°F	89mm	1.6 in.	10
April	13°C	61°F	3°C	47°F	38mm	1.3 in.	8
May	17°C	70°F	7°C	55°F	51mm	0.9 in.	6
June	20°C	79°F	10°C	63°F	61mm	0.8 in.	5
July	22°C	84°F	12°C	68°F	74mm	0.7 in.	3
August	22°C	83°F	12°C	69°F	61mm	0.7 in.	4
September	19°C	77°F	9°C	63°F	81mm	1.1 in.	6
October	14°C	67°F	7°C	56°F	104mm	2.0 in.	7
November	9°C	58°F	3°C	48°F	76mm	2.3 in.	11
December	6°C	50°F	1°C	43°F	71mm	2.8 in.	14

ATHENS

MONTH	AVG. HIGH TEMP.		AVG. LOW TEMP.		AVG. RAINFALL		AVG. NUMBER OF WET DAYS
January	13°C	56°F	7°C	45°F	34mm	1.3 in.	13
February	13°C	56°F	7°C	44°F	28mm	11 in.	10
March	16°C	60°F	8°C	47°F	34mm	1.3 in.	10
April	24°C	67°F	16°C	53°F	22mm	0.9 in.	8
May	24°C	76°F	16°C	60°F	9mm	0.4 in.	6
June	29°C	85°F	20°C	68°F	3mm	0.1 in.	4
July	32°C	90°F	23°C	73°F	7mm	0.3 in.	2
August	32°C	90°F	12°C	54°F	3mm	0.1 in.	1
September	28°C	83°F	20°C	67°F	7mm	0.3 in.	3
October	23°C	74°F	16°C	61°F	22mm	0.9 in.	7
November	18°C	65°F	12°C	54°F	62mm	2.4 in.	10
December	14°C	58°F	9°C	48°F	52mm	2.0 in.	12

GREEK ISLANDS

AVG. TEMP. (LOW/ HIGH), PRECIP.	JANUARY			APRIL			JULY			OCTOBER		
	°C	°F	mm	°C	°F	mm	°C	°F	mm	°C	°F	mm
Mykonos	6/12	43/54	135	11/18	52/64	58	21/30	70/86	18	15/22	59/72	167
Andros	10/14	50/57	42	13/19	55/66	12	22/27	72/81	1	18/22	64/72	18
Santorini	9/14	48/57	114	12/19	54/66	28	22/28	72/82	1	16/22	61/72	61

To convert from degrees Fahrenheit to degrees Celsius, subtract 32 and multiply by 5/9. To convert from Celsius to Fahrenheit, multiply by 9/5 and add 32.

°CELSIUS	-5	0	5	10	15	20	25	30	35	40
°FAHRENHEIT	23	32	41	50	59	68	77	86	95	104

essentials

measurements

Like the rest of the rational world, Greece and Turkey use the metric system, except in Greece certain beverages, like wine, are measured in kilos. The basic unit of length is the meter (m), which is divided into 100 centimeters (cm) or 1000 millimeters (mm). One thousand meters make up one kilometer (km). Fluids are measured in liters (L), each divided into 1000 milliliters (mL). A liter of pure water weighs one kilogram (kg), the unit of mass that is divided into 1000 grams (g). One metric ton is 1000kg.

MEASUREMENT CONVERSIONS	
1 inch (in.) = 25.4mm	1 millimeter (mm) = 0.039 in.
1 foot (ft.) = 0.305m	1 meter (m) = 3.28 ft.
1 yard (yd.) = 0.914m	1 meter (m) = 1.094 yd.
1 mile (mi.) = 1.609km	1 kilometer (km) = 0.621 mi.
1 ounce (oz.) = 28.35g	1 gram (g) = 0.035 oz.
1 pound (lb.) = 0.454kg	1 kilogram (kg) = 2.205 lb.
1 fluid ounce (fl. oz.) = 29.57mL	1 milliliter (mL) = 0.034 fl. oz.
1 gallon (gal.) = 3.785L	1 liter (L) = 0.264 gal.

language

TURKISH

Turkish has its roots in Central Asia with many loanwords from Arabic and Persian. It has no grammatical gender and has extensive honorifics depending on the age, familiarity and social status of the addressees.

Pronunciation

Turkish words are spelled with an adapted Roman alphabet. The language is phonetic; each letter has only one sound that is always pronounced distinctly. Nouns are the same in the singular are plural. Words are usually accented on the last syllable; special vowels, consonants, and combinations include:

PHONETIC UNIT	PRONUNCIATION	PHONETIC UNIT	PRONUNCIATION
c	*j* as in **j**acket	ş	*sh* as in **sh**ort
ç	*ch* as in **ch**eck	u	*oo* as in b**oo**t
ğ	lengthens adjacent vowels	â	dipthong of *ea*, or faint *ya*
ı/I	(no dot on the "i") *i* as in cous**i**n	ū	*ew* as in c**ue**
i/İ	*ee* as in b**ee**t	ay	*eye* as in p**ie**
j	*zh* as in pleasure, or *j* as in French **j**adis	oy	*oy* as in t**oy**
ö	*eu* as in French d**eu**x	uy	*oo-ee* as in ph**ooey**

Phrasebook

ENGLISH	TURKISH	PRONUNCIATION
Hello!	Merhaba!	mehr-HA-bah!
Goodbye (during the day)	İyi günler	ee-yee goon-lehr
Goodbye (in the evening)	İyi akşamlar	ee-yee ak-SHAM-lahr
Yes.	Evet.	eh-veht
No.	hayır	hyer
Please	Lütfen	loot-fahn
Pardon me.	Pardon.	par-dohn
Thank you.	Teşekkur ederim	tesh-ekur edeh-rim
You're welcome/It's nothing.	Bir şey değil.	beer shay dee-eel
Do you speak English?	İngilizce biliyor musun	een-gul-EEZ-je beel-ee-YOR muh-SUN
I don't speak Turkish	Turkçe okuyorum	Toork-che BEEL-mee-YOR-uhm
I don't understand.	Anlamadım	Ahn-luh-mah-dim
My name is...	İsmim...	Ees-meem...
What's up/new?	Ne haber?	nah-behr
Where is the bathroom?	Tuvalet nerede?	too-walet nehr-e-de
EMERGENCY/HEALTH		
Go away!	Git başımdan!	git bah-shim-dahn!
Help!	İmdat!	EEM-dat!
Call the police!	Polis çağırın!	po-LEES cha-girin!
I need a doctor!	Doktor ihtiyacim!	dohk-tor eeh-tee-ya-cheem!
Where is a pharmacy?	Eczane nerede?	Ej-ZAH-ne neh-reh-de
My stomach hurts.	Midem ağriyor.	bash-uhm ahr-ee-yohr
I have a cold.	Nezlem var.	Nehz-lem vahr.
I have diarrhea.	İshalım var.	EES-hahl-uhm vahr.
FOOD		
Do you have food without meat?	Etsiz yemek var mı?	eht seez yemek vahr mih?
I'm a vegetarian	Vejetariyanım	vej-e-tar-iyan-im
Check, please.	Hesap, lütfen.	hesahp, loot-fahn.
I want a glass of water.	Bir bardak su istiyorum.	beer bahr-dak soo eest-ee-yor-uhm
What's in...?	...neler içinde, acaba?	...neh-lehr eech-een-deh, a-jah-bah
cheese	peynir	pay-neer
Are you open/closed?	Açık/kapalı mısın?	a-chik/kah-pah-li misin?
SLEEPING/GETTING AROUND		
Where is...?	...nerede?	nehr-eh-deh?
I am looking for...?	...için ariyorum.	...eecheen ahr-ee-yohr-uhm.
Where is the bus station/airport/ferry?	otogar/hava lımanı/feribot nerede?	oh-tow-gahr/hah-vah lumahnu nehr-e-deh?
Which bus goes to...?	...a hangi otobüs gider?	...a hahn-gee oto-boos GEE-dehr
When is the next bus?	Sonraki otobus kaçta kalkiyor?	sohn-rah-kee oto-boos kach-tah kahlk-EE-yohr?
How long does it take?	Kaç zaman sürür?	kach zahmahn suOOR-oor
I am going to...	...ya gidiyorum	...yah geed-EE-yohr-uhm.
Is there an available room?	Boş odanız var mı?	bosh odaniz vahr mih?
single/double/triple room	tek/çift/üç kişilik	tehk/cheeft/ooch kee-shee-leek
Is there hot water?	Sicak su var mı?	sijak soo vahr mi?
Is there a room with a shower?	Duşlu oda var mı?	DOOSH-loo odah vahr mi?
Can I see it?	Bakabilirmiyim	buhk-ah-dah kamp e-deh-bee-LEER mee-yeem

essentials

GREEK

Alphabet

The Greek alphabet has 24 letters. In the chart below, the left column gives the name of each letter in Greek, the middle column shows capital and lower case letters, and the right column shows the pronunciation. Greek words often have an accent mark called a tonos (τόνος). The tonos appears over the vowels of multisyllabic words and tells you where the stress lies. The stress can change the meaning of the word, so the tonos is essential for understanding and communication. The semicolon (;) is the Greek question mark (?). Really; Really.

SYMBOL	NAME	PRONOUNCED	SYMBOL	NAME	PRONOUNCED
A α	alpha	*a* as in f**a**ther	N ν	nu	*n* as in **n**et
B β	beta	*v* as in **v**elvet	Ξ ξ	xi	*x* as in mi**x**
Γ γ	gamma	*y* or *g* as in **yo**ga	O o	omicron	*o* as in r**o**w
Δ δ	delta	*th* as in **th**ere	Π π	pi	*p* as in **p**eace
E ε	epsilon	*e* as in j**e**t	P ρ	rho	*r* as in **r**oll
Z ζ	zeta	*z* as in **z**ebra	Σ σ/ς	sigma	*s* as in **s**ense
H η	eta	*ee* as in qu**ee**n	T τ	tau	*t* as in **t**ent
Θ θ	theta	*th* as in **th**ree	Y υ	upsilon	*ee* as in gr**ee**n
I ι	iota	*ee* as in tr**ee**	Φ φ	phi	*f* as in **f**og
K κ	kappa	*k* as in **k**ite	X χ	chi	*h* as in **h**orse
Λ λ	lambda	*l* as in **l**and	Ψ ψ	psi	*ps* as in oo**ps**
M μ	mu	*m* as in **m**oose	Ω ω	omega	*o* as in Let's G**o**

Pronunciation

Greek has a few sounds that are not intuitive for English speakers. For example, *gh* marks a muted "g" sound produced from the back of the throat. *Dth* denotes a hard "the" as in "thee," as opposed to a soft "th," in "three." Delta is most often pronounced with a hard "th." Below is a list of challenging double consonants and vowels that do not follow the above pronunciations.

PHONETIC UNIT	PRONUNCIATION	PHONETIC UNIT	PRONUNCIATION
αι	*eh* as in "**e**lement"	μπ	*b* as in **b**aby
αυ	*ahf/ahv* as in "**puff**in"/"im**prov**"	ντ	*d* as in **d**une
γγ	*ng* as in E**ng**lish	ου	*oo* as in s**oo**n
γκ	*g* as in **g**od	οι	*ee* as in b**ee**t
ει	*ee* as in b**ee**t	τζ	*tz* sound or *j* as in **j**ockey
ευ	*ef/ev* as in **eff**ort/**ev**er	υι	*ee* as in b**ee**t

Phrasebook

ENGLISH	GREEK (PRONUN-CIATION)	ENGLISH	GREEK (PRONUNCIA-TION)
Yes/No	Neh/Oh-hee	Sorry/pardon me	sig-NO-mee
Okay	en-DAH-kse	Please/You're welcome.	pah-rah-kah-LO
Thank you (very much).	Ef-hah-ree-STO (po-LEE)	Help!	vo-EE-thee-ah!
Good morning/day.	kah-lee-MEH-rah	Good night.	kah-lee-NEEH-tah
Hello/goodbye (polite plural)	yah sahs	Hello/goodbye (familiar)	yah-soo
I am ill.	EE-meh AH-rose-tose	What is your name?	pos seh LEH-neh?
I don't speak Greek.	dthen meel-AOH eh-lee-nee-KAH	My name is...	meh LEH-neh
I don't understand.	dthen kah-tah-lah-VEH-no	Do you speak English?	mee-LAH-teh sng-lee-KAH
FOOD			
bread	pso-MEE	cheese	ti-REE
chicken	ko-TO-poo-lo	egg-lemon soup	ahv-gho-LEH-mono
lamb	ar-NA-kee	stew with meat and onions	stee-FAH-dho
milk	GHAH-lah	*mezzedes* (assorted appetizers)	meh-ZEH-dthes
Greek meatballs	kef-TEH-dhes	ice cream	pah-gho-TO
SLEEPING/GETTING AROUND			
How much does it cost?	PO-so KAH-nee	I am going to...	pee-GHEE-no sto...
I am lost	HA-thee-kah	I need a ticket.	hree-AH-steh to me-tree-TEE
here/there	eh-DTHO/eh-KEE	bus	leh-o-fo-REE-o
airplane	GHAH-lah	ferry	PLEE-o
passport	dthaya-vah-TEE-ri-o	suitcase	vah-LEE-tsah
open/closed	ah-nee-KTO/klee-STO	police	as-tee-no-MEE-a
room	dtho-MAH-tee-o	Can I see a room?	bo-RO nah dtho E-nah dtho-MAH-tee-o
good/bad	kah-LO/kah-KOS	Cheers!	yah mahs!

essentials

glossary

TURKEY

ada: island
Akdeniz: Mediterranean Sea
altın: gold
ayran: salty yogurt drink
bay: man (as it is written on bathrooms)
bayan: woman (see above)
bedesten: bazaar
bilet: ticket
burada: here
çay: tea
durak: stop
Ege Deniz: Aegean Sea
et: meat
gar: train station
hamam: Turkish bath
kahve: coffee
kilim: tapestry woven mat
lahmacun: often called Turkish pizza-bread topped with ground meat and spices
lokum: Turkish Delight
mescit/camii: mosque
meydan: town square
namaz: open-air mosque, espcially for the army
nargile: water pipe
pide: bread filled with cheese or meat
sarhoş: drunk
saz: stringed instrument used in Turkish folk music
Sufi: an adherent to mystical Islam
tekke: Sufi lodge
yasak: forbidden, prohibited

GREECE

acropolis: fortified high place atop a city
amphora: two-handed vessel for oil/wines storage
atrium: Roman house's interior courtyard
basilica: church containing a saint's relic
capital: top of a column
Cyclopean walls: massive, irregularly cut Minoan and Mycenaean stones walls
domatia: rooms to rent in private homes
Faneromeni: term used in Orthodox symbolism for the revealed Virgin Mary
frieze: decorated middle part of a temple exterior (in particular, the entablature)
heroon: shrine to a demigod
iconostasis: screen that displays Byzantine icons
Katharevusa: snooty, "pure" Greek literary langugae
kore: female statue
kouros: male nude statue
KTEL: intercity bus service
malaka: common obscenity connoting masturbation
meltemi: unusually strong north wind in the Cyclades and Dodecanese
odeon: semi-circular theater
OSE: Greece's national railway
palaestra: Classical gymnasium
pantheon: collective of mythological gods
periptero: streetside kiosk selling everything from phone cards to candy bars
plateia: town square
portico: colonnade
stoa: public building fronted by rows of columns in ancient marketplaces

let's go online

Plan your next trip on our spiffy website, 🖥www.letsgo.com. It features full book content, the latest travel info on your favorite destinations, and tons of interactive features: make your own itinerary, read blogs from our trusty Researcher-Writers, browse our photo library, watch exclusive videos, check out our newsletter, find travel deals, follow us on Facebook, and buy new guides. Plus, if this Essentials wasn't enough for you, we've got even more online. We're always updating and adding new features, so check back often!

essentials

BEYOND TOURISM

If you are reading this, then you are a member of an elite group—and we don't mean "the literate." You're a student preparing for a semester abroad. You're taking a gap year to save the trees, the whales, or the dates. You're an 80-year-old woman who has devoted her life to egg-laying platypuses and figuring out what the hell is up with that. In short, you're a traveler, not a tourist; like any good spy, you don't observe your surroundings—you become an active part of them.

Your mission, should you choose to accept it, is to study, volunteer, or work in Athens or Istanbul as laid out in the dossier—er, chapter—below. More general wisdom, including international organizations with a presence in many destinations and tips on how to pick the right program, is also accessible by logging onto the Beyond Tourism section of ▣www.letsgo.com. We leave the rest (when to go, whom to bring, and how many changes of underwear to pack) in your hands. This message will ▨**self-destruct** in five seconds. Good luck.

greatest hits

- **MONEY DOES GROW ON TREES.** Get paid to work on one of over 45 organic farms in Turkey (p. 236).

- **JACK, WE NEED TO GET BACK TO THE ISLAND.** Take a 3-week poetry class held on the island of Spetses, two hours off of Athens (p. 229).

- **PICK UP MORE THAN JUST CHICKS.** Dig the Athenian agora and take part in an archaeological excavation (p. 232).

- **INTERNATIONAL GROOVE SOUNDS.** Have your own radio show at Istanbul University (p. 231)!

- **FAMILY VALUES.** Work and learn alongside a native family in Athens and Istanbul (p. 231).

- **THEY TRIED TO MAKE THE MONK SEAL GO TO REHAB...** And you said no, no, no, and helped the species survive (p. 233)!

studying abroad

While studying abroad with a hangover in certain Europe cities has become a staple for certain American college students, Athens and Istanbul provide a new—albeit historically significant—option for adventurous learners. While other European destinations are known primarily for their party scenes and nightlife, both Athens and Istanbul attract students looking to have a good time as well as learn from the vast amount of action that has happened within each city. Despite each having over 3,000 years of history, Athens and Istanbul are relatively new destinations for international students.

Athens is the perfect haven of humanities for students interested in philosophy, history, architecture, and the classics. Like other global capitals, it offers various public and private universities with immersion programs taught in both modern Greek and English. For even more venturesome travelers, Istanbul is the ideal crossroads of culture between Europe and the Middle East—not to mention a great location for students interested in traveling to two different continents during their stay. Located on the Bosphorus strait, Istanbul houses 20 of the best public and private universities in Turkey with classes in English and Turkish. While history and archaeology programs abound, Istanbul is the fifth largest city in the world and offers courses in virtually any subject.

Researching your options may at first seem like a Herculean task: credit requirements, cost, and length of stay are all factors when choosing a program in these cities. When looking into programs, find out who your peers will be during your stay. If you are looking for a full-immersion language program or even just an introduction to the city, you want to be with a group of students with like-minded goals. Most programs offer accommodations through a host university, particularly in Istanbul; however, a family stay can be an incredibly rewarding experience as you can encounter the day-to-day life of a real family in your chosen country.

visa information

While rules for legally staying in Greece and Turkey vary, both countries require foreigners on extended stay (over three months) to obtain a visa before departing their home country. This visa is what makes you a legal, official person and acts as your "get out of jail free and don't get deported" card. To get this all-important paperwork, you need to cut through some serious red tape and present pieces of identification that you never even knew existed. For both countries, make sure to have your passport, completed application, permanent resident card, and a passport-like photograph. Fortunately, many travel or study abroad programs point you in the right direction and help with this process, so check with these institutions before you start the process. For both Athens and Istanbul, contact the consulate nearest your permanent address for the most up-to-date information, and make sure your passport is valid for up to six months after your expected stay. If you are from an EU country, you will need a visa if you plan on staying in another member country longer than three months. Check with your consulate to see if your country has specific rules and visas for travel within these two countries. Make sure to specify if you will be traveling outside of the country you are applying for during your stay. Visa applications often have ▮fees which can range from $20-120.

UNIVERSITIES

Some American and European universities have affiliates or approved universities in Athens and Istanbul that focus on history, archaeology, or the classics. You can find programs of varying lengths taught in English in these destinations, but both Greek and Turkish, respectively, are offered. If you are a native or fluent speaker, you can enroll directly in one of these foreign institutions. Check with your current school to make sure these programs are legit and recognized so your credits don't crumble like feta cheese back at home.

International Programs

ARCADIA CENTER FOR HELLENIC, MEDITERRANEAN AND BALKAN STUDIES

450 South Easton Rd., Glenside, PA ☎866-927-2234 🖳www.arcadia.edu/abroad

Small-group classes with field-study excursions to historical sites. Courses entirely in English except for Greek language courses.

i 3.0 min. GPA. $ Semester $14,490+.

THE AMERICAN SCHOOL OF CLASSICAL STUDIES AT ATHENS

6-8 Charles Street, Princeton, NJ 08540 ☎609-683-0800 🖳www.ascsa.edu.gr

While the year-long program is limited to graduate students in affiliated universities, upper-level undergrads and teachers of the classics can apply to their intensive introduction to Greek track.

i Check website for eligibility and requirements. $ Membership fees vary by age and tenure, but room and board costs around $2,500-4,500. Full year approx. $22,910.

AHA INTERNATIONAL, UNIVERSITY OF OREGON

70 NW Couch St., Suite 242 Portland, OR 97209 ☎800-654-2051 🖳www.ahastudyabroad.org

Aha! Experience Athens from the inside by taking classes at the Athens Centre through the University of Oregon. Classes taught in English and Modern Greek. Rolling applications for summer session; fall and spring semesters offered.

i College students in good academic standing who have completed at least 1yr. $ Semester $11,150; summer $3,850.

AMERICAN FIELD SERVICE

71 West 23rd Street, 17th Floor, New York, NY 10010 ☎212-352-9810 🖳www.afs.org

Run by a network of volunteer organizations in over 50 countries, AFS offers various immersion programs for high school students in Istanbul. Contact the office in your home country for more details.

i Prices and available spots vary over time; consult the website for up-to-date information. Scholarships available.

THE ATHENS CENTRE

Archimidous 48, Athens 116 36 ☎21070 12 268 🖳www.athenscentre.gr

Offers language, classics, poetry, and theater classes of varying lengths throughout the year. Many universities around the world are affiliated with this institution. For the venturesome, check out the 3-week workshops in poetry and art held on the island of Spetses, 2hr. from Athen's main port.

$ 3-5wk. €350-650; summer €1800-2200.

COLLEGE YEAR IN ATHENS

2464 Mass. Ave., Suite 316, Cambridge, MA 02140 ☎617-868-8200 🖳www.cyathens.com

Started in 1962, College Year in Athens is the oldest English study-abroad program in Greece. Modern Greek Language classes offered as well as three different levels of courses; study travel programs to Crete, Peloponnesse, and other parts of Greece offered within curriculum.

i Check website for eligibility and requirements. $ Semester $17,550; full year $31,800. Fees include room and board.

HARVARD SUMMER ABROAD IN ISTANBUL, TURKEY

51 Brattle St., Cambridge, MA   ☎617 495 4024 ▇www.summer.harvard.edu

This program combines students and faculty from Sabanci University of Turkey and Harvard, fostering an eight-week intercultural exchange both inside and outside of the classroom. Students select two courses in the humanities and social sciences.

i *Obtain transfer credit from your home institution. Harvard students given preference during application.* Ⓢ *Summer $7350.*

LEXIA STUDY ABROAD PROGRAMS

6 The Courtyard, Hanover, NH, 03755   ☎800-77-LEXIA ▇www.lexiaintl.org

With courses taught at renowned Bogazici University, Lexia offers students courses in all levels of Turkish as well as history and sociology classes on Turkish culture and Istanbul. Emphasizes various excursions and research projects throughout the term to explore the city first-hand.

i *2.7 min. GPA in field of study.* Ⓢ *Semester $15,750.*

RUTGERS STUDY ABROAD

102 College Ave., New Brunswick, NJ   ☎732 932 7787 ▇www.studyabroad.rutgers.edu

With Athens as a home base, this course taught in English by three Rutgers professors offers students a chance to travel throughout Greece and learn from its historic monuments and cities.

i *Check with your university for transfer credit.* Ⓢ *NJ residents $5500; non-NJ residents $6500.* ⌚ *Programs last 5 weeks.*

UNIVERSITY OF INDANAPOLIS ATHENS CAMPUS

Syntagma Square, Athens 105 57   ☎21032 37 077 ▇www.uindy.gr

Study alongside both Greek and other international students at the University of Indianapolis's Odyssey in Athens program. Offers summer and intersession programs as well as semester study-abroad programs for graduate and undergraduate students looking to earn credit abroad. Become PADI Open Water Diver certified with the Odyssey in Athens Scuba Diving Program.

i *Check with your home university for requirements and credit transfer.* Ⓢ *Semester $9995; full year $22,985; summer $3490; winter session $2995. Prices include room and board, tuition, and group travel.*

Greek and Turkish Programs

While it may be easier to apply through an international study abroad program, both Greece and Turkey have domestic programs for the international student looking for complete immersion. Beware: the programs listed below are full-fledged, verifiable institutions in these countries, and you'll be learning and studying alongside locals in their environment.

ATHENS UNIVERSITY OF ECONOMICS AND BUSINESS

76, Patission St., GR10434 Athens, Greece   ☎21082 03 911 ▇www.aueb.gr

Acting as the college stomping grounds for many industry leaders in Greece, AUEB provides classes in all kinds of business to undergraduates, graduates, and executive students. Their large Erasmus program helps them boast of being the "most per-capita-intensive" exchange program in Greece.

i *If from EU, check with home university for Erasmus information; otherwise, consult their website* Ⓢ *Tuition and accommodations vary by program and chosen term.*

BEYKENT UNIVERSITY

Sisli Ayazaga Mahallesi, Hadim Koru Yolu, 34396 ☎90 212 867 50 77 ▇www.beykent.edu

With over 28 departments in the sciences and liberal arts, this university offers undergraduate and graduate programs taught in English. If from the EU, ask about their Socrates and Erasmus programs.

i *Must have high school or lycee diploma or equivalent and certain standardized test results.* Ⓢ *Full year $5,292.*

ISTANBUL UNIVERSITY

34452 Beyazit, Eminonu, Istanbul ☎212 440 00 00 💻www.istanbul.edu.tr/english

Located alongside Beyazit Square, Istanbul University celebrated its 550th anniversary in 2003. With over 60,000 undergraduate and 8,000 graduate students enrolled with its 17 faculties, everything from a radio station to athletic teams are offered to international students.

[i] Consult website for Erasmus and other international programs, tuition fees, and admissions requirements.

LANGUAGE SCHOOLS

As renowned novelist Gustave Flaubert once said, "Language is a cracked kettle on which we beat out tunes for bears to dance to." While we at *Let's Go* have absolutely no clue what he was talking about, we do know that the following are good resources for learning modern Greek and Turkish.

ATHENS GREEK SCHOOL (OFFERED THROUGH AMERISPAN STUDY ABROAD)

1334 Walnut St., 6th Fl., Philadelphia, PA 19107 ☎215 751 1100 💻www.amerispan.com

Located near the National Archaeological Museum in Athens, this school offers air-conditioned classrooms and a matching service for host families. Group classes meet 4hr. per day.

[i] Airport pick-up, weekend excursions, and one-on-one classes offered at extra cost. [$] 2 weeks $2245; 4 weeks $4315. Fees include homestay and breakfast.

A2Z LANGUAGES: AZ ATHENS

3219 East Camelback Rd. #806, Phoenix, AZ ☎888 417 1533 💻www.a2zlanguages.com

AZ Athens offers two types of Greek language programs, the Greek Immersion Program during the summer, and the Accelerated Greek Program throughout the rest of the year. Each class utilizes two teachers that stress vocabulary and grammar rules.

[i] Limited apartment accommodations offered on a first come basis. [$] 3-4 weeks $1,000-1,200.

EFINST TURKISH CENTRE

1 Levent, Istanbul, Turkey ☎90212 282 90 64 💻www.turkishlesson.com

Established in 1992 for mostly foreign business people, EFINST focuses on the communication aspect of language and shuns lecture-like teaching. EFINST provides accommodations varying from hotels and hostels to apartments and host families. Be sure to sign up for an executive host family to get meals M-F.

[i] See website for specific programs. [$] Application fee of €50 per student. Program costs range from €264-528 (group courses) to €348-1,680 (1-on-1 lessons). ⏰ Program lengths vary; study and holiday courses available

GREEK LANGUAGE INSTITUTE

Nat. Registration Center, PO Box 1393, Milwaukee, WI ☎414 278 0631 💻www.nrcsa.com

With a branch in Athens, this institute offers immersion-based classes in modern Greek in conjunction with the University of Wales.

[i] See website for FAQs and to request information. [$] Classes from $1,100-2,200, depending on group size. Program fees include homestay. ⏰ Program durations vary; consult website for information.

KENTRO ELLINIKOU POLITSMOU (HELLENIC CULTURE CENTER)

Tilemahou 14, Athens 11472 ☎210 52 38 149 💻www.hcc.edu.gr

Classes offered in beginner, intermediate, and advanced levels of modern Greek; or, make your own class with private tutoring.

[i] Consult the website for seasonal classes. [$] Program fees between €370-450 (1 week) and €740-900 (2 week).

DILMER DIL OGRETIM MERKEZI LANGUAGE TEACHING CENTER

Inonu Cad. S. Tunaya Tarik Zafer Sk., Istanbul ☎90 212 292 96 96 🖳www.dilmer.com

Offering 4- and 8-week immersion language programs, Dilmer gives instruction in 7 levels of Turkish with books and resources prepared by their own staff.

i Website offers complete list of courses and schedules; placement tests first day of class. $ 4- to 8-week courses anywhere from €288-384 (72-96hr. of instruction)

OMILO

Tsaldari 13, Maroussi 15122 ☎210 612 2896 🖳www.omilo.com

Located in Maroussi, this program offers biweekly lessons in the mornings and evenings year-round as well as intensive courses that last 4hr. per day during certain months.

i Must be at least 17 years old for group courses. $ Programs cost €370 (1 week intensive), €400 (8-10 weeks). See website for private lesson rates.

DIGGIN' FOR GLYPHS IN ATHENS

Students who find their way to study abroad in Athens are often those interested in the classics and archaeology. There is no better way to learn about the past than by actually finding it and digging it up. The **Archaeological Institute of America**, 656 Beacon St., Boston, MA 02215 *(☎617 353 9361; 🖳www.archaeological.org)*, annually publishes the *Archaeological Fieldwork Opportunities Bulletin*, which includes listings of dig sites in Greece. Print editions of the bulletin cost $20 and can be bought from David Brown Book Co., *(PO Box 511, Oakville, CT 06779 ☎800 791 9354; 🖳www.oxbowbooks.com)*. If you are on more of a budget, the **Hellenic Ministry of Culture** *(🖳www.culture.gr)* maintains a complete and free list of archaeological sites in Greece. Below is a list of organizations that can help you find an archaeological dig in Athens.

THE AMERICAN SCHOOL OF CLASSICAL STUDIES AT ATHENS

Souidias 54, Athens 10676 ☎21072 36 313 🖳www.ascsa.edu.gr

Since 1881, American graduate students and professors have flocked here to participate in ongoing excavations of ancient sites, including the ancient Athenian agora. A 6-week summer program allows undergraduates to work at its sites and others.

i Applicants selected based on academic achievement and previous fieldwork experience. Application deadline for summer digs set in Dec. of previous year. $ Room and a small daily stipend are given to admitted volunteers who can provide their own travel arrangements.

ARCHAEOLOGY ABROAD

31-34 Gordon Sq., London WC1H, UK ☎20 85 37 08 49 🖳www.britarch.ac.uk/archabroad

This annual guide about archaeology contains information on fieldwork opportunities and offers periodic emails to keep its subscribers up-to-date.

i See website for information on buying a subscription. $ Guides for individual use £27-33, institutional use £33-37.

BRITISH SCHOOL IN ATHENS

O. Souidias 52, Athens 10676 ☎21072 10 974 🖳www.bsa.gla.ac.uk

Courses and internships for undergraduates, postgraduates, and teachers as well as annual fieldwork in Athens. See website for various seminars offered at their Athens location.

i See website for membership info and subscription fees.

CANADIAN INSTITUTE IN GREECE

Dion. Aiginitou 7, Athens 11528 ☎21072 232 01 🖳www.cig-icg.gr

Provides information and membership for Canadians interested in fieldwork and seminars on Greek archaeological studies.

GERMAN ARCHAEOLOGICAL INSTITUTE

Fidiou 1, Athens 10678   ☎21033 07 400 ▦www.dainst.org

Offers an archaeological database of current and past excavations as well as scholarship aid to academics and graduate students. Holds seminars, colloquia, and congresses throughout the world.

i Consult website for scholarship opportunities and fieldwork/research programs

volunteering

While there exist many educational programs and classes in both Athens and Istanbul, there is no better way to give back to these historic cities than by pulling up your sleeves and helping them out with your own two hands. If that last research paper put you over the edge, if those lectures are almost as potent as a prescription sleeping drug, or if you are looking for opportunities to volunteer during your gap year, both cities offer different community service programs that will prove to be beneficial to both you and the city. In Athens, Mediterranean wildlife, including endangered sea turtles and monk seals, need your help before they become extinct. Most opportunities in Greece are short-term with organizations that make use of drop-in and summer volunteers. In Istanbul, volunteer groups target poverty and antiquated infrastructures to help the less fortunate in their society. More often than not, these programs will either provide accommodation or put you in the right direction for finding cheap, nearby room and board. While programs vary seasonally, the listings below should help you with your quest for international service—or at least help you rationalize prolonging your trip for a few more weeks.

WILDLIFE CONSERVATION

ARCHELON SEA TURTLE PROTECTION SOCIETY

3h Marina Glyfadas, 166 75, Glyfada   ☎210 89 82 600 ▦www.archelon.gr

This organization provides the opportunity to volunteer at three different turtle nesting areas on the beaches of Zakynthos, Crete, and the Peloponnese as well as a rehab center in Athens. Volunteers live free of charge on camp sites.

i 18+. Must have a health insurance plan and speak English; consult website for application process.

HELLENIC ORNITHOLOGICAL SOCIETY

Vas. Irakleiou 24, Athens 106 82   ☎21082 27 937 ▦www.ornithologiki.gr/en/enmain.htm

This group plans volunteering opportunities from field work to office help in order to protect endangered species of birds.

i See website for over 16 volunteering positions throughout Greece.

HELLENIC SOCIETY FOR THE STUDY AND PROTECTION OF THE MONK SEAL

18 Solomou, Athens 106 82   ☎2105 22 2888 ▦www.mom.gr

Volunteer on the rehab team, the education volunteer team, or the development and communications team to help save the endangered Mediterranean monk seal. Conducts information sessions for local fishermen and the public about conservation, and provides an adopt a monk seal program for people around the world.

i 18+. Must have insurance to volunteer.

THE MEDITERRANEAN ASSOCIATION TO SAVE THE SEA TURTLES

Likavitou 1c, Athens, 106 72   ☎21036 40 389 ▦www.medasset.org

Helps rescue and secure the natural habitats of sea turtles throughout the Mediterranean, with sites at Zakynthos and Kephalonia. While no funding is given through the association, working in its Athens office can provide free lodging for a few weeks, and international funding is available through other organizations.

i Placement usually starts in September; academic credit for undergraduate internships.

SOCIAL WELFARE

THE EXPERIMENT IN INTERNATIONAL LIVING

PO Box 676, 1 Kipling Rd, Battleboro, VT 05302 ☎800-257-7751 🖥 www.worldlearning.org

5-week immersion program focusing on community service, travel, and regional exploration; departs from New York. Includes homestay in Istanbul and a traditional Anatolian village.

i High school students. $$5,700. Fees include international transportation and some meals.

HABITAT FOR HUMANITY TURKEY

Zochova 6-8, Bratislava 811 03, Slovenia ☎421 233669000 🖥 www.habitat.org/intl

The grandaddy of them all, Habitat for Humanity keeps its international acclaim and name brand appeal with destinations around the world. Although the company doesn't currently have an opportunity in Turkey, it has in the past and might provide service projects in the future.

VOLUNTEERS FOR INTERNATIONAL PARTNERSHIP

70 Landmark Hill, S. 204, Brattleboro, VT ☎802 246 1154🖥www.partnershipvolunteers.org

Offering various volunteer opportunities throughout Turkey, VIP sets up a homestay and orientation for its volunteers. Volunteer programs range from helping the environment to assisting those with disabilities to art preservation.

i Request information on their website to find out which programs are currently offered. $ Program fees vary by destination and duration.

working

From backpackers wanting to finance the next leg of their trip with short-term work to teachers looking for a long-term international position, all levels of instructors can find English language teaching jobs in Athens and Istanbul. University students should talk to their foreign language departments and study abroad offices for connections to jobs abroad, while people with friends and family in Greece should see if their loved ones can expedite work permits or arrange work-for-accommodation deals. With the current financial issues in Greece, it may be more difficult to find a job in today's Athenian economy.

For budding working stiffs already on the road, some hostels have bulletin boards with recent job openings in their neighborhoods, and websites like www.jobsabroad.com and www.travel-to-teach.org often help match people and schools. **City News** (*🖥athens.citynews.com/Employment.html*) is a database of employment listings in Athens. Some programs require you to have either a college degree or be EFL qualified, so make sure you have the required credentials when applying.

LONG-TERM WORK

If you plan on working for more than three months in Greece or Turkey, begin your search for a job well in advance as both long-term jobs and work permits are hard to find. **International placement agencies** can help travelers find jobs abroad, especially for teaching English. The **AIESEC International** promotes international jobs in 100+ countries, including Greece and Turkey (*☎21036 28 236; 🖥www.aiesec.org*).

TEACHING ENGLISH

Although you won't be making millions teaching English abroad, some elite American schools offer competitive salaries for instructors, and some jobs come with a daily stipend to help with living expenses. Usually, you will need to have at least a bachelor's degree in English or Literature to be a full-time teacher, but volunteer teachers and undergrads can often find summer positions teaching or tutoring their native tongue. Some language programs require teachers to hold a **CELTA (Certificate in English Language**

Teaching to Adults). To obtain a teaching license in Greece, you will need your diploma, passport, and CV translated into Greek; for current requirements contact the **Hellenic Ministry of Education**, Mitropoleos 15, Athens 10185 (📧*www.ypepth.gr*). Other schools require a prospective teacher to hold a **TEFL**, or a **Teaching English as a Foreign Language** certificate, but they are not always necessary. In Istanbul, make sure to have copies of your passport, CV, and language certificates when applying for a teaching license. Contact your local Turkish and Greek consulate for up-to-date requirements—especially in Athens with its current tumultuous economic issues.

- **DILKOENGLISH** A chain of language schools in Istanbul offering classes in Standard English (North Americans take note—this means English); no teaching experience required (☎*90 538 320 3116;* 📧*www.dilko.com.tr*).

- **INTERLANG** With five branches in Istanbul, this private language school helps its English instructors find housing; teachers usually need a university degree and CELTA certification (☎*90 212 244 8643;* 📧*email liz@interlang.com.tr*).

- **TEFL INSTITUTE** Take courses from this institute that offers certification programs and job placement in Athens for English teaching jobs that last 6-12 months (📧*www.teflinstitute.com*).

- **DAVE'S ESL CAFE** A 2-sided marketplace for ESL teachers and employers, Dave's ESL Cafe has listings around the globe. Free for teachers but fees for schools and recruiters (📧*www.eslcafe.com*).

- **OFFICE OF OVERSEAS SCHOOLS** This website of the US Department of State keeps a list of schools and agencies abroad that arrange for Americans to act as instructors (☎*202 261 8200;* 📧*www.state.gov/m/a/os*).

AU PAIR WORK

Usually women in their late teens or twenties, au pairs work as live-in nannies in exchange for room, board, and a small spending allowance. If you're a man, you can still try applying to be an au pair—just realize that au pairs are traditionally women. This line of work allows you to live and work with natives and really get to know Athens or Istanbul without the high expenses of travel, but the experience really depends on your host family. Au pairs in these cities generally work 30-45hr. per week, including a few evenings, and payment depends on family size, family income, and qualifications. Below are a few agencies that match families to potential au pairs—the *au-lmost* pairs.

- **ANGLONANNIES:** Database for au pair and nanny openings in Istanbul and Athens (☎*90 212 265 4340;* 📧*www.anglonannies.com*).

- **AU PAIR.COM:** Families post listings directly to this website for aspiring au pairs (*www.aupair.com*).

- **AUPAIRCONNECT:** This website matches families and au pairs by location and country for free (📧*www.aupairconnect.com*).

- **GREAT AU PAIR:** With thousands of au pairs and families worldwide, this matching site includes both Athens and Istanbul. 30-day membership $60 (☎*775 215 5770;* 📧*www.greataupair.com*).

- **NINE MUSES:** An agency with online applications that helps place EU nationals with families in Athens and other parts of Greece (📧*www.ninemuses.com*).

SHORT-TERM WORK

Seeing a lot of zeros in your bank account? Pockets frayed from spending so much cash during your last few weeks of travel? Finding short-term work is your best bet to avoid backpacker bankruptcy. While working without a permit is illegal in the EU, many establishments will hire people illegally for a short period of time. Certain industries like hospitality and tutoring have high turnover rates, so working as a bartender, waiter, or private tutor is a great way to work for money or room and board. The easiest way to find these jobs is by asking hostels, hotels, and restaurant front desks as well as other backpackers. Just remember that *Let's Go* doesn't recommend working illegally in any capacity.

more visa information

Depending on the type and duration of your work in Greece and Turkey, you will need some sort of a working visa. For finding the most up to date information and starting the process to become a bonefide international breadwinner (or maybe just an unpaid intern), contact your local Greek and Turkish consulates. Most EU citizens will need a working Schengen visa that corresponds to their length of stay and their home countries relationship with these nations. Sound a little confusing? It is. Make sure to start your visa application the moment you know you are working in Athens or Istanbul as the process is long and arduous. First check with your employer or any contacts in these cities about permits—usually they are easier to obtain from government organizations within the city limits.

- **BACK DOOR JOBS:** Offering "short-term job adventures," this site has paid and unpaid opportunities. Make sure you follow the breadcrumbs to the international page (*www.backdoorjobs.com*).
- **EASY EXPAT:** This site offers international openings for the traveler looking to earn some quick coin in the near future; passport, visa, and work permit information included (*www.easyexpat.com*).
- **SEASONWORKERS.COM:** Focusing on seasonal opportunities for full-time work in both Turkey and Greece, this website acts as a database for current job openings available to foreigners; provides visa information (*www.seasonworkers.com*).
- **WORKAWAY:** Site includes listings for paid and unpaid jobs for internationals. Check out the jobs on the Mediterranean for a possible summer on the beach (*www.workaway.info*).
- **WORLD WIDE OPPORTUNITIES ON ORGANIC FARMS:** With farming opportunities surrounding Istanbul and throughout Turkey, this website is a great resource for those looking for an unconventional but meaningful experience abroad (*www.wwoof.org*).

tell the world

If your friends are tired of hearing about that time you saved a baby orangutan in Indonesia, there's clearly only one thing to do: get new friends. Find them at our website, *www.letsgo.com*, where you can post your study-, volunteer-, or work-abroad stories for other, more appreciative community members to read. There's also a Beyond Tourism section that elaborates on non-destination-specific volunteering, studying, and working opportunities. If you liked this chapter, you'll love it; if you didn't like this chapter, maybe you'll find the website's more general Beyond Tourism tips more likeable, you non-likey person.

beyond tourism

INDEX

index

MAP INDEX

map index

MAP LEGEND

▪ Sight/Service	👑 Castle	🖥 Internet Cafe	🚔 Police
✈ Airport	⛪ Church	📖 Library	✉ Post Office
⌂ Arch/Gate	⚑ Consulate/Embassy	Ⓜ Ⓜ Metro Station	🎿 Skiing
💲 Bank	✝ Convent/Monastery	⛰ Mountain	✡ Synagogue
🏖 Beach	⚓ Ferry Landing	🕌 Mosque	☎ Telephone Office
🚌 Bus Station	(347) Highway Sign	🏛 Museum	🎭 Theater
✪ Capital City	✚ Hospital	℞ Pharmacy	ⓘ Tourist Office
			🚉 Train Station

The Let's Go compass always points NORTH.

| Pedestrian Zone | | Park | | Water | | Beach |
| Stairs | | | | | | |

THE STUDENT TRAVEL GUIDE

These Let's Go guidebooks are available at bookstores and through online retailers:

EUROPE

Let's Go Amsterdam & Brussels, 1st ed.
Let's Go Berlin, Prague & Budapest, 2nd ed.
Let's Go France, 32nd ed.
Let's Go Europe 2011, 51st ed.
Let's Go European Riviera, 1st ed.
Let's Go Germany, 16th ed.
Let's Go Great Britain with Belfast and Dublin, 33rd ed.
Let's Go Greece, 10th ed.
Let's Go Istanbul, Athens & the Greek Islands, 1st ed.
Let's Go Italy, 31st ed.
Let's Go London, Oxford, Cambridge & Edinburgh, 2nd ed.
Let's Go Madrid & Barcelona, 1st ed.
Let's Go Paris, 17th ed.
Let's Go Rome, Venice & Florence, 1st ed.
Let's Go Spain, Portugal & Morocco, 26th ed.
Let's Go Western Europe, 10th ed.

UNITED STATES

Let's Go Boston, 6th ed.
Let's Go New York City, 19th ed.
Let's Go Roadtripping USA, 4th ed.

MEXICO, CENTRAL & SOUTH AMERICA

Let's Go Buenos Aires, 2nd ed.
Let's Go Central America, 10th ed.
Let's Go Costa Rica, 5th ed.
Let's Go Costa Rica, Nicaragua & Panama, 1st ed.
Let's Go Guatemala & Belize, 1st ed.
Let's Go Yucatán Peninsula, 1st ed.

ASIA & THE MIDDLE EAST

Let's Go Israel, 5th ed.
Let's Go Thailand, 5th ed.

Exam and desk copies are available for study-abroad programs and resource centers.

Let's Go guidebooks are distributed to bookstores in the U.S. through Publishers Group West and through Publishers Group Canada in Canada.

For more information, email letsgo.info@perseusbooks.com.

ACKNOWLEDGMENTS

JONATHAN ROSSI THANKS: In no particular order: Anna Boch, Marykate Jasper, the whole Let's Go office, Grace Sun, Michal Labik, Jocey Karlan, Mark Warren, Christa Hartsock, Elyssa Spitzer, my family, all the food establishments in Harvard Square, the Los Angeles Lakers, the Kevin & Bean radio show, Winthrop E-21, Winthrop G-42, Antoine Dodson, and coffee.

ANNA BOCH THANKS: In a very particular order: all the kick-ass RW's, Jonathan Rossi, Marykate Jasper, the Snuggie, Caturday, Iya Megre, honey-stung fried chicken, the Winthrop-Eliot Dramatic Society, Marcel Moran, friends-list, Lucy, Waffle, and Moustafa the smoothie guy in the T-stop.

LET'S GO masthead

DIRECTOR OF PUBLISHING   Ashley R. Laporte
EXECUTIVE EDITOR   Nathaniel Rakich
PRODUCTION AND DESIGN DIRECTOR   Sara Plana
PUBLICITY AND MARKETING DIRECTOR   Joseph Molimock
MANAGING EDITORS   Charlotte Alter, Daniel C. Barbero, Marykate Jasper, Iya Megre
TECHNOLOGY PROJECT MANAGERS   Daniel J. Choi, C. Alexander Tremblay
PRODUCTION ASSOCIATES   Rebecca Cooper, Melissa Niu
FINANCIAL ASSOCIATE   Louis Caputo

DIRECTOR OF IT   Yasha Iravantchi
PRESIDENT   Meagan Hill
GENERAL MANAGER   Jim McKellar

ABOUT LET'S GO

THE STUDENT TRAVEL GUIDE

Let's Go publishes the world's favorite student travel guides, written entirely by Harvard students. Armed with pens, notebooks, and a few changes of clothes stuffed into their backpacks, our student researchers go across continents, through time zones, and above expectations to seek out invaluable travel experiences for our readers. Because we are a completely student-run company, we have a unique perspective on how students travel, where they want to go, and what they're looking to do when they get there. If your dream is to grab a machete and forge through the jungles of Costa Rica, we can take you there. If you'd rather bask in the Riviera sun at a beachside cafe, we'll set you a table. In short, we write for readers who know that there's more to travel than tour buses. To keep up, visit our website, www.letsgo.com, where you can sign up to blog, post photos from your trips, and connect with the Let's Go community.

TRAVELING BEYOND TOURISM

We're on a mission to provide our readers with sharp, fresh coverage packed with socially responsible opportunities to go beyond tourism. Each guide's Beyond Tourism chapter shares ideas about responsible travel, study abroad, and how to give back to the places you visit while on the road. To help you gain a deeper connection with the places you travel, our fearless researchers scour the globe to give you the heads-up on both world-renowned and off-the-beaten-track opportunities. We've also opened our pages to respected writers and scholars to hear their takes on the countries and regions we cover, and asked travelers who have worked, studied, or volunteered abroad to contribute first-person accounts of their experiences.

FIFTY-ONE YEARS OF WISDOM

Let's Go has been on the road for 51 years and counting. We've grown a lot since publishing our first 20-page pamphlet to Europe in 1960, but five decades and 60 titles later, our witty, candid guides are still researched and written entirely by students on shoestring budgets who know that train strikes, stolen luggage, food poisoning, and marriage proposals are all part of a day's work. Meanwhile, we're still bringing readers fresh new features, such as a student-life section with advice on how and where to meet students from around the world; a revamped, user-friendly layout for our listings; and greater emphasis on the experiences that make travel abroad a rite of passage for readers of all ages. And, of course, this year's 16 titles—including five brand-new guides—are still brimming with editorial honesty, a commitment to students, and our irreverent style.

THE LET'S GO COMMUNITY

More than just a travel guide company, Let's Go is a community that reaches from our headquarters in Cambridge, MA, all across the globe. Our small staff of dedicated student editors, writers, and tech nerds comes together because of our shared passion for travel and our desire to help other travelers get the most out of their experience. We love it when our readers become part of the Let's Go community as well—when you travel, drop us a postcard (67 Mt. Auburn St., Cambridge, MA 02138, USA), send us an email (feedback@letsgo.com), or sign up on our website (www.letsgo.com) to tell us about your adventures and discoveries.

For more information, updated travel coverage, and news from our researcher team, visit us online at www.letsgo.com.

- **PINK PALACE.** Corfu Island, Greece. ☎30 26610 53103 or 53104. 🖥www. thepinkpalace.com.

HELPING LET'S GO. If you want to share your discoveries, suggestions, or corrections, please drop us a line. We appreciate every piece of correspondence, whether a postcard, a 10-page email, or a coconut. Visit Let's Go at **www.letsgo.com** or send an email to:

feedback@letsgo.com, subject: "Let's Go Istanbul, Athens & the Greek Islands"

Address mail to:

Let's Go Istanbul, Athens & the Greek Islands, 67 Mount Auburn St., Cambridge, MA 02138, USA

In addition to the invaluable travel advice our readers share with us, many are kind enough to offer their services as researchers or editors. Unfortunately, our charter enables us to employ only currently enrolled Harvard students.

Distributed by Publishers Group West.
Printed in Canada by Friesens Corp.
Maps by Let's Go and Avalon Travel
Design Support by Jane Musser, Sarah Juckniess, Tim McGrath

ISBN-13: 978-1-59880-740-0
First edition
10 9 8 7 6 5 4 3 2 1

Let's Go Istanbul, Athens & the Greek Islands is written by Let's Go Publications, 67 Mt. Auburn St., Cambridge, MA 02138, USA.

Let's Go® and the LG logo are trademarks of Let's Go, Inc.

quick reference

YOUR GUIDE TO LET'S GO ICONS

☎	Phone numbers	⊘	Not wheelchair-accessible	❄	Has A/C
▣	Websites	(ᵗ)	Has internet access	♯	Directions
💳	Takes credit cards	☁	Has outdoor seating	*i*	Other hard info
⊛	Cash only	▼	Is GLBT or GLBT-friendly	$	Prices
♿	Wheelchair-accessible	⍦	Serves alcohol	⏲	Hours

PRICE RANGES

Let's Go includes price ranges, marked by icons ❶ through ❺, in accommodations and food listings. For an expanded explanation, see the chart in How To Use This Book.

GREECE	❶	❷	❸	❹	❺
ACCOMMODATIONS	under €22	€22-33	€34-45	€46-60	€60+
FOOD	under €6	€6-12	€13-19	€20-25	€25+

TURKEY	❶	❷	❸	❹	❺
ACCOMMODATIONS	under €35	€36-50	€51-70	€71-100	€100+
FOOD	under 10TL	11-16TL	17-25TL	26-40TL	40TL+

IMPORTANT PHONE NUMBERS

GREECE EMERGENCY: POLICE 100, FIRE 199, ANYTHING 112			
Tourist Police in Greece	171	Ambulance in Greece	178

TURKEY EMERGENCY: POLICE 155, FIRE 110, ANYTHING 112			
Tourist Police in Istanbul	0212 527 4503	International operator in Turkey	115

GREEK ALPHABET

SYMBOL	NAME	SYMBOL	NAME	SYMBOL	NAME	SYMBOL	NAME
A α	alpha	H η	eta	N ν	nu	T τ	tau
B β	beta	Θ θ	theta	Ξ ξ	xi	Υ υ	upsilon
Γ γ	gamma	I ι	iota	O o	omicron	Φ φ	phi
Δ δ	delta	K κ	kappa	Π π	pi	X χ	chi
E ε	epsilon	Λ λ	lambda	P ρ	rho	Ψ ψ	psi
Z ζ	zeta	M μ	mu	Σ σ/ς	sigma	Ω ω	omega

TURKISH LETTERS AND PRONUNCIATION

SYMBOL	PRONUNCIATION	SYMBOL	PRONUNCIATION	SYMBOL	PRONUNCIATION
c	*j* as in **j**acket	ı/İ	*ee* as in b**ee**t	u	*oo* as in b**oo**t
ç	*ch* as in **ch**eck	j	*zh* as in plea**s**ure	â	dipthong of *ea*, or faint *ya*
ğ	lengthens adjacent vowels	ö	*eu* as in French d**eu**x	ü	*ew* as in c**ue**
ı/I	*i* as in cous**i**n	ş	*sh* as in **sh**ort	uy	*oo-ee* as in ph**ooey**

MEASUREMENT CONVERSIONS

1 inch (in.) = 25.4mm	1 millimeter (mm) = 0.039 in.
1 foot (ft.) = 0.305m	1 meter (m) = 3.28 ft.
1 mile (mi.) = 1.609km	1 kilometer (km) = 0.621 mi.
1 pound (lb.) = 0.454kg	1 kilogram (kg) = 2.205 lb.
1 gallon (gal.) = 3.785L	1 liter (L) = 0.264 gal.